New Perspectives on the History of Political Economy

Robert Fredona · Sophus A. Reinert
Editors

New Perspectives on the History of Political Economy

palgrave
macmillan

Editors
Robert Fredona
Harvard Business School
Boston, MA, USA

Sophus A. Reinert
Harvard Business School
Boston, MA, USA

ISBN 978-3-030-09628-1 ISBN 978-3-319-58247-4 (eBook)
https://doi.org/10.1007/978-3-319-58247-4

Printed on acid-free paper

This Palgrave Macmillan imprint is published by Springer Nature
The registered company is Springer International Publishing AG
The registered company address is: Gewerbestrasse 11, 6330 Cham, Switzerland

Contents

Editors and Contributors

About the Editors

Robert Fredona is a Research Associate at Harvard Business School, USA, and an Associated Member of the Centre for Evolution of Global Business and Institutions at the York Management School, UK. Robert is interested in the intersection of law, politics, and commerce in the pre-modern world.

Sophus A. Reinert is Marvin Bower Associate Professor of Business Administration in the Business, Government, and the International Economy Unit at Harvard Business School, USA. A student of political economy, Sophus works on the long histories of capitalism, globalization, development, and business-government relations from the Renaissance to today's emerging markets.

Contributors

C.N. Biltoft Graduate Institute, Geneva, Switzerland

Robert Fredona Harvard Business School, Boston, USA

Walter A. Friedman Harvard Business School, Boston, USA

Erik Grimmer-Solem Wesleyan University, Middletown, USA

Bernard E. Harcourt Columbia University, New York, USA

Diana Kim Edmund A. Walsh School of Foreign Service, Georgetown University, Washington, USA

Jeffrey Miner Western Kentucky University, Bowling Green, USA

Arnaud Orain University of Paris 8, Paris, France

Laura Phillips Sawyer Harvard Business School, Boston, USA

Steve Pincus Yale University, New Haven, USA

John Shovlin New York University, New York, USA

Corey Tazzara Scripps College, Claremont, USA

Carl Wennerlind Barnard College, Columbia University, New York, USA

Introduction: History and Political Economy

Robert Fredona and Sophus A. Reinert

The first decade of the twenty-first century, bookended by the terrorist attacks of 9/11 and by a global financial crisis with aftershocks still resonating throughout the world, witnessed the clamorous and urgent return of both "the political" and "the economic" to historiographical debates. For some, this return could not have come sooner. Economics (both academic and "popular") had, many argued, largely embraced increasingly abstract formal methods in the preceding decades. So much so that one economic historian could recently argue that

> the debate about the role of mathematics in economic theory can hardly be said to be of much significance in the modern literature, since there are no longer any leading economists who believe that academic economics can be a nonmathematical discipline.[1]

Yet, even if this debate is truly closed, an unanswered question remains: is mathematics *enough*? Whatever their role within economics as an academic field, these deracinated methods, for intrinsic but also complex sociological and political reasons, have tended to buttress clusters of interrelated ideological programs and proposals favoring *laissez-faire* policies and their global institutionalization. And these policies, associated with the so-called "Washington Consensus," had been implemented with decidedly varying results.[2] At the same time, the historical profession—ideally well positioned to provide realist grounding for theoretical extremes—undertook (or fell under the sway of) its "cultural turn," generally leaving historical economic analysis behind and relegating it to an arid subfield of economics in the academic establishment.[3] The sheer consequentiality of subsequent events, and what many—including, remarkably, even the rather partial *The Economist* magazine [Fig. 1]—have seen as the manifest crisis of economic theory as such, reopened the eyes of scholars and laymen alike to the need for a more historical (or at least more historically aware) approach to economic phenomena.[4] And, although far from moribund, the so-called "free trade" paradigm in Anglo-American economic thought on the one hand and the wider dominance of cultural concerns in the academic study of history on the other are at last beginning to fragment. As the cracks and fissures in their foundations continue to grow, it is becoming more important than ever to rethink the historical role of politics (and, indeed, of government) in business, economic production, (re)distribution, and exchange, not to mention in the complex array of processes brought together under the umbrella of globalization.[5] Indeed, although career prospects for young historians remain challenging at best, leading universities are increasingly hiring scholars working on "the history of political economy" in addition to "the history of capitalism," elevating the historical analysis of economic ideas and practices to new heights.[6] To be blunt, "political economy" has again become something of an academic catchphrase, and it is now seen to offer an important vantage point on the turmoil of our time.

Fig. 1 The Economist, July 18–24, 2009. Jon Berkeley for The Economist

New Perspectives on the History of Political Economy contributes to this resurgent historiography and suggests new avenues and agendas for research on the political-economic nexus as it has developed in the Western world since the end of the Middle Ages. Far from procrustean, the volume brings together purposefully selected young and established scholars from a wide variety of disciplinary backgrounds—history, economics, law, and political science—in an effort to continue the ongoing reconceptualization of the origins and history of political economy through a variety of still largely distinct but complementary approaches—legal and intellectual, literary and philosophical, political and economic—and from a variety of related perspectives: debt and state finance, tariffs and tax policy, the encouragement and discouragement of trade, accounting and bookkeeping, merchant communities and companies, smuggling and illicit trades, mercantile and colonial systems, empires and special economic zones, economic cultures, and the history of doctrines more traditionally construed.

There are, of course, many ways of engaging with the history of political economy, and it is purposefully not our wish to suggest that there are right and wrong ways of so doing: Herodotus' house can, happily, be as vast and sprawling as Borges' "Library of Babel." Historiographically speaking, it seems important to us, not only given recent trends but also recent events, to purposefully encourage a widening of historical perspectives. There is a time for tightly focalized volumes, surely, but an argument can now be made for broader temporal approaches and looser disciplinary boundaries. Though such an approach may lose something in the way of coherence, this is, we believe, a price worth paying when the ultimate dividend is a richness of detail and variety of insight unlikely if not impossible inside the "box" of strict chronological and essentialist disciplinary bounds. As varied as they are, all of the essays in this volume nonetheless share some crucial points of convergence and the area of conceptual overlap is greater than the areas of disparateness. And John Maynard Keynes was right, during the Great Depression that marked the end of the last major period of *laissez-faire* globalization, to warn against "the silliness of the doctrinaire."[7] That said, different approaches to the history of political economy serve divergent purposes, inviting different possibilities and challenges alike. As many have pointed out before, historians of economic analysis have frequently pursued *internalized* economic genealogies, essentially approaching the history of economics from the perspective of contemporary theory.[8] Though the influence of the history of science and other traditions has certainly broadened the historiography of economics in recent years, it remains that the history of economic analysis has often been approached as a purely intellectualized trajectory from analytical falsity to truth.[9] Mark Blaug, after all, called his major work *Economic Theory in Retrospect*, and even as erudite and wide-ranging a scholar as the MIT economist Paul Samuelson gave a keynote lecture to the History of Economics Society towards the end of the Cold War in which he forcefully argued that the

> history of economics [should] more purposefully reorient itself towards studying the past from the standpoint of the present state of economic science. To use a pejorative word unpejoratively, I am suggesting a Whig Economic History of Economic Analysis.[10]

As Sir William J. Ashley, something of a British envoy of the German Historical School of Economics almost a century earlier, memorably opined of such methods, they ran the risk of making the history of economics little but "a museum of intellectual odds and ends, where every opinion is labelled as either a surprising anticipation of the correct modern theory or an instance of the extraordinary folly of the dark ages."[11] Quentin Skinner has rightly argued that such intellectual endeavors can be "labelled the mythology of prolepsis, the type of mythology we are prone to generate when we are more interested in the retrospective significance of a given episode than in its meaning for the agent of the time."[12] Such proleptic thinking is at best idealistic (in the philosophical sense) and at worst hopelessly anachronistic, so we might be wise to always keep in mind the historian Carlo Ginzburg's *obiter dictum* that anticipations (or *precorrimenti* as they are called in Italian) should always be interpreted as questions rather than answers.[13]

The essays that follow are preponderantly externalizing rather than internalizing, and if at times they do explore the "odds and ends" of the historical record, they uniformly do so to understand rather than to pass judgment. Beyond these caveats, however, the internalist approach, which of course can be illuminating and which to this day has many brilliant followers, risks being dismissive of the real causes as well as consequences of past political economy almost by default, particularly as born from or applied in policy.[14] Uniquely vulnerable to charges of anachronism, as we have suggested, the method furthermore courts teleology; it risks, in other words, completely losing hold of the very historical axis it purportedly seeks to embrace.[15] Even the Austrian Harvard economist Joseph A. Schumpeter, whose seminal *History of Economic Analysis* in many ways remains unsurpassed, could be quick to dismiss a long dead economist who did not pass his theoretical muster as owing "his survival" merely to the refutations of a more famous thinker, completely ignoring that the "bad" theories in question might have had unfortunate consequences.[16] That was simply not his interest, though there are good reasons to argue it should be ours.

Of course economic ideas often *have* had disastrous effects on people when translated into policy, from François Quesnay's failed physiocratic reforms in eighteenth-century France all the way through Stalinist communism to the famous "flaw" Alan Greenspan identified in his approach to regulation that allowed the 2008 financial crisis to occur and the ways in which tentative (and miscalculated) connections between public debt and low economic growth were used to justify austerity measures in its wake, by some accounts negatively influencing the lives of quite literally hundreds of millions of people.[17] This lattermost was, perhaps, a moment when in the face of uncertain equilibria it would have been humane to remember (and not only figuratively) Oscar Wilde's admonition that "to recommend thrift to the poor is both grotesque and insulting. It is like advising a man who is starving to eat less."[18] Indeed, as several of the following essays point out, we may have just as much to learn from the history of "bad" political economy as we do from charting the genealogies of currently fashionable ideas, and quite possibly much more. Such studies may point to the quintessentially contingent and political nature of much economic thinking, and, as the Columbia economist Joseph Dorfman long ago put it,

> since in the final analysis men's minds may be read most clearly in their actions, the practical ambitions and political interests of the molders of economic thought must constantly be kept in view by those who seek to understand what successive generations have put into the public record.[19]

An openness to the variety of approaches and justifications currently characterizing the history of political economy, and a rejection of the theoretical dogmatism that has characterized much thinking about economic matters and their history in recent decades does not mean the volume completely lacks a central coherence. Instead, the contributors different approaches represent complementary perspectives on some of the central questions of economic and political life, and particularly so regarding the nature, legitimation, contention, and neutralization of *power* in a world increasingly driven by economic concerns. From Jeffrey Miner's opening chapter on Medieval Genoese debates regarding public debt to Erik Grimmer Solem's analysis of Germany's violent call for a "place in the sun" on the eve of the Great War and Bernard Harcourt's exploration of the genealogy of morals in the history of political economy, the chapters offer compelling alternate narratives of power—economic, political, military, territorial, and cultural—as they relate to the theories and practices of political economy in the period since economic matters first became a question of political survival. Since, in the Scottish philosopher David Hume's celebrated phraseology, "trade" first became "an affair of state."[20]

For Hume that moment occurred in the seventeenth century, and he was confounded by the lack of engagement with trade by political writers in antiquity and among the "Italians."[21] We to the contrary suspect that trade has been inextricably and momentously linked with politics from the beginnings of recorded history, but privilege two historical moments in Europe, the height of the so-called "commercial revolution" of the late Middle Ages and the "Economic Turn" of the mid-eighteenth century, which saw an explosion of printed texts and translations of a political-economic character and which quantitatively and qualitatively changed the scale of political-economic discussions.[22] All told, trade's life-or-death centrality to "the state" seems as old as the state itself, however we choose to understand that term. Pierre Bourdieu's understanding of the genesis of the (modern) state as a process of the accumulation or concentration of different species of "capital" is especially compelling, but where Bourdieu sees taxation and levies at the heart of the "economic capital" subsumed by the emergent state, we prefer to look at the ways the state managed commerce, giving (through privileges and protection) as much as taking, or even liberated it.[23]

Financial and corporate structures in the European world developed alongside governmental ones, and the story of the origins of political economy is not a one-sided one, in which states or proto-states simply regulated production and trade. Nor is it a teleological one, with the neoliberal internationalist state waiting for us at the end. Rather, it is a dynamic and contentious story in which the power of creditors and of capital, and of economic ideas and practices, shaped and were shaped by political communities. It is, in short, the story of wealth and power in the West and the world it often violently created; of how human beings thought about, grappled with, and overcame material hardship; organized their political and economic communities, and struggled for dominance on an increasingly larger global stage. With the rise of China as an economic superpower, "state capitalism" has rushed to the center of the economic discourse.[24] But this is nothing new—the history of state capitalism, of truly political economy, is also the history of the global hegemony of the West over the past 700 years as well as of the rise of the proverbial rest.[25] We maintain that a good way of gaining greater clarity with regards to this vital history—its manifest successes and egregious limitations—is to examine the intricate ways in which politico-economic ideas and practice intertwined in the city-states of late medieval Italy as much as in the oceanic empires that birthed the vexed geopolitical world in which we live. In fact, the essays contained in this volume help tell precisely this story, through snapshots from a truly global array of individuals, business enterprises, states, empires, and from the idealized domain of theories themselves.

In his classic *American Capitalism* (1952), John Kenneth Galbraith presented a suggestive theory of "countervailing powers" in market societies, arguing that the United States had ceased to be (if it ever had been) a perfectly competitive market because of oligopolistic business practices, suggesting a solution in the countervailing influences of corporations, states, and trade unions.[26] These would be the de facto building blocks of much subsequent historiography, even in fields and for periods far distant from Galbraith's own, to the extent that they eventually came to be taken for granted: the world was made up of firms, states, and workers.[27] Today, however, these categories of analysis are increasingly being questioned and indeed exploded, allowing for the reconstruction of a far richer—and more nuanced—history of power in which an array of state and non-state actors, not to mention theories, dogmas, and ideologies, vie for supremacy in a world characterized by relentless economic competition. The fact that something close to the Weberian "State" for a time gained a near monopoly on the legitimacy of power should, as many of the following essays make clear, not blind us to the contentious process that gave birth to our world, the many sources of its regulation, or the continuing relevance of non-state and trans-state power in shaping it.[28] The state, then, need not be the central actor in a sophisticated history of political economy, and perhaps, some day in the future, glancing at the grim outlines of international capital in a world of diminished nation-states and diminished discourses of legitimacy, one redolent of an earlier and formative age, we can begin to sketch a new and compelling metaphor for power, one that is plural where the state is singular: as Herman Melville wrote to Nathaniel Hawthorne, "Leviathan is not the biggest fish;—I have heard of Krakens."[29]

For the sake of clarity, it must be said that this volume's use of the term "political economy" does not reflect current sectarian uses of it, whether by Marxists or by Chicago-school public choice theorists.[30] Rather, it is a conscious resurrection of "political economy" in its original designation and a glimpse at its prehistory (and perhaps future). Adam Smith famously defined the discipline as a "branch of the science of a statesman or legislator" in his 1776 *Inquiry into the Nature and Causes of the Wealth of Nations*, forever linking politics, economics, and law to the legitimacy of power.[31] The term 'legitimate' is related to the Latin *legitimus*, or "lawful," itself in turn emerging from the etymological varieties of "law," meaning "rule," perhaps in the earliest instance derived from Proto-Germanic or Indo-European roots signifying "putting" or "laying." So fitting is the widespread historical phraseology of "giving" or "laying down the law" as a metaphor for conquest and a way of conceptualizing hierarchies of power in a variety of contexts from the commercial to the cultural. Linguistically speaking, then, law *is* power, and political economy was long considered its pre-eminent "science."[32]

The questions posed, in a variety of ways, by the contributors to this volume regard the nature, legality, and consequences of such power in historical time, as well as attempts to navigate, manage, project, usurp, and neutralize it. Needless to say, this process is, and must be, ongoing, but the intellectual history of such political economy is a topic too important to be left to policy makers and economists unaware of this past. This raises, however obliquely, the perennial questions of intentionality and relevance in—and of—the history of political economy. On the one hand, historians find themselves scrambling for "relevance" in the face of the proverbial "crisis of the humanities," and have, perhaps naturally, turned to the histories of capitalism and political economy *en masse* in the wake of the 2008 financial meltdown, not unlike how the study of economic history came into being and has since been strengthened during previous periods of economic crisis—theoretical as well as practical.[33] On the other hand, many historians remain deeply vexed by such calls for "relevance," the pressures of "presentism," and their collateral danger of "anachronism."[34]

We do not pretend to speak for the contributors to this volume, and respect deeply their individual approaches and perspectives, but we believe that their works—independently but particularly in concert—simultaneously elucidate our complex past, clarify the problems of the present, and adumbrate future concerns. As Skinner has argued, "if they simply ply their trade," intellectual historians help "prevent us from becoming too readily bewitched."[35] And bewitched we have been. Yet we would venture to argue that, in the vast constellation of the history of ideas, the past plays an *even* more organic and integral role for the study of political economy than for many other intellectual endeavors. Already at its very outset as an academic enterprise in the eighteenth century, "history" was considered one of the principal sources of authority in economic debates because it grounded theories in what many might still consider the realm of "facts."[36] As Italy's third professor of political economy taught his students in the early 1770s, "There is no better way of understanding the uses of a machine," in his example the politics of the world economy, "than to observe the process of its construction."[37] Similar sentiments have frequently resurfaced in the labyrinthine history of the subject, and the Cambridge historian and political philosopher Istvan Hont, one of the principal architects of the history of political economy over the past four decades, was utterly unapologetic about writing "with eyes firmly fixed on the challenges of today," justifying his work on the grounds that "the globalization debate of the late twentieth and early twenty-first centuries lack[ed] conceptual novelty."[38] To study the history of political economy was, in his opinion, to engage with the principal political and economic questions of the day; as he once asked, "why else would you do it?."[39] Nor by any means was Hont the first to suggest this: "A careful study of economic history," wrote business historian Edmond E. Lincoln in the vexed early years of the 1930s, "reveals surprisingly few new 'problems'."[40] Even Schumpeter himself, late in life, expressed hope that the historical study of political economy would "result in a new wing being added to the economist's house."[41] Though it may be an architectural pipe dream, it remains one worthy of our attention. For, since economics cannot *but* be political, its history should be considered not merely a foil against bewitchment but the ballast of its very endeavor.[42]

There can be no doubt that we find ourselves now at a proverbial crossroads of capitalism, and that many central assumptions regarding the nature, purpose, and future of political economy are being actively rethought across the world.[43] Whether with respect to long-term dynamics, like the recent peaking of international trade and subsequent decline of aggregate trade flows, or to singular yet momentous events such as Britain's decision by popular referendum to leave the European Union and the election of Donald Trump to the US Presidency—symptoms and causes of what some have come to call "the Rage of 2016"—everything suggests we are living through a period of long unprecedented change as neglected economic forces, which scientism failed to identify and address, trigger surprising political results with real and widespread social consequences.[44] Yet this is hardly the first time we find ourselves in this position, nor, bar the direst of recent predictions coming to pass, will it be the last.[45]

In a classic study of the history of economic thought, the economist and economic historian William J. Barber proudly proclaimed that "few things on this earth approach immortality so closely as a taut set of economic ideas."[46] When we are no longer so certain about the certainties, when ideologies have failed, our only lodestar is and must be history. The artifacts of pre- and early modern political economy, not to mention of the postwar period, remain monuments of perennial importance for understanding how human beings organized their political and economic communities, won great wealth and lost it, conquered and were conquered. We must understand this past, the history of business, politics, and economics, on its own terms and, indeed, in its own terms, not for reasons of antiquarianism but because they shed precious light on some of the most pressing challenges of our own time, including how we got "here," wherever that happens to be. The following essays testify to the rich and powerful lessons to be had from such a historical understanding of political economy, and will hopefully serve as inspiration for further work on the role of power in our long economic age.

* * *

Although the road was winding and somewhat bumpy, this volume emerged from a conference we organized at Harvard Business School in the fall of 2013, and we are grateful to that institution, and particularly to the Faculty Chair of its Business History Initiative, Geoffrey Jones, for making the event possible. In addition to the contributors represented here, the success of that conference owed to the extraordinary participation of S.M. Amadae, David Armitage, Lawrin Armstrong, Ed Balleisen, Paul Cheney, Rebecca Henderson, Geoffrey Jones, Julius Kirshner, Michael Kwass, Sreemati Mitter, Isaac Nakhimovsky, Emma Rothschild, Jacob Soll, Anoush Terjanian, and Richard Tuck. Kate Jenkins and Jayanthi Narayanaswamy also provided invaluable assistance during the editing of this volume.

In December of 1941, just weeks after the United States entered World War Two and while the Great Depression was still spurring new investigations of the economy and its history, N.S.B. Gras, the "father of business history" and the school's first Isidor Straus Professor of Business History, presented a paper titled "Capitalism—Concepts and History" at the American Historical Association's annual meeting. As his respondent, Gras personally chose Raymond de Roover, his former M.B.A. student, who was then a Ph.D. candidate in Economics at the University of Chicago. De Roover's reply played with one of Gras's central economic-historical conceits—the transition from petty capitalism to commercial capitalism, and a corresponding shift from the central importance of the traveling to the sedentary merchant—and laid out the remarkable case for a "commercial revolution" in the thirteenth century, first among the Italians and then in the Low Countries.[47] De Roover, especially with his 1963 magnum opus *The Rise and Decline of the Medici Bank*, would go on to become one of the driving forces in the economic historiography of the late Middle Ages and Renaissance. When Wallace K. Ferguson surveyed the field of Renaissance economic history in 1960, he made a point of mentioning Gras's importance in the development of the field. Business history, "in the sense in which Professor Gras envisaged it," he argued, encompassed works from Armando Sapori's seminal studies of the medieval Bardi, Peruzzi, and del Bene firms; to most of De Roover's work; to Frederic Lane's study of the Renaissance Venetian merchant Andrea Barbarigo; and even Iris Origo's *Merchant of Prato*.[48] That this volume should have originated at Harvard Business School is, then, more than a happy coincidence. We have brought together "Business Historians" and historians of many other stripes precisely because we share the broadness of vision that brought together Gras and De Roover, one we believe still remains fruitful for historical research to this day.

And it is also important that this volume begins in the commercial republics of premodern Italy. According to Emma Rothschild, David Hume's well-known 1754 essay "On Refinement in the Arts" proposed nothing less than a "Florentine Model" of political economy; Florence, whose history Hume loved, represented for him a paradigmatic form of the "opulent republic" in which democracy and commerce were united.[49] Whether or not this is actually true of the historical Florence, Enlightenment thinkers found in the Renaissance (and especially in the commercial and industrial cities of Northern and Central Italy) models for understanding how wealth and virtue, luxury and political moderation could coexist. Hume's essay was just one entry in the then raging debate over luxury and its presumably deleterious effects on public virtue. We are again faced with questions, as pressing as ever in human history, about the corrupting influence of wealth and the practices that produce it on our polities. These are civilizational questions and, indeed, existential ones. And they are also personal and moral questions. When so many ask simply how do we get rich, we should again be asking what it means for us to be both rich and good. With Hume we assert that wealth and virtue are not incompatible, and with him we look to the past in order to understand where we are and where we might be headed.

Robert Fredona
Sophus A. Reinert

Notes

1. Angmar Sandmo, *Economics Evolving: A History of Economic Thought* (Princeton: Princeton University Press, 2011), 464.
2. On the mathematization of economics see E. Roy Weintraub, *How Economics Became a Mathematical Science* (Durham: Duke University Press, 2002). For an early statement of the so-called "Washington Consensus," see John Williamson, "What Washington Means by Policy Reform," in Williamson, ed., *Latin American Adjustment: How Much Has Happened*, (Washington, DC: Institute for International Economics, 1990), 7–38. For perspectives on its earlier history, see Philip Mirowski and Dieter Plehwe, eds., *The Road from Mont Pèlerin: The Making of the Neoliberal Thought Collective* (Cambridge, MA: Harvard University Press, 2009). For early critical works on the phenomenon, see Joseph Stiglitz, *Globalization and Its Discontents* (New York: Norton, 2002); David Harvey, *A Brief History of Neoliberalism* (Oxford: Oxford University Press, 2005); Erik S. Reinert, *How Rich Countries Got Rich… and Why Poor Countries Stay Poor* (London: Constable, 2007). The 2008 crisis of course magnified the (already more than extensive) literature substantially, but see for a pugnacious take Philip Mirowski, *Never Let a Serious Crisis Go to Waste: How Neoliberalism Survived the Financial Meltdown* (London: Verso, 2013).
3. See, among many others on this, Francesco Boldizzoni, *The Poverty of Clio: Resurrecting Economic History* (Princeton: Princeton University Press, 2011), 169–70; Marc Parry, "Shackles and Dollars: Historians and Economists Clash over Slavery," *The Chronicle of Higher Education*, 28 October 2016, https://www.chronicle.com/article/ShacklesDollars/238598.
4. For an emblematic statement of this crisis, see the remarkable list of contrarian works by mainstream economists discussed in Noah Smith, "The Writing That Shaped Economic Thinking in 2016,"

Bloomberg, 20 December 2016, https://www.bloomberg.com/view/articles/2016-12-20/the-writing-that-shaped-economic-thinking-in-2016.

5. The many globalizations have many histories, but see the essays in Anthony G. Hopkins, ed., *Globalisation in World History* (London: Pimlico, 2002) and more recently Sebastian Conrad, *What Is Global History?* (Princeton: Princeton University Press, 2015).
6. A veritable cottage industry has sprung up to address the "crisis of the humanities," but for a refreshing perspective on it see Peter Mandler, "Rise of the Humanities," 17 December 2015, https://aeon.co/essays/the-humanities-are-booming-only-the-professors-can-t-see-it. On the academic resurgence of the history of capitalism, see among others Jennifer Schuessler, "In History Departments, It's Up with Capitalism," *The New York Times*, April 6, 2013.
7. Jorge Luis Borges, "The Library of Babel," in id., *The Total Library: Non-Fiction 1922–1986,* trans. Eliot Weinberger (London: Allen Lane, 2000), 214–16; John Maynard Keynes, "National Self-Sufficiency," *The Yale Review* 22, no. 4 (1933): 755–69, now in id., *The Collected Writings of John Maynard Keynes*, ed. Elizabeth Johnson and David Moggridge, 30 vols., vol. XXI, *Activities 1931–1939; World Crises and Policies in Britain and America* (London: Macmillan *et al* for the Royal Economic Society, 1971–1989), 233–46, 244. For a varied perspective on how to write the history of economics today, see E. Roy Weintraub, "How Should We Write the History of Twentieth-Century Economics," *Oxford Review of Economic Policy* 15, no. 4 (1999): 139–52.
8. See for example Sandmo, *Economics Evolving*, 7.
9. On such approaches see among many others Riccardo Faucci, *L'economia politica in Italia: Dal cinquecento ai nostri giorni* (Turin: UTET, 2000), 5–6. On the importance of the history of science for the history of political economy see Margaret Schabas, "Coming Together: History of Economics as History of Science," *History of Political Economy*, Annual Supplement to vol. 34 (2002): 208–25.
10. Mark Blaug, *Economic Theory in Retrospect*, 4th ed. (Cambridge: Cambridge University Press, 1985); Paul A. Samuelson, "Out of the Closet: A Program for the Whig History of Economic Science; Keynote Address at History of Economics Society Boston Meeting, June 20, 1987," *History of Economics Society Bulletin* IX, no. 1: 51–60, 52, and see generally for his perspective on the essays in id., *Paul Samuelson on the History of Economic Analysis: Selected Essays*, ed. Steven G. Medema and Anthony M. C. Waterman (Cambridge: Cambridge

University Press, 2014). For a take on Blaug's tentative conversion late in life, see Antonio Magliulo, "Amintore Fanfani e la storiografia del pensiero economico," in *Amintore Fanfani storico dell'economia e statista: Economic Historian and Statesman*, ed. Angela Maria Boci Girelli (Milan: Franco Angeli, 2013), 49–70, 66–67.

11. William J. Ashley, *An Introduction to English Economic History and Theory*, 2 vols., vol. II (New York: G.P. Putnam's Sons, 1893), 381, on whom see Bernard Semmel, "Sir William Ashley as 'Socialist of the Chair'," *Economica* 24 (1957): 343–53; Gerard M. Koot, *English Historical Economics, 1870–1926: The Rise of Economic History and Neomercantilism* (Cambridge: Cambridge University Press, 1987), particularly 113–15. The quote is beautifully discussed in Lars Magnusson, *Mercantilism: The Shaping of an Economic Language* (London: Routledge, 1994), 13 and id., *The Political Economy of Mercantilism* (London: Routledge, 2015), 7. On the German Historical School generally, see among others Yuichi Shionoya, *The Soul of the German Historical School: Methodological Essays on Schmoller, Weber and Schumpeter* (Dordrecht: Springer, 2005) and the masterful Erik Grimmer-Solem, *The Rise of Historical Economics and Social Reform in Germany 1864–1894* (Oxford: Oxford University Press, 2003). For a profound engagement with the purpose of such historical economics, see Nicholas W. Balabkins, *Not by Theory Alone... The Economics of Gustav von Schmoller and Its Legacy to America* (Berlin: Duncker & Humblot, 1988).
12. Quentin Skinner, "Meaning and Understanding in the History of Ideas," in id., *Visions of Politics*, 3 vols., vol. 1, *Regarding Method* (Cambridge: Cambridge University Press, 2002), 57–89, 73. For the history of economics being particularly prone to this, see also Richard Whatmore, *What Is Intellectual History?* (Cambridge: Polity, 2016), 88–89.
13. Carlo Ginzburg, "Machiavelli, the Rule and the Exception," in *Renaissance Letters and Learning*, ed. Dilwyn Knox and Nuccio Ordine (London and Turin: Warburg Institute and Nino Aragni, 2012), 73–92, 81. For the context of Italian thought on *precorrimenti* and idealism, see Ferruccio de Natale, "Storicità della filosofia e filosofia come storiografia," in *Dentro la storiografia filosofica. Questioni di teoria e didattica*, ed. Giuseppe Semerari (Bari: Dedalo, 1983), 101–48.

14. On theoretically internalist and "absolutist" versus contextually "relativist" approaches to the history of political economy, see among others Robert B. Ekelund and Robert F. Hebert, *A History of Economic Theory and Method*, 4th ed. (New York: McGraw-Hill, 1997), 61.
15. See, for example, the memorable statement in the epochal Charles Gide and Charles Rist, *Histoire des doctrines économiques depuis les physiocrates jusqu'à nos jours* (Paris: J.B. Sirey, 1909), vii, that "in this book the history of facts will not be discussed beyond the measure to which it seemed indispensible to us for understanding the appearance or the eclipse of such and such a doctrine." On the dimension of time in the history of economics, see furthermore Graeme Donald Snooks, "What Can Historical Analysis Contribute to the Science of Economics?," in id. ed., *Historical Analysis in Economics* (London: Routledge, 1993), 1–25.
16. Joseph Alois Schumpeter, *History of Economic Analysis*, (Oxford: Oxford University Press, 1994 [1954]), 344f7. That long forgotten economist was Marc' Antonio de Santis. Jacob Viner's own verdict regarding Schumpeter's posthumous work remains apt: "there is, as we shall see, much in this book which is redundant, irrelevant, cryptic, strongly biased, paradoxical, or otherwise unhelpful or even harmful to understanding. When all this is set aside, there still remains enough to constitute, by a wide margin, the most constructive, the most original, the most learned, and the most brilliant contribution to the history of the analytical phases of our discipline which has ever been made." See Jacob Viner, "Schumpeter's History of Economic Analysis," *The American Economic Review* 44, no. 5 (1954): 894–910, 894–95. One may still ask, however, with George J. Stigler, "Why Schumpeter or Anyone else Should want to Write on such a Scale," see his "Schumpeter's History of Economic Analysis," *Journal of Political Economy* 62, no. 4 (1954): 344–45, 344.
17. On the failure of Physiocracy, see the classic work of Steven L. Kaplan, *Bread, Politics, and Political Economy in the Reign of Louis XV*, 2nd ed. (London: Anthem, 2015). On Stalinism, see for an exemplary study Stephen Kotkin, *Magnetic Mountain: Stalinism as Civilization* (Berkeley: University of California Press, 1995); on the theoretical causes of the financial crisis see David Sington, *The Flaw: Markets, Money, Mortgages, and the Great American Meltdown* (New York: New Studio Group et al., 2011); for the miscalculations see Carmen

M. Reinhart and Kenneth S. Rogoff, "Growth in a Time of Debt," *American Economic Review: Papers & Proceedings* 100 (2010): 573–78, which astoundingly concluded by claiming their (tentative and erroneous) correlations "should be at the forefront of public policy concerns," 578. On the subsequent brouhaha see John Cassidy, "The Reinhart and Rogoff Controversy: A Summing Up," *The New Yorker*, April 26, 2013. See also L. Randall Wray, "Why Reinhart and Rogoff Results Are Crap," *EconoMonitor*, April 20, 2013, http://archive.economonitor.com/lrwray/2013/04/20/why-reinhart-and-rogoff-results-are-crap/. On austerity in general see Mark Blyth, *Austerity: The History of a Dangerous Idea* (Oxford: Oxford University Press, 2013); Florian Schui, *Austerity: The Great Failure* (New Haven: Yale University Press, 2014). On economists making mistakes, see Alessandro Roncaglia, *Economisti che sbagliano: Le radici culturali della crisi* (Rome-Bari: Laterza, 2010).

18. Oscar Wilde, "The Soul of Man Under Socialism," in id., *The Soul of Man Under Socialism & Selected Critical Prose*, ed. Linda Dowling (London: Penguin, 2001), 125–60, 130. For an illuminating take on how "anyone" still believing in self-regulating markets "must have been asleep for the past five or six years," see Raymond Geuss, "Economies: Bad, Good, Indifferent," in id., *Reality and Its Dreams* (Cambridge, MA: Harvard University Press, 2016), 117–47, 143.
19. Joseph Dorfman, *The Economic Mind in American Civilization*, 3 vols. vol. I (New York: Viking, 1946–1949), ix.
20. David Hume, "Of Civil Liberty," in id., *Political Essays*, ed. Knud Haakonssen (Cambridge: Cambridge University Press, 1994), 51–57, 52.
21. On the limitations of Hume's viewpoint, see Sophus A. Reinert, "Introduction" to Antonio Serra, *A Short Treatise on the Wealth and Poverty of Nations (1613)*, trans. Jonathan Hunt (London, New York, and Delhi: Anthem, 2011), 1–86, 19–21.
22. The idea of a medieval "commercial revolution" is perhaps most strongly linked to Roberto S. Lopez's late survey *The Commercial Revolution of the Middle Ages, 950–1350* (Cambridge: Cambridge University Press, 1976). On the "Economic Turn," see Steven L. Kaplan and Sophus A. Reinert, "The Economic Turn in Enlightenment Europe," introduction to Kaplan and Reinert, eds., *The Economic Turn: Recasting Political Economy in Eighteenth-Century Europe*, 2 vols. (London: Anthem, forthcoming 2018).

23. Pierre Bourdieu, *Sur l'état: Cours au Collège de France, 1989–1992* (Paris: Seuil, 2012), 300–347, but still very useful is id., "Rethinking the State: Genesis and Structure of the Bureaucratic Field," in *State/Culture: State Formation after the Cultural Turn*, ed. George Steinmetz (Ithaca and London: Cornell University Press, 1999), 53–75.
24. See among others Aldo Musacchio and Sergio G. Lazzarini, *Reinventing State Capitalism: Leviathan in Business, Brazil and Beyond* (Cambridge, MA: Harvard University Press, 2014).
25. See, again among others, Erik S. Reinert, "The Role of the State in Economic Growth," *Journal of Economic Studies* 26, no. 4/5 (1999): 268–326; Chalmers Johnson, *MITI and the Japanese Miracle: The Growth of Industrial Policy, 1925–1975* (Stanford: Stanford University Press, 1982); Robert Wade, *Governing the Market: Economic Theory and the Role of Government in East Asian Industrialization* (Princeton: Princeton University Press, 1990); and Alice H. Amsden, *The Rise of "The Rest:" Challenges to the West from Late-Industrializing Economies* (Oxford: Oxford University Press, 2001).
26. John Kenneth Galbraith, *American Capitalism: The Concept of Countervailing Power* (New York: Houghton Mifflin, 1952). On Galbraith, see among others Richard Parker, *John Kenneth Galbraith: His Life, His Politics, His Economics* (New York: Farrar, Straus and Giroux, 2005).
27. For a related argument, see John O'Neill, *The Market: Ethics, Knowledge and Politics* (London: Routledge, 1998), 2.
28. For a happy reminder of which see Philip J. Stern, *The Company-State: Corporate Sovereignty and the Early Modern Foundations of the British Empire in India* (Oxford: Oxford University Press, 2011); Sophus A. Reinert, "Rivalry: Greatness in Early Modern Political Economy," in *Mercantilism Reimagined: Political Economy in Early Modern Britain and Its Empire*, ed. Philip J. Stern and Carl Wennerlind (Oxford: Oxford University Press, 2013), 248–370, now also as "Economic Emulation and the Politics of International Trade in Early Modern Europe," in *Handbook of Alternative Theories of Economic Development*, ed. Erik S. Reinert, Jayati Ghosh, and Rainer Kattel (Cheltenham: Edward Elgar, 2016), 42–62, particularly 55–56.
29. Herman Melville, *Correspondence*, ed., Lynn Horth, Evanston and (Chicago: Northwestern University Press and the Newberry Library, 1993), letter of [17?] November 1851, 213.

30. On these varieties of political economy see Peter Groenewegen, "'Political Economy' and 'Economics'," *The New Palgrave: A Dictionary of Economics*, 2nd ed., 8 vols., vol. III, ed. Steven N. Durlauf and Lawrence E. Blume (Basingstoke: Palgrave Macmillan, 2008), 904–7. The histories of how the term evolved are many, but see among others Dimitris Milonakis and Ben Fine, *From Political Economy to Economics: Method, the Social and the Historical in the Evolution of Economic Theory* (London: Routledge, 2009).
31. Adam Smith, *An Inquiry into the Nature and Causes of the Wealth of Nations*, 2 vols. in one, vol. I, ed. Edwin Cannan (Chicago: University of Chicago Press, 1976), 449.
32. See Sophus A. Reinert, *Translating Empire: Emulation and the Origins of Political Economy* (Cambridge, MA: Harvard University Press, 2011), 26–29 for a discussion of this idiom.
33. Boldizzoni, *Poverty of Clio*, 3 and *passim*; Alon Kadish, "Economic History and the Contraction of Economics," in id., *Historians, Economists, and Economic History* (London: Routledge, 1989), 221–45.
34. For different caveats regarding these challenges, see Quentin Skinner, *Liberty before Liberalism* (Cambridge: Cambridge University Press, 1998), 101–20; Lynn Hunt, "Against Presentism," *Perspectives on History*, May 2002; and Nick Jardine, "Uses and Abuses of Anachronism in the History of the Sciences," *History of Science* 38 (2000): 251–70.
35. Quentin Skinner, *Liberty Before Liberalism* (Cambridge: Cambridge University Press, 1997), 116, 118.
36. Sophus A. Reinert, "Authority and Expertise at the Origins of Macroeconomics," in *Antonio Serra and the Economics of Good Government*, ed. Rosario Patalano and Sophus A. Reinert (Basingstoke: Palgrave Macmillan, 2016), 112–42, 113 and *passim*.
37. Agostino Paradisi, "Lezioni di economia civile [1771]," Biblioteca Panizzi, Reggio Emilia, Italy, MSS. REGG: E 139, vol. II, f. 102–3. On Paradisi, see Sophus A. Reinert, "Lessons on the Rise and Fall of Great Powers: Conquest, Commerce, and Decline in Enlightenment Italy," *The American Historical Review* 115, no. 5 (2010): 1395–1425.
38. Istvan Hont, "Jealousy of Trade: An Introduction," in id., *Jealousy of Trade: International Competition and the Nation-State in Historical Perspective* (Cambridge, MA: Harvard University Press, 2005), 1–156, 5, 155.

39. Raymond Geuss, "István Hont (1947–2013)," in id., *Reality and Its Dreams*, 85–90, 89.
40. Edmond E. Lincoln, "Applied Economic History: Some Relations between Economic History and Modern Business Management," in *Facts and Factors in Economic History: Articles by Former Students for Edwin Francis Gay*, ed. Arthur H. Cole, A. L. Dunham, and N. S. B. Gras (Cambridge, MA: Harvard University Press, 1932), 640–65, 665.
41. Joseph A. Schumpeter, "Comments on a Plan for the Study of Entrepreneurship," in id., *The Economics and Sociology of Capitalism*, ed. Richard Swedberg (Princeton: Princeton University Press), 406–28, 408.
42. As Wilhelm Roscher argued in 1843, economic science had by default to be "a political science, by which the main thing is: to judge people and to rule over them." See his *Grundriß zu Vorlesungen über die Staatswirthschaft. Nach geschichtlicher Methode*, Göttingen, 1843, iv, quoted in Thanasis Giouras, "Wilhelm Roscher: The 'Historical Method' in the Social Sciences; Critical Observations for a Contemporary Evaluation," *Journal of Economic Studies* 22, no. 3/4/5 (1995): 106–26, 120. For an impressionistic sample of sentimentally similar, though practically greatly different, justifications for the history of political economy by less seminal authorities, see, among *many* others, Giulio Capodaglio, *Sommario di storia delle dottrine* economiche (Bologna: Zanichelli, 1937), 1–5; Lucas Beltran, *Historia de las doctrinas económicas* (Barcelona: Editorial Teide, 1960), 7–8; R. D. Collison Black, "Introduction," in Collison Black, ed., *Ideas in Economics* (Houndmills: Macmillan, 1986), ix–x, ix.
43. For a salutary reminder of the relationship between economics and the public sphere, see Harro Maas, *Economic Methodology: A Historical Introduction*, trans. Liz Waters (London: Routledge, 2014), 174.
44. Binyamin Appelbaum, "A Little-Noticed Fact About Trade: It's No Longer Rising," *The New York Times*, October 30, 2016; Roger Cohen, "The Rage of 2016," *The New York Times*, December 5, 2016.
45. See, among others, Martin Rees, *Our Final Century? Will the Human Race Survive the Twenty-First Century?* (London: Heinemann, 2003); Mark Lynas, *Six Degrees: Our Future on a Hotter Planet* (New York: HarperCollins, 2008); and Elizabeth Kolbert, *The Sixth Extinction: An Unnatural History* (New York: Henry Holt, 2014).

46. William J. Barber, *A History of Economic Thought* (London: Penguin, 1967), 9.
47. N. S. B. Gras, "Capitalism—Concepts and History," *Bulletin of the Business Historical Society* 16 (1942): 21–42, including the responses of De Roover and Henrietta Larson. For the personal request to De Roover to serve as respondent, see Norman S. B. Gras Papers, Baker Library, Harvard Business School, carton 1, folder 54, letters dated 5 and 9 March 1941. On Gras, see Robert Fredona and Sophus A. Reinert, "Business and Economics in Historical Perspective: The Harvard Research Center in Entrepreneurial History and the Daimonic Entrepreneur," *History of Political Economy* 49 (2017): 267–314. On De Roover, see the essays of Richard Goldthwaite and Julius Kirshner in De Roover, *Business, Banking, and Economic Thought in Late Medieval and Early Modern Europe*, ed. Kirshner (Chicago: University of Chicago Press, 1974).
48. Wallace K. Ferguson, "Recent Trends in the Economic Historiography of the Renaissance," *Studies in the Renaissance* 7 (1960): 7–26, 17.
49. "Faith, Enlightenment, and Economics" in *Natural Law, Economics, and the Common Good: Perspectives from Natural Law*, ed. Samuel Gregg and Harold James (Exeter: Imprint Academic, 2012), 17–23.

Genoa, Liguria, and the Regional Development of Medieval Public Debt

Jeffrey Miner

Beginning in the late thirteenth century, the commune of Genoa went massively and irrevocably into debt, running up a seemingly endless series of long-term obligations whose collective face value surpassed 3 million Genoese lire by 1400. Across this formative period, the various individual debts were periodically consolidated, occasionally reformed, and very rarely paid down. Then, between 1407 and around 1450, the lion's share of the remaining capital was consolidated into a single mass, administered by an institution that would come to be known as the Casa di San Giorgio. A marvel of premodern public finance and political economy, the Casa was a kind of shareholders' consortium that would play the lynchpin role in Genoa's communal finances for nearly four hundred years, until it was abolished by Napoleon around the turn of the nineteenth century.

The precocity, scale, and endurance of premodern Genoa's communal debt attracted the notice of contemporaries. It continues to draw modern and scholarly interest as well. Commentators and opinions have run the gamut from Machiavelli, who famously praised the Casa di San Giorgio by calling it a "state within a state," to Karl Marx, who saw in

J. Miner (✉)
Western Kentucky University, Bowling Green, USA
e-mail: jeffrey.miner@wku.edu

R. Fredona and S.A. Reinert (eds.), *New Perspectives on the History of Political Economy*, https://doi.org/10.1007/978-3-319-58247-4_1

Genoa's and Venice's experiments with public credit the birth of "one of the most powerful levers of primitive accumulation."[1] Sovereign debt and lending to states continue to be major, if contentious, features of the modern political economy, and scholarship on the subject continues to generate new questions and lines of research.[2] For those interested in the historical roots of modern political and economic conditions, the experiences of the independent city-states of premodern Italy (Genoa, Venice, and Florence) continue to be a popular starting point.[3]

However, it remains an open question whether or not we should take medieval and Renaissance Italy seriously as the origin point of "modern" political economy or as a major stage in the development of public finance in particular. On the one hand, Italy remains a major point of reference in symposia, general syntheses, and new research.[4] On the other hand, scholars of Italy have voiced some of the strongest objections to broad lines of interpretation, preferring to emphasize diversity and discontinuity over general similarities or common patterns of development.[5] Of these objections, the most significant was raised by Anthony Molho.[6] A detailed reconstruction of the Florentine case in the fifteenth and sixteenth centuries, Molho argued, showed two things. First, that Florentine experiments in public finance were less modern than they initially appeared. Second, that the transition to a supposedly more bureaucratic and modern (and therefore powerful and effective) fiscal regime under republican government was undone more or less completely by the Medici, indicating that progress in public finance was neither inevitable nor irreversible. On the back of this analysis, he concluded that change in public finance depended on complex internal political developments, a conclusion that ran counter to much of what had been previously accepted—that all European states faced what amounted to evolutionary pressures from warfare, pressures that resulted in either modernization or elimination.[7]

This chapter considers Genoa's experience from roughly 1200 to 1450, alongside recent research on other cities, both Italian and non-Italian. It argues that the modernity of late medieval Italian political economy is both more and less real than it seems. Over the course of the fourteenth century, the Genoese created what amounted to a permanent public debt for their republic. In line with the findings of social scientific literature, this does seem to have amounted to a revolution in the realm of political economy, as the commune of Genoa shifted permanently and heavily to debt as a means of communal finance, resulting in the creation of a permanent public debt. However, this major transition enshrined practices, principles, and ideas that ran precisely counter to what we might expect a modernizing state to have sought—relative autonomy for regional subjects, a basically contractual notion of Genoese sovereignty over Liguria. This counter-intuitive consequence of the invention of permanent public indebtedness was a result of the distinctive contours of Genoa's political regime and its position in the Mediterranean. At the same time, a shift to permanent indebtedness did move Genoese ideas about citizenship and political membership closer to ideas we would recognize as familiar—a citizen body as the set of taxpayers, rather than a citizen body as all adult males eligible to bear arms. In light of Genoa's unique position between regional and pan-Mediterranean circuits of exchange, the chapter will close with a brief comparative consideration of the importance of regional economies to different cities' experiences with medieval public finance.

What Were the Compere?

It is critically important to start with the medieval vocabulary. Otherwise thoughtful scholars have at times put forward explanations of Genoa and its public finances that are flawed, because they have been led astray by modern vocabularies that only partially approximate the past they purport to describe. This is particularly true for social scientists who have most often used Genoese history as part of a longer-term investigation of the connection between property rights, political institutions, and economic change.

Compere, what scholars usually mean by Genoa's "public debt," appear in historical records as early as the mid-twelfth century.[8] In this period, a *compera* referred to a short-term purchase of communal fortresses or taxes to be collected. Over time, however, the Genoese adapted the *compera*, changing it into the instrument that would eventually form the basis of a permanent communal debt. In the late twelfth century, partly due to imperial pressure and influence, Genoa and other northern Italian cities began to experiment with new taxes, especially direct taxes based on assessments of propertied wealth (called an *estimo* elsewhere, but more often an *avaria* in Genoa).[9] Everywhere direct taxation was tried, it provoked serious social tensions. In Genoa, these were resolved by combining a forced one-time contribution to the commune (the *avaria*) with a *compera*: The new *compera* required individuals to pay a given amount, but compensated contributors with an annual percentage (usually 10%, sometimes lower) of their contribution until the original sum was repaid. This annual percentage was obtained from the income of one or more communal taxes, which were specifically assigned to participants (*partecipes* in the Latin). Unlike earlier versions of a *compera*, this new form allowed participants to freely transfer their shares and the associated income to a third party, and a lively secondary market in *compera* shares quickly developed.

This combination of contribution, compensation, and market proved fruitful and expedient for the commune, which was able to raise much larger sums of ready cash than by other available means. As has often been the case, the need for immediate funds quickly outstripped the income or funds assigned for repayment.[10] In a few bursts of acute need from the late thirteenth through late fourteenth centuries, Genoa created so many *compere* that the city was effectively left with a permanent communal debt, despite the fact that legal documents creating new *compere* continued to optimistically include clauses allowing for eventual repayment.[11] By 1400, the mass of *compere*, now totaling over 3 million Genoese lire in face value, had become unwieldy and burdensome. For a variety of political and economic reasons, the commune of Genoa and the administrators of the *compere* consolidated the vast majority into a single body, the *compere* of San Giorgio, later called the Casa di San Giorgio or simply "San Giorgio." This not only simplified the administration of tax collection, but it also standardized the compensation promised to participants at 8%.[12] Borrowing, however, continued apace and by the mid-fifteenth century, the commune was borrowing against future *paghe*, or interest payments and issuing *lire di paghe*, a kind of promissory note for the seized payments. Here, too, a lively secondary market developed and *lire di paghe* (deferred payments on the commune's consolidated debt) could also be used as a kind of substitute currency in the regional economy.

In fact, exactly what terms should be used to describe the *compere* is a matter of disagreement among scholars.[13] Traditionally, the *compere* have simply been called the "debito pubblico" or public debt. At times, they are more specifically designed as Genoa's "funded debt," because specific incomes were assigned to service the debt, or at others the "long-term debt," which distinguishes the *compere* from short-term loans at interest contracted with individual bankers.[14] These terms have not proven satisfying to all, and some scholars have advocated avoiding the term "public debt" altogether, preferring to refer to the *compere* as "forced loans" instead.[15] These scholars would prefer to reserve the term public debt for voluntary loans to the state. This has the advantage of highlighting the fact that the *compere* were not bonds, as much contemporary public debt is, and shares in a *compera* were not usually initially acquired voluntarily. Instead, a sum of money was demanded by the commune, which then could require payment from the citizens, often in proportion to an estimate of their propertied wealth.[16]

Yet while "forced loan" is mostly correct, it still fails to capture the full diversity and flexibility of the *compera* instrument. In some cases, contributions actually were voluntary. In one case, communal officers took out a regular, voluntary loan. Lenders were to be exempted from an upcoming direct tax (an *avaria*) in exchange for their contribution. When the direct tax failed to be collected, the voluntary loan was converted into a *compera*.[17] In other cases, the commune assigned shares in a new *compera* directly to individuals who armed or constructed galleys for a communal fleet, compensating armed service directly and omitting altogether the forced loan portion of the transaction.[18] So although public debt, forced loan, bond and other modern terms cover part of the Genoese fiscal system, none is a perfect fit and, to make matters more complicated, what term fits best changes depending on what period one considers.

The problem is less the possibility for miscommunication between scholars using different vocabularies, but rather assumptions that are brought in the wake of identifying the *compere* too closely with a neat modern concept. This has been most often true in social scientific literature that looks to use the late medieval or Renaissance past as a laboratory in which to explore commitment problems between sovereigns and their lenders.[19] These studies often begin from a highly stylized hypothetical problem (in this case, how lenders can safely extend credit to an absolute sovereign with the power to repudiate all debts with impunity) and a solution that is known to exist in advance (some form of constraint on the sovereign), and then try to work backward.[20] This opens up the road to problems raised by subtle differences between complicated premodern realities and simplifying modern vocabularies.

One such case is the use of the term "interest" to describe income to shareholders in the *compere*. In the modern world, the interest rate on sovereign debt reflects the workings of international markets for credit and debt, so that states that are better creditors pay lower interest rates on their debt than those who are relatively worse. Thus, the rate of interest charged on public debt can be used as a measure of how credibly states commit to repay their debts.[21] The *compere* paid a percentage of their value to participants every year, which does look like a rate of interest. However, the rate of return on a share in a *compera* (whether before or after the consolidation of the Casa di San Giorgio) was not an interest rate in the way scholars have assumed.[22] The rate of return was theoretically fixed, but varied in practice every year, depending on the income from the various taxes assigned to the debt. In effect, when scholars look at declining rates of return and see declining interest rates, they assume that what they are looking at is a successful accommodation between the state and its creditors. Although that is possible, what this declining rate more directly reflects is the declining importance of Genoa's port and, possibly, the ineffectiveness of taxation.[23]

Treating Genoa's public debt as a commitment problem also assumes a clearer distinction between the "public" and "private" portions of the institutions than the sources warrant. It is necessary analytically for the two to be separated so one can act as a "check" on the other, but the *compere* and the Casa are not necessarily easy to categorize in this way.[24] Medieval Genoa was a city that, even more than its peers, organized communal life in ways that are extremely difficult to disentangle. Unlike nearly all modern public debts, in Genoa the commune did not directly collect the taxes it used to pay the creditors. Instead, it farmed the collection of taxes out to private individuals or groups in exchange for a flat fee up front.[25] This is particularly the case after the founding of the Casa di San Giorgio, when the *compere* passed into a single body administered by a group of creditors, and then as the Casa came to collect taxes on behalf of the republic, and at times also operate like a public bank.[26] Occasionally, the Casa, as in previous arrangements such as the two *maone* of Chios, took over the administration of Genoese territory directly.[27] For some, the *compere* look less like a public debt (retained and administered by the state) than a consortium of individuals sucking away resources that properly belonged to the state (with all the moral judgment this implies).[28] Rather than a public debt that enhanced the borrowing power of the state, the *compere* were, in this reading, a tool for exploitation by private interests.

How one distinguishes the private from public elements of the system is critical for longer-term analyses, many of which focus on trying to establish how external bodies can constrain sovereigns not to default on their debts, thus enabling stable long-term borrowing.[29] But as with the issues of labeling the *compere* as forced loans and their annual payments as interest, the historical reality is too complex for easy analytical clarity. Careful attention to the individuals involved shows series interpenetration and relations that belie any sense of the *compere* as "privatized" or separate from the commune. To pick only one example: Tommaso Ottone was a Genoese notary who became the collector of a *compera* in the 1360s, as the culmination of a career that appears first in documents when he was the scribe of a communal war fleet. Later, he obtained a significant stake in the *compere*, used his shares as security to purchase a tax farm, served for a time on the doge's governing council, and even represented a Genoese inhabitant of the Byzantine Empire in a dispute with the commune regarding taxes.[30] Thus, whatever institutional mechanisms may on paper have secured Genoa's *compere*, the practical reality is that default was prevented by multiple, overlapping social bonds as much as by any formal institutional structure.

In light of these difficulties, what should be made of the *compere*? Were they a public debt? I would argue that they were, for in all their various configurations, they were long-term, interest-bearing communal obligations. Granted, it is essential to avoid anachronism if we are to understand properly how medieval Genoa's debt practices developed in response to its particular historical circumstances. But given that the *compere* fulfilled many of the same political and economic functions for the Genoese commune as modern public debts do for nation-states (providing access to credit for the commune, allowing short-term cash to be raised based on longer-term tax receipts), it seems unhelpful to stand so firmly on semantic differences. Whether or not "revolution" is the appropriate term for what took place, a major transition occurred in Genoa across the long fourteenth century.[31] The capacity of the commune to commit itself to long-term financial arrangements with individuals in exchange for a share of its take from taxation led to a permanent state of indebtedness as a normal and (mostly) acceptable part of the regional political economy. Genoa did undergo something like a financial revolution, but it was not driven by changes in property rights, nor did it result in a massive expansion of communal power. Instead, the transition to permanent public indebtedness had its origins in the distinctive intersection between the political economy of Genoa's dominions in Liguria and the demands of long-distance trade in the Mediterranean.

Communal Debt, Regional Subjects, Taxation, and Membership

The transition from a commune that paid its debts to a commune that lived in a permanent state of arrears was significant. However, the effects on Genoa and its dominions was not the creation of a modern or centralized state. Those who caution against anachronism are correct in general, even if the move to cut the medieval and early modern past off semantically from later experiments in public indebtedness is probably not the correct one. Interestingly, Genoa seems to undercut the assumption that strong states and stable debts are closely linked. In fact, Genoa's greatest expansion of its public debt took place in a period known rather for the weakness than the strength of central authority.[32]

In order to understand the relationship between Genoa's communal debt and its political economy, it is necessary to step outside the city walls and think about the place of Genoa's port in its regional (Ligurian) and Mediterranean contexts. The effectiveness of the *compere* stemmed at least as much, if not more, from the taxes and income that paid the participants than it did from Genoese cleverness in figuring out that short-term cash could be obtained in exchange for long-term streams of income. What makes the Genoese experiment in borrowing interesting is that it shows clearly how a set of pressures common to many cities in the period (military expenditure), though met with a broadly similar response (borrowing against future tax revenue), ultimately produced such a highly distinctive outcome.[33]

The basic structures that shaped the power and potential of long-term debt in Genoa lay in its *districtus* or regional state. A major watershed moment in the creation of a regional dominion came in the period from 1199 to 1204.[34] Although the Genoese had made efforts to exert influence and control over their regional neighbors before, both along the coast and in the mountains, during this period a major segment of its regional dominion was crystallized in a series of pacts between Genoa and the other towns of the Riviere. Although the specific terms of the treaties varied somewhat, the key provisions were all basically identical: Subject towns were to provide military aid, to pay *collecte* (extraordinary taxes), to contribute to the maintaining of a garrison at Bonifacio on Corsica, and to allow legal disputes between men of the town to be judged in Genoa, according to Genoese law.[35] The most important element for Genoa's future political economy, however, was the requirement that subjects obey Genoese regulations concerning navigation, particularly the requirement to visit Genoa first, before traveling beyond Barcelona or Sardinia. This last was critical as it meant all Ligurian ships would pay Genoese port taxes before engaging in long-distance trade. After the turn of the thirteenth century, although it took another couple of generations to firm up the boundaries of Genoa's dominion, the essential configuration of Genoa's regional dominion remained stable.

One of the most remarkable things about this configuration was that it did not attempt to exclude Genoa's regional subjects from the privileges, exemptions, and other trading advantages that the Genoese fought so hard to extract from sovereigns around the Mediterranean, beginning in the period after the first crusade (ca. 1100).[36] Agreements with smaller towns in Liguria frequently offered regional subjects the right to enjoy any "honors, immunities, franchises, graces, privileges and benefits of all kinds conceded to the commune of Genoa or the men of Genoa, now and in the future."[37] When treaties secured advantageous terms, they often applied to, "every Genoese or person who is held or reputed to be Genoese, is ruled by the Genoese or who enjoys the benefits of the Genoese."[38] When this status was restricted, it was at the behest of local rulers jealous of their tax receipts, not that of the Genoese. In the thirteenth century Treaty of Nymphaeum between Genoa and the Byzantine emperor, any Genoese in Pera or Constantinople were required to present some kind of documentation in order to enjoy the tax exemptions conceded to their community.[39] Interestingly, this was not included at the instigation of the Genoese, but of the emperor, who was well aware of how merchants might strategically position themselves as members of this or that community depending on the rules of the customs house.[40] This state of affairs seems to have continued, for we know that Venetian representatives in Constantinople in the fourteenth century worried that restricting access to Venice's privileges would induce many merchants to "turn Genoese."[41] One of the key goals of Genoese rule, then, was to co-opt its regional subjects into a subordinate position in Mediterranean trade, eliminating them as rivals but also subjecting them to the port taxes that were essential to its system of political economy.

Without this system, and its capacity to extract labor and value from long-distance commerce, Genoa's experiment with long-term debt would never have begun. The ability to borrow successfully did not spring into being from abstract fiscal know-how or political will. Instead, it depended on the capacity of taxes to meet the demands of *compere* participants. This capacity was, in turn, secured by a Mediterranean-wide system of privileged trade. Genoa's fiscal innovations were not produced by a "capitalist" attitude to wealth, but by a set of political, demographic, and economic circumstances which focused Genoa's fiscal system on its own port above all else.[42]

The insistence that regional subjects put into port in Genoa was absolutely essential to the city's Mediterranean ambitions, though it was less about eliminating competitors than it was about ensuring that as many people as possible paid the all-important port taxes. By diverting more traffic to Genoa itself, the architects of Genoa's dominions ensured that their city would be poised to capitalize on their region's most abundant resource—knowledge of navigation and the sea.[43] Those regional subjects who did wish to travel abroad could do so safely, at least relatively so, under the umbrella of the mother city's military, diplomatic, and legal protections. This political and economic blurring of boundaries was expressed in cultural and ideological terms as well.[44] That Genoa sucked up a greater share of its region's population than its peers elsewhere in Italy is another sign of the underlying limits of the economy and the way the Genoese actively shaped their region to focus economically on the capital.[45]

Focusing traffic on the capital city and taxing, it was a sensible choice, born of the basic problem that Liguria produced only a very few products for export. Small ports along the western coast produced various agricultural goods. Sanremo, for example, had about a thousand hearths in its whole territory in the sixteenth century, when it was known as a grower and exporter of a variety of citrus products.[46] The eastern Riviera was known already in the Middle Ages for its wines. Vernazza wine was praised by Boccaccio, Dante, and Petrarch.[47] Unsurprisingly, it was singled out for high export duties.[48] Nevertheless, there was not a great deal of underlying productivity to tap in order to finance long-term public debt.[49] Instead, the Genoese fiscal system focused on controlling key points of intersection in broader economic networks. The profits from most of Genoa's possessions in the region seem to have been meager, and the amount of income they brought in was often far outweighed by the costs of acquiring them.[50] Tighter fiscal and economic controls on the hinterland, then, would have cost more time and effort than could be recouped in tax or tribute.

The effort spent focusing Liguria on Genoa created a strong and interconnected web of economic and political relations. When the commune began to create more debts, and thus more taxes to pay the interest, this web was critically important in shaping the outcome. Although the growth of debt was closely connected with the demands of warfare in the fourteenth century as traditional accounts have it, when Genoa transitioned to a political economy based on permanent indebtedness, the result was not simply a strengthening of the state. It had the effect of intensifying certain relationships at the expense of others. This can be most clearly seen by considering two major periods of challenge to Genoa's regional dominion in the fourteenth century, one in the late 1360s and another in the early 1380s. These challenges were important enough to merit recording in the city's *Libri Iurium* or books of privileges.[51] Both disputes were direct responses to decisions about war finance, and they were significant for two reasons. First, they forced the Genoese and their subjects to articulate explicitly the benefits and obligations attendant on both subjects and rulers in the regional state. Second, they show how and why the rising tide of debt pushed the Genoese commune to intensify its fiscal attention in the capital instead of trying to intensify its controls in Liguria more broadly. Here, the analysis will focus on one town, Sanremo, because it was a key protagonist in both periods and the documents bear witness to the issues most clearly.[52]

In 1361, Sanremo was one of the several towns to protest against what they saw as excessive demands by the commune of Genoa, in this case for military support against a different rebellious town in the hinterland.[53] Their argument was particularist—it depended on a close reading of the specific terms of the lordship Genoa had purchased over the town.[54] Essentially, they argued that their specific relationship to the dominant city did not include the right to demand military service in the mountains. The representatives of Genoa, by contrast, based a key part of their argument on what we might consider general or state-level terms: Because Sanremo and its men enjoyed the privileges of the Genoese "in diverse parts of the world," they could thus reasonably be expected to defend Genoese interests wherever they might be.[55] The result was ultimately a compromise—while it recognized that Genoa's representatives were correct in principle, the legal officials charged with the case limited what could be demanded of the subject town and reaffirmed that they were not, in fact, to be subjected to taxes or impositions not covered in their earlier submission to Genoa.

The compromise that preserved the *status quo ante* of Genoa's Ligurian dominions in 1361 itself became a bone of contention in

1381. In the meantime, fiscal matters had changed substantially. The second round of dispute took place under strained circumstances, shortly after Genoa snatched crushing defeat from the jaws of nearly certain victory in the War of Chioggia (1378–1381). During this conflict, the Genoese had shifted heavily toward financing war using *compere*, rather than the sorts of direct impositions that had caused the earlier controversy with Sanremo and other subject towns.[56] In the 1350s, just after being decimated by the plague, the commune had created about 450,000 lire worth of *compere*, also fighting Venice. Around 1380, the commune mustered the astronomical sum of 1.2 million lire, increasing the face value of the commune's public debt by something between a third and half in the space of 3 years. In part, the legal disputes of the 1360s likely played a role in this shift, as they indicated the difficulty that could arise in compelling or even requesting subject cities to contribute manpower to Genoese military endeavors. The *compere* may have been nominally a "forced" loan, but the possibility of compensation meant that the amount of passive and active resistance would be lessened. As a result, the Genoese preferred to raise taxes in the port itself and reinforce communal monopolies over commodities like salt, which needed to be imported.[57] In part, this no doubt also reflects the long-term influences of the plague. As in Florence, the effect of the plague must have meant that coin, rather than labor, was relatively plentiful and thus encouraged the use of *compere*, rather than attempting to force subject cities to provide (military) labor, when preparing a communal fleet or army.[58]

As a result, when the men of Sanremo returned to court in the early 1380s, arguing that the specific terms of the 1361 settlement had exempted them from Genoese taxation everywhere in the world because of specific terms in the earlier treaty, the arbitrators sided decisively with the representatives of Genoa. In a clever, if tendentious, reading of the previous dispute, the men of Sanremo argued that when the arbitrators had declared them free from "new impositions" in 1361, this, in combination with the earliest treaty between the communities, made them immune from Genoese taxation throughout the world.[59] Not only that, but they also argued that the arbitrators' sentence had absolved them of the need to put into port at Genoa before sailing out of the district.[60]

These arguments, if accepted, would have preserved the rights of the Sanremesi to benefit from the Genoese system, while exempting them from contributing to it in any way. Unsurprisingly, the hand-picked representatives of Genoa's commune put in charge of the case disagreed. In the 1380s, the cumulative effect of generations of pressure on the other cities of Liguria—political and military pressure at first, but also the politically reinforced economic gravity of the dominant city—created a situation in which aid in kind was both resented and less effective than it had been in 1200. Sanremo had been effective at resisting the requirement to contribute men and arms. Attempting to avoid port taxes was another matter entirely.

Yet the transition toward debt finance and away from levies of men and arms took place within the long-established framework of relations and pattern of interactions. This emerges clearly from the content of a burst of legal activity undertaken by Genoa in the same years, as a special commission was appointed to review the cases of individuals, towns, and corporations claiming exemptions of any kind from the many different forms of communal taxation.[61] In a little over a year from spring 1384 through the summer of 1385, this group, clearly responding to pressures created by the massive increase in taxation that had taken place in 1378–1381, reviewed about fifty cases, rejecting, revising, and approving exemptions claimed by feudal nobles, subject communities, men with more than 12 children, and those granted exemptions for exemplary military service to the commune. Because of the moment in which it took place, we might expect this to have been a move to rationalize the collection of taxes by eliminating exemptions and pushing subjects toward paying port taxes rather than making direct contributions to military activity. Instead, what took place was a careful review of existing treaties, bargains, and privileges to make sure that the letter of the law was respected.[62] The committee seems to have paid particularly close attention to commercial taxes, dating carefully each exemption granted and limiting its scope to taxes already in existence, taking care to preserve the reach of the most recently imposed duties, and thus the income of the city's creditors.

Inside the city, the long-term consequences of this system had helped push the wealth of the Genoese abroad, into Mediterranean commerce.

By encouraging and supporting its own citizens' Mediterranean ambitions, the commune of Genoa had enhanced the shaping force of Liguria's marginal agricultural productivity on the city's economy and fiscal policies. As one of Genoa's own rulers noted in 1363, the wealth of the Genoese was so deeply invested in trade that even an assessment of their goods and property was a far from a simple matter.[63] This made measures like Florence's famous *catasto*, which inventoried the goods of its subjects down to the last cow, both difficult practically and unpopular politically.[64] Not only that, but even in the weakened economic conjuncture of the later fourteenth century, with the lingering effects of the plague and multiple expensive and inconclusive wars with Venice, Genoa's port was still profitable enough to support a huge burst of borrowing against its taxes.[65]

The need to tap the wealth of the capital's citizens in order to perpetuate the system itself encouraged changes in the nature of citizenship and membership in the community. Membership in the community continued to entail the legal protection of the commune, but it came increasingly to be identified with supporting the burden of taxation and borrowing imposed by the city in times of need. In one well-documented case, a man from Lucca who had obtained Genoese citizenship was kidnapped and held for ransom by members of the Spinola clan, one of Genoa's feudal lineages living in the hinterland.[66] He was able to secure communal sanctions against his attackers, who had challenged his citizenship, because he was able to produce physical documentation of his having paid the *avaria*.[67] The quality of his legal representation and social network was clearly inferior to that of his opponents, but participating in public finance was enough to call the commune to his defense and secure its judgment against his opponents. Interestingly, the damages he was able to recover from the Spinola came in the form of shares in the *compere*, suggesting another way in which public debt may have affected social and economic relations in Liguria.[68]

The reverse side of this linking of citizenship with public finance was that communal officials increasingly attempted to revoke or withdraw the privileges of citizenship from those individuals who attempted to flout the law and, especially, to avoid communal taxation. When, in 1372, Genoa's doge heard that there were ships avoiding the port because they did not wish to pay taxes, he wrote in no uncertain terms to condemn their attitude. He and his council threatened that,

> the ships and their passengers will not be treated as Genoese, they will not enjoy the benefits or immunities which the Genoese enjoy, neither will justice be done for them by any Genoese magistrate in Genoa or any part of the world whatsoever. If they are attacked or suffer damage from any person, Genoese or not, they will not receive justice and no such legal case will be heard.[69]

This was the corollary of the tighter nexus between fisc and citizen—if citizenship was a status predicated on certain economic arrangements, then refusal to participate might invalidate that status.[70] Although the pressure of rising public debt did not transform Liguria into a more recognizably modern state, the effects within Genoa do seem to have exerted pressure to transform an older model of citizenship, predicated on active military service, into one that looks more familiar—a tax-based and economic model of citizenship.[71]

In sum, the expansion of Genoa's temporary debts into a permanent public debt across the later Middle Ages had multiple causes and effects. Despite what can be identified in retrospect as pointillist "progress" away from something that looks like a "domain state" (finance based on communal possessions, and impositions of service) toward a "tax state," long-term transitions of this kind are not discernable in particular moments like Genoa's reform of privileges in the 1380s. The capacity of Genoa's commune to sustain a remarkable amount of permanent debt was a product of two logics that intersected in the city's port: military support of privileged trade abroad in the Mediterranean and a local dominion that focused Ligurian patterns of political and economic life on Genoa as much as possible. The burden of debt was sustainable, or at least serviceable because of the tight nexus between these two. The expansion of the *compere* enhanced the commune's military capability, but it also led to a tightening of bonds between the commune and its Genoese creditors. In Genoa's dominion, by contrast, the capital city's debts ultimately reinforced existing relations and the system of individual privileges and treaties of a patchwork dominion, rather than driving a search for a reformed or intensified regional state. In subsequent centuries, the Genoese elite would use the Casa di San Giorgio to try and tighten fiscal control, and to rationalize tax collection in the city and its territory. However, this was more a response to the weakening economic foundations of Genoa's port than anything else. The lowered rate of return on the *compere*, then, should be first attributed to an erosion of revenue as opposed to strengthening bonds of fidelity between the commune and its creditors.

Fiscal Change and Regional Dynamics

Medieval Genoa's state of permanent indebtedness was the result of a combination of factors. Most notably, these were a distinctive regional geography and the political choice of its civic elite to invest heavily, politically, and economically, in long-distance trade. As broad models of fiscal change have suggested, warfare was critically important in driving borrowing. The specific configurations of that borrowing, however, had a distinctively Genoese cast, linking urban creditors, regional taxation, and Mediterranean exchange in ways that do not fit neatly into modern analytical vocabularies. Rather than a property of Genoa's urban environment alone, the *compere* suggest the critical effect of public finance on the late medieval political economy should be sought in regional interactions, even if the region in question was not always politically independent (as in Iberia or the Low Countries) or unified politically.

In line with what has been suggested by other scholars, the Genoese experience suggests that changes in medieval political economy may be better understood as the outcome of regional dynamics, more so as the outcome of either the strictly internal dynamics of a particular city or the generalized fiscal pressure generated by warfare. As Genoa did in adapting a known credit instrument, the *compera*, to shifting circumstances, Valencia modeled its civic debt on the *censal*, the most widely used form of personal credit in its region.[72] When the cities in the Low Countries began selling voluntary annuities called *rentes* or *renten*, this was, unsurprisingly, an extension of an already popular form of agricultural credit, the *census* contract.[73] In city after city, a link can be found between the demands of war finance and changes in public credit. At the same time, civic public debts were expressions of pre-existing and underlying practices typical of regional economies than strictly urban novelties.[74]

The regional dimension is even more critical in trying to understand the subsequent effects of this broad move to urban public credit. In Liguria, Genoa's rising indebtedness in the fourteenth century tended to reaffirm its relatively decentralized and privilege-based configuration. This was, in no small part, due to the fact that the regional economy had already been shaped by multiple generations worth of political choices to focus relatively intensely on the port of Genoa. Tuscany, by contrast, was home to multiple powerful urban centers jockeying among themselves and each developing its own civic finances in competition and comparison with each other.[75] Here, Genoa, like Venice, may prove to be even more of an outlier, for neither of the two Italian maritime republics possessed a substantial agrarian base, making both dependent on and invested in a long-distance trade to an extent unmatched by any other community in Europe.[76]

The medieval Genoese set up institutions of credit and debt that retain a very familiar cast, despite the centuries that have passed. The problem with teleological readings of late medieval public finance, readings that either trace an evolutionary genealogy to the present or set up abstract and ahistorical "problems" to be solved by reaching an already-given endpoint, is not simply that they make a vocabulary mistake, using "public debt" when it is inappropriate. The problem with teleological readings is that they misunderstand the meaning of the institutions they analyze, because they assume that the phenomena that are most familiar to us must be those phenomena that led to us. Instead, what emerges from a more detailed consideration of premodern public finance is a renewed sense for the divergent ways complexes of institutions, especially regional complexes, rather than single specific traits or practices, shaped historical outcomes.

Notes

1. Niccolò Machiavelli, *Le istorie fiorentine*, ed. Giovan Battista Niccolini (Florence: Le Monnier, 1990), 419; Carlo Taviani, "'Hanno levato l'amore dal comune e postolo a San Giorgio.' L'immagine del comune e della Casa di San Giorgio di Genova (XV–XVI sec.)," in *Libertà e*

dominio: Il sistema politico genovese, le relazioni esterne e il controllo del territorio, ed. Matthias Schnettger and Carlo Taviani (Rome: Viella, 2011).

2. For one recent overview of research on sovereign debt in the contemporary world, see Ugo Panizza, Federico Sturzenegger, and Jeromin Zettelmeyer, "The Economics and Law of Sovereign Debt and Default," *Journal of Economic Literature* 47, no. 3 (2009): 651–98.
3. For two popular and contrasting accounts of the medieval origins of modern conditions, see David Graeber, *Debt: The First 5000 Years* (Brooklyn, NY: Melville House, 2011), esp. 290–93; Niall Ferguson, *The Ascent of Money: A Financial History of the World* (New York: Penguin, 2009). See also Michael Veseth, *Mountains of Debt: Crisis and Change in Renaissance Florence, Victorian Britain and Postwar America* (Oxford and New York: Oxford University Press, 1990); and James MacDonald, *A Free Nation Deep in Debt: The Financial Roots of Democracy* (New York: Ferrar, Straus, and Giroux, 2003). One popular way scholars attempt the same is to link the city republics with seventeenth-century England, arguing that the Italian cities underwent a "financial revolution" akin to that hypothesized for the English crown. Michele Fratianni and Franco Spinelli, "Italian City-states and Financial Evolution," *European Review of Economic History* 10 (2006): 257–78; Ann E. Davis, "Bringing Politics Back In: Violence, Finance, and the State," *Journal of Economic Issues* 47 (2013): 219–46, particularly 230–31. For Genoese scholars, the temptation to lionize their city's history can be hard to resist. Giuseppe Felloni and Guido Laura, *Genova e la storia della finanza: una serie di primati?/Genoa and the History of Finance: A Series of Firsts?* (Genoa: Banco di San Giorgio, 2004).
4. For one influential program that attempted to synthesize across national boundaries, see Richard Bonney, ed., *Economic Systems and State Finance*, The Origins of the Modern State in Europe, Thirteenth to Eighteenth Centuries (Oxford: Clarendon Press, 1995). The Italian cities also provided the archetype of "capital" in Charles Tilly's much-discussed *Coercion, Capital and European States, A.D. 900–1990* (Cambridge, MA: Blackwell, 1992). For one recent program, looking at recent research and considering long-term perspectives and examples, Katia Béguin, ed., *Ressources publiques et construction étatique en Europe XIIIe–XVIIIe siècle* (Paris: Comité pour l'histoire économique, 2015).
5. Patrizia Mainoni, "Finanza pubblica e fiscalità nell'Italia centro-settentrionale fra XIII e XV secolo," *Studi storici* 40 (1999): 449–70; Maria Ginatempo, *Prima del debito: Finaziamento della spesa pubblica e*

gestione del deficit nelle grandi città toscane (1200–1350 ca.), Biblioteca storica toscana, 38 (Florence: Olschki, 2000).

6. Anthony Molho, "Tre città-stato e i loro debiti pubblici. Quesiti e ipotesi sulla storia di Firenze, Genova e Venezia," in *Italia 1350–1450: tra crisi, trasformazione, sviluppo* (Pistoia: Centro Italiano di studi di storia e d'arte, 1993).
7. Jean-Philippe Genêt, "Which State Rises?," *Historical Research* 65 (1992): 119–33, particularly 131.
8. Heinrich Johann Sieveking, *Studio sulle finanze genovesi nel medioevo e in particolare sulla Casa di S. Giorgio*, vol. 1, Atti della società ligure di storia patria, v. 35 pt. 1 (Genoa: Società Ligure di Storia Patria, 1905), 47–50.
9. Patrizia Mainoni, "A proposito della 'rivoluzione fiscale' nell'Italia settentrionale del XII secolo," *Studi storici* 44 (2003): 5–42.
10. For an overview of the system as it stood after the reforms of 1340, see Steven A. Epstein, *Genoa and the Genoese, 958–1528* (Chapel Hill: University of North Carolina Press, 1996), 206. See also Giovanna Petti Balbi, *Simon Boccanegra e la Genova del '300* (Genoa: Edizioni scientifiche italiane, 1995), 97–133.
11. See, for example, the *Compera magna venetorum*, or "Great *compera* of the Venetians," which allowed for the repayment of *compera* shares at face value. Archivio di Stato di Genova, *Manoscritti*, Membranaceo VII, 7r. Interestingly, it also assigned some of the income to paying the salaries of key communal officials and to the upkeep of militarily significant points within Liguria.
12. For a full overview of this institution and its multiple economic functions, see Jacques Heers, *Gênes au XVe siècle, activité économique et problèmes sociaux* (Paris: S.E.V.P.E.N., 1961), 97–192.
13. For a brief and helpful introduction to the modern terms, see the glossary in MacDonald, *A Free Nation Deep in Debt: The Financial Roots of Democracy*, 483–86.
14. The basic reference work remains Sieveking, *Studio*. It is also worth noting that in modern economic literature, the "public debt" refers to *all* debts contracted by sovereign entities, so that Genoa's "public debt" would include the *compere* but also any additional shorter-term or other obligations the commune incurred.
15. Julius Kirshner, "States of Debt," paper presented to the Mellon Sawyer Seminar on Debt, Sovereignty, and Power at the University of Cambridge, 18 November 2006. See also Julius Kirshner, "Authority, Reason and Conscience," 115–18. For an argument against the

use of the term "public debt" see Luciano Pezzolo, "The Venetian Government Debt, 1350–1650," in *Urban Public Debts: Urban Government and the Market for Annuities in Western Europe (14th–18th centuries)*, ed. Marc Boone, Karel Davids, and Paul Janssens (Turnhout: Brepols, 2003). Pezzolo names as the defining characteristic the "primary open market" and the unrestricted freedom to invest as they wish, which excludes forced loans.

16. For an overview, see Domenico Gioffrè, *Il debito pubblico genovese. Inventario delle compere anteriori a San Giorgio o non consolidate nel Banco (Sec. XIV–XIX)* (Milan: Giuffré, 1967).
17. The *Compera tertii pluris* (The Compera of Three More) was so named because the initial capital was augmented by a third to cover lenders' losses. See ibid., 178–79.
18. See for one example, Archivio di Stato di Genova, *Compere e mutui* 1018, 20r.
19. The classic case study is Douglass C. North and Barry R. Weingast, "Constitutions and Commitment: The Evolution of Institutions Governing. Public Choice in Seventeenth-Century England," *Journal of Economic History* 49 (1989): 803–32. On Genoa, see Michele Fratianni, "Government Debt, Reputation and Creditors' Protections: The Tale of San Giorgio," *Review of Finance* 10 (2006): 487–506; Fratianni and Spinelli, "Italian City-states and Financial Evolution"; and David Stasavage, *States of Credit: Size, Power and the Development of European Polities* (Princeton: Princeton University Press, 2011).
20. For a critique, see Francesco Boldizzoni, *The Poverty of Clio: Resurrecting Economic History* (Princeton: Princeton University Press, 2011). For a helpful definition and critique of teleological reasoning, see William H. Sewell Jr., *Logics of History: Social Theory and Social Transformation* (Chicago: University of Chicago Press, 2005), 83–91.
21. The classic case study is North and Weingast, "Constitutions and Commitment: The Evolution of Institutions Governing. Public Choice in Seventeenth-Century England."
22. Fratianni, "Government Debt, Reputation and Creditors' Protections: The Tale of San Giorgio"; Stasavage, *States of Credit: Size, Power and the Development of European Polities.*
23. Thomas Allison Kirk, *Genoa and the Sea: Policy and Power in an Early Modern Maritime Republic, 1559–1684* (Baltimore: Johns Hopkins University Press, 2005).

24. Stasavage's turn to consider merchant oligarchy, effectively a socio-political state of affairs, rather than a representative institution marks a major advance over previous attempts. Stasavage, *States of Credit: Size, Power and the Development of European Polities.*
25. Domenico Gioffrè, ed., *Liber institutionum cabellarum veterum Communis Janue*, Acta Italica (Milan: Giuffré, 1967).
26. On the bank, see Giuseppe Felloni, "Ricchezza privata, credito e banche: Genova e Venezia nei sec. XII–XIV," *Atti della Società Ligure di Storia Patria* CXV, n.s. XLI (2001): 295–318; Giuseppe Felloni, "I primi banchi pubblici della Casa di San Giorgio (1407–1445)," *Atti della Società Ligure di Storia Patria* 38 (1999): 225–46.
27. Carlo Taviani, *Superba discordia: guerra, rivolta e pacificazione nella Genova di primo Cinquecento* (Rome: Viella, 2008). The *maona* of Chios is a particularly interesting case, on which see Philip P. Argenti, *The Occupation of Chios by the Genoese and Their Administration of the Island, 1346–1566*, 3 vols., vol. 1 (Cambridge: Cambridge University Press, 1958). The *maona* of Chios was initially created as a *compera*-funded military expedition but when its target disappeared without a fight, the fleet was sent to the east to do something useful. It wound up capturing the island of Chios and setting it up as a quasi-public, quasi-private possession of Genoa that nominally belonged to the commune but was practically run as a private possession by a consortium of the participants in the original expedition.
28. Gioffrè, *Il debito*, 7.
29. Fratianni, "Government Debt, Reputation and Creditors' Protections: The Tale of San Giorgio." Stasavage, *States of Credit: Size, Power and the Development of European Polities.*
30. Jeffrey D. Miner, "Lest We Break Faith with Our Creditors: Public Debt and Civic Culture in Fourteenth-century Genoa" (Ph.D. diss., Stanford University, 2011), 100–102.
31. For a criticism of approaches to public finance that overemphasize balance sheets and are too hasty to see revolutionary change in less dramatic moments of technical change, see Jean-Claude Waquet, *Le grand-duché de Toscane sous les derniers Médicis: Essai sur le système des finances et la stabilité des institutions dans les anciens États italiens* (Rome: Ecole français de Rome, 1990), 175. Waquet's notion of "fiscal systems" is distinct from Bonney's "fiscal constitution," which is the state's own "general theory of income." Bonney, *Economic Systems*, 431–32.

See also Jean-Claude Waquet, "Conclusione: Qualche proposta per un'altra storia delle finanze pubbliche," *Cheiron* 12 (1995): 137–40.

32. Petti Balbi, *Simon Boccanegra*. For the ongoing weakness of state institutions vis à vis family, clan and other ties, see Osvaldo Raggio, *Faide e parentele: lo stato genovese visto dalla Fontanabuona*, Microstorie, 18 (Turin: Einaudi, 1990).
33. On the importance of local and regional difference in the Italian context, Stephan R. Epstein, "Cities, Regions and the Late Medieval Crisis: Sicily and Tuscany Compared," *Past and Present* 130 (1991): 3–50. See also Davis, "Bringing Politics Back. In: Violence, Finance, and the State." On important variations in fiscal decisions, Maria Ginatempo, "Il finanziamento del deficit pubblico nelle città dell'Italia centro-settentrionale (XIII–XV secolo)," in *Debito pubblico e mercati finanziari in Italia: Secoli XIII–XX*, ed. Giuseppe De Luca and Angelo Moioli (Milan: Franco Angeli, 2007).
34. Romeo Pavoni, *Liguria medievale: da provincia romana a stato regionale* (Genoa: ECIG, 1992); Gabriella Airaldi, *Genova e la Liguria nel medioevo* (Turin: Frilli, 1986).
35. See, for example, Dino Puncuh, ed., *I Libri Iurium della Repubblica di Genova*, vol. I/3 (Rome: Ministero per i beni culturali, 1998), 3–7.
36. For a recent summary of the way the Genoese trading nations developed and were organized, see Giovanna Petti Balbi, *Negoziare fuori patria nazioni e genovesi in età medievale* (Bologna: CLUEB, 2005).
37. Michaela Lorenzetti and Francesca Mambrini, eds., *I Libri Iurium della Repubblica di Genova*, vol. II/2, Fonti per la storia della Liguria (Genoa: Società Ligure di Storia Patria, 2007), 265.
38. Francesca Mambrini, ed., *I Libri Iurium della Repubblica di Genova*, vol. II/3, Fonti per la storia della Liguria (Genoa: Società Ligure di Storia Patria, 2011), 573.
39. Steven A. Epstein, *Purity Lost: Transgressing Boundaries in the Eastern Mediterranean, 1000–1400*, Johns Hopkins University Studies in Historical and Political Science (Baltimore: Johns Hopkins University Press, 2006), 109.
40. The "flag of convenience" was an important element in organizing trans-Mediterranean trade in the Middle Ages and beyond. What has less often been appreciated is that changing affiliation from one community to another was not an economically parasitic activity, but actually had important benefits for the group whose flag was adopted.

On the phenomenon, see David Abulafia, "The Levant Trade of the Minor Cities in the Thirteenth and Fourteenth Centuries: Strengths and Weaknesses," in *The Medieval Levant. Studies in Memory of Eliyahu Ashtor (1914–1984)*, ed. Benjamin Z. Kedar and Avrom L. Udovich, Asian and African Studies (Haifa: Heinemann Insitute, 1988), 188–91. For an example of a similarly cautious attitude by Manfred, King of Sicily, in 1261, specifically excluding "Provençals, Romans, Tuscans, Venetians, Pisans, and inhabitants of our kingdom who call themselves Genoese," see Mambrini, *Libri Iurium*, 584.

41. Benjamin Z. Kedar, *Merchants in Crisis: Genoese and Venetian Men of Affairs and the Fourteenth-Century Depression* (New Haven: Yale University Press, 1976), 8.
42. Genoa plays a major role in Tilly's *Coercion, Capital and European States* but he assumes throughout that cities are basically "economic" and stand in for market forces, so that the fact that cities' economic primacy might itself be due to compulsion or political exploitation never enters into his analysis. Tilly, *Coercion*, 17–19. For a critique, see Epstein, "Cities, Regions and the Late Medieval Crisis: Sicily and Tuscany Compared."
43. Valeria Polonio, "Dalla marginalità alla potenza sul mare: un lento itinerario tra V e XIII secolo," in *Storia della Liguria*, ed. Giovanni Assereto and Marco Doria (Rome: Laterza, 2007).
44. See, for example, the Genoese Anonymous's multiple poems in praise of Genoese victories at sea over the Venetians. Luciana Cocito, ed., *Poesie: Edizione critica, introduzione, commento e glossario* (Rome: Edizioni dell'Ateneo, 1970), 234. The constant circulation of people between Genoa and its satellite towns also makes it difficult to trace individuals by toponymic surnames, as Genoa was the home of many individuals styled "of" this or that town. Benjamin Z. Kedar, "Toponymic Surnames as Evidence of Origin: Some Medieval Views," *Viator* 4 (1973): 123–30.
45. On population distribution in Italy generally, see Stephan R. Epstein, *Freedom and Growth: The Rise of States and Markets, 1300–1700* (New York: Routledge, 2000), 89–105. *Freedom and Growth*, 89–105 on population generally in Italy.
46. Agostino Giustiniani, Vincenzo Canepa, and Giovanni Battista Spotorno, *Annali della repubblica di Genova di Monsignor Agostino Giustiniani*, vol. 1 (Genoa: Canepa, 1854), 26.

47. Luigi Tommaso Belgrano, *Della vita privata dei genovesi* (Genoa: Fratelli Frilli, 2003), 124–25.
48. For the trade in wine, see Epstein, *Genoa & the Genoese*, 176. The tax on Vernazza wine was over four times as high (25 solidi) as that charged for other wines from the region (6 soldi). Archivio di Stato di Genova, Manoscritti, Membranaceo VII, 5v–6v.
49. Ibid.
50. The clearest way to see this is to look at towns whose lordship Genoa purchased. For example, in the 1350s, Sanremo and Genoa split the costs of purchasing the town from its lords, several members of Genoa's Doria family. The total amount came to around 14,000 lire, and the income from the town's lordship seems to have been only about 150 lire annually. Lorenzetti and Mambrini, *Libri Iurium*, 465–66, 476, 481. For an example involving a mountain, rather than coastal town, see Epstein, *Genoa & the Genoese*, 133–37.
51. Antonella Rovere, "I 'Libri Iurium' dell'Italia comunale," *Atti della Società Ligure di Storia Patria* 29 (1989): 157–95.
52. This is due to the fact that Sanremo had only recently been acquired by Genoa as a subject, although the town did have a long-standing agreement with Genoa that dated to around 1200 as described above.
53. Lorenzetti and Mambrini, *Libri Iurium*, 499–504.
54. See, for example, the way the men of Sanremo kept careful record of the specific terms they served militarily under Accelino Doria, knowing that their action was likely to be cited later as a precedent. Ibid., 498–99.
55. Ibid., 503.
56. For a summary of the raw figures, see Gioffrè, *Il debito.*
57. Domenico Gioffrè, "Il commercio del sale ed il monopolio fiscale genovese nel secolo XIV," *Bolletino ligustico per la storia e la cultura regionale* X (1958): 3–32. For similar practices in other Italian cities, see Patrizia Mainoni, ed., *Politiche finanziarie e fiscali nell'Italia settentrionale (Secoli XIII–XV)* (Milan: Unicopli, 2001).
58. Richard A. Goldthwaite, *The Building of Renaissance Florence* (Baltimore: Johns Hopkins University Press, 1980), 29–66.
59. Lorenzetti and Mambrini, *Libri Iurium*, 517.
60. Ibid., 516–17.
61. For Sanremo's documents, ibid., 513. See also Mambrini, *Libri Iurium*, 788–972.

62. See, for example, the decision regarding Ovada and Rossiglione, which were exempt from taxes on goods produced in their districts, but required to pay the *pedagium* of the port of Genoa, all in accordance with multiple pre-existing treaties and agreements. Mambrini, *Libri Iurium*, 892–902, esp. 901.
63. *Historiae patriae monumenta*, vol. 18 (1901), col. 348.
64. Giuseppe Petralia, "Fiscality, Politics and Dominion in Florentine Tuscany at the End of the Middle Ages," in *Florentine Tuscany: Structures and Practices of Power*, ed. William J. Connell and Andrea Zorzi (Cambridge: Cambridge University Press, 2000).
65. For an analysis of the fragmentary records of the port taxes, see John Day, *Les douanes de Gênes*, 2 vols., vol. 1 (Paris: S.E.V.P.E.N., 1963). At times, however, the underlying taxes did fail to produce the required payments. See Miner, "Lest We Break Faith," 201. In this case, the commune voted to find new sources of income to pay the participants, another sign that the *compere* were acknowledged as a public debt and not the sale of rights to a private consortium.
66. For a transcription of the documents, see Ausilia Roccatagliata, ed., *L'Officium Robarie del comune di Genova (1394–1397)*, 3 vols., vol. 3, Collana storica di fonti e studi (Genoa: Università di Genova, 1989), 971–1063.
67. The requirement to bear the burdens of communal finance was ubiquitous in citizenship practices in the Italian cities. On citizenship, see William M. Bowsky, "Medieval Citizenship: The Individual and the State in the Commune of Siena, 1287–1355," *Studies in Medieval and Renaissance History* 4 (1967): 193–243; James Grubb, "Piero Amadi Imitates His Betters: 'Original Citizenship' in Venice," in *A Renaissance of Conflicts: Visions and Revisions of Law and Society in Italy and Spain*, ed. John A. Marino and Thomas Kuehn (Toronto: University of Toronto Press, 2004); Julius Kirshner, "*Civitas sibi faciat civem*: Bartolus of Sassoferrato's Doctrine on the Making of the Citizen," *Speculum* 48 (1973): 694–713; Diego Quaglioni, "The Legal Definition of Citizenship in the Late Middle Ages," in *City States in Classical Antiquity and Medieval Italy: Athens and Rome, Florence and Venice*, ed. Anthony Molho, Kurt Raaflaub, and Julia Emlen (Stuttgart: Steiner, 1991); Nicolai Rubenstein, "Reprisals and Citizenship in Law Suit at Lucca After the Death of Castruccio Castracani," in *Studi di storia medievale e moderna per Ernesto Sestan* (Florence: Olschki, 1980);

and Giacomo Todeschini, "La reputazione economica come fattore di cittadinanza nell'Italia dei secoli XIV–XV," in *Fama e publica vox nel medioevo*, ed. Isa Lori Sanfilippo and Antonio Rigon (Rome: Istituto Storico Italiano per il Medio Evo, 2011).

68. Roccatagliata, *L'Officium Robarie*, 1044–45.
69. ASG, *Manoscritti, Membranaceo IV*. 364r. For refusing to bring the ship into port, the captains were to be fined 1000 florins and the scribes 400. If a new voyage was planned, the captain faced a 1000 florin penalty, the scribe and officers 400 florins, the sailors 50 florins, and the merchants 500. Any goods loaded on the ship became property of the commune.
70. For a consideration of economic status and citizenship, see Jan Luiten van Zanden and Maarten Prak, "Towards an Economic Interpretation of Citizenship: The Dutch Republic between Medieval Communes and Modern Nation-states," *European Review of Economic History* 10 (2006): 111–45.
71. See Paolo Prodi, "Identità civiche e identità economiche in Italia fra Medioevo ed Età moderna," in *Identità cittadina e comportamenti socio-economici tra Medioevo ed Età moderna*, ed. Paolo Prodi, Maria Giuseppina Muzzarelli, and Stefano Simonetta (Bologna: CLUEB, 2007), 11–17.
72. Juan Vicente García Marsilla, *Vivir a crédito en la Valencia medieval: De los orígines del sistema censal al endeudamiento del municipio* (Valencia: Universitat de València, 2002), 137–232.
73. James D. Tracy, "On the Dual Origins of Long-Term Urban Debt in Medieval Europe," in *Urban Public Debts: Urban Government and the Market for Annuities in Western Europe (14th–18th centuries)*, ed. Marc Boone, Karel Davids, and Paul Janssens (Turnhout: Brepols, 2003); John H. A. Munro, "The Usury Doctrine and Urban Public Finances in Late-Medieval Flanders (1220–1550): *rentes* (annuities), Excise Taxes, and Income Transfers from the Poor to the Rich," in *La Fiscalità nell'economia Europea secc. XIII–XVIII: Fiscal Systems in the European Economy from the 13th to the 18th Centuries*, ed. Simonetta Cavaciocchi (Florence: Firenze University Press, 2007).
74. One way to integrate the study of Italy into broader European patterns, despite its political fragmentation, is to treat Europe itself as composed of a series of regional economic circuits, not all of which were well integrated with each other. Stephan R. Epstein, "Storia economica e storia

istituzionale dello Stato," in *Origini dello Stato: Processi di formazione statale in Italia fra medioevo ed età moderna*, ed. Giorgio Chittolini, Anthony Molho, and Pierangelo Schiera (Bologna: Il Mulino, 1994).
75. Ginatempo, *Prima del debito*. For a view of Florentine public finances and their effect on one of its neighbors, see William P. Caferro, *Mercenary Companies and the Decline of Siena* (Baltimore: Johns Hopkins University Press, 1998). Even smaller Italian cities tended to leverage their credit markets to dominate their political and economic hinterlands. See Paolo Gabriele Nobili, *Alle origini della città: credito, fisco e società nella Bergamo del Duecento* (Bergamo: Fondazione per la storia economica e sociale, 2011).
76. For a discussion of the full range of credit operations in Venice, including its various forms of public debt, see Reinhold C. Mueller and Frederic Chapin Lane, *The Venetian Money Market: Banks, Panics, and the Public Debt, 1200–1500* (Baltimore: Johns Hopkins University Press, 1997).

Author Biography

Jeffrey Miner is Assistant Professor in History at Western Kentucky University. Jeffrey is a historian of late medieval Europe, broadly interested in social and economic change in the premodern Mediterranean. His book in progress, *Public Debt and Civic Culture in Fourteenth-Century Genoa,* examines how the fourteenth-century explosion of public indebtedness in Genoa inflected both private and public life, drawing on a wide variety of methodologies and sources including financial records, legal privileges, sermons and poetry.

Angelo degli Ubaldi and the Gulf of the Venetians: Custom, Commerce, and the Control of the Sea Before Grotius

Robert Fredona

Trinidad and Tobago's position is that Barbados could not acquire fishing rights by virtue of the long and continuous artisanal fishing practices of Barbadian nationals in waters near Tobago because those waters formerly had the status of high seas and were res communis.

—*Barbados v. Republic of Trinidad & Tobago*, Permanent Court of Arbitration, Award of April 11, 2006, 144, 45 I.L.M.800, 823 (2006).

It is impossible to imagine a more canonical figure, one whose foundational reputation in his given field is more secure, than Hugo Grotius. Explicitly apotheosized by the Dutch in the eighteenth century, he would go on to receive almost universal acclaim as the inaugurator of

Martine van Ittersum and Nicola Lorenzo Barile provided crucial and generous assistance during the drafting of this essay; the author wishes also to thank David Butterfield, Julius Kirshner, John M. Najemy, Sophus A. Reinert, Jacob Soll, and Richard Tuck for their help and encouragement at an early stage. In the text and notes, the Justinianic *Corpus iuris civilis* is cited using the abbreviations D. [Digest], C. [Code], and I. [Institutes].

R. Fredona (✉)
Harvard Business School, Boston, MA, USA
e-mail: rfredona@hbs.edu

R. Fredona and S.A. Reinert (eds.), *New Perspectives on the History of Political Economy*, https://doi.org/10.1007/978-3-319-58247-4_2

"modern international law" in the nineteenth century.[1] Indeed, to read nineteenth-century historical surveys of international law is to enter a sprawling minefield in which volatile phrases like these cannot be side-stepped: "Modern international law, of which Grotius must be considered the father…"; "Grotius, the father of the science of international law"; "Hugo de Groot is regarded as the father and founder of international law"; and so on.[2] Even today, and even among the very best scholars, Grotius's influence is cast as both field-defining *and* epoch-defining: "Dutch and English overseas expansion in the early modern period," we read in a rightly highly regarded 2006 book, "is *literally inconceivable* without Grotius's … theories."[3] Twentieth- and twenty-first century scholarship has thus not questioned Grotius's canonical character, even as it continued to highlight the influences of his predecessors, men like the Italo-English jurist Alberico Gentili and the leading lights of the School of Salamanca.[4] But scholars largely—almost entirely—continue to ignore, or at best to pay fleeting lip service to, one of the most important practical sources of "international law" before Grotius, namely the works of thirteenth- to sixteenth-century *ius commune* (Roman and canon law) jurists, often Italians, and in particular their ad hoc opinions (*consilia*) as opposed to their doctrinal and trattistic works.[5] I find this omission somewhat perplexing because Grotius cites few, if any, authorities more than these jurists and Roman Law texts in his famous *Mare liberum* or *Free Sea* of 1609, with which he is purported to have first sired the field.

The technical legal character of the *Mare liberum* and its scholarly apparatus cannot be doubted: Averaging 1.5 mentions per page, Grotius cites no source more than the *Digest* of Justinian, often mediated through the interpretative lens of medieval glosses, lectures, commentaries, and *consilia*. Indeed, the *Digest* alone is cited more than all of Grotius's other classical, late antique, and pagan sources combined, from Aristotle to Virgil. If you include all the source texts of Roman, Canon, and Feudal law, we reach an average of 2.25 mentions per page. More striking, though, is Grotius's extensive references to and struggle against medieval works of interpretation: The works of the fourteenth-century Italian jurists Bartolo and Baldo are cited more often than those of Cicero, Grotius's most cited classical author; the authoritative mid-thirteenth-century Gloss of Francesco Accorso is cited more often than Pliny, his second most cited classical author, and

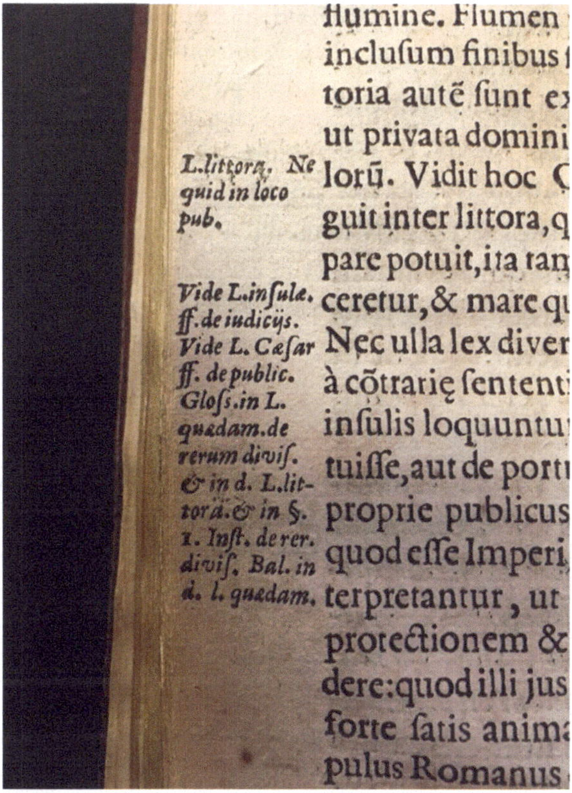

Fig. 1 Medieval legal citations; *Mare liberum* (Leiden: Ludovicus Elzevirius, 1609), p. 26. *Source* Harvard College, Houghton Library

so on.[6] Figure 1 shows marginal citations from p. 26 of the first 1609 edition, including references to two thirteenth-century glosses (on D. 1.8.2 and D. 43.8.2) and to a lecture of Baldo (on D. 1.8.2). It is well known that Grotius also routinely imported arguments, citations, and *exempla* from other intermediary works (like those of Gentili, Francisco de Vitoria, and Rodrigo Suárez), sometimes doing so with a kind of voracious sangfroid (as in the case of Vázquez). The preponderance of these sources and, crucially, of *their* sources and interlocutors—Alessandro Tartagni, Felino Maria Sandeo, Baltasar Ayala, Diego Covarrubias, to name but a few—emerged from Southern European

Rechtsräume, zones and approaches defined by affinity or compatibility with the long scholastic and *ius commune* traditions, in which jurists and other writers confronted legal-political problems not, as it were, head-on, but obliquely—finding them embedded already in a complex and often extraordinarily recursive array of inter- and intra-textual citations, a kind of hypertextual sea navigated through printed indices, headnotes, and cross-references but also, crucially, by locating the most authoritative jurists of the past and present who had addressed a given point (almost always including Bartolo, the *monarcha iuris* and *lucerna iuris*, the king and lantern of the law), employing them like highly-visible landmarks, or seamarks, for confident orientation and piloting.[7]

Historians have often given us a distorted picture of sixteenth-century European jurisprudence, Grotius's immediate background, by focusing, in a teleological fashion, on the innovative but still relatively marginal (and often university-bound) trends, such as legal humanism and legal nationalism, which would transform the practice and theory of law in the seventeenth century.[8] Well into the 1620s, the major centers of European legal publishing—Cologne, Frankfurt, Lyon, and Venice—overwhelmingly printed and reprinted works of traditional jurisprudence, which has come to be called the Bartolist tradition or the Italian custom, the *mos italicus*.[9] The point here is not to suggest that Grotius was a traditional jurist, even in the first decade of the century, far from it; only that many of the issues at stake in the *Mare liberum* had been in large part invented, raised, addressed, and disputed in theoretical and practical works of late medieval and early Renaissance Italian jurisprudence, works that created the living frameworks employed by Grotius's Iberian intermediaries; that grappling with these texts (or, indeed, appearing to have grappled with them[10]) was crucial for Grotius, his sources, and his opponents and should thus be no less so for us; and that ignoring these texts is to risk misunderstanding Grotius's arguments, the world in which he wrote, and, indeed, the whole heritage of premodern commercial-legal thought.

In this necessarily impressionistic essay, I will begin to make this case by looking in some detail at a single argument for maritime dominion addressed by Grotius in the *Mare liberum* and the longer manuscript work *On Prize Law* (*De iure praedae*) from which it was excerpted.[11] Some of the arguments for Portuguese control of the seas have been treated at great length—for instance, the arguments that dominion springs from discovery, from the laws of war, or from papal privilege. The argument I will treat, likely because of its more technical legal character, has received relatively little attention in spite of the fact that Grotius devotes the second-longest chapter of the *Mare liberum*, the seventh, to refuting it.

Great as Grotius was, and I surely do not deny his greatness, he was also not without his scholarly failings and I would rank his dismissiveness of theoretical opponents and his often sloppy, indirect scholarship high on the list. The latter was repeatedly pointed out in the eighteenth century by the French translator and editor of Grotius's *On the Law of War and Peace*, Jean Barbeyrac, who at one point, in a long note on a faulty quotation Grotius had copied from the sixteenth-century humanist jurist Jacques Cujas, added, "It is good to point out here a rather obvious example of the way authors copy other authors, without saying a word, and so run the risk of adopting and perpetuating the mistakes of others."[12] The former and latter defects can both be seen by examining a pointed and powerful but little known bit of *ad hominem* from Chap. 7, in which Grotius argues that the Portuguese have no legal title to control the sea by custom or prescription (a technical term of law that will be explored below):

> Thus it seems that Angelus, and those who have agreed with Angelus in saying that the Venetians and the Genoese were able to acquire through prescription a certain right over the maritime gulf adjacent to their shores, are either deceived or guilty of deceit, as is all too often the case with jurists when they exercise the authority of their sacred profession, not in the interests of law and reason, but for the gratification of those in power.[13]

Of course, such criticisms of lawyers survive to this day, but they already formed an enduring commonplace much earlier, in the Middle Ages: Lawyers, for instance, were called "deceivers" by such august men as Bernard of Clairvaux and John of Salisbury, and routinely called much worse—whores, vultures, vipers, and so on—by lesser poets and chroniclers. Is it any surprise that Thomas More, himself a jurist and a patron saint of lawyers, banished them "utterly" from *Utopia*?[14]

And that lawyers are friends of the powerful, and indeed friends of power, is no less obvious for no briefer a stretch of time: when Franco Sacchetti, the fourteenth-century Florentine writer of comic tales (*novelle*), has a man tell his nephew, just returned from studying *ragione* (literally "reason," but the term meant law in the medieval vernacular) for a decade in Bologna, that he should instead have studied *forza* there, we would still get the joke—even if Sacchetti would not spell it out for us: "it does not matter who is right"—who has *ragione*, he says—"for if one party has more power than the other, the law is useless, and today one sees penalties imposed on the poor and powerless easily; but on the rich and powerful with difficulty."[15] So the criticism is not new, and surely it is true in some cases, but what about this one?

First things first, who is this Angelus? This might seem unnecessarily pedantic, but to show how little attention Grotius scholars have until recently paid to his medieval Italian legal sources, I must point out that more than one edition[16] of the *Mare liberum* printed in this and the last century misidentified this Angelus—making him the noted fifteenth-century jurist and criminalist Angelo Gambiglioni of Arezzo instead of the correct Angelus, Angelo degli Ubaldi of Perugia, who was active in the second half of the fourteenth century (he died around 1407, but possibly as early as 1400), who was a likely student of Bartolo and the brother of the more famous Baldo degli Ubaldi, and who like his brother was a professor and prolific legal consultant. Angelo spent most of his career teaching in landlocked Perugia and Florence, but he was called to Padua by its lord Francesco I Carrara (called "il Vecchio") in the mid-1380s, serving as Ordinary Professor in the University there in 1384–1386.[17] In the Venetian orbit, Padua's law faculty was regularly tasked with exploring Venice's expansive jurisdictional and proprietary claims, both in the *terraferma* and at sea. Indeed, in an important essay, Aldo Mazzacane has persuasively argued that Padua's position meant that jurists there were naturally predisposed to defend Venetian claims against those of other regional powers.[18] I should stress that Grotius himself does not make the misidentification (Angelus Aretinus for our Angelus Perusinus), but there is nonetheless no reason to believe Grotius ever actually read the opinion on which he heaps so much scorn. In fact, there is evidence that Grotius actually copied the reference from another work: the treatise *On Prescriptions* by the sixteenth-century jurist Giovanni Francesco Balbo of Turin. In order to avoid diving too deeply into erudite *minutiae*, suffice it to say that Grotius repeatedly borrows citations—seven in all—from Balbo in this chapter and even carries over some of Balbo's idiosyncrasies and errors.[19] Not to mention the curious fact that Grotius always seem to have access to the same edition used by Balbo even when, as here in the case of Angelo's opinion, Balbo is using what would, a century later, have been an outdated and somewhat rare incunabular version of a text regularly reprinted and widely available in modern printed editions throughout the sixteenth century. It is also worth noting that although scholars have shown that Grotius regularly added legal citations after the fact to adorn his completed work, the marginal references to Balbo and to Angelo's opinion appear in Grotius's manuscript *On Prize Law* to have been written at the same time as the associated text, suggesting that Grotius was composing with Balbo's *On prescriptions* immediately at hand (Fig. 2).[20]

Angelo's opinion has come down to us as a *consilium*, a kind of ad hoc consultation usually written for a price on behalf of a party in a dispute or at the behest of a civic magistracy.[21] In the edition of Angelo's *Consilia* used and cited by Balbo (and then by Grotius), it is numbered as *consilium* 289, but in most subsequent printings it is numbered 290 (Fig. 3).[22] Had Grotius read the opinion itself, instead of relying on the summary of it he copied from Balbo and the criticisms of its arguments that he found in Fernando Vázquez de Menchaca, the Spanish jurist who authored one of Grotius's favored sources, the late sixteenth-century compilation entitled *Illustrious Controversies*,[23] he would have realized that (1) instead of aiming simply at the gratification of the powerful, in this case the Venetians, the opinion actually curbs and checks Venetian control of the Adriatic, and (2) instead of being a *pro parte* opinion for a Venetian client (or even a *consilium sapientis* for a Venetian official or magistracy), it is actually an academic exercise, a disputation as Angelo plainly calls it, printed later as a *consilium* (Fig. 4).[24] Indeed, at the end of the opinion, Angelus declares openly and simply *non sum consultus*, "I am not acting as a legal consultant," and that were he a consultor in this matter he would address other sorts of questions.[25]

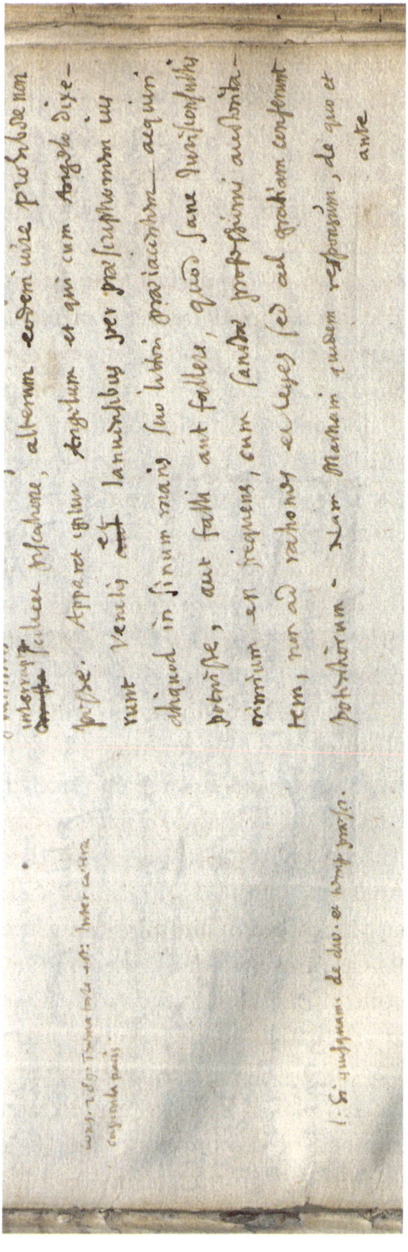

Fig. 2 Grotius citing Angelo's opinion; Ms. BPL 917, *De iure praedae commentarius* (autograph manuscript), folio 109r, detail. *Source* Leiden University Library

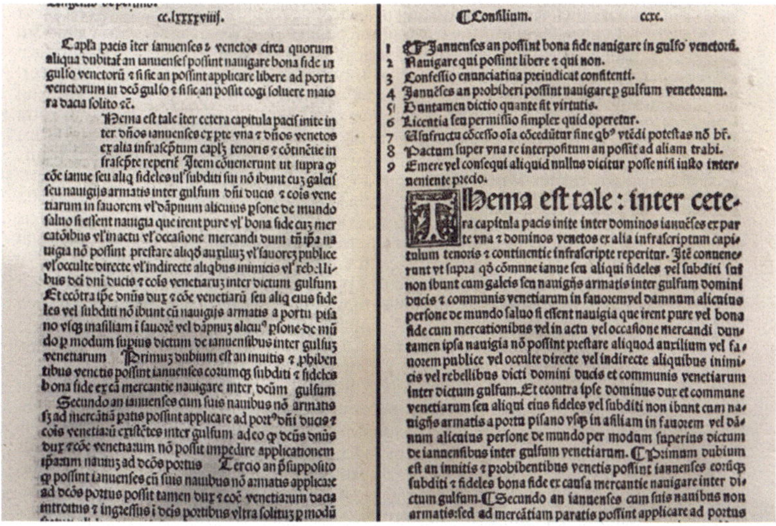

Fig. 3 Beginning of Angelo's *consilium* misnumbered 299 (correctly 289, at left) and numbered 290 (at right); from *Consilia et responsa* (Venice: Giovanni Rossi, 1487), n.f., and *Consilia seu responsa* (Lyon: Jean Moylin, 1539), folio 123r. *Source* Historical & Special Collections, Harvard Law School Library

A "long fourteenth century," stretching from 1298 to 1406, witnessed nearly constant struggles between Venice and Genoa for control of lucrative Mediterranean sea lanes and uninterrupted supplies of grain, raw materials, and luxury goods.[26] More specifically, between 1351 and 1355, Venice and her allies waged a (largely commercial) war at sea, in the words of one of their several pacts of cooperation, "for the confusion, destruction, and final extermination of the Genoese."[27] The war ended not with Genoa's extermination but with an uneasy and costly peace, and with the ultimate mastery of maritime trade in the Mediterranean still undecided. The peace treaty ratified in 1355 dealt explicitly with commerce and the control of the sea, stating, among its many provisions:

> Furthermore, [the parties] agreed, that the commune of Genoa… will not enter with galleys or armed ships into the gulf of the … Duke and

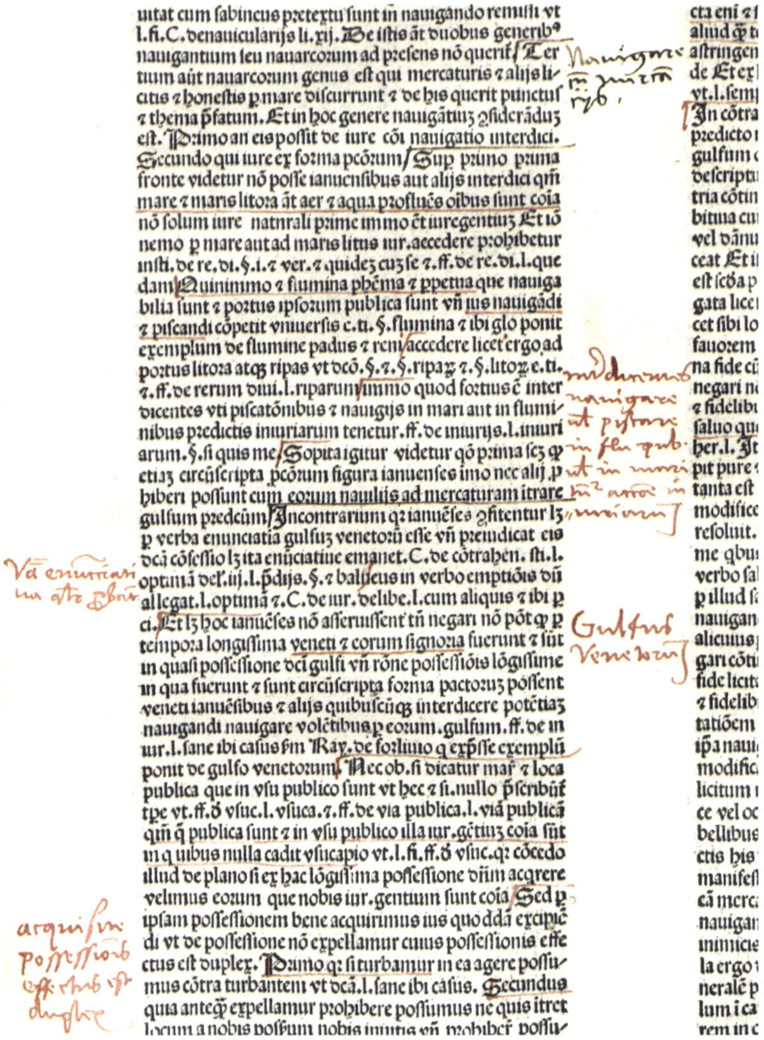

Fig. 4 Angelus, *Consilia et responsa* (Venice: Giovanni Rossi, 1487), consilium 289, n.f., detail, heavily annotated by Konrad Peutinger. *Source* Baverische Staatsbibliothek, 2 Inc.c.a. 1963 a, fol. s3 recto

> Commune of Venice, either to aid or harm any person in the world: this may occur if there are ships that go purely and in good faith with merchandise, or are in the act or opportunity of trade, provided that these ships cannot provide any help or favor publicly or secretly, directly or indirectly, to any enemies or rebels of the said Duke and Commune of Venice in the said gulf.

Less than a quarter century later, not surprisingly, Venice and Genoa were again at war. And when this conflict—the so-called War of Chioggia—ended in 1381, the peace agreement, signed in Turin on 8 August, declared "that the Genoese can and may freely sail in the Gulf of the Venetians just as and in the same manner as is contained in the old peace celebrated between the two parties on Monday 1 June 1355."[28] The terse and legalistic language of this treaty provision left many questions unanswered—questions about the very nature of Venice's control of the Adriatic, referred to here, as in nearly all contemporary documents, as the "gulfus venetiarium."[29] For Angelo at Padua, as for other jurists within the wider Venetian world, questions about Venice's dominion at sea were naturally, and properly, questions about commerce. According to Angelo, in his opinion, three questions or essential doubts arose from the *tenor* and content of this particular article: First, whether the Venetians can prohibit the Genoese to sail in the Adriatic "in good faith and for the sake or trade"? Second, whether the Genoese can put into Venetian ports with unarmed trading ships? And, third, supposing the Genoese can enter these ports, whether the Venetians can increase their "dues and entrance and exit charges beyond what is customary" for other ships?[30]

I want to address the second two questions first, since we can see here the extent to which Grotius's criticism of Angelo (if not his followers) is largely uncalled for, if not deceptive. So, what about the Venetian ports? Here the words of the pact seem to favor the Venetians, since it is a basic principle of Roman law that a contract about one thing cannot be extended to cover others things not originally considered. But to the contrary, Angelo invokes the authority of the consensus of jurists (*communis opinio doctorum*) that "if a license of going to a place is granted to anyone, the license is understood to have been granted of staying at the place and leaving it, because otherwise it would bring no convenience but rather inconvenience, uncertainty, trouble ... and the danger of death," a condition not unlike slavery.[31]

And, what about the third question, can the Venetians burden good faith Genoese merchant ships with additional taxes and fees? In proper professorial fashion, Angelo first presents the argument—ornamented with laws and legal citations—that, indeed, Venice cannot tax at all, since this power is retained by Caesar—that is, by the Emperor—alone. Only to quickly dismiss this as laughably legalistic, saying, "because all … cities and lords who rule for themselves impose taxes, dues, and gabelles as is observed *de facto*, we should not dispute further *de iure* lest our disputation meet derision." So if it is a given, de facto, that the Venetians can impose taxes and other charges, it remains only to be decided whether and to what extent they can increase them. "Whether" is the easy question, for the simple power to impose implies a related and linked power to extend, augment, and increase. But can the Venetians impose taxes so high as to effectively prohibit Genoese trade? A matter, he says, that should not be "left to the hungry appetite of the Venetians." Being forced to pay uncustomarily "grave and immoderate" entrance and exit taxes is the equivalent to being forbidden to sail the gulf, and the *rigor* of the article itself and natural equity state that Venice should not be able to subvert the intention of the pact by means of wickedness, deceit, or lack of good faith.[32]

Now let's return to Angelo's answer to the first question, and his reasoning there, from which emerged the entire argument against which Grotius argues in Chap. 7—such that we might call Angelo degli Ubaldi the *father and founder* of the argument for maritime dominion through prescription.[33] Can the Venetians prohibit the Genoese from sailing in the Adriatic? Without a doubt, Angelo asserts, the Venetians can forbid some types of navigators from entering their gulf—namely pirates, the wicked enemies of the Christian and the human race—and certainly cannot forbid others—namely those who sail *ex causa necessaria*, for urgent and essential reasons, and thus have the "fullest freedom to sail," such as ships bringing grain supplies.[34] But what about captains carrying merchandise and other honest wares? The specific article in the peace agreement seems to suggest that honest Genoese tradesmen cannot be stopped, but it also—and in the words consciously agreed upon by both parties—declares (by the use of the phrase "gulfus venetiarum," the gulf *of the* Venetians, employing the genitive of possession) that the body of water *is* the Venetians' or *belongs* to them in some way. Although the words of the pact do not explicate or expand upon this phrase, and the Genoese did not explicitly admit anything more, "nevertheless it cannot be denied (*tamen negari non potest*)" that "for the longest of times (*per tempora longissima*) the Venetians and their *signoria* have been and are in effective possession (*in quasi possessione*) of the gulf."[35] Angelo's carefully chosen language points to the Roman legal doctrine of *longi temporis praescriptio*, a kind of defense based on the long passage of time, and a variation on *usucapio*, or acquisition through possession or use for a fixed time.[36] By effectively and continuously using and controlling the Adriatic for a long time, Angelo asserts, the Venetians acquired a title of possession to it and this title was referenced and accepted by the very words of the Genoese in agreeing to call the sea "the gulf of the Venetians."

But Angelo has a big problem, namely that Roman law and the law of nations, the *ius gentium*, not to mention natural and primeval law, all declared the sea (along with the air, the seashore, and flowing water) "common to all."[37] Angelo's way out of this requires a subtle and curious step. The sea being "common to all" does not mean that it is owned by everyone, he claims, but rather that ownership of it is barred *to no one*. So the Venetians could own the Adriatic along, in theory, with everyone else. As owners, even as common owners, the Venetians could thus avail themselves of a legal exception or defense against those disturbing their possession or attempting to expel them from their property. "Before we are expelled," Angelo argues, "we can prohibit someone from entering a place possessed by us against our will and therefore we can by reason of possession prohibit sailing of the sea ... common to us by the law of nations."[38]

There is another problem for Angelo—or better, we might say, for the Venetian cause: "it is clear that those who contracted [the article of the treaty] wanted sailing for the sake of trade and in good faith, simply and indistinctly, to be permissible, provided that those sailing abstained from providing help or favor to the enemies of or rebels against the Doge and Commune of Venice" even though the very same article called the sea in question the gulf *of the Venetians*. In other words, sailing for trade is explicitly willed in the treaty by the Venetians in their capacity as *longi temporis* possessors of the gulf. And therefore what the Venetians could forbid by law, they do not allow themselves to forbid by treaty.[39]

It is hard to evaluate Angelo's argument from the possessive language of the then common name for the Adriatic, but I think he meant it—and later sympathetic jurists read it—less as an argument than as evidence for the longness, continuousness, and certitude of Venice's possession. The phrase "gulfus venetiarum" or "gulfus venetorum," the Gulf of the Venetians, is indeed widely attested already in the literature of the thirteenth century, in Venetian and non-Venetians sources. Even Genoese chronicles used the term unproblematically, as in the late thirteenth-century supplement to the Genoese *Chronicle* of Iacopo da Verazze [de Voragine], the city's famed archbishop.[40] Nor did this usage abate over the next century. But it was not, of course, the only available term: when in the 1330s, the German traveler Wilhelm von Boldensele crossed this contentious body of water he wrote, "I passed over the *sinus Adriaticus* or *mare Adriaticum*"—the Adriatic gulf or sea—"which today is called (*hodie appellatur*) the Gulf of the Venetians (*gulfus venetiarum*)."[41] The Genoese chancellor Giorgio Stella, writing in the early fifteenth century, used similar expressions.[42] And alternating expressions just like this—the Adriatic, today called the Gulf of the Venetians—would appear in chronicles, histories, and geographies well into the eighteenth century. And Renaissance maps of the region, not surprisingly, often employed similar terminology, whether drawn by Italians or not—in the 1570s and 1580s, for example, Flemish maps added "now the Gulf of Venice (*nunc Golfo di Venetia*)" to the ancient terms *Mare Adriaticum* or *Superum* (Fig. 5).[43]

The argument by genitive of possession was not long-lived. The crucial claim to both supporters and deniers of Angelo's argument was that the sea can be possessed by *praescriptio*, or something like it. The fact that Angelo offered this opinion in his role as academic and not as official consultant may be important in understanding how his doctrine of *longi temporis* prescription of the sea came about. It was widely accepted doctrine from the thirteenth century in that judges and legal consultants, in their official capacities, were required to follow widely accepted juridical consensus, the so-called *communis opinio doctorum*, but that jurists were free to innovate, to invent new doctrine in disputations and in university teaching.[44] So strong was this rule that penalties as well as financial and other liability could attach to practical judgments or opinions that deviated from consensus. The sixteenth-century Paduan jurist Pace Scala concluded his famed

Fig. 5 Detail from the map of Italy in Gerard de Jode, *Speculum Orbis Terrarum* (Antwerp, 1578). *Source* Private collection

treatise on offering expert opinions, the *De consilio sapientis* of 1560, by rhetorically stressing the importance of this rule: consensus doctrine, he argues, should "be followed as if it were religion" and all who deviate from it are "damned."[45] But what began as innovative doctrines in the schools appeared, in time, in legal consultations and judgments. This process was eloquently described in a much-quoted phrase by the sixteenth-century Roman humanist jurist Mario Salamonio, who wrote "consensus opinions are born in schools, grow there, become old there, and die there, and they exit from schools into the courts and are approved."[46] At some point in the life cycle of a new opinion, it gains enough support or is cited enough by enough jurists to enter the world of real practice. We can see a crucial aspect of this process at work in Angelo's theory of sea prescription and its reception.

As is well known, the publication of Grotius's *Mare liberum* instigated, or perhaps better, sped up what has been called a "battle of the books."[47] In less than half a century, more than a dozen major works and numerous minor ones took up the issue of maritime dominion, many explicitly addressing Grotius's arguments, on one side or the other. Several, including works by Cornelio Frangipane, Giulio Pace, and Paolo Sarpi, focused particularly on Venice's dominion in the Adriatic, but all addressed Angelo's argument about prescription.[48] Since it is impossible to lay out the entire history of the reception of this argument, I would like to simply outline three aspects of its development: first, some possible sources of it; second, how it was used before Grotius's assault; and finally, the origins of the argument that ultimately overcame or replaced it.

Although it is right to call the notion of maritime *praescriptio* Angelo's idea, he was not without forerunners in suggesting customary possession of the sea. With its repeated assertions that the sea was *res communis*, openly admitted by Angelo, a strict understanding of Roman Law seems the greatest obstacle in the way of rightfully occupying sea spaces, but the *Digest* also offered tantalizing hints that the Romans considered themselves lord of what they called their sea (*mare nostrum*), as well as that individual sea spaces and coastal spaces could be appropriated. For the latter, the crucial passage was the text that Angelo and the lawyers called the *lex Sane si maris* (D. 47.10.14), which records the words of the second-century jurist Paulus:

> Of course if someone has a particular right (*proprium ius*) in the sea, he can use the interdict *uti possidetis* if prevented from exercising his right because this matter pertains to private and not public law.[49]

The interdict *uti possidetis* (literally, "as you possess") was a double interdict, issued by the Praetor to both parties in a civil dispute over immoveable property, which would maintain the possessory *status quo* until trial.[50] So, in other words, the lex *Sane si maris* contemplated a situation in which personal rights to the sea could be upheld in a legal process. Historians now suggest that this law reflected a situation in the Eastern Empire where individuals could have monopolies over private coastal fisheries with fixed nets or perhaps salt evaporation pans,[51] but the medieval lawyers who confronted the passage could only take it at face value—that a possessory right in the sea itself existed (or could exist) under Roman Law. And if such a right existed, where did it come from? The thirteenth-century glossator Azo or Azzone of Bologna left a brief and controversial gloss on the law, stating, "let this [i.e., particular right in the sea] pertain to two situations: privilege and long custom."[52] The latter notion, that property rights in the sea could arise from long custom nonetheless seemed contrary to the spirit of the law according to which the sea is held in common. Venice always presented a test case, for Venice's relationship with the sea was special: For the lawyers, Venice (and thus its *libertas*) was *fundata* or *aedificata in mari*, "built on the sea," and so, even if it were not free by Imperial privilege, it would be free on the basis of that fact alone. Precisely because it exists, and has always existed, in a space outside of ordinary territorial dominion, it can itself claim dominion over that space.[53] The central figure in the creation of the juridical doctrine of *fundatio in mari* seems, not by chance, to have been Angelo's brother Baldo degli ubaldi. Commenting upon the *lex Summa* (D. 1.8.1), which held that "a building erected in the sea becomes private property," Baldo presented the kernel of the case for Venice's independence: "according to the law of nations, cities built on the sea belong to those who built them" and "the Venetians claim their liberty with this argument: because they did not build on another's soil."[54] But the mechanism by which Azo's "long custom" could become a property right was not clear. Nor was it clear exactly what "long" might mean in this case. Angelo suggests that the mechanism by which custom becomes right is *praescriptio*, but he was not likely the first to do so. That innovation possibly belongs to the earlier fourteenth-century commentator Raniero Arsendi of Forlì, who, in Angelo's words, "expressly gave the example of the gulf of the Venetians" in his own lecture on *Sane si maris*. Just as Angelo would be later, Raniero had been brought to the Paduan *studium* in the 1340s, by Ubertino I da Carrara, and there, like Angelo, dealt not surprisingly with the unique problems of Venice's dominion.[55] If *Sane si maris* and thus the interdict *uti possidetis* were applicable to "the gulf of the Venetians" in Raniero's argument, lawful possession in the sea would have had to emerge from something like *usucapio*. *Longi temporis praescriptio*, which medieval lawyers often understood as a kind of *usucapio* for immovables, then, seemed the right form to Angelo—especially since it required only 10 or 20 years, depending on a variety of technical factors, and the Venetian claim was based on a much longer period of continuous possession.[56]

The core of Angelo's argument is simple, but subtle. To summarize: For Angelo, as we have already seen, it was impossible (even, presumably, for the Genoese) to deny that "for the longest of times the Venetians and their *signoria* have been and are in effective (*quasi*) possession of the gulf." To this Angelo immediately adds, "by reason of very long possession (*ratione possessionis longissimi*)... the Venetians can forbid the right of sailing to the Genoese and to any others who wish to sail through their gulf," alleging the *lex Sane si maris* and noting that Raniero Arsendi before him had understood that *lex* to apply in the case of the Venetians and their gulf.[57] Angelo clearly felt that the logic of *Sane si maris* applied and that a right to the sea (of the sort that could be defended with the interdict *uti possidetis*) emerged from long possession, a process to which the closest analogue was obviously *longi temporis praescriptio*. This right is, of course, not ownership (*dominium*). Angelo knows that *usucapio* and its analogues do not apply to the sea or to things held in common or for public use, so it is impossible to legally acquire ownership (*dominium*) in the sea by means of possession, even by means of very long possession (*longissima possessione*) like that of the Venetians. Grotius, at the start of Chap. 7, when he says that such things "cannot be acquired as a result of possession," would then seem initially to be almost entirely in agreement with Angelo, assuming that acquisition implies resultant ownership.

"But," Angelo argues, although we cannot acquire ownership, "by such possession we properly acquire a right of exception (*ius quoddam excipiendi*) such that we are not expelled from possession," and this right has a twofold effect: First, "if we are disturbed in it, we can act against the person causing the disturbance" and, second, "before we are expelled we can prohibit someone from entering a place possessed by us against our will: therefore we can, by reason of possession, prohibit sailing and fishing of the sea and a river common to us by the law of nations," And "I conclude," says Angelo, "that not by the law of ownership but by that of the possession which the Venetians have of the said gulf, they can impede and prohibit sailors for as long as they are in possession of it," with the exception of ships carrying grain and so on, as discussed earlier.[58]

Grotius treats Angelo's argument here as if it were distinct from his saying that the Venetians were able "to acquire through prescription a certain right (*per praescriptionem ius aliquod... acquiri*)," the claim which had shown him to be "deceived or guilty of deceit." "Furthermore," and on this new point, Grotius adds

> Angelus propounded a thoroughly foolish doctrine when he maintained that even if prescription could not serve to produce ownership, nevertheless, an exception should be given to a possessor. For Papinian [*marginal note:* d. l. ultima = *D. 41.3.45*] distinctly denies the existence of such exceptions; nor would it have been possible for him to take a different stand, since prescription itself, in his day, was nothing else but an exception.[59]

The passage of Papinian included in the *Digest* and cited by Grotius declared that "prescription by long possession is not conceded by the law of nations for the acquisition of public land."[60] The language of Grotius's invective against Angelo is clearly indebted to Vàzquez, whom he quotes at great length, and who speaks of the arguments in favor of prohibiting sea access as absurd delusions ("But the opinion of all these persons are no less wildly erroneous than the opinions of those who are wont to embrace a very similar delusion in regard to the Genoese and the Venetians. The absurdity of all such beliefs...," etc.).[61] Both Vàzquez and Grotius were also participating in a long tradition of humanist invective against medieval lawyers that was already underway in the mid-fifteenth century.[62] This sort of dismissive rhetoric was for Grotius liberating: It allowed him to address the medieval jurists and their arguments, but absolved him of the responsibility of dealing with them as authorities; it also thereby allowed him a direct appeal to the texts of the *corpus iuris*, understood historically rather than synchronically (*ipsius saeculo*, he says of Papinian). Backed by the unequivocal statement of Papinian, Grotius, in his dispute with Angelo (*apud* Balbo), seems to have only one worry, the *lex Si quisquam* (D. 44.3.7), a snippet from Aelius Marcianus's third book on the *Institutiones*, which held that someone who had "for several years (*pluribus annis*)" fished in a small stream of a public river "may prevent (*prohibet*) another person from exercising the same right." Of course, it had been this law that suggested the contours of Angelo's *ius excipiendi*, with its right to prohibit. "[T]he *responsum* of Marcianus," writes Grotius concerning *Si quisquam*, "if duly coupled with the words of Papinian, is certainly susceptible to no other interpretation than the one approved in former times by Johannes [Bassianus] and by Bartolus, and accepted now by all the learned authorities" namely that the right to prohibit discussed by Marcianus ceases if it is interrupted and

> once such an interruption occurs, occupation loses its force, though it may have continued previously for a thousand years. Moreover, even if Marcianus had meant to say that a prescriptive title is conceded wherever occupation is conceded, although one can scarcely believe that he entertained such a position, it would still be absurd to apply a statement regarding a public river to the common sea, or one regarding a small river fork to a gulf; for prescription affecting the sea or a gulf would impede the use of something that is common property by the law of nations, whereas in the other cases mentioned prescription would result in no great impediment to public use. The other argument of Angelus, drawn from [texts on an] aqueduct, is rightly rejected by all on the ground that it is (as the same Castrensis [Paolo da Castro] points out) entirely extraneous to the question.[63]

Grotius here wants to be seen looking backward and forward at the same time. Backward: to the twelfth-century Giovanni Bassiano, to Bartolo, and to the fifteenth-century Paolo da Castro; back, in other words, to the medieval Italian jurisprudential tradition. Forward: to "all the *learned* authorities (*doctis omnibus*)"—citing passages from the works of François Douaren, Hugues Doneau, and Jacques Cujas; in other words, to the forebears of the *avant garde* humanist jurists opposed to the medieval Italian tradition. But Grotius took his references to Giovanni Bassiano and to Bartolo from Cujas, secondhand, just as he had taken his understanding of Angelo's opinion (and probably the Paolo da Castro reference) from Giovanni Francesco Balbo.[64]

Scholars have long treated Grotius as a father, as a beginning, and in doing so have elided what came before him. Perhaps a perspective that centers on Angelo degli Ubaldi, to take just one example, or that treats him as an endpoint, can allow us new glimpses at the history of international law and the history of political economy. To state the obvious: at the point of their creation, every work is an endpoint, a culmination of earlier arguments, works, and traditions. The search for origins, and the search for "fathers," in the history of ideas is a mug's game. On the small matter of *praescription* and the control of the sea, we can learn more by looking not at Grotius, but at his direct source on the issue, Giovanni Francesco Balbo's treatise *On prescriptions*. For Balbo, in addressing the question of "whether those things that relate to the law of nations can be prescribed," the most important references are the lengthy 1491 *repetitio* of the Pavian law professor Giasone del Maino on the *lex Quominus* (D. 43.12.2) and Bartolo's own earlier *repetitio* on the same law. The *lex Quominus* (a snippet from the Roman jurist Pomponius included in the Justinianic *corpus* declaring that water can be drawn from public rivers, except when this would affect their navigability or when the water is already devoted to some public use) was employed as a kind of springboard for dealing with the legal aspects of rivers and river rights.[65] Giasone found in Bartolo's teaching on the issue of prescribing public rivers a set of insoluble contradictions, contradictions that Balbo set out to harmonize:

> But indeed Bartolus can be entirely saved from contradiction and the texts of the *lex finalis* [D. 41.3.45] and of *lex Si quisquam* [D. 44.3.7] can be harmonized, for Bartolus does not say in *Si quisquam* that prescription should proceed by reason of the effective possession of the right of fishing. He says instead that when someone is in effective possession of fishing that person alone and at a small bend or part of a public river can prohibit another by his right of preoccupation (*praeoccupationis iure*)... But if he is not in the said effective possession, he cannot prevent another occupant, for however long a time in the past he has possessed it, and this is said concerning the *lex finalis*. It is clear therefore that in *Si quisquam* the prescription of ten or twenty years is not required for someone to be able to prohibit another from fishing, indeed preoccupation and effective possession of the right of fishing for the present are sufficient, as is stated by the words of this law, where no word at all about prescription occurs. And when such an effective possession is lost, the right of prohibition ceases...[66]

Bartolo, in his commentary on the *lex finalis* (D. 41.3.45), had presented a question: If my mill is destroyed by a flood and someone else wants to build a mill, above or below it on the river, which would injure me if I rebuilt my mill in its place, can I prohibit him from doing so? Bartolo had encountered a similar case in Le Marche and the lawyers there, he says, ignorantly argued that the owner of the destroyed mill would lose his right to prohibit another after a period of 10 years of nonuse had elapsed, following the rule in *lex Sicut* (C. 3.34.13) on the expiration of servitudes. A servitude, similar to an "easement" in English law, was a kind of property right in Roman law that, for example, allowed someone to restrain another person from doing something that would negatively affect his use of the property. But, Bartolo affirms "*praescriptio longi temporis* is of no use insofar as the use of a river, common according to the law of nations, is concerned, as in this case."[67] In his commentary on *Si quisquam*, Bartolo simply distinguished the case presented in that law from the case of the destroyed mill: in the former, the fisherman had effective possession, so he could prohibit another from fishing in his section of the river; in the latter, the man whose mill had been destroyed did not have effective possession.[68] So Balbo's harmonization of the apparently contradictory texts of Bartolo allows him to present a rule (*regula*) and the first of three exceptions (*limitationes* in the juridical idiom of the sixteenth century) to it: "Therefore there exists a rule that those things that are part of the law of nations are not prescribed. First, limit that rule so that it applies in terms of prescription but not with respect to custom." Borrowing the term (in this particular application) from several fifteenth-century jurists, Balbo transforms *praeoccupatio* (acquiring first or before) and *quasi possessio* into custom (*consuetudo*). The logic of prohibition in *Si quisquam* is then clear, "for many years a single person has fished in a certain part of a public river and has prohibited others, doing so with the knowledge of the people and without anyone contradicting this; he has the requested right by the tacit consent of the people, and indeed henceforth he alone should be able to fish there and to prohibit others."[69] Reconciling *Si quisquam* with the broader Roman law principle that rivers were public and common to all had preoccupied jurists from at least the middle of the twelfth century.

There is evidence of this in the apparatus to *§Flumina autem omnia* (I. 2.1.2), which declared "all rivers and ports are also public, and thus the right of fishing in a harbor or in streams is common to all"; there, one gloss to the last word (*omnibus*) of the paragraph added that neither could someone who had been fishing there a long time (*longo tempore*) repel another coming along, while another gloss attributed to Giovanni Bassiano argued that *Si quisquam*, which allowed repulsion, should be followed if the fisherman was "*in possessione piscandi.*" For although the right to fish (*ius piscandi*) was free to all in rivers, in Giovanni's view it was subject in any case, and at a particular spot in the river, to possession from which the right to repel another fisherman would emerge.[70] Balbo's second exception to the rule brings us back to Angelo. Although things pertaining to the law of nations cannot be prescribed in the usual way, i.e., through a term of 10 or 20 years, "nevertheless they are prescribed by a time so long that its beginning is not remembered to the contrary, this is an exception made by Angelus [on D. 41.3.45] where he reports that the Venetians prescribed the gulf of the sea for so long a time." For prescription based in immemorial possession, Angelo alleged the gloss on the word "constitutum" in the *lex Usum aquae* (C. 11.43.4), which held that "the established (*constitutum*) use of water, based upon old and long ownership (*dominio*)" should not be disturbed, since the gloss clarified that such use could be established either by the Emperor or "indeed by custom of which there is no memory."[71] Balbo's third and final exception is nothing other than what Grotius called Angelo's "thoroughly foolish doctrine," which explains why Grotius treated it separately in Chap. 7.[72]

Perhaps the fullest elaboration and explication of Angelo's theory would come not in Grotius or the "battle of the books," but in the work of the fifteenth-century ambassador and jurist Bartolomeo Cipolla who, in his treatises *On Rustic and Urban Servitudes*, devoted a number of important passages to Venice's control of the sea by prescription. Not surprisingly, the two treatises emerged from Bartolomeo's 1460–1461 lectures in Padua, just as Raniero and Angelo had addressed the Adriatic when they were in Padua.[73] Following the arguments of earlier jurists, Bartolomeo clears a path through the conflicting passages of the *Digest* and glosses, relying on an oft-quoted distinction made in the second half of the fourteenth century by Angelo's brother Baldo, "the sea is common in terms of use, it is no one's (*nullius*) in terms of property according to Jacobus de Ravennis, but in terms of jurisdiction it is Caesar's."[74] Since the Venetians recognized no superior, they could act *in loco Caesaris* and claim jurisdiction over the sea, and, like the Emperor, could lay servitudes on immovables held in common. More pressing (at least for our purposes) was the issue of whether actual property could be carved out of the sea by prescription. Using the standard scholastic *pro-et-contra* matrix, Bartolomeo argues *no* for all the reasons we would expect, chief among them that the law of nations forbids laying property claims on the sea. But,

> to the contrary it seems that it can be acquired for so great a time [that memory of it does not exist], because at sea there is jurisdiction just as on the earth, therefore it can be prescribed. Likewise, this is so because possession or effective possession, the memory of which does not survive, has the force of a title, privilege, or constitution. But by title and privilege, the Prince can grant that some private person has jurisdiction at sea, therefore possession or quasi-possession for a said time perishes like a privilege, or another title, but because the sea and other rivers can be prescribed and acquired by custom, therefore they could also be prescribed by possession for so great a time that the memory of it does not survive, which has the force of custom.[75]

At that point, Bartolomeo cites Angelo's "consilium" and his commentary on *lex Sane si maris* (D. 47.10.14) and the *lex finalis* of the title *De usucapionibus* (D. 41.3.45), taking the key point—that immemorial possession or effective (*quasi*) possession can have the force of custom, title, or privilege—but setting it within a framework of jurisdiction and princely (Imperial) power. He continues:

> The Venetians have occupied the gulf of the Adriatic Sea (*gulphum maris Adriatici*), the memory of which does not survive, and have prescribed the sea in terms of its jurisdiction. And likewise the people of Genoa in the case of their sea. But I understand the foregoing to be true when the title or privilege of an emperor is alleged, because he believes that he or his heirs had the right at sea. It is different if he confesses that he and

> his ancestors never had any title or any right but only prescribed it for a certain amount of time. … Likewise, understand the foregoing in relation to jurisdiction but not to ownership, because it cannot be prescribed by any prescription or custom, because things governed by the law of nations and public law, and in public use like the sea and navigable rivers, are not acquired at any time unless the grant of Caesar or the Senate should intervene.[76]

In Bartolomeo's treatise, Angelo's arguments are still relevant and still alive, though they have been adapted to a new framework.

> But it can be doubted that someone is said to have possessed or effectively possessed the sea or some jurisdiction over it. Say that he who has power over the sea (*ille qui habet imperium in mari*) is said to possess the sea. For I alleged against the people of Brescia that the Lago di Garda was entirely in the territory of Verona, because the Veronese people and the princes who ruled at Verona had always exercised power (*imperium*) and jurisdiction over the whole lake. And this was the judgment of the illustrious Consiglio dei Rogati at Venice. And I say the same about the gulf of the sea that is guarded by the Venetians: they have exercised and do exercise jurisdiction in that gulf.[77]

It is impossible to know whether Bartolomeo's arguments (or, through him, Angelo's) had any impact on the 1455 decision of the Venetian Senate that settled the jurisdictional dispute between Verona and Brescia, but this reference speaks loudly to the fact that the issues at stake in the academic jurisprudence of the fourteenth and fifteenth centuries were anything but purely academic.

Bartolomeo was, of course, neither the first nor the last jurist to approvingly cite and embellish Angelo's argument: We see it, for example, in Giovanni Piazza and in the other Angelus, Angelo Gambiglioni, both lecturing in the fifteenth century on the *lex* containing the *§Flumina*, which was adorned with the very gloss of Giovanni Bassiano that had provided Angelo degli Ubaldi with the seed of his argument.[78] We see it also in the Corfu-born Venetian jurist Tommaso Diplovatazio's ca. 1528 *On the Liberty of the City of Venice and the Dignity of its Rule*. The apologetic treatise, written in a Venetian cultural milieu shaped by the city's disastrous 1509 defeat at Agnadello, compiled a sprawling argument for Venice's sovereignty (including its control of the Adriatic) from a wide range of diplomatic and legal sources, among them Angelo's consilium and his lectures (Fig. 6).[79] And in time, Angelo's argument, when it was recapitulated, came not to rely on the technicalities of *longi temporis* prescription, which Grotius had anyway likely overstated because Balbo, his source, had appropriately focused on them in his treatise *On prescriptions*, nor on Bartolomeo Cipolla's Baldo-inspired idea of jurisdiction, but on the simple and potent logic of immemorial possession. So when in the 1550s Benvenuto Stracca, one of the first systematizers of commercial law, approvingly described Angelo's opinion in his treatise *On Commerce*, he says "Angelus responds that the Venetians have the right to prohibit navigation in the Adriatic gulf (*in Hadriatico sinu*) because they acquired it through time, the origin of which exceeds the memory of men," leaving out the possessive phrase *gulfus venetiarum* and the details of prescription entirely. And in 1635, when Selden quoted Angelo's *consilium* with approval, listing the long train of followers who agreed with it, he did so as well.[80]

As in the poetic description I mentioned earlier, in its own way, Angelo's teaching was born, and matured, and died. Even if it was kept on life support, as it were, during the battle of the books initiated with Grotius's *Mare liberum*. But it was not Grotius's arguments and those of his followers that ultimately overcame it. Figure 7, for instance, is a map showing Italy's lawful claims to the sea around Venice. They are, as you likely already know, limited to a thin band of waters adjacent to the coast, which we call territorial. The notion that jurisdiction, if not ownership, extends outward from the coast to a fixed distance may well be the innovation of another fourteenth-century Italian jurist, the profoundly influential Bartolo of Sassoferrato, who advanced it in his extraordinary legal-geometrical treatise *On the Tiber*.[81] In spirit, if not in detail, the system which now prevails is both Bartolist *and* Grotian. Like success, "international law" has many fathers, and the story of its paternity neither begins in the seventeenth century nor resumes there after a long dark age. Indeed, Grotius's real interest was not in gulfic spaces at all—not in coasts, inlets, and bays—but in pelagic ones: "the

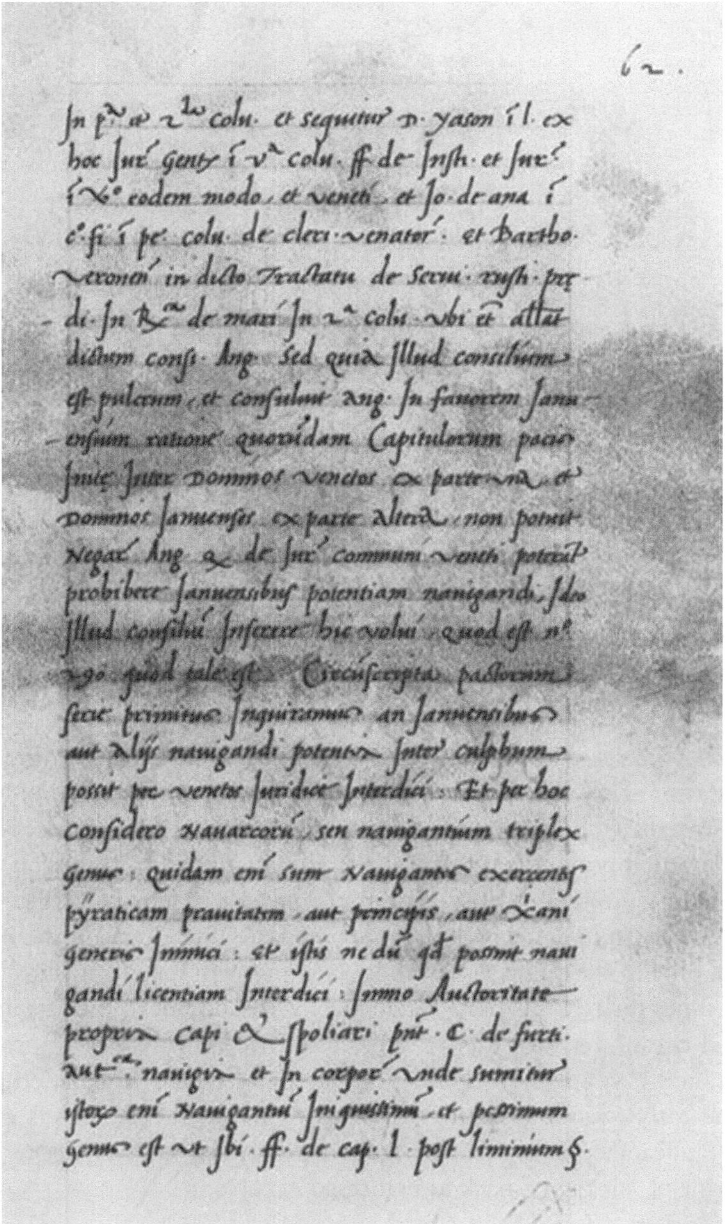

Fig. 6 Tommaso Diplovatazio discussing Angelo's opinion; Cod. Lat. XIV, 74 [4056], *De Venetae Urbis libertate*, folio 62r. *Source* Bibliotheca Nazionale Marciana, Venice

Fig. 7 Detail from "Table of Baselines and Limit of Territorial Sea (according to Presidential Decree No. 816, April 26, 1973)." *Source* The Sea: Supplement to Hydrocarbons and Geothermal Resources Official Bulletin 57.2 (Rome: Ministero dello sviluppo economico, 2013)

ocean, immense, infinite, the father of created things, bounded only by the heavens."[82] But the (literal and metaphorical) size of Venice's gulf and, more importantly, the size of the arguments for its dominion over it (and the prestige of their authors) could not be ignored. The arguments of Bartolo and his contemporaries were interested, on the other hand, only in the gulfic spaces, those teeming with merchant ships (and sometimes pirates), in coasts, bays, and rivers, and not in the vast unexplored ocean. Yet they exerted great influence into the age of oceanic trade, and beyond. Even in the great "battle of the books" that erupted in the early twentieth century over air rights, medieval lawyers made their appearance, with scholars and international lawyers tracing the doctrine of "air rights" back to Francesco Accorso.[83]

I certainly do not wish to argue that 600- or 700-year-old lawyers have discrete or practical lessons to teach us, but my hortatory suggestion is this: until we take the jurists of the thirteenth through the sixteenth centuries seriously, we remain ignorant of the bulk of the prehistory (no, history) of the practical and theoretical interactions of government and merchants, of states and commerce, indeed of "political economy" *avant la lettre*. Studies of Grotius and other canonical figures continue to be published at a ferocious pace, but—among the many possible sources for new perspectives—the vast corpus of premodern juridical materials remains largely unstudied. It has long been known that the sea is not a single thing but many, whether we think of Isidore of Seville's seventh-century definition—a "congregation of many waters"—or of the many "liquid plains" that formed Braudel's Mediterranean.[84] The history of international law, the history of state and commercial interactions, is a congregation of many waters as well. We have charted again and again the gulfs, the waters of the coasts, the inlets and straits and bays, the waters closest to us, which we know very well. But there are rich and deep oceans for which we have as yet no reliable chart.

Notes

1. For a visual example of this apotheosis, see the title page of volume 1 of Caspar Brandt and Adriaen van Cattenburgh, *Historie van het leven des Heeren Huig de Groot* (Amsterdam and Dordrecht: Van Braam and Onder de Linden, 1727), reproduced in Peter Borschberg's important recent book *Hugo Grotius, the Portuguese and Free Trade in the East Indies* (Singapore: NUS Press, 2011), 104. The covert and at times even overt linkage between canonicity and apotheosis is, I suspect, by now self-evident and, faced with such canonical figures, we are left with two ways of proceeding, to "venerate from afar or more actively wrestle with" them, as Edward Said states in *Humanism and Democratic Criticism* (New York: Columbia University Press, 2004), 25–26.
2. Thomas Joseph Lawrence, *Essays on Some Disputed Questions in International Law*, 2nd ed. (Cambridge, UK: Deighton, Bell, 1885), 204; Karl Ludwig Theodor Brater, entry "International Law," 715–27,

in John J. Lalor, ed., *Cyclopædia of Political Science… by the Best American and European Writers*, vol. 2 (Chicago: Melbert B. Cary, 1883), 725; Charles Russell (Baron Killowen), *International Law and Arbitration* (Philadelphia: n.p., 1896), 14. From among innumerable similar sentiments, I have chosen these three in particular because they each introduce discussions of Grotius's precursors, indicating the eternally vexed nature of intellectual paternity.

3. Martine van Ittersum, *Profit and Principle: Hugo Grotius, Natural Rights Theories and the Rise of Dutch Power in the East Indies* (Leiden: Brill, 2006), xxxvii, my emphasis.
4. Richard Tuck's *The Rights of War and Peace: Political Thought and the International Order from Grotius to Kant*, revised edition (Oxford: Oxford University Press, 2001), is exemplary in this regard, with chaps. 1 and 2, on Humanist and Scholastic ideas before Grotius, respectively, 16–77. See also Anthony Pagden, *Lords of All the World: Ideologies of Empire in Spain, Britain and France, c. 1500–1800* (New Haven: Yale University Press, 1998) and the essays in Benedict Kingsbury and Benjamin Straumann, eds., *The Roman Foundations of the Law of Nations: Alberico Gentili and the Justice of Empire* (Oxford: Oxford University Press, 2010).
5. Stephen C. Neff, *Justice among Nations: A History of International Law* (Cambridge, MA: Harvard University Press, 2014), 73, has recently (and suggestively) pointed to this very lacuna; but like the late Wilhelm G. Grewe, *Epochs of International Law*, trans. Michael Byers (Berlin: de Gruyter, 2000), 37–50, whose focus was more "medieval" than most, Neff deals with these jurists only on the well-trodden ground of grand political theory, especially on the nature of and relationships among empire, papacy, kingship, and free cities.
6. The calculations are my own. For the text (and in most cases the translation) of the *Mare liberum*, I use Robert Feenstra, ed., *Mare Liberum, 1609–2009*, which includes a facsimile of the first 1609 edition. I cite this work below simply as *Mare liberum*, giving page numbers according to the page of Feenstra's edition with the page of the 1609 edition in square brackets when helpful. Feenstra's is the first edition to accurately identify Grotius's legal sources and should be strongly preferred, in that area, to those of James Brown Scott [New York: Carnegie Endowment, 1916] and David Armitage [Indianapolis: Liberty Fund, 2004].

7. For the epithets associated with Bartolo, see, for example, Thomas Diplovatatius, *Liber de claris iuris consultis. Pars posterior*, ed. Hermann Kantorowicz (Bologna: Institutum Gratianum, 1968) [=*Studia Gratiana* 10 (1968)], 274; Guidus Panzirolus, *De claris legum interpretibus* (Leipzig: J.F. Gleditsch, 1721), 506–11. On Bartolo generally, see Ennio Cortese, *Il diritto nella storia medievale*, vol. 2 (Rome: Il Cigno, 1995), 425–36; on his immense later stature, and even his elevation to source of law in Spain and Portugal, see Francesco Calasso, "Bartolismo," in *Enciclopedia del diritto*, vol. 5 (Milan: Giuffrè, 1959), 71–74. On the wider issue of Renaissance and Early Modern textual practices as they relate to "information management," see Ann Blair, *Too Much to Know: Managing Scholarly Information before the Modern Age* (New Haven: Yale University Press, 2010); Maria Gioia Tavoni, *Circumnavigare il testo: Gli indici in età moderna* (Naples: Liguori, 2009), although neither deals adequately with juridical practices. David A. Salomon, *An Introduction to the* Glossa Ordinaria *as Medieval Hypertext* (Cardiff: University of Wales Press, 2012), has made the case for the medieval *Ordinary Gloss* of the Bible as a hypertext; a much stronger one could be made for the sources of medieval Roman and Canon law.
8. This distortion is apparent in even the best recent surveys, like Peter Stein, *Roman Law in European History* (Cambridge: Cambridge University Press, 1999), 71–103; Randall Lesaffer, *European Legal History: A Cultural and Political Perspective* (Cambridge: Cambridge University Press, 2009), 338–71. In the Anglophone world, Donald Kelley's influential *Foundations of Modern Historical Scholarship* (New York: Columbia University Press, 1970) remains perhaps the crucial reference point for it. My own view is sketched out in the entry "Roman Law" in the *Encyclopedia of Renaissance Philosophy*, ed. Marco Sgarbi (forthcoming from Springer International Publishing).
9. A point forcefully made in Douglas Osler, "Images of Legal Humanism," *Surfaces* 9 (2001): 101–6.
10. Recent studies of Grotius's working methods have highlighted his use of intermediary sources (indices, dictionaries, *florilegia*, the notes of friends, etc.) and his lack of direct interaction with many of the sources he cited; see, for example, Martine van Ittersum, "The Working Methods of Hugo Grotius: Which Sources Did He Use and How Did He Use Them in His Early Writings on Natural Law Theory?"

in *Reassessing Legal Humanism and Its Claims: Petere Fontes?*, ed. Paul J. Du Plessis and John W. Cairns (Edinburg: Edinburgh University Press, 2016), 154–93.

11. Leiden University Ms. Bibliotheca Publica Latin 917 (hereafter BPL 917) was printed for the first time only in 1868, but its twelfth chapter was revised, at the behest of the Dutch East India Company, by Grotius in 1608 for publication the next year as *Mare liberum*; Martine van Ittersum, "Preparing *Mare Liberum* for the Press: Hugo Grotius' Rewriting of Chap. 12 of *De Jure Praedae* in November–December 1608," *Grotiana*, new series, 27–28 (2005–2007): 246–80.
12. Barbeyrac, trans. and ed., *Le Droit de la guerre et de la paix par Hugues Grotius*, vol. 2 (Basel: Thourneisen, 1746), 79, n. 3 (to II.xx. 24.1).
13. *Mare liberum*, 101 [39].
14. James A. Brundage, "Vultures, Whores, and Hypocrites: Images of Lawyers in Medieval Literature," *Roman Legal Tradition* 1 (2002): 56–103, *passim* but especially 68, 75 and 85.
15. Franco Sacchetti, *Il Trecentonovelle*, ed. Emilia Faccioli (Turin: Einaudi, 1970), novella 40, 109. Francesco Serdonati's seventeenth-century collection of popular Italian proverbs included a similar sentiment in verse: "contra forza, val poco/ragione in ogni loco"; Piero Fiorelli, "'Ragione' come 'diritto' tra latino e volgare," in Id., *Intorno alle parole del diritto* (Milano, Giuffrè, 2008),129–83, 181–83.
16. In *Mare liberum*, LXI, Feenstra addresses these misidentifications, see especially n. 180–82.
17. On Angelo degli Ubaldi and the details of his career, see Carla Frova, "Angelo degli Ubaldi sr. (Perugia, 1327/8-ivi, 1407)," in *Dizionario biografico dei giuristi italiani (XII–XX secolo)*, vol. 2, ed. Italo Birocchi et al. (Bologna: Mulino, 2013), 68–71; Stefania Zucchini, *Università e dottori nell'economia del Comune di Perugia: I Registri dei Conservatori della moneta (secoli XIV–XV)* (Perugia: Pliniana, 2008), *passim*; Torquato Cuturi, "Angelo degli Ubaldi in Firenze," *Bollettino della R. Deputazione di Storia Patria per l'Umbria* 7 (1901): 189–221, adding to it the discoveries of Enrico Spagnesi, *Utiliter edoceri: Atti inediti degli ufficiali dello Studio fiorentino (1391–96)* (Milan: Giuffrè, 1979), 52–54, 105–7; and Paolo Colliva, "Angelo degli Ubaldi e le *Constitutiones Aegidianae,*" *Archivio giuridico* 184 (1973): 103–20.

18. Mazzacane, "Lo Stato e il dominio nei giuristi veneti durante il 'secolo della terraferma,'" in *Storia della cultura veneta*, vol. 3, *Dal primo Quattrocento al Concilio di Trento*, ed. Girolamo Arnaldi and ManlioPastore Stocchi (Vicenza: Pozza, 1980), 576–650. A similar though broader point is also stressed in Mario Ascheri, *The Laws of Late Medieval Italy (1000–1500): Foundations for a European Legal System* (Leiden: Brill, 2013), 267–68. On the juridical milieu in Padua, see Annalisa Belloni, *Professori giuristi a Padova nel secolo XV: Profili bio-bibliografici e cattedre* (Frankfurt am Main: Klostermann, 1986).
19. For an error copied from Balbo, see *Mare liberum*, 107 [42; third marginal reference from the top], where Grotius follows Balbo in changing a Roman law citation (in the commentaries of the other Angelo, Gambiglioni) from "Inst." to "ff.," i.e., from a reference to the *Institutes* to one to the *Digest.*
20. Leiden University BPL 917, 109r (using the folio number in the topmost right). This folio corresponds to H.G. Hamaker, ed., *Hugonis Grotii De jure praedae commentaries* (Hague: Martinus Nijhoff, 1868), 232–33. On the pitfalls of using Hamaker's edition and the need to examine BPL 917, see Jan Waszink, "Using the Work: Remarks on the Text of *De iure praedae*," *Grotiana* 26–28 (2005–2007): 215–45. I base my judgment on the comparison of ink color between text and marginal notes, following the method used by Martine van Ittersum, "Dating the Manuscript of *De jure praedae* (1604–1608): What Watermarks, Foliation and Quire Divisions Can Tell Us about Hugo Grotius' Development as a Natural Rights and Natural Law Theorist," *History of European Ideas* 35 (2009): 125–93, 139.
21. On the late medieval *consilium* genre, see the essays in Mario Ascheri et al., eds., *Legal Consulting in the Civil Law Tradition* (Berkeley: The Robbins Collection, 1999).
22. Robert Feenstra has noted, correctly, that "Grotius literally copied the reference [to Angelo's opinion on the Venetian control of the Adriatic] from Balbo"; see *Mare liberum*, 101, n. e. But Feenstra, using a late sixteenth-century edition of Angelo's *Consilia* [Frankfurt: Andreas Wechelus, 1575], does not seem to have had at hand any of the "old edition[s]" in which the opinion is numbered 289 instead of 290, instead basing his surmise on a note in the Italian translation of Alberico Gentili's 1589 *De iure belli libri tres*: Pietro Nencini, trans., *Il diritto di guerra* (Milano: Giuffrè, 2008), 132, n. 57.

23. For Grotius's use of Vázquez, see van Ittersum, "Working Methods," n. 35. We might say such copying on Grotius's part is less an incidence of plagiarism per se than of what, in a fine turn of phrase, the American pulp writer H.P. Lovecraft called "second-hand erudition," a failing he attributed to Poe. See Lovecraft, *Selected Letters,* vol. 4 *(1932–1934)*, ed. August Derleth and James Turner (Sauk City, WI: Arkham House, 1976), 162. On Lovecraft, see the important recent study by Sophus A. Reinert, "The Economy of Fear: H.P. Lovecraft on Eugenics, Economics and the Great Depression," *Horror Studies* 6 (2015): 255–82.
24. Angelus, *Consilia*, cclxxxix, $2v^b$, using the phrase "nostra disputatio." The opinion (incipit: *Thema est tale inter cetera capitula pacis*) is misnumbered as *consilium* CCLXXXXVIIII (299) but it comes between 288 and 290, in the early edition printed in Venice in 1487 by the printer Giovanni Rossi of Vercelli, which is accompanied by an index (*tabula*), notes, and dedication (to Bishop Iacopo Zeno) by Giovanni Battista Sambiasi of Lecce, professor of law at Padua. Since I have been unable to find an extant manuscript of the opinion, all quotations from this opinion below are from this *incunabulum*, which is not paginated or foliated. I cite it as Angelus, *Consilia*, cclxxxix, giving a folio number as if the opinion were self-contained and numbered internally, i.e., 1v–3r, column a or b. In addition to the copy at Harvard Law School, I have had the pleasure of using the copy of it in Munich once found in the personal library of the Augsburg humanist and jurist Konrad Peutinger (d. 1547), which bears valuable marginalia in his hand; Bayerische Staatsbibliothek, 2 Inc.c.a. 1963a. On the book's provenance, see Hans-Jörg Künast and Helmut Zäh, eds., *Die autographen Kataloge Peutingers: Der juristische Bibliotheksteil*, vol. 2, *Die Bibliothek Konrad Peutingers: Edition der historischen Kataloge und Rekonstruktion der Bestände* (Tübingen: Niemeyer, 2005), 66.
25. Angelus, *Consilia*, cclxxxix, $3r^a$. Angelus gave other disputations while in Padua on pressing politico-commercial matters, see e.g., Biblioteca Apostolica Vaticana, Vat. lat. 10726, f. 61r (dated 1386), but the opinion on the control of the Adriatic is not in this collection.
26. The contours of this struggle, from the perspective of Venice, are laid out in Michel Balard, "La lotta contro Genova," in *Storia di Venezia dalle origini alla caduta della Serenissima*, vol. 3, *La formazione dello*

stato patrizio, ed. Girolamo Arnaldi et al. (Rome: Istituto della Enciclopedia Italiana, 1997), 87–126; I paraphrase Balard's "lungo secolo" from p. 87.

27. The agreement, with the King of Aragon, called for Aragonese ships to harass Genoese fleets in the western Mediterranean; see the account of Ioannes VI Kantakouzenos, *Historiōn biblia D[=4]*, 4.30–32 and 39, in *Corpus scriptorum historiae byzantinae* 20.3 (Bonn: Weber, 1832), 219–36, 289.
28. For the two conflicts and their historical-chronicle sources, see still Heinrich Kretschmayr, *Geschichte von Venedig*, vol. 2 (Gotha: Perthes, 1920), 207–15, 604–5 (Third Genoese War) and 229–42, 608–11 (War of Chioggia). The pacts are printed in *Liber iurium reipublicae genuensis* [=*Monumenta historiae patriae* 7], vol. 2 (Turin: Officina regia, 1857), columns 617–27, quotation at 624 [CCVIII, 1 June 1355] and 858–906, quotation at 874 [CCLVI, 8 August 1381]. The latter agreement is carefully summarized in Luigi Agostino Casati, *La g uerra di Chioggia e la pace di Torino: Saggio storico con documenti inediti* (Florence: Le Monnier, 1866), after 248, see especially 253–54 for the provision relating to the earlier pact.
29. The interpretation of statutes and similar government acts lay at the very center of juristic activity in Venice, as in the rest of north and central Italy, even though Venice's legal system was in many respects unique; broadly, see Giorgio Zordan, *L'Ordinamento giuridico veneziano: Lezioni di storia del diritto veneziano con una nota bibliografica* (Padua: CLEUP, 1980), but on Venice's ca. 1300 break from the rest of the *ius commune* world, see Karin Nehlsen von Stryk, "'Ius commune', 'consuetudo' e 'arbitrium iudicis' nella prassi giudiziaria veneziana del Quattrocento," in *Diritto comune, diritti commerciale, diritto veneziano*, ed. Stryk and Dieter Nörr (Venice: Centro Tedesco di Studi Veneziani, 1985), 107–40. *Ius commune* jurists like Angelo often approached such questions creatively, especially in academic settings, but always within a complex, received interpretive framework best described in the classic work of Mario Sbriccoli, *L'Interpretazione dello statuto: contributo allo studio della funzione dei giuristi nell'età comunale* (Milan: Giuffrè, 1960), though Sbriccoli's ideological biases demand a gentle corrective, as in the form of Mario Ascheri, "Il 'dottore' e lo statuto: Una difesa interessata?," *Rivista di storia del diritto italiano* 69: 95–113.

30. Angelus, *Consilia*, cclxxxix, 1v[b].
31. Ibid., 2v[ab]. The contractual rule is an extension of D. 2.14.27[4]. Of course, if the Geneoese were "enemies of Venice," they could anyway be prohibited by the terms of the treaty, but Angelo decided not to address that matter, saying: "It remains to be seen who should be called 'enemies', those to whom neither help nor favor can be shown even in the course of trade. And this should be investigated especially regarding those who made peace with the Venetians, among whom there is a fervent rancor lying latent in their souls, which began before the articles of peace"; 3r[a].
32. Angelus, *Consilia*, cclxxxix, 1v[b]. The de facto-*de iure* distinction was crucial in the jurisprudence of the Italian city-states only nominally under the authority of the Emperor; Joseph Canning's sensitive reading of the distinction in the political thought of Angelo's brother Baldo is illuminating; *The Political Thought of Baldus de Ubaldis* (Cambridge: Cambridge University Press, 1987), *passim* but, for a good example, 65.
33. Of course, the argument *in nuce* preceded Angelo; see, for example, the discussion of Raniero Arsendi below. And, indeed, as we will also see below, Angelo's argument was less interested in prescription than in a right to prohibit derived from immemorial possession, an idea which traced back at least to the twelfth-century glossator Giovanni Bassiano.
34. Angelus, *Consilia*, cclxxxix, 1vb–2ra. With the wide diffusion of printed editions of his collected *Consilia*, Angelo's discussion of pirates here came to be a standard reference point on the topic; see, for example, Ioannes Bonifacius, *Liber de furtis* (Venice: Amadeus, 1619), §1, 15, n. 59, and Doctor [Orazio] Marta, *Tractatus de iurisdictione* (Mainz: Albinus, 1609), II.xxiv, 219, n. 3. Also on navigation generally, as in Dominicus Tuschus, *Practicae conclusiones iuris*, vol. 5 (Rome: Paulini, 1606), N, conc. XIV, 871, citing Angelo's take on the types of permitted and forbidden navigation. The political and human stakes of grain provisioning were, as they had been since antiquity, high in Trecento Italy; Charles M. de la Roncière, "L'Approvisionnement des villes italiennes au Moyen Age (XIVe–XVe siècles)," in *L'Approvisionnement des villes: De l'Europe occidentale au Moyen Age et aux temps modernes* (Auch: Le Centre, 1985), 33–51.
35. Angelus, *Consilia*, cclxxxix, 2r[a]. Angelo follows the logic of Cino da Pistoia on the prejudicial power of the words of an agreement; Cynus Pistoriensis, *In Codicem... commentaria* (Frankfurt am Main:

Feyerabend, 1578), on C. 6.30.21, f. 388v. How geographical features are named has always been and remains a pressing matter of cultural and political significance; the best known example today is surely the Persian (or Arabian) Gulf; see for historical background Sultān bin Muhammad Al-Qāsimī, *Power Struggles and Trade in the Gulf, 1620–1820* (n.p. but Exeter: Forest Row, 1999), especially 2–3; Karen Zraik, "Persian (or Arabian) Gulf Is Caught in the Middle of Regional Rivalries," *New York Times*, January 13, 2016, A8.

36. On *longi temporis praescriptio*, see the essential pages of Max Kaser, *Das römische Privatrecht*, vol. 2 (Munich: Beck, 1959), 285–88, as well as Giovanni Pugliese, *Istituzioni di diritto romano* (Turin: Giappichelli, 1998), 339–40; recognized in a rescript of AD 199, it allowed a possessor after an undisturbed period of possession of 10 or 20 years to defend his claim; it is, in other words, an exception or defense rather than a way of acquiring property like *usucapio*.
37. On the Roman law of seas and rivers, both ancient and to some extent medieval (as at pages 427–84), see Mario Fiorentini, *Fiumi e mari nell'esperienza giuridica: Profili di tutela processuale e di inquadramento sistematico* (Milan: Giuffrè, 2003). Still valuable is the classic essay of Muzio Pampaloni, "Sulla condizione giuridica delle rive del mare in diritto romano e odierno: Contributo all teoria delle 'res communes omnium,'" *Bollettino dell'Istituto di diritto romano* 4 (1892): 197–246. On the more specific question of *praescriptio* and the seashore (and D. 41.3.45 pr.), see Hans Ankum, "'Litora maris' et 'longi temporis praescriptio,'" *Index* 26 (1998): 361–82; as these Roman doctrines relate to Grotius, see Alberto Mieli, "'Res publica', 'res communis omnium', 'res nullius': Grozio e le fonti romane sul diritto del mare," *Index* 26 (1998): 383–87.
38. Angelus, *Consilia*, cclxxxix, 2r[a].
39. Angelus, *Consilia*, cclxxxix, 2r[b].
40. Giovanni Monleone, ed., *Jacopo da Varagine e la sua Cronaca di Genova dalle origini al MCCXCVII* (Rome: Tipografia del Senato, 1941), 479, "Gulfus veneciarum." For a variety of other uses, including Genoese ones, see the entry "Gulfus" in Charles du Cange et al., eds., *Glossarium mediae et infimae latinitatis*, vol. 4 (Niort: Favre, 1883), column 137c.
41. "Itinerarius Gulielmi de Boldensele," ed., Carl Ludwig Grotefend, "Die Edelherren von Boldensele oder Boldensen," *Zeitschrift des Historischen*

Vereins für Niedersachsen 1 (1855): 209–86, 239. More than a century later the Venetian humanist and statesman Paolo Morosini would use a similar phrase; Paulus Maurocenus, "Defensio venetorum ad Europae principes contra obtrectatores," in *Bibliotheca manuscripta ad S. Marci Venetiarum*, ed. Joseph [Giuseppe] Valentinelli (Venice: Commercii, 1868), 180–230, 217, "what had earlier been called the Adriatic was named the Venetian gulf [*venetus sinus sive gulfus*]".

42. Giovanna Petti Balbi, ed., *Georgii et Iohannis Stella Annales Genuenses* (Bologna: Zanichelli, 1975), 35, "they had crossed into the gulf of the Adriatic sea (*maris Adriatici sinum*), which sailors speak of as the gulf of the Venetians (*gulfum Venetiarum*)"; 180, "*ubi gulfum Venetiarum vulgares appellant.*" On Stella, see Giovanna Petti Balbi, "Giorgio Stella e gli Annales Genuenses," *Miscellanea storica ligure* 2 (1961): 123–215.
43. Gerard de Jode, "Italiae totius orbis" (Antwerp, 1577); Abraham Ortelius, "Italiae novissima descriptio" (Antwerp, 1598), and many others; more purely classicizing maps, like the "Tabula nova Italiae" and "Tabula V Europae" (both Strasbourg, 1535) of Lorenz Fries, omitted the Venetian claim, using the terms "Mare Adriaticum" and "Sinus Hadriaticus" respectively; Italian cartographers sometimes gave precedence to the modern terminology, as in Giacomo Gastaldi's "Dalmacia nova tabula" (Venice, 1548), "sinus venetus antea adriaticus."
44. For various formulations of the medieval rule, see Woldemar Engelmann, *Die Wiedergeburt der Rechtskultur in Italien durch die wissenschaftliche Lehre* (Leipzig: Koehler, 1938), 213–27. Such a rule did not, for the most part, guide classical Roman jurists; Antonio Marongiu, "Legislatori e giudici di fronte all' autorità dei giuristi," in *Studi di storia e diritto in onore di Enrico Besta*, vol. 3 (Milan: Giuffrè, 1939), 441–64, especially at 459. Divining the *communis opinio* became central to Renaissance jurisprudence; the best introduction to the topic is Luigi Lombardi [Vallauri], *Saggio sul diritto giurisprudenziale* (Milan: Giuffrè, 1967), 164–82.
45. Pax Scala, *De consilio sapientis in forensibus causis adhibendo libri IV* (Hamburg: Burdelius, 1560), cap. 24, nn. 3–4, 351.
46. Marius Salomonius Alberthescus, *In l. Gallus et in § responsa prudentum paradoxa* (Rome: Stefano Guillery, 1519), 97rv.
47. The famed expression comes from Ernest Nys, "*Une bataille de livres*, an Episode in the Literary History of International Law," *Juridical Review* 3.1–3.2 (1891): 1–11, 131–37.

48. The best introduction to arguments about Venice's control of the Adriatic remains Roberto Cessi, *La repubblica di Venezia e il problema adriatico* (Naples: Edizioni scientifiche italiane, 1953), on which see Egidio Ivetic, "L'Adriatico nella venezianistica di Roberto Cessi," *Mediterranea: Ricerche Storiche* 28 (2013): 231–48. See also, for lists of such works, Emanuele Antonio Cicogna, *Saggio di bibliografia veneziana* (Venice: Merlo, 1847), 128–31. Paolo Sarpi has received the most scholarly attention; see recently Ivone Cacciavillani, *Paolo Sarpi: La guerra delle scritture del 1606 e la nascita della nuova Europa* (Venice: Corbo e Fiore, 2005), though this particular *guerra*, a pamphlet war, was instigated by the 1606 papal interdict of Venice.
49. *The Digest of Justinian*, trans. Allan Watson, vol. 2 (Philadelphia: University of Pennsylvania Press, 1985) at D. 47.10.14, n.p., is the source of this translation and all others from the Digest. For how medieval jurists referenced the sources of Roman law, see Herman Kantorowicz, "Citations in the Later Middle Ages," in *Dictionary of Sigla and Abbreviations to and in Law Books before 1607*, 2nd corrected printing (Buffalo: Hein, 1996), 3–16, especially 7–8 on citing the Digest. An excellent introduction to the sources of medieval Roman and Canon Law is Eltjo J.H. Schrage (with the participation of J.H. "Harry" Dondorp), *Utrumque ius: Een inleiding tot de studie van de bronnen van het middeleeuwse geleerde recht* (Amsterdam: Uitgeverij, 1987).
50. A clear discussion of *uti possidetis* may be found in Adolf Berger, "Interdictum," columns 1609–1707, in August Pauly, Georg Wissowa et al., eds., *Realencyclopädie der classischen Altertumswissenschaft*, vol. IX.18 (Stuttgart: Metzler, 1916), at col. 1682. *Uti possidetis* remains as a principle in international law; Christiane Simmler, *Das uti possidetis-Prinzip: Zur Grenzziehung zwischen neu entstandenen Staaten* (Berlin: Duncker & Humblot, 1999).
51. See for example Peter Ørsted, "Salt, Fish and the Sea in the Roman Empire," in *Meals in a Social Context: Aspects of the Communal Meal in the Hellenistic and Roman World*, ed. Inge Nielsen and Hanne Sigismund Nielsen (Aarhus: Aarhus University Press, 2001), 13–35, 18–20.
52. Azo, gloss on the word "Sane," D.47.10.14; *Digestum novum* (Venice: Jenson, 1477), column 1117 (not numbered), k.
53. Ugo Petronio, "Civitas Venetiarum est edificata in mari," in *Studi veneti offerti a Gaetano Cozzi* (Venice: Cardo, 1992), 171–85; Christian

Mathieu, *Inselstadt Venedig: Umweltgeschichte eines Mythos in der Frühen Neuzeit* (Cologne: Böhlau, 2007), 212–23, which expands on Petronio's work.

54. Baldus de Ubaldis, *Commentaria in primam Digesti veteris partem* (Venice: Giunti, 1572), 48r.
55. Angelus, *Consilia*, cclxxxix, 2r[a]. On Raniero, see Roberto Abbondanza, entry "Raniero Arsendi," in *Dizionario Biografico degli Italiani*, vol. IV (Rome: Istituto dell'Enciclopedia Italiana, 1962), 333–39. The widely available printed text of Raynerius de Forlivio, *Utilis ac fecunda lectura super prima et secunda parte ff. novi* (Lyon: Vincent de Portonariis de Tridino, 1523), contains no mention of Venice at D. 47.10.14, 115. Raniero lectured on the *Digestum novum* in Padua in 1356–1357, near the end of his life in 1358; Andrea Gloria, *Monumenti della Università di Padova (1318–1405)*, vol. 1 (Padua: Forni, 1972 [1888]), 120–24.
56. Helmut Coing, "Zur Eigentumslehre des Bartolus," *Zeitschrift der Savigny-Stiftung für Rechtsgeschichte: Romanistische Abteilung* 70 (1953): 48–71, especially 63–65 for Bartolo's influential understanding of *praesciptio longi temporis*.
57. Angelus, *Consilia*, cclxxxix, f. 2r[a].
58. Angelus, Consilia, cclxxxix, f. 2r[a]. *Mare liberum*, 99–101 [38–39]. Percy Thomas Fenn Jr., *The Origin of the Right of Fishery in Territorial Waters* (Cambridge, MA: Harvard University Press, 1926), 142–43, appears to attribute Angelo's "sweeping" argument to Balbo (or to a whole class of jurists he summarizes), who recites it, noting that such a *ius excipiendi* would nullify the rule it is meant to modify, i.e., that the sea is *res communis*.
59. *Mare liberum*, 105 [41].
60. D. 41.3.45 presented cases where this rule was applied: "when the building which he had erected on the seashore is totally destroyed (or perhaps he pulled it down or abandoned it), a man opposes another subsequently building and occupying in the same place, or again, if a person, because he alone has fished in a reach of a public river for some years, refuses someone else the right." Note that there is some difference of opinion about how exactly to read the passage and whether a particular phrase was a later interpolation; see Gaetano Scherillo, *Lezioni di diritto romano* (Milan: Giuffrè, 1945), 81; Fiorentini, *Fiumi e mari*, 368, n. 191. Grotius, who discusses it at length, *Mare liberum*, 101

[39], calls this *lex* the *lex ultima*, i.e., the last law in its particular title of the *Digest*, but contemporary editions of the *Digest* included further laws (41.3.46–49), suggesting that Grotius took the citation second-hand from an earlier work, likely Balbo, which used the vulgate text. At a different place in the text, Grotius corrected his error in the manuscript; see Feenstra, *Mare liberum*, 73, n.a. Earlier jurists commonly called it the *lex finalis* and knew title 3 of book 31 of the *Digest* as *De usucapionibus et usurpationibus*, and those terms are reversed in modern editions.

61. *Mare liberum*, 113–15 [45–46].
62. A high (or low) point in this invective is the infamous letter of Lorenzo Valla to Pier Candido Decembrio attacking Bartolo, translated in Osvaldo Cavallar et al., eds., *A Grammar of Signs: Bartolo da Sassoferrato's Tract on Insignia and Coats of Arms* (Berkeley: Robbins Collection, 1994), 179–200. Manlio Bellomo, *The Common Legal Past of Europe 1000–1800*, trans. Lydia G. Cochrane (Washington: Catholic University of America Press, 1995), 215, speaks in an excellent turn of phrase of "acid-tongued humanists who vented their critical humors by coining picturesque insults for the jurists of the thirteenth and fourteenth centuries." Grotius himself is often classed with the so-called "Dutch Elegant School" of jurists, exponents of the *jurisprudentia elegantior* who carried on the work of the French legal humanists in the Netherlands, but see Douglas Osler, "The Myth of European Legal History," *Rechtshistorisches Journal* 16 (1997): 393–410, especially 394–98.
63. *Mare liberum*, 101–3 [39–40].
64. Iacobus Cuiacius, *Commentaria in Pandectarum titulos*, vol. 2 of his *Opera quae de iure fecit* (Frankfurt: Wechel, 1623), on D. 41.3.45, at columns 282–83.
65. Franciscus Balbus, *Tractatus de praescriptionibus* (Cologne: Gymnich, 1590 [1565]), V.4, question 6, 467. Annabel Brett, *Liberty, Right, and Nature: Individual Rights in Later Scholastic Thought* (Cambridge: Cambridge University Press, 1997), 186–87, and especially note 64, has highlighted the direct relationship between Renaissance trattistic approaches to *praescriptio* and an increasingly historicist awareness of the importance of custom as a source of law, an awareness associated with the so-called *mos gallicus*. Balbo, although influenced by new approaches, is working very much in what is called

the *mos italicus*. For the ancient context of the *l. quominus* and the distinction between public and private water sources, see Christer Bruun, "Water Use and Productivity in Roman Agriculture: Selling, Sharing, Servitudes," in *Ownership and Exploitation of Land and Natural Resources in the Roman World*, ed. Paul Erdkamp et al. (Oxford: Oxford University Press, 2015), 132–49, 133–36.

66. Balbus, *Tractatus*, 468. Giasone's lengthy *repetitio* was printed alone a number of times beginning in 1492 (Pavia: Gaspar de Balditionibus), but see Iason Maynus, *In primam Digesti novi partem commentaria* (Lyon: Compagnie des libraires, 1582), where it is appended at 161v–170r.

67. Bartolus de Saxoferrato, *Commentaria in primam digesti novi partem* (Lyon: [n.p. but Compagnie des libraires], 1555), on D. 41.3.45, f. 121r. On servitudes as they pertain to rivers in Roman law, especially the *servitus acquae ductus*, see Christer Bruun, "Water Use," 145–49. Disputes pertaining to mills were common, as testified to by their presence in countless *consilia*; see Osvaldo Cavallar, "The Wheels of Watermills and the Wheel of Fortune: A Consilium of Donatus Ricchi de Aldighieris," *Rechtsgeschichte* 13 (2008): 80–116, especially 83, where he provides a list of Baldo's *consilia* on the topic, for the "kaleidoscopic range of quarrels" involving mills. Baldus de Ubaldis, *Consilia sive responsa*, vol. 4 (Venice, 1575; rept: Turin: Bottega d'Erasmo, 1970), vol. IV, f. 16r, is of particular interest here. Watermills also figured prominently in Bartolo's academic work; see, for example, his lengthy *repetitio* on the *lex Quominus* (D. 43.12.2), discussed in Osvaldo Cavallar, "*Quod de Tibere dicetur*: Fiumi, incrementi fluviali, mulini ad acqua e giuristi," in *La civiltà delle acque tra Medioevo e Quattrocento*, ed. Arturo Calzona and Daniela Lamberini (Florence: Olschki, 2010), 91–120, especially at 115–16. For the repetition, Javier Barrientos Grandon, "*Repetitio* a la *Lex Quominus, de fluminibus* (D.43.12.2): Introducción, traducción y comentario," *Revista de Derecho de Aguas* IV (1993): 97–125. In Bartolo's legal imagination, moreover, questions about rivers were inextricably linked to political ones, and his three most famous political treatises were connected by means of his treatise on rivers, the *Tiberiadis*; Cavallar, "Personaggi in cerca di 'editore': Una proposta di lettura per alcuni degli ultimi trattati bartoliani," *Rivista internazionale di diritto comune* 15 (2004): 97–142; Bartolo's original organizational conceit is followed in Harvard

Law School Library Ms. 75. For the three political treatises: Diego Quaglioni, *Politica e diritto nel Trecento italiano: Il De tyranno di Bartolo da Sassoferrato (1314–1357). Con l'edizione critica dei trattati* De Guelphis et Gebellinis, De regimine civitatis, *e* De tyranno (Florence: Olschki, 1983).

68. Bartolus de Saxoferrato, *Commentaria in primam digesti novi partem*, on D. 44.3.7, 188v. *Quasi possessio* [=*possessio iuris*] implied a right to use, like a usufruct.
69. Balbus, *Tractatus*, 469. At 469–70, he explains further: "and to introduce such a custom it will be necessary to prove that someone has fished for a long time, i.e., for at least 10 years, in such a part of a public river, and that he has prohibited others from fishing during that time, namely done so twice, with the knowledge and acceptance of the people or the majority (*maiori parte*) of them and without their contradiction, or that it has probably passed into the knowledge of the people or the majority of them, because these things are required for the proof of custom."
70. Inst. 2.1.2; *Institutiones* (Venice: Jacobus Rubei, 1478), f. 17r, gloss z.
71. Ibid., 470. And see Angelus de Perusio, *Lectura aurea super prima ff. novi* (Lyon: Moylin, 1534), 36r, citing C. 11.43.4 (along with the *glossa* on the word "constitutum") and C. 11.43.9. Angelo lectured on the *Digestum novum* in Perugia in 1395–1396; Archivio di Stato di Perugia, *Conservatori della moneta* 33, 6v. For the text of the gloss, see *Volumen legum* (Lyon: Cardon, 1604), column 160. Cf. Fenn, *Origin of the Right*, 135–43.
72. Balbus, *Tractatus*, 473.
73. Bartolomeo's treatises, for which he is famous, began to be printed as early as 1473 (in Rome by the "printer of the *Mercuriales questiones*"); I use Bartholomaeus Caepolla, *Tractatus de servitutibus tam urbanorum quam rusticorum praediorum* (Cologne: Gymnich, 1579), especially chap. 26 "De mari," 658–70. On Bartolomeo, see the essays in Giovanni Rossi, ed., *Bartolomeo Cipolla: Un giurista veronese del Quattrocento tra cattedra, foro e luoghi del potere: Atti del convegno internazionale di studi, Verona, 14–16 ottobre 2004* (Padua: CEDAM, 2009), especially, on the *tractatus*, Stefano Barbacetto, "Il giurista, la città e i quattro elementi: Sull'ordine espositivo dei Tractatus de servitutibus," 317–56. On chap. 26 and its context, see Christian Zendri, "*Mare passim omnibus patet*: Il diritto del mare agli inizi dell'età

moderna (secc. XV–XVII)," *Archivio Scialoja-Bolla: Annali di studi sulla proprietà collectiva* 1 (2007): 93–121, especially at 101–10.

74. Baldus Ubaldus, *Commentaria in primam Digesti Veteris partem* (Lyon: Compagnie des libraries, 1585), on D. 1.8.2, 51r.
75. Caepolla, *Tractatus*, 662–63. I have removed the legal citations.
76. Ibid., 663–64.
77. Ibid., 664–65. For the judgment of the Venetian Senate, see *Raccolta di privilegj, ducali, giudizj, terminazioni, e decreti pubblici sopra varie materie giurisdizionali, civili, criminali, ed economiche, concernenti la città, e provincia di Brescia* (Brescia: Bossini, 1732), 9 December 1455, 360.
78. Ioannes de Platea, *Super quatuor Institutionum libris commentaria* (Lyon: Moylin, 1539), 26rv, n. 7; Angelus a Gambilionibus, *In quatuor Institutionum Iustiniani libros commentaria* (Venice: Liechtenstein, 1568), 59r, nn. 4–5.
79. Biblioteca Nazionale Marciana, Venice, Cod. Lat. XIV, 74 [4056]: Thomas Diplovataccius, *Tractatus de Venetae Urbis libertate et eiusdem Imperii dignitate*; Angelo's works are discussed at 55r–64v, with a lengthy discussion of the consilium beginning at 62r. This manuscript is the expanded presentation copy that Diplovatazio deposited with the Council of Ten; his autograph manuscript [Cod. Lat. XIV, 77 (2991)] is also kept at the Marciana; both are incomplete. On Diplovatazio and his treatise, see Mazzacane, "Lo Stato e il dominio nei giuristi veneti," 622–38.
80. Benvenutus Stracca, *De mercatura seu mercatore tractatus* (Venice: [n.p., but with an Aldine printer's mark], 1553), 166. On the *De mercatura*, see Charles Donahue, "Benvenuto Stracca's *De Mercatura*: Was there a Lex Mercatoria in Sixteenth-Century Italy?," in *From Lex Mercatoria to Commercial Law*, ed. Vito Piergiovanni (Berlin: Duncker & Humblot, 2005), 69–120; Ioannes Seldenus, *Mare clausum seu dominio maris libri duo* (Leiden: Maire, 1636), 56.
81. On Bartolo's *Tiberiadis* generally, see the beautiful essay of Osvaldo Cavallar, "River of Law: Bartolo's *Tiberiadis* (*De alluvione*)," in *A Renaissance of Conflicts: Visions and Revisions of Law and Society in Italy and Spain*, ed. John A. Marino and Thomas Kuehn (Toronto: University of Toronto Press, 2004), 31–82. Nineteenth-century international lawyers established Bartolo's priority; see, for example, Walther [Max Adrian] Schücking, *Das Küstenmeer im internationalen Rechte: im*

Völkerrechte, wie im internationalen Privat- und Strafrechte (Göttingen: Dieterich, 1897), 1.2, 6–14; A[lbert de] Geouffre de Lapradelle, "Le droit de l'État sur la mer territoriale," *Revue générale de droit international public* 5 (1898): 264–84, 270. Nonetheless, the earliest printed "views of the representative publicists" belong to Grotius, Van Bynkershoek, and Vattel in Henry Graham Crocker (ed.)'s monumental assemblage *The Extent of the Marginal Sea: A Collection of Official Documents and Views of Representative Publicists* (Washington: [U.S.] Government Printing Office, 1919); Ralph J. Gillis's important *Navigational Servitudes: Sources, Applications, Paradigms* (Leiden and Boston: Nijhoff, 2007), 239–40, dispatches with the pre-Grotius history in a single sentence. With the notable exception of Fenn, *Origin of the Right*, most scholars who have dealt with the subject in the last century and a half have either treated Grotius as an historico-analytical *terminus post quem* or treated earlier jurists secondhand, just as Grotius did.

82. *Mare liberum*, 81.
83. See, for example, John Cobb Cooper, "Roman Law and the Maxim *Cujus est solum* in International Air Law," *International Air Law* 1 (1952): 23–65, *passim* but especially 41 (citing Accorso, on Digest 8.2.1 and 43.24.22.4, who seemed to apply the logic of restricting servitudes over public roads to private property generally).
84. Wallace M. Lindsay, ed., *Isidori Hispalensis episcopi Etymologiarum sive originum libri XX*, 2 vols. (Oxford: Clarendon Press, 1911), XIII.14, 2:15; Fernand Braudel, *La Méditerranée et le monde méditerranéen à l'époque de Philippe II* (Paris: Colin, 1949), 73–99. For one take on this and similarly oxymoronic or even catachretic expressions in Braudel, see Hans Kellner, "Disorderly Conduct: Braudel's Mediterranean Satire," *History and Theory* 18 (1979): 197–222, 209–10.

Capitalism and the Special Economic Zone, 1590–2014

Corey Tazzara

Special economic zones are one of the dirty secrets of modernity. After standing near the brink of extinction at the end of World War II, when only thirty or so existed, they have proliferated with wild abandon in recent decades. One survey from 2006 found some 3500 such zones, and their number continues to grow.[1] The transformation of the global economy during and after decolonization, which formally redefined the nature of international trade, is responsible for their resurgence. Some are famous for their economic miracles; many are infamous for their relaxation of labor and environmental standards, as the scandals over the iPhone supply chain or the fires in Bangladeshi factories illustrate.[2] There is no doubt that the West has been complicit in the spread of these places: One need only think of the relationship between the USA and the Maquiladora towns of northern Mexico, whose lawlessness and misery were movingly portrayed in Roberto Bolaño's novel *2666*.[3]

We are in fact living through the second age of special economic zones. A special zone may be defined as any enclave carved out of the national territory and endowed with its own administrative and

C. Tazzara (✉)
Scripps College, Claremont, USA
e-mail: ctazzara@scrippscollege.edu

R. Fredona and S.A. Reinert (eds.), *New Perspectives on the History of Political Economy*, https://doi.org/10.1007/978-3-319-58247-4_3

economic policies, usually of a liberal or even libertine cast. Their lineal ancestors were called free ports. Despite a marked diversity of forms, most free ports were basically commercial, that is, geared to the deposit, transit, or sale of merchandise. The modern special zone tends to be an industrial town brimming with cheap labor.[4] In both cases, however, scholars have argued that special zones are tools of weak, marginal, or developing states and serve the interests of the rich world more than that of the poor.

I shall argue that this grafting of the early modern and the contemporary is deeply misleading. The Italian free port system—the first well-articulated one in history—was not a close concomitant of the global economic system. Regional geopolitical context was more important in accounting for the spread of free ports in the Italian sphere. While regional considerations remain somewhat topical today, the basic differences in economic character between free ports and the modern free zone are contingent on those twin beasts of modernity, the bureaucratic state with its capacity to redraw boundaries; and modern capitalism, with its global appetite for cheap labor and consumer-oriented manufacturing.

Decoupling the present from the past does not mean that special zones are incommensurable across the temporal abyss. Despite their differences, all special zones face a challenge that few regimes have met: integrating a zone into the larger civil and administrative apparatus of the host state. Zones foster interest groups committed to preserving their liberties against state interference. This problem cuts across the modern/premodern divide and prompts us to reconsider the supposedly rational or uniform nature of the modern state.[5] Through a process of what I call "administrative relimitation," the modern state in recent decades has proven almost as generous as its premodern ancestor in endowing certain people and territories with special privileges. And as in the past, there is little reason to believe that entitled groups will voluntarily surrender their privileges when the state has had a change of heart.

Regional Competition and the Free Port System of Early Modern Italy

The Italian free port system began amid commercial rivalries between Tuscany and Genoa in the late sixteenth century and over the following hundred and 50 years grew to encompass Savoy, France (through its port of Marseille), the Papal States, Venice, the Kingdom of Naples, and the Austro-Hungarian Empire (through Trieste). By 1740, all major and most minor ports in a kind of "greater Italy" were free ports.[6] Commentators have not been kind to them. The eighteenth-century mercantilist Carlo Antonio Broggia accused Italian states of "prostituting" their commerce to foreigners, and there is no question that English merchants in particular pushed regimes to establish free ports, from the Savoyard port of Nice around 1620 to papal Ancona a century later.[7] A quasi-colonial attitude on the part of the British became explicit by the end of the eighteenth century, especially in the Caribbean and East Asia. As one English official put it in 1787: Free ports gave "all the advantages of the foreign colonies without being exposed to the expense of establishing or protecting them."[8] Free zones became a kind of discount imperialism that receded during the European landgrabs of the nineteenth century but reappeared in the wake of decolonization.

Scholars have treated free ports as a function of the rise of the Atlantic World: displacement of economic growth from the Mediterranean to the Atlantic; deindustrialization of Italy as it moved to export agricultural produce; and political domination of the Italian peninsula, formally by Spain and later Austria and informally by England, France, and the Netherlands. It is as though historians cannot resist speaking about Italy in the language of world-systems analysis: A former core that slipped into the semi-periphery and was in danger of further slippage.[9] It is thus possible to assimilate early modern and contemporary economic zones as two phases in the evolution of the global economy. Free ports (in this story) were at first a response to the loss of foreign markets and the decline in native Italian shipping; that is, free ports were the best way for states to stay connected to global markets. What began as a rearguard defense of commerce ended in tragedy, as these zones facilitated the foreign penetration of Italian markets.

The world-systems perspective harbors problematic assumptions about what "ought" to have happened in Italy—namely that Italian states ought to have cultivated an active merchant marine, ought to have conserved their urban industries, and ought to have protected their medieval trade monopolies; and that the failure to fulfill these "obligations" had devastating consequences on Italian economic and political life. In fact, while changes in the international system did make it impossible for city-states to maintain their old monopoly systems, the spread of free ports owed a great deal to traditional regional and institutional dynamics, and their legacy was much more mixed than scholars have supposed.

In lowering port tariffs and welcoming foreigners, Italy's free ports multiplied the number of entrepôts throughout the peninsula. These entrepôts increased Italy's access to international maritime commerce and probably promoted its integration into Atlantic markets.[10] Whether integration into international markets was a good thing depended on whether one had benefited or not from the prior arrangements.[11] The most profound implication of free ports was the dismantling of the old monopoly systems of the Middle Ages. From the eleventh century on, Italian port cities were vicious competitors with one another. They sought to impose trade monopolies on their own territories and on their trading partners. Venice, for instance, controlled exchange within the Adriatic while also ensuring its pre-eminence in the Eastern Mediterranean; Genoa sought with less success to do the same in the Tyrrhenian, but it did manage to subordinate all other ports in Liguria to its needs.[12]

The collapse of trade monopolies owed to competition in international commercial and industrial markets undergoing a deep transition from about 1500 to 1620 or even later. Changes began with the loss of competitiveness in shipping in the face of superior Atlantic-style vessels. The appearance of Dutch and English shipping in the Mediterranean did not in itself damage overall Italian competitiveness:

Much of the capital for the shipping came from Italian merchants, who also owned much of their cargo. But two developments undid the old hegemony. The growth of the Dutch maritime empire succeeded in doing what the Portuguese never managed to do: put the overland route to Europe out of business. Venice in particular suffered from losing its position as lord of the spices. More profoundly, textile producers in northwestern Europe outcompeted Italian woolens in the Levant through the sale of cheaper imitations. Since wool production was a core export industry throughout north-central Italy, the loss of eastern markets had a profound effect on external trading relations.[13]

But what looked like decline to Genoa and Venice—and certainly was the loss of monopoly rent—created an arc of opportunity for other ports in the region: for Livorno, Ancona, and Trieste above all, not to mention the larger region. From the perspective of the wider Italy, then, and not only those powers whose medieval success has long attracted the attention of historians, free ports may have improved access to commodity markets and made it easier to export one's goods. Above all, the terms "Genoa" and "Venice" create a false impression: The medieval regime had really benefited only a restricted class of patricians and their urban artisans. Free ports may have been bad for certain bourgeois citizens; it is less clear that they were bad for the larger population of Italians who had not benefited from the monopolies of the Middle Ages.

To all appearances, the Italian economy in the aggregate neither declined nor grew in the seventeenth century. The pie was cut differently. The unmaking of the commercial monopolies shifted the locus of power from capital city elites to new entities—from Genoa to communities in the Ligurian Riviera; from Venice to other Adriatic cities (Ancona and Trieste) and to mainland towns in the Veneto; from Florence to the coastal complex of Pisa and Livorno; Le Marche, which could now export its produce more readily, was especially successful.[14] An indication of these transformations may be found in the demographic changes experienced by Italian cities during the early modern period (Table 1). It shows the relative growth of such places as Pisa or Livorno (in the seventeenth century) and Trieste or Ancona (in the eighteenth century). It also shows that while the status of Venice

Table 1 City population in select Italian regions, 1500–1800

		1500	1600	1700	1800
A. City population in select Italian regions, 1500–1800 (in thousands)					
Liguria					
	Genoa	83%	87%	90%	80%
	Other	17%	13%	10%	20%
	Total (N)	84	75	71	95
Tuscany					
	Livorno/Pisa	7%	11%	20%	30%
	Other Tuscany	93%	89%	80%	70%
	Total (N)	118	169	173	226
The Veneto					
	Venice	45%	43%	47%	35%
	Trieste	3%	2%	2%	6%
	Other Veneto	52%	55%	51%	59%
	Total (N)	226	324	295	389
Le Marche					
	Ancona	22%	13%	9%	11%
	Other Le Marche	78%	87%	91%	89%
	Total (N)	69	77	101	137
	Total (N)	497	645	640	847
	Change from prior		30%	−1%	32%
B. City population in select Italian regions, 1500–1800 (by percent)					
Liguria		17%	12%	11%	11%
Tuscany		24%	26%	27%	27%
The Veneto		44%	49%	45%	43%
Trieste		1%	1%	1%	3%
Le Marche		14%	12%	16%	16%
Total (including Trieste)		497	645	640	847

Source Paolo Malanima, "Italian Urban Population 1300–1861," accessible at http://www.paolomalanima.it/default_file/Page646.htm
Note Trieste is excluded from the "Veneto" calculations in Table 1B because Trieste was not part of the Venetian state

and Genoa as capital cities preserved their relative weight in their own territories, as a whole Liguria and the Veneto saw a decline in its urban population vis-à-vis the other regions in the set.

This gradual transformation constituted a political problem of the first order because it affected the fiscal pacts that defined relations between center and periphery, that is, between the old monopolists and their subjugated territories. To give one example: In the Middle Ages, Genoa had not permitted subject cities to engage in international trade.

In theory, residents of the localities had to trade as Genoese citizens when abroad and through the port of Genoa itself. This arrangement had made it possible to tax local commerce heavily, since Ligurian towns had little choice but to make their purchases in Genoa. But the spread of free ports in nearby regions made it easier to defraud this fiscal system, which Genoa was no longer capable of policing. In any case, what did the localities have to gain by submitting to a Genoese monopoly that had ceased to pay dividends? In the seventeenth century, Ligurian towns traded more on their own count and paid fewer commercial taxes to Genoa than during the Middle Ages.[15]

While this brave new world may have been an economic boon to many communities, it menaced fiscal stability in the old monopolists, exposing the inadequacy of the patchwork of municipal privileges on which Italian territorial states had been constructed. Unfortunately, it was hard to change fiscal arrangements even when they no longer functioned. Administrators in Venice and Genoa found it impossible to embrace free port policies without radically reshaping the entire fiscal structure of their states, which had long depended on import and export duties. In both places, there was a movement toward consumption taxes that paralleled developments toward the excise in England or the Netherlands. Conversely, regimes had the most leeway to craft a free port when their maritime cities were less implicated in the old monopolies: Livorno, Ancona, and Trieste as newcomers found themselves less entangled in the fiscal mess of the late Middle Ages. The freedom of action that rulers enjoyed there enabled them to construct more effective free port institutions, largely through the informal delegation of decision making to local merchant and government elites.[16]

Transformations in the international trading regime promoted a move toward freer trade in Italy, although local institutional factors exerted a powerful effect on just how far ports actually opened their gates to foreign goods and merchants. But why did this movement toward free ports happen in Italy rather than throughout Europe? The answer, in a word, was regional political geography. Many states, many ports, and a central spot in the landscape of Mediterranean commerce: This was the predicament of early modern Italy. Under these circumstances, states either needed to enforce a monopoly against their neighbors by violence or had to relinquish themselves to the pressures of competition. Monopoly after the sixteenth century was no longer feasible; states had little choice but to confront the rigors of competition. As the eminent Neapolitan economist Antonio Genovesi put it: "If all or almost all of our neighboring nations have a free port, then we have no choice but to have one as well: for he who remains alone is deserted."[17] This was the choice of the rich but small states of northern Italy.

Regional competition and the collapse of the old monopolies were the basic conditions for the Italian free port system. Yet perhaps geography was the more important of the two since the spread of the free port in Italy recalls earlier patterns of regional integration. The ravages wrought by the Black Death and by the interminable wars fought among communes during the fourteenth century laid the foundation for integration within the boundaries of the state.[18] The free ports continued this impulse toward a more unified economic space, albeit with respect to maritime trade and global markets. The freezing of Italian political boundaries in the mid-sixteenth century did not put an end to integration, in other words, but diverted it into a different modality. The process bore some resemblance to the earlier phase of integration, too, when political fragmentation and an abundance of alternative routes encouraged cities to create fairs or minimize transit duties. Relentless commercial competition is one of the red threads running through Italy's history before and after the Renaissance, with fairs strung on it like so many hundreds of beads. One customs official unwittingly alluded to a deeper truth when he called Livorno in 1645 a "continuous fair of foreigners."[19]

Early modern Europe, like the larger world, had a polycentric economy with several core areas. The ultimate success of the Dutch and English did not owe to the unfolding of an intrinsic logic of capitalism, but to a set of conjunctures—including commercial rivalries in Italy that long antedated the rise of the Atlantic World. Even if certain British officials saw free ports as part of an informal imperial project, they were not their architects. The chain of causality moved in the opposite direction: The Netherlands and England were the beneficiaries rather than creators of the Italian free port system. We should therefore be cautious about speaking of their economic "dominance" in the central Mediterranean. In the poorly integrated markets of early modern Europe, the notion of hegemony obscures the realities of much international trade.

World-systems analysis is not very helpful in explaining patterns of global change before 1750 or even 1800. The dichotomies that pair the rich world with manufacturing and the poor world with agriculture are seriously misleading for the early modern period.[20] The fact that Italian agricultural exports in wine or olive oil were on the rise in the seventeenth century while industry was in (modest) decline cannot be read in light of the contemporary world system, with its stark structural contrasts between core and periphery.[21] In any case, north-central Italy remained an exporter rather than an importer of manufactured goods until the late eighteenth century.[22] The region fully met the criteria of a core economy.[23] No wonder, then, if its commercial space continued to be shaped by intra-urban rivalries within Italy rather than by supposedly asymmetric relations with northwestern Europe. Where a free port appeared depended on considerations that powerful countries could scarcely control, much less dictate.

Administrative Relimitation and Contemporary Capitalism

Despite the importance of changing patterns of global commerce, which helped usher in the collapse of Italian trading monopolies, Italian free ports emerged as a part of a regional rather than global dynamic. The global economic system is, however, critical for understanding contemporary special economic zones. Not that geography is unimportant: The relationship between the Mexican maquiladoras and the USA is obviously dependent on vicinity. But the creation of global marketplaces in labor, commodities, and consumer goods, as well as the radically cheaper costs of long-distance transit, has made the old style of regional customs competitions less important. In that sense, the early modern system of free ports—associated with the fragmented political landscape and dense maritime networks of Italy, the North Sea region, and the Caribbean—differs markedly from that of the contemporary free zone, such a conspicuous feature of the decolonized world. The new zones are an alternative to the import-substitution policies common among developing countries in the 1960s and 1970s. Regimes even target specific industries or sectors for "export-led growth," so that the dizzying variety of zone names reflects diverse industrial and commercial goals. In general, willingness to endow a place with the proper cocktail of policies and infrastructure is the major factor in whether a special zone is successful or not.[24] Whether success is a good thing for local workers and the integrity of the host state is more doubtful.

"How did a small, unremarkable Central American country with a turbulent political past (and, indeed, present) manage to become a leading exporter of clothing and apparel to the USA and, in doing so, create in excess of 100,000 new jobs?" So begins an awestruck article on the free zones in Honduras. The answer to the riddle? Honduras began establishing free zones in 1976. In 1998, its Congress declared the entire national territory a Free Zone Area, allowing private *Zonas Industriales de Procesamiento* to be established anywhere within state boundaries. Such zones are exempt from all federal, city, and commercial taxes. In-house customs officials enable "rapid and simplified customs procedures." Zone operators, customs officers, and central government officials are deeply complicit. As one operator put it, "a customer [foreign investor] who gets exposed to government-related corruption and other problems gets scared and wants to leave. The *maquila* operator functions as the interface that sorts out all the issues behind the scene, leaving the companies to do what they do best, which is manufacturing." This striking abdication of national sovereignty, along with massive infrastructural investments by the state, has worked its magic. In 2007, the country enjoyed $219.6 million in foreign direct investment (77% by Canada or the USA), most of it in textiles and oriented toward the North American apparel market. Some 75% of labor was female, meaning poorly paid and poorly protected. Over 60% of all Honduran exports were generated out of its free zones and were entirely beyond the reach of the Fisc.[25]

The free zones of Honduras are not unusual. Despite numerous lacunae and a certain (by now) antiquity, the most complete exploration of contemporary special zones is that of Jean-Pierre Singa Boyenge, compiled for the International Labor Office (ILO) in 2007. Boyenge's catalog required some finessing while transferring it to an electronic database.[26] His thirty-two different designations for a special zone were eliminated, in part because most zones are export processing zones, but above all because the distinctions between zone types are not clear. His data on investment and export values also had to be discarded due to idiosyncratic data entry. It is also worth noting that his sector lists are difficult to use, because where an activity falls along a supply chain is more important than what industry it belonged to. For instance, the vast majority of those working in "textiles" or "electronics"—terms that appear frequently in the catalog—are low-end factory workers, not fashion designers or engineers (Table 2).

Table 2 Special economic zone statistics (2007)

Top-ten category	Average number of zones per country	Average number of zone workers	Average percent female	Average zone exports as percent of total exports	Percent reporting in Boyenge database
Female participation	21	230,198	**79**	65	25
Workforce size	87	**1,360,495**	58	66	76
Zone exports	52	200,403	57	**85**	45
Total database	25	237,368	60	25	100

Source Boyenge, "ILO Database"
Note I have put the key statistic for each category in bold. "Percent reporting" refers to the percentage of cases for which the key statistic is included in the database, which has 108 entries. The countries with the highest female participation are Nicaragua, Jamaica, Cape Verde, Bangladesh, El Salvador, Sri Lanka, Honduras, the Philippines, Madagascar, South Korea, Guatemala, and Panama; those with the highest workforce size (excluding China) are the Philippines, Mexico, Malaysia, Vietnam, Pakistan, Indonesia, the Czech Republic, the United Arab Emirates, and South Africa; those with the highest percentage of zone exports as a percentage of total exports were Yemen, Brazil, Argentina, the Czech Republic, Puerto Rico, Kenya, Algeria, Mozambique, Malaysia, Madagascar, the Dominican Republic, Vietnam, Macao, Gabon, Zimbabwe, Mali, and Lesotho. Some "top-ten" lists had more than ten countries due to identical values

It is impossible to produce global averages of such statistics as the number of zone workers, the percent of female zone workers, or the portion of the world's production and commerce that passes through zones. Instead, I have made "top-ten" lists to get a sense of the extremes of the phenomenon (Table 2). The data confirm a few striking facts. Free zones are concentrated in relatively poor countries, with the exception of the USA (which has hundreds of bonded warehouse zones). Free zones often have hundreds of thousands of workers, sometimes more: as many as six million in Indonesia and forty million in China. A striking proportion of zone workers moreover are women: as much as 90% in Nicaragua or 85% in Bangladesh (the average over the whole database is 60%). These figures do not herald a victory for feminism. Women are concentrated in the lowest paid, hardest working sectors such as textiles, electronics assembly, packaging, and food processing. In general, the zones are crucial to their host countries' export economies, although to varying degrees many remain outside of the state's control. Overall, zones accounted for 64% of total exports from countries in the database. For a number of countries, zones accounted for almost *all* exports. In short, special zones are pockets of low-tech industry absolutely central to manufacturing and export, but often removed from a state's ordinary fiscal and administrative apparatus.

Removed for whose benefit? Boyenge's catalog shows that the most common investors in special zones are western Europe, the USA, and China; others are local or regional to the zone in question. More importantly, the USA and Europe dominate the market for zone exports. While it is a truism that in recent decades the West has exported its industries and their externalities to the developing world, it is less known that much of this industry takes place in special economic zones. Thus, it is fair to say that "spatialization" is an important element of contemporary capitalism, ultimately made possibility by cheap transport and communications. Certainly, the West would no longer tolerate within its own borders the exploitation of huge numbers of female workers. But the spread of free zones reveals another dimension of contemporary capitalism, its capacity to exploit state weakness to create enclaves exempt from the prevailing rules. We might call this process "administrative relimitation." Although dressed up in the language of economic liberalism, relimitation is another term for the political economy of privilege.

The term "relimitation" is borrowed from law, where it means the reassignment of property rights subject to a special disposition (as in a will). More generally, it indicates a redefinition or scaling back of prevailing norms. The OED provides this illustration: "I would support proposals made by Michael Graetz to relimit the reach of the income tax to the rich and to impose a value added tax ... on everybody else."[27] But the relimitation I have in mind is administrative rather than legal; zonal privileges are not the outgrowth of an inegalitarian legal regime but the product of modern bureaucratic states. On the other hand, we cannot describe the process as one of intensified bureaucratization (bureaucracy's scope is deliberately limited in a special zone) or rationalization (the movement promotes state lumpiness rather than uniformity). Administrative relimitation is the strategic retreat of bureaucracy in the service of economic growth or, more to the point, business interests. My term evokes the transformation in boundaries and regulations that characterizes the contemporary free zone.[28]

The special economic zone offers an unusual case of rent seeking in the name of freedom. Typically, we imagine monopolists exploiting legal privileges or market share to cut out competitors and sell to consumers at higher prices. The special zone, by contrast, allows firms to compete for commodities and labor in a global environment. So far, those who hail zones as avatars of economic freedom are correct. But thanks to relaxed labor, environmental, and fiscal policies, the same firms enjoy distinct advantages over businesses located in a state's regular administrative space. Ordinary firms accordingly have difficulty competing with their lean, tax-unburdened cousins in the free zones. Free zones, far from *necessarily* catalyzing liberalization in the larger economy, concentrate capital investment within their enclaves—and employment opportunities, too.[29] Job creation in special economic zones (and unemployment elsewhere) is not the result of market forces, but of deliberate choices of state policy reminiscent of the age of mercantilism.

Another way of phrasing this point: Free zones only promote general liberalization if a host state continually adds free zones or alters its own political economy. The "if" implies further political and bureaucratic interventions that should not be taken for granted. Occasionally, whether because of state weakness (as in Honduras) or deliberate policy making, free zones *have* multiplied. For weak states, the contagious spread of special-zone liberalism may result in a fatal sacrifice of state sovereignty. For strong states, free zones may indeed catalyze the spread of free markets—but of such a libertine cast that it is hard to see them as an unalloyed good for the workers who toil in their factories.

In this context, it is important to examine China's use of the special economic zone to promote gradual liberalization: What Deng Xiaoping called "crossing the river by touching the stones." The process began with the relimitation of a few coastal areas in 1978, came to encompass the entire coastal region by about 1988, and spread inland in the following decades. Today, over 300 special zones are found throughout almost the entire country. The zones promoted foreign direct investment while pioneering capitalist property rights and labor contracts. The increasingly dynamic sectors of the economy in the special zones exacerbated economic inequalities between the zones and the regular space, and between the coastal areas (where zones were most dense) and inland areas. As a result, to maintain their competitiveness, many of China's state-owned enterprises were permitted to shed workers and otherwise liberalize. Further reforms also liberalized ordinary administrative space, such as the lowering of general tariffs and the privatization of the agricultural economy. The end point? Phenomenal GDP growth fueled by low-wage export industries. As of 2006, the five initial special economic zones alone accounted for 9% of foreign investment and 22% of exports. Zone workers have experienced higher wages, but also brutal working conditions, insecure employment tenure, intensified managerial control, and the collapse of collective bargaining rights. Lest we think democracy and capitalism walk hand in hand into the bright future, all of this change occurred without compromising one-party rule.[30]

Chinese success has seduced observers into elevating its policies into a model (Fig. 1). In their view, liberalization in the zones stimulates pressure to liberalize a state's ordinary administrative space; in turn, a more competitive host state exerts further reciprocal pressure on the

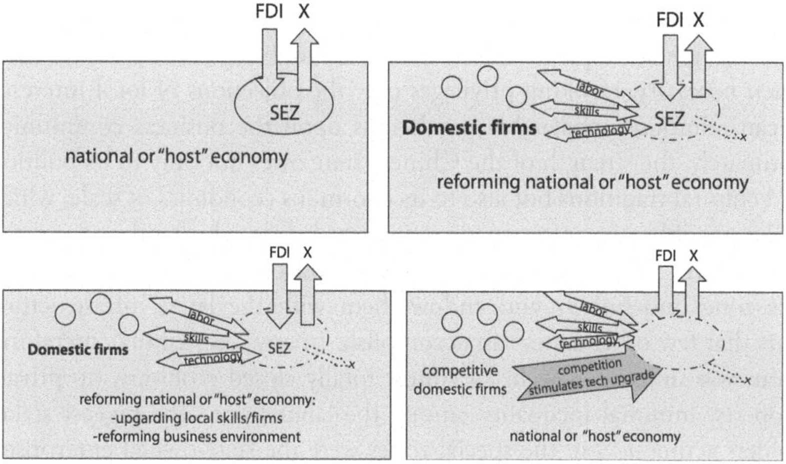

Fig. 1 Model for how a special economic zone might transform the host economy (based on the example of Shenzhen, China). I explain in text why the model does not have general applicability. *Source* Justine White, "Fostering Innovation in Developing Economies through SEZs," in *Special Economic Zones*, 183–205: 200–201

zonal economies to remain innovative. The process is meant to encourage technological progress and a gradual ascent up the value-added chain, so that developing countries are not forever manufacturing low-wage, labor-intensive goods.

Even in China, much of the second half of this program—clawing up the economic food chain—remains in the domain of the optative mood. Although high-tech industry has begun to blossom in some cities, problems of transitioning from a low-wage to a high-wage economy, with improving the social well-being of workers inside and outside zones, remain to be solved. A sad legacy of the special zones is the massive deracination of rural workers, many of whom remain unregistered in their new cities (and hence ineligible for certain social benefits). Some observers use Pollyannaish language to describe the relationship between workers and the special zone, for instance by terming the latter "an important innovative solution to the employment problems" in China.[31] But misery is still common.

China, despite its boosters, is not a model. It possesses an exceptionally strong state capable of imposing free zone regulations at will and, when necessary, revoking privileges over the objections of local interests. It can reimpose unpalatable regulations upon the business community. Ultimately, the strength of the Chinese state owes not only to its political and cultural traditions but also to its enormous economies of scale, which make possible vast infrastructure projects before which other countries would balk. These factors have made it possible for China to multiply free zones indefinitely and endow them with the latest infrastructure: feats that few other states can accomplish. In any case, China's prereform status was unusual as well: an almost totally closed economy, no private property, minimal inequality among the labor force. The biggest stakeholders acting *against* the special zones were the state-owned enterprises, but the strength of the Chinese state, as well as the gradual "sequencing" by which liberalization occurred, made it possible to circumvent their opposition. All of which enabled "some people to get rich first," as Deng Xiaoping put it.[32] Other countries have to cope not only with poverty, but also massive initial inequality in the ownership of capital.

The proliferation of free zones reflects willingness to compromise on market principles: Firms and governments will gladly alight in free trade zones when they cannot secure universal liberalization. Yet the free zone is not a typical case of embedded liberalism, in which government regulations seek to contain the evils of an untrammeled market.[33] Instead, the free zone facilitates a shift from high-paid male labor to low-paid female labor. The feminization of industry has been accompanied by the renegotiation of workers' rights and privatization (and insecurity) in such matters as housing, healthcare, childcare, working hours, and tenure of contract.[34] Society has been more often threatened than protected by its special zones.

One hopes that prosperity will radiate outward from the zones and downward from industrial elites. Yet the conditions that make zones possible also create pressure to extend industrial privileges at the expense of competing social goods. An industrial enterprise must be located in a specific place. In today's environment, low labor costs produce development and over the long term raise wages beyond that of the competition (e.g., China vis-à-vis Vietnam or Bangladesh). This means that interest groups are under perpetual threat from the outside: Their only recourse is to find *further* ways to liberalize and to distinguish themselves from the host state and from competitors. For states to safeguard the well-being of their workers and the natural environment, they must be able to fetter local business interests.

Whether a state succeeds in controlling its offspring or surrenders its authority remains to be seen, although there is a reason to fear that the fate of Honduras will be more common than that of China. If so, it is difficult to maintain that the international regime is dominated by states and only secondarily by corporate interests. On the contrary, the spread of free zones owes to ad hoc bargaining between owners of capital and poor states. Powerful nations, if they had been capable of controlling outcomes, would have preferred a multilateral reduction of barriers to investment and trade. Accordingly, the vertiginous rise of free zones challenges any characterization of international political economy as a conflict between trading blocs such as the North American Free Trade Agreement (NAFTA) or a universal market as envisioned by the World Trade Organization (WTO).[35] In huge swathes of the developing world, and even some parts of the rich world, it is the free zone that has been the vehicle of liberalization. Behind every poor state's "choice" to endow a zone lies the hunger of international capital for cheap labor, the knowledge that capital will seek those places where regulations are minimal and property protections maximal, and the desire—shimmering like a desert mirage—of becoming a prosperous nation.

Special Zones, Special Interests

The survival of "the city" as an administrative category makes inter-urban rivalries possible, and with them, the proliferation of distinct policy environments: what I have called administrative relimitation. But whereas in the Renaissance, the city and its privileges were explicit categories of economic analysis, economic theory today takes the firm and (reluctantly) the state as its primary actors. Municipal independence is often seen as urban self-help in the face of state failure rather than what it is: constitutive of the system. All cities are potentially special economic zones to the extent that they possess their own government, their own elite, their own fiscal rules, and their own commercial infrastructure.[36] Even as cities in the western world have lavished tax breaks and infrastructure on corporations, regimes in the developing world have rushed to create export processing zones and other industrial infernos. Both processes, proceeding in tandem, have buttressed business elites everywhere. But what kind of societies will best be able to stand up to entitled local interests, contentious democracies, or strong absolutist regimes? The battles over free zones in India versus the quiescence of opposition in China suggest that, for good or ill, absolutist regimes may have the advantage both in conjuring up a zone and in putting it to sleep when it has outlived its purpose. And even they may have a devilishly hard time of it.[37]

Rulers of early modern free ports discovered that it was difficult to make local merchants come to heel. In Livorno, for instance, officials complained that merchants enjoyed a "despotic liberty" to import and export whatever they chose, and on whatever terms they chose.[38] Throughout the long eighteenth century, the Tuscan government proved incapable of imposing key policies on the refractory merchant class of Livorno. "The character and nature of the commerce of Livorno are not susceptible to systems or rules. It is entirely foreign, having to do with transit, and depends on the will of foreigners," explained the city's governor in 1765. "So the only projects and systems that can affect the commerce of Livorno, are ones that increase its favors and conveniences, and which leave merchants a full liberty to direct their businesses as they see fit."[39] It was even impossible to collect trade statistics from merchants, because such questions amounted to an "interrogation," a "trial against one or more merchants of this marketplace."[40] For all their liberties, Livorno merchants were on cozy terms with local officials and were consulted with lavish deference whenever the government contemplated a change in policy: From technical matters of customs collection to the general welfare of the port and its relations with Tuscany, the (mostly foreign) merchants enjoyed a dominant voice in the determination of local policy. Even the grand duke admitted that it was an "illusion" to administer the city in any other way.[41]

Despite the differences between free ports and their modern descendants, every free area creates a class of businessmen whose interests constitute the *raison d'être* of the zone. In China, for example, municipalities often delegate decision making and even legislation to a special committee sympathetic to business.[42] Firms are encouraged to organize to protect their collective interests, as when the Wenzhou footwear firms united against charges of dumping their wares on the Indian market; worker unionization is prohibited or feckless.[43] Free zones exist *solely* to promote economic growth. This fact legitimates strategies centered on economic prosperity and delegitimizes alternative goals—such as the well-being of individual workers, the preservation of cultural heritage, the expansion of participatory democracy, or the preservation of sovereignty. As one scholar sympathetic to free zones commented without qualification: "longer government procedures and lower government efficiency" was the consequence of Tianjin Municipality gradually recapturing some of its authority over its zone.[44] Efficiency is one of the altar gods of the special economic zone. Special interests readily master its ritual language.

Roberto Bolaño's *2666* is one of the great modernist novels of our time. Much of the narrative takes place in the city of Santa Teresa, a fictionalized version of Ciudad Jaurez on the Mexican-American border. The most memorable portion of *2666* is the long segment detailing the crimes that led to the death or disappearance of some three hundred women. The reader learns a lot about Santa Teresa in the course of the investigation. It is a booming city, owing to its factories and proximity to the USA. It has one of the lowest unemployment rates in Mexico. Most of the victims are women working at the local maquiladoras, that is, factory women: "disposable at any moment or for any reason or hint of a reason."[45] The criminals belong to the class of industrialists, drug cartels, and politicians who run the city. Whenever a police investigation touches on one of their interests, it is quietly discouraged; many a kidnapped woman is last seen stepping into one of the sleek black sports cars favored by the city's playboys. Santa Teresa is the kind of place where the rich can indulge their vices with impunity and without compromising their profits. The poor are defenseless, overworked, and expendable.

Bolaño makes it clear who was really in charge in Santa Teresa. Before making an arrest of the prime murder suspect, a German-born American citizen named Klaus Haas, the police chief calls a meeting with his top detectives, a judge, the city mayor, and—naturally—a representative of the chamber of commerce. The businessman is skeptical of their presentation. He affects not to understand the details of the case. "Anything is possible, but there's no need to descend into chaos, no need to lose our bearings." When the mayor finally commands the police chief "to put an end to this goddamn business" by arresting the culprit, Bolaño gives the last word to the man from the chamber of commerce: find him, yes, "but discreetly, if I may make one request, without sending anyone into a panic."[46] Haas is arrested. No other man of wealth or power suffers a similar fate. The murders continue unabated. Business is good.

The epigraph of *2666* comes from Baudelaire's *Le Voyage*: "An oasis of horror in a desert of boredom." Bolaño's Santa Teresa is typical of special economic zones throughout the world, with pervasive physical and structural violence against the poor.[47] Have we at last found the dividing line between the special economic zone and its ancestor? Certainly, there was little horror in early modern free ports, those colorful places of cosmopolitan toleration. And yet there is something curiously Ancien Regime about the special economic zone. It belies the myth of the modern state, with its supposed tendencies to level distinctions and create a uniform bureaucratic space in the service of capitalism. Today, as in early modern Italy, it is privilege—a peculiar administrative and customs realm, complete with its own entitled interest groups—that makes possible the commercial miracles, political failures, and social tragedies of the special economic zone.

Notes

1. Richard S. Thoman, *Free Ports and Foreign-Trade Zones* (Cambridge: Cornell Maritime Press, 1956), 128; Robert J. McCalla, "The Geographical Spread of Free Zones Associated with Ports," *Geoforum* 21, no. 1 (1990): 121–34; and Jean-Pierre Boyenge, "ILO Database

on Export Processing Zones (Revised)," accessed June 28, 2011, http://www.ilo.org/public/libdoc/ilo/2007/107B09_80_engl.pdf. Estimating growth of free zones at 2% per year between 2007 and 2014, there would now be 4100 such zones; estimating free zone growth at 4% per year (which was the rate between 2002 and 2006 according to Boyenge), there were would now be 4790 zones.

2. See, for instance, *The Guardian*, January 25, 2013, "Child Labour Uncovered in Apple's Supply Chain"; and *The New York Times*, November 26, 2012, "Fatal Fire in Bangladesh Highlights the Dangers Facing Garment Workers."
3. Dennis A. Rondinelli, "Export Processing Zones and Economic Development in Asia: A Review and Reassessment of a Means of Promoting Growth and Jobs," *American Journal of Economics and Sociology* 46, no. 1 (1987): 89–105; John R. McIntyre, Rajneesh Narula, and Len J. Trevino, "The Role of Export Processing Zones for Host Countries and Multinationals: A Mutually Beneficial Relationship?," *The International Trade Journal* 10, no. 4 (1996): 435–66; Dorsati Madani, "A Review of the Role and Impact of Export Processing Zones" (n.d.); for a focus particularly on the appetite for unskilled labor, Mauricio Jenkins, Gerardo Esquivel, and Felipe Larraín, *Export Processing Zones in Central America*, Development Discussion Papers, Central America Project Series (Harvard University: Harvard Institute for International Development, 1998); Enrique Blanco De Armas and Mustapha Sadni Jallab, *A Review of the Role and Impact of Export Processing Zones in World Trade: The Case of Mexico* (Institute of Development Studies, 2002); Yue-man Yeung, Joanna Lee, and Gordon Kee, "China's Special Economic Zones at 30," *Eurasian Geography and Economics* 50, no. 2 (2009): 222–40; Thomas Farole and Gokhan Akinci eds., *Special Economic Zones. Progress, Emerging Challenges, and Future Directions* (New York: The International Bank for Reconstruction and Development, 2011); and Dara Orenstein, "Foreign-Trade Zones and the Cultural Logic of Frictionless Production," *Radical History Review* no. 109 (2011): 36–61.
4. Paul Masson, *Ports francs d'autrefois et d'aujord'hui* (Paris: Hachette, 1904); Bruno Minoletti, *I porti franchi* (Turin: Einaudi, 1939); Johannes Hovy, *Het voorstel van 1751 tot instelling van een beperkt vrijhavenstelsel in de Republiek. (Propositie tot een Gelimiteerd Porto-franco)* (Groningen: J. B. Wolters, 1966), esp. 161–81; and Louis Dermigny, "Escales, échelles et ports francs au moyen âge et aux temps moderns," in *Les grandes escales* (Bruxelles: Recueil de la Société Jean Bodin, 1974), 521–26.

5. See Max Weber, *Economy and Society*, ed. Guenther Roth and Claus Wittich, 2 vols. (Berkeley: University of California Press, 1978), 956–1044; Michael Mann, *The Sources of Social Power, vol. II, The Rise of Classes and Nation-States, 1760–1914* (Cambridge: Cambridge University Press, 1993), 444–78; on institutional structure, see Douglass Cecil North and Robert Paul Thomas, *The Rise of the Western World: A New Economic History* (Cambridge: Cambridge University Press, 1973); Douglass Cecil North and Barry Weingast, "Constitutions and Commitment: Evolution of Institutions Governing. Public Choice in Seventeenth-Century England," *Journal of Economic History* 49 (1989): 803–32; Hilton L. Root, *The Fountain of Privilege: Political Foundations of Economic Markets in Old Regime France and England* (Berkeley: University of California Press, 1994); and Daron Acemoglu et al., "The Rise of Europe: Atlantic Trade, Institutional Change and Economic Growth," *American Economic Review* 95, no. 3 (2005): 546–79.
6. On Italian free ports, see Mario Baruchello, *Livorno e il suo porto. Origini, caratteristiche e vicende dei traffici livornesi* (Livorno: Società Anonima Editrice Riviste Tecniche, 1932); Alberto Caracciolo, *Le port franc d'Ancône, croissance et impasse d'un milieu marchand au XVIIIe siècle* (Paris: SEVPEN, 1965); Giulio Giacchero, *Origini e sviluppo del portofranco genovese* (Genova: Sagep, 1972); Lucia Frattarelli Fischer, "Livorno città nuova: 1574–1609," *Società e storia* XI (1989): 873–93; idem, "Livorno 1676: La città e il porto franco," in *La Toscana nell'età di Cosimo III*, ed. Franco Angiolini et al. (Firenze: EDIFIR, 1993); Massimo Costantini, "La regolazione dei dazi marittimi e l'esperienza del 'portofranco' a Venezia tra il 1662 e il 1664," in *La finanza pubblica in età di crisi*, ed. Antonio Di Vittorio (Bari: Cacucci, 1993), 77–88; and Thomas Allison Kirk, *Genoa and the Sea: Policy and Power in an Early Modern Maritime Republic, 1559–1684* (Baltimore: Johns Hopkins University Press, 2005), 176–85.
7. Carlo Antonio Broggia, *Trattato de' tributi, delle monete, e del governo politico della sanità* (Napoli: Pietro Palombo, 1743), 98–101; Caracciolo, *Le port franc d'Ancône,* 165; and Gigliola Pagano De Divitiis, *English Merchants in Seventeenth-Century Italy* (Cambridge: Cambridge University Press, 1997), 117.
8. Quoted by Frances Armytage, *The Free Port System in the British West Indies. A Study in Commercial Policy, 1766–1822* (London: Longmans, Green, 1953), 58.

9. See Immanuel M. Wallerstein, *The Modern World-System*, vol. 2 (New York: Academic Press, 1976–1989), 50n, 193–200; Fernand Braudel, *Civilization and Capitalism, 15th–18th Century* (Berkeley: University of California Press, 1982–1984), vol. 3, *The Perspective of the World*, 175–76; idem, *Out of Italy: 1450–1650* (Paris: Flammarion, 1991), 202; and Massimo Costantini, *Porto navi e traffici a Venezia 1700–2000* (Venice: Marsilio, 2004), 21–24.
10. Giulio Giacchero, *Storia economica del Settecento genovese* (Genova: Apuania, 1951), 54, 59, 66–67, 72; idem, *Il seicento e le compere di San Giorgio* (Genoa: Sagep, 1979), 606–8; Edoardo Grendi, "Traffico e navi nel porto di Genova fra 1500 e 1700," in *La repubblica aristocratica dei genovesi* (Bologna: Mulino, 1987), 327–31, 345, 352; Caracciolo *Le port franc de Ancône*, 117–18; Jean Georgelin, *Venise au siècle des lumières* (Paris: École des hautes études en sciences sociales, 1978), 90–91, 99–101. The econometric work done by Perrson suggests that the Pisan grain market became more integrated, first in the decades around 1600 with the expansion of Livorno, and later around 1700—perhaps because of increased competition among Italian ports? Karl Gunnar Persson, *Grain Markets in Europe, 1500–1900* (Cambridge: Cambridge University Press, 1999), 98–99, 110–11. For the fitful process of early modern integration, see Stephan R. Epstein, *Freedom and Growth. The Rise of States and Markets in Europe, 1300–1750* (London: Routledge, 2000), 38–72, 147–68; K. H. O'Rourke and J. G. Williamson, "When Did Globalisation Begin?," *European Review of Economic History* 6 (2002): 23–50; Klas Rönnbäck, "Integration of Global Commodity Markets in the Early Modern Era," *European Review of Economic History* 13 (2009): 95–120; and Regina Grafe, *Distant Tyranny: Markets, Power, and Backwardness in Spain, 1650–1800* (Princeton: Princeton University Press, 2012), 86–102.
11. Since internal tolls remained, maritime integration affected port cities and their surrounding regions more than states as a whole.
12. On the Venetian system, see Frederic C. Lane, *Venice: A Maritime Republic* (Baltimore: The Johns Hopkins University Press, 1973), esp. 22–117; on Genoa, Claudio Costantini, *La repubblica di Genova* (Torino: UTET, 1978), 364–70; and Jeffrey Miner, "Lest We Break Faith with our Creditors: Public Debt and Civic Culture in Fourteenth-century Genoa" (Ph.D. dissertation, Stanford University, 2011), 103–33.
13. R. T. Rapp, "The Unmaking of the Mediterranean Trade Hegemony: International Trade Rivalry and the Commercial Revolution," *Journal*

of Economic History 35 (1975): 499–525; Paolo Malanima, *La fine del primato. Crisi e riconversione nell'Italia del Seicento* (Milano: Bruno Mondadori, 1998).

14. See Caracciolo, *Le port franc de Ancône*, 163–64, 183–96, 241–47; *Livorno e Pisa: due città e un territorio nella politica dei Medici: Livorno, progetto e storia di una città tra il 1500 e il 1600* (Pisa: Nistri-Lischi e Pacini, 1980); and Paola Lanaro, ed., *At the Centre of the Old World: Trade and Manufacturing in Venice and on the Venetian Mainland, 1400–1800* (Toronto: Centre for Reformation and Renaissance Studies, 2006).
15. The Casa di San Giorgio's battle against fraud during the seventeenth century sheds a lot of light on the capital's relationship with subject towns. Giacchero, *Settecento*, 21; idem, *Compere*, discussion of 1590 balance sheet; 338, 128–32, 412–17; 431–33; 573–85; and idem, *Origini e sviluppo*, 155–59; and also Heinrich Sieveking, *Studio sulle finanze genovesi e in particolare sulla casa di San Giorgio* (Genova: Tip. della Gioventù, 1905), 219–20; Edoardo Grendi, "The Political System of a Community in Liguria: Cervo in the Late Sixteenth and Early Seventeenth Century," in *Microhistory and the Lost Peoples of Europe*, ed. Edward Muir and Guido Ruggiero (Baltimore: Johns Hopkins University Press, 1991), 119–58; and more generally, Corey Tazzara, "State Formation, Market Development, and Customs Fraud in Seventeenth-Century Liguria," in William Caferro, ed., *The Routledge History of the Renaissance* (London: Routledge, 2017), 358–72.
16. Corey Tazzara, "Managing Free Trade in Early Modern Europe: Institutions, Information, and the Free Port of Livorno," *Journal of Modern History* (September, 2014).
17. Antonio Genovesi, *Delle lezioni di commercio o sia d'economia civile*, vol. 1 (Naples: I Fratelli Simone, 1765), 319. Broggia, *Trattato* 104, 115, 117–18 makes a similar point.
18. Stephan R. Epstein, "Market Structures," in *Florentine Tuscany. Structures and Practices of Power*, ed. William J. Connell and Andrea Zorzi (Cambridge: Cambridge University Press, 2000), 90–121; idem, *Freedom and Growth*, 59–60, 73–88.
19. ASF, MP, 2160, from an undated memorandum appended to 01/16/1645 [AD], Pandolfo Attavanti to Domenico Pandolfini.
20. See Kenneth Pomeranz, *The Great Divergence: Europe, China, and the Making of the Modern World Economy* (Princeton: Princeton University Press, 2000), esp. 253–63.

21. Italy's much-discussed industrial "decline" was very modest—only a couple of percent, according to Malanima.
22. See, for instance, Pagano De Divitiis, *English Merchants*, esp. 126, 127, and 144; Paolo Malanima, *La decadenza di un'economia cittadina: l'industria di Firenze nei secoli XVI–XVIII* (Bologna: Il Mulino, 1982), esp. 305; Domenico Sella, *Crisis and Continuity: The Economy of Spanish Lombardy in the Seventeenth Century* (Cambridge: Harvard University Press, 1979), esp. 116–23; and in general, Carlo Poni, *La Seta in Italia. Una Grande Industria Prima Della Rivoluzione Industriale* (Bologna: Il Mulino, 2009). The situation in the south of Italy was rather different: see Sophus A. Reinert, *Translating Empire. Emulation and the Origins of Political Economy* (Cambridge: Harvard University Press, 2011), 186–232.
23. That is relatively free markets, extensive market-oriented handicraft industries, and commercialized agriculture.
24. In addition to the works cited above, see for institutional factors George T. Crane, *The Political Economy of China's Special Economic Zones* (Armonk, NY: East Gate, 1990) and Triyakshana Seshadri and Virgil Henry Storr, "Knowledge Problems Associated with Creating Export Zones," *The Review of Austrian Economics* 23 (2010): 347–66; on export-led growth, see Robert Gilpin, *Global Political Economy: Understanding the International Economic Order* (Princeton: Princeton University Press, 2001), 316–29.
25. The quotes are from Michael Engman, "Success and Stasis in Honduras' Free Zones," in *Special Economic Zones*, 47, 57, and 60. The statistics are from ibid., 51–53; and Boyenge, *ILO Database*, 13. For the contemporary history of Honduras, see Thomas M. Leonard, *The History of Honduras* (Santa Barbara, CA: Greenwood Press, 2011), 156–76.
26. The spreadsheet and tables are posted on my website, http://community.scrippscollege.edu/ctazzara/.
27. From the OED's second definition of relimit: "2. trans. To set new limits for; to restrict again." [...] 2002 Yale Law Jrnl. 111 1413. OED Online. June 2014. Oxford University Press, accessed August 07, 2014. http://www.oed.com/view/Entry/161961.
28. Administrative relimitation unfolds at one extreme of contemporary political practice, in which the state voluntary surrenders (some of) its control over a territory; the other extreme is the "zomia" described by

James Scott, in which the state is incapable of exerting any control at all over a territory. See James C. Scott, *The Art of Not Being Governed: An Anarchist History of Upland Southeast Asia* (New Haven: Yale University Press, 2010).

29. See David Harvey, *A Brief History of Neoliberalism* (Oxford: Oxford University Press, 2005), 130–33.
30. The quote is from Douglas Zhihua Zeng, "How Do Special Economic Zones and Industrial Clusters Drive China's Rapid Development?", in *Building Engines for Growth and Competitiveness in China: Experience with Special Economic Zones and Industrial Clusters* (Washington, DC: The International Bank for Reconstruction and Development, 2010), 8; the 2006 data are from ibid., 13. For data on the proliferation of Chinese zones, see Jim Wang, "The Economic Impact of Special Economic Zones: Evidence from Chinese Municipalities," *Journal of Development Economics* 101 (2013): 133–47, 136–37. For the condition of workers, see Mary Elizabeth Gallagher, *Contagious Capitalism: Globalization and the Politics of Labor in China* (Princeton: Princeton University Press, 2005), esp. 96; and Leslie T. Chang, *Factory Girls: From Village to City in a Changing China* (New York: Spiegel & Grau, 2008).
31. Yiming Yuan et al., "China's First Special Economic Zone: The Case of Shenzhen," in *Building Engines for Growth*, 55–85, 66.
32. Quoted by Gallagher, *Contagious Capitalism*, 12.
33. Karl Polanyi, *The Great Transformation* (Boston: Beacon Press, 2001).
34. Altha J. Cravey, *Women and Work in Mexico's Maquiladoras* (Lanham, MD: Rowman and Littlefield, 1998), *passim*, esp. 18.
35. See Gilpin, *Global Political Economy*, 196–233, 341–61.
36. The key Renaissance figure was Giovanni Botero; see the recent translation of his *On the Causes of the Greatness of Cities* by Geoffrey Symcox (Toronto: University of Toronto Press, 2012). Modern economists have not neglected cities entirely, but as Paul Krugman notes, their study remains adventitious to the discipline. See *Geography and Trade* (Cambridge: MIT Press, 1991), 4–10. The special economic zone is one form of the "urban entrepreneurialism" discussed by David Harvey in *Spaces of Capital: Towards a Critical Geography* (New York: Routledge, 2001), 345–68.

37. On special zones in India, see Laura Alfaro and Lakshmi Iyer, "Special Economic Zones in India: Public Purpose and Private Property," *Harvard Business School*, 2012. I am grateful to Sophus A. Reinert for access to this document. For an analysis of how optimal political economy changes over time, see Jean-Laurent Rosenthal and R. Bin Wong, *Before and Beyond Divergence. The Politics of Economic Change in China and Europe* (Cambridge, MA: Harvard University Press, 2011).
38. ASF, MP, 2198, 12/09/1675, Camillo Capponi to Ferdinando Bardi.
39. ASL, Governo, 1, ff. 500–528, *Relazione del governo civile, del commercio, e della marina mercantile di Livorno*. The quotations are from ff. 509–10.
40. ASL, Governo, 964, p. 95, 03/11/1768, Bourbon del Monte to Orsini Rosenberg.
41. Pietro Leopoldo d'Asburgo Lorena, *Relazioni sul governo della Toscana*, vol. 3, ed. Arnaldo Salvestrini (Firenze: Olschki, 1974), 60–71. Rulers of other free ports faced similar problems. See Junko Thérèse Takeda, *Between Crown and Commerce: Marseille and the Early Modern Mediterranean* (Baltimore: The Johns Hopkins University Press, 2011); and Caracciolo, *Le port franc d'Ancône*, 237–61.
42. Zeng, ed., *Building Engines for Growth*, 10, 17, 37, 80–81, 116.
43. See Jici Wang, "Industrial Clustering in China: The Case of the Wenzhou Footwear Sector," in *Building Engines for Growth*, 151–79, 175; Zeng, "How Do Special Economic Zones," 35.
44. Xiaoxi Li et al., "A Case Study of Tianjin Economic-Technological Development Area," in *Building Engines for Growth*, 87–121, 116.
45. Roberto Bolaño, *2666* (New York: Farrar, Straus, and Giroux, 2008), 527. For the maquiladora system in Mexico and its US entanglements, see Leslie Sklair, *Assembling for Development: The Maquila Industry in Mexico and the United States* (San Diego: Center for US-Mexican Studies, 1993).
46. All quotes from Bolaño, *2666*, 471.
47. See Cravey, *Women and Work*, esp. 81–86, where she describes official collusion in silencing worker grievances; 96–98, on health violations; and 106 on sexual abuse in the company dormitories.

Author Biography

Corey Tazzara is Assistant Professor of History at Scripps College. He received his Ph.D. from Stanford University in 2011. Corey's publications include "Managing Free Trade: Institutions, Information, and the Free Port of Livorno," *The Journal of Modern History* (86: 2014); "Capricious Demands: Artisanal Goods, Business Strategies, and Consumer Behavior in Seventeenth-Century Florence," in *Early Modern Things. Objects and Their Histories, 1500–1800,* ed. by Paula Findlen (New York: Routledge, 2012); and a translation with Brad Bouley of Renata Ago, *A Gusto for Things: A History of Objects in Seventeenth-Century Rome* (Chicago: University of Chicago Press, 2012). His first monograph, *The Free Port of Livorno and the Transformation of the Mediterranean World, 1574–1790*, has recently been published by Oxford University Press.

Theatrum Œconomicum: Anders Berch and the Dramatization of the Swedish Improvement Discourse

Carl Wennerlind

Introduction

A variety of improvement discourses shaped the contours of early modern capitalism. Whether labeled Mercantilism, Colbertism, Cameralism, Physiocracy, or Classical Political economy by posterity, early modern improvement discourses shared a fundamental focus on progress through material expansion.[1] The commercial opportunities, destabilizing social experiences, and transformative political trends experienced throughout Europe inspired leading reform writers to address the same general themes and questions. In networks spanning national borders, they shared insights and strategies, creating a considerable intellectual coherence on topics including property, wealth and virtue, jealousy of trade, population, education, employment, fiscal management, and

The author thanks Ken Carpenter, Monica Miller, Erik Reinert, Philipp Rössner, Lisa Tiersten, Andre Wakefield, and Sophie Wilkowske for comments on earlier drafts. Thanks to Mårten Granert and Jenny Svennås-Gillner for generous assistance with images and Christel Kraft for helping with archival material.

C. Wennerlind (✉)
Barnard College, Columbia University, New York, USA
e-mail: cwennerl@barnard.edu

R. Fredona and S.A. Reinert (eds.), *New Perspectives on the History of Political Economy*, https://doi.org/10.1007/978-3-319-58247-4_4

nature.[2] Yet, each nation developed its own discourse—or in some instances multiple discourses—focusing on a specific set of themes that addressed the nation's most pressing challenges and considerable advantages.

In Sweden, the dominant improvement discourse centered on the development of economically useful natural knowledge.[3] Starting in the 1640s, as a result of Sweden's remarkable success in the Thirty Years' War, Swedish elites called for a new vision for Sweden's future. It was clear to everyone that Sweden had to find an abundant source of wealth if the nation were to retain its newfound geopolitical power. Inspired by the pan-European universal reformation movement and the Swedish tradition of *Gothicism*, generations of Swedish reformers posited strategies for the nation's improvement.[4] Over the next century, a discernably Swedish discourse of improvement emerged, centered on the advancement of natural knowledge as the key to improvement.

The development of new knowledge was essential, as was the thorough dissemination of this knowledge throughout the nation. As many people as possible had to be given access to the most sophisticated natural knowledge available and be encouraged to incorporate it into their daily interactions with nature. The cheapening of print, the development of a postal system, and the remaking of the nation's educational curriculum contributed importantly to the dissemination of useful knowledge. Yet simply circulating knowledge was not enough. In order for people to fully embrace and implement new ideas, more effective pedagogies for the transmission of knowledge were necessary.

One of the most intriguing moments of the dissemination of the Swedish improvement discourse was the creation of Anders Berch's *Theatrum Œconomicum* at Uppsala University. Convinced that useful natural knowledge could not be taught by words alone, or even by illustrations, Sweden's first professor of political economy spent years assembling a large collection of materials, commodities, and mechanical devices, both domestic and foreign, to be used in his teaching. The collection included thousands of samples of different woods, textiles, metals, stones, leather, potteries, and papers, as well as models of plows, seeders, and other mechanical devices.[5] He tried to acquire samples from every stage of the production process of popular commodities, so that he could describe the transformation of nature in as much detail as possible. By staging critical moments in the life cycle of a commodity, Berch invited his students to become spectators in a performance of knowledge. By *seeing* the transformation of nature *performed* in front of their eyes, students came to understand the principles and properties of nature and realize both the potential and the limitations of existing knowledge. Similar to how anatomical theaters across Europe were used to transmit knowledge about the human body (Olof Rudbeck had established such a theater in Uppsala in 1663), Berch's *Theatrum Œconomicum* was designed to dramatize knowledge about the component parts of wealth—the commodity. While Berch's epistemological spectacle may not have been as sensational as the dissection of human cadavers, the pedagogical rationale was in many ways the same: to teach the audience about the inner structure of complex bodies through public demonstration.

While historians of science have for some time studied the spatiality of knowledge production and consumption, in particular laboratories, museums, and "the field," historians of political economy have paid less attention to the spaces and pedagogies of dissemination.[6] This paper explores not only what constituted oeconomic knowledge in early modern Sweden, but also how and where this knowledge was taught. I show how Berch, both through his writings and his *Theatrum Œconomicum,* publicized, promoted, and performed knowledge integral to the flourishing of agriculture, mining, manufacturing, and trade—the most integral ingredients, he argued, of Sweden's improvement.

The Swedish Improvement Discourse

Sweden emerged from the Thirty Years' War as a militarily powerful nation. Political, economic, and intellectual elites realized that Sweden quickly had to develop its economic base in order to support the nation's newfound geopolitical prominence. Queen Christina and Lord High Chancellor Axel Oxenstierna invited foreign scientists and philosophers to Stockholm to invigorate the intellectual climate and to redesign the nation's educational curriculum. To the dismay of the Lutheran clergy, Sweden hosted both Catholics and radical Protestants, as well as

Paracelsian and Rosicrucian mysticists.[7] Efforts to turn Stockholm into an *Athens of the North* led the city to play host to a vibrant discussion of improvement ideas, with conversations ranging across the confessional and philosophical spectrum. Soon an indigenous vision for the nation's improvement emerged. Drawing heavily on foreign intellectual authorities—including Jan Comenius, Samuel Hartlib, Johann Becher, and René Descartes—and Olof Rudbeck, Johannes Bureus, and George Stiernhielm's version of *Gothicism*, Swedish reformers combined natural knowledge, spirituality, and political economy to develop a strategy for improvement uniquely designed to fit the nation's circumstances and challenges.[8] While each of the most prominent Swedish reform writers, including Johan Risingh (1617–1672), Urban Hiärne (1641–1724), Christopher Polhem (1661–1751), and Carl Linnaeus (1707–1778), contributed their own specific insights, they shared a conviction that knowledge about nature was key to the enrichment and improvement of the nation and its people.[9]

As Sweden transitioned from the *Age of Greatness* (1632–1718) to the *Age of Liberty* (1719–1772)—a shift characterized by a change in political culture and the loss of its Baltic empire—the emphasis on natural knowledge remained strong, as reflected by the formation of the *Royal Academy of Science* [Kungliga Vetenskapsakademien] and the creation of Sweden's first university professorship in political economy, or, more precisely, in *jurisprudentiæ, œconomiæ, et commerciorum,* at Uppsala University. Both the Royal Academy and the aforementioned first professor of political economy, Anders Berch (1711–1774), were dedicated to the advancement of natural knowledge in the service of material improvement. Less interested in engaging in abstract philosophical reasoning at the center of the natural law and civic humanist traditions, the pedagogical mission of the Swedish reformers was to deepen students' understanding of nature—in particular, the ways whereby nature could be transformed into useful commodities. The institutionalization of the union between scientific and material progress continued apace during the middle decades of the eighteenth century, producing both a steady stream of scientific breakthroughs and generations of students with economically applicable expertise of nature.[10]

Anders Berch

Anders Berch was born in 1711 in the Swedish province of Dalarna.[11] Berch moved to Uppsala in his teens, where he studied experimental physics with Daniel Menlös (1699–1743) and mathematics with Samuel Klingenstierna (1698–1765). He completed his dissertation, titled *The Nation's Happiness Promoted through Economic Prosperity* (1731) [*De Felicitate Patriae Per Oeconomiam Promovenda*], under the

direction of the famous scientist Anders Celsius (1701–1744). Through his mentors and his brother Carl Reinhold, Berch was introduced to *Bokwetts Gillet*, a leading learned society at Uppsala dedicated to the advancement of useful scientific knowledge. The society was a continuation of *Collegium Curiosorum*, formed by Eric Benzelius, Jr., (1675–1743) and Christopher Polhem in 1710. Polhem had also contributed to the post-Rudbeck intellectual culture of Uppsala by forming, with the help of Emmanuel Swedenborg (1688–1772), Sweden's first scientific publication, *Daedalus Hyperboreus,* in 1715. In addition to operating in the same circles as Polhem and Swedenborg, Berch most likely would have crossed paths with Linnaeus, born in the same year, during their student days at Uppsala. The familial ties between their respective mentors—Anders Celsius, Berch's mentor, was the nephew of the Uppsala botanist Olof Celsius, who taught Linnaeus—made such an encounter all but inevitable.

Uppsala's intellectual life was particularly vibrant during the first few decades of the eighteenth century, in part because of *Bokwetts Gillet.* Like many of its foreign counterparts, the society was interested in the promotion of ideas that might illuminate nature and reveal its uses to humanity. Early on, the society began advocating for the establishment of a professorship in *œconomie* at Uppsala, an idea that the young Berch had called for in his dissertation.[12] While Berch was busy working, first for the *Board of Trade* and later for the *Parliamentary Council for Trade and Manufacturing*, the newly ascendant political party, *The Hats*, succeeded in convincing Parliament to create such a professorship. In 1741, the chair was offered to Berch.[13] He became the first professor of *œconomie* in Sweden and the fourth in Europe, after Simon Peter Gasser in Halle, Justus Christoph Dithmar in Frankfurt an der Oder, and Johann Furstenau Hermann in Rinteln.[14]

As part of the parliamentary debates regarding the creation of a professorship in *œconomie*, an anonymous tract was published that listed the ideal qualities that such a professor must possess. As Berch's later writings would reveal, he was very much in agreement with the anonymous author, so much so that it is plausible to suspect that Berch may have had a hand in its drafting. The ideal professor had to be competent in mathematics, physics, mechanics, hydraulics, and natural history.

Moreover, he must be an expert in agriculture and mineralogy, as well as possess a deep knowledge of manufacturing. Lastly, the professor must be well-versed in all matters pertaining to trade, including navigation, shipbuilding, trade regulations, and customs. The professor must lecture in Swedish and organize his teaching around practical demonstrations. He should have access to a plot of land on which to demonstrate the most recent techniques and should be provided with the latest tools and equipment used in manufacturing. Students should be exposed to actual devices or miniature reproductions of the tools and equipment used in agriculture, mining, and manufacturing, as well as samples of all kinds of raw materials and commodities.[15] The Parliamentary Council Berch had previously served on issued a statement as to what the students should take away from their educational experience. Most fundamentally, they should be provided with knowledge conducive to the "improvement of the nation's commodities, enhancement of the soil, cultivation of the useful arts, and refinement of both oeconomie and manufacturing."[16] In short, the professorship was designed to help spread the Swedish improvement discourse throughout the nation.

Berch was the ideal candidate for the position. He would not only become one of the most influential synthesizers of the Swedish improvement discourse, but he was also a product of it. His writings and pedagogical project were firmly grounded in the already well-established Swedish discourse. The catalog of his 508-volume library reveals a deep familiarity with the Swedish tradition, containing works by Johan Risingh, Anders Nordencrantz, A.G. Duhre, Carl Linnaeus, Lars Salvius, Pehr Chisternin, Pehr Kalm, and Erik Salander, among many others.[17] Berch was also inspired by German writers, having read the works of Christian Wolff, Johann Becher, J.R. von Rohr, Justus Dithmar, and Gottfried Leibnitz.[18] But this was not his only foreign influence. He was also familiar with both the English and the French traditions; his library contained books by many English authors, including Thomas Mun, Charles Davenant, William Petty, Josiah Child, William Wood, and John Houghton, as well as some by French writers, including Jean-François Melon and Nicholas Dutot. Yet, while Berch was never afraid of incorporating ideas from foreign authors, his most important intellectual debts were to the Swedish improvement writers that came before him.

Introduction to General Householding

Berch published his immensely popular textbook, *Introduction to General Householding: Including the Foundations for Politie, Œconomie, and the Cameral Sciences,* in 1747. It remained the principal textbook at Uppsala for nearly a century. The book was also widely read and admired in Germany, where the Cameralist professor Daniel Gottfriend Schreber had published a translation.[19] The stated aim of Berch's book was to promote the greatest possible happiness among the nation's inhabitants. He articulated a simple yet powerful analytical framework, explaining the relationship between scientific knowledge and material prosperity, between civil society and politics, and between the four main sources of economic prosperity: agriculture, mining, manufacturing, and trade. Improvement, for Berch, was based on the development of knowledge that enabled humanity to take advantage of nature's abundance. People should be taught how to "acquire, maintain, and multiply" any knowledge that might promote success in agriculture, mining, manufacturing, and trade.[20] Berch explored these issues under the rubric of *Œconomie.* While material abundance was absolutely essential to the well-being of humanity, it was not the only component of happiness. For Berch, it was necessary for people to be raised appropriately, enjoy a sensible lifestyle, and uphold the social order at all times. Only then was it possible for them to enjoy a sound heart and mind, a healthy and secure body, and a sense of material comfort and ease.[21] Once a nation's inhabitants achieved a sufficiently healthy and comfortable life, they became even more productive, suggesting a favorable dynamic between health, wealth, and happiness. Berch explored these concerns under the rubric of *Politie.* In the third and shortest part of the book, Berch examines how the state could raise enough money to meet its obligations and responsibilities. He argued that a properly developed *Cameral Science* was essential to the state's capacity to provide defense, infrastructure, and education, without which all of the previous lessons would be irrelevant. A well-organized polity, combined with a sophisticated command of the Cameral Sciences, was therefore essential to the prosperity of the nation. Yet, it was the vibrancy of the *œconomie* that constituted the primary engine of progress and improvement.

The centerpiece of Berch's book was the discussion of *œconomie.* Whether *œconomie* was considered an "art, wisdom, science, education, or something else," its main purpose was to enhance the population's general welfare and riches, as well as the nation's "sustainable power, reputation, and wealth."[22] The most fundamental key to prosperity was that all people strove to put their property to use in a manner that generated the greatest possible benefit and gain.[23] To be considered beneficial, the multiplication of property had to have an impact not just on the individual, but on the community at large—a condition that was met by agriculture, mining, manufacturing, and trade.[24] These four components of wealth mutually reinforced each other. Berch explained,

> Agriculture and Mining provide the foundation to all other sources of wealth: Manufacturing is entirely based on them and Trade requires the aid of all three: Agriculture and Mining without Manufacturing and Trade are ineffectual: Manufacturing without Trade never expands the nation's wealth: Trade without Manufacturing is always damaging or at least leads to a loss of revenues.[25]

Berch concluded that every part of "this chain" was indispensable and contributes to "the same end and sets the other parts in proper motion."[26] Indeed, to Berch, the idea of prioritizing one productive activity over the others was absurd. He noted, "all bickering over whether one source of wealth is more important than the other is merely a war of words."[27] The key was to ensure that there was a dynamic and vibrant interplay between them, which was best promoted by allowing a growing population to freely engage in whatever economic pursuit they wanted and by ensuring that they had proper access to all useful knowledge.[28]

While some of the writers who laid the foundation for the Swedish improvement discourse had a tendency to emphasize specific scientific pursuits—among them Hiärne (chemistry), Polhem (mechanics), and Linnaeus (botany)—Berch insisted that all forms of knowledge with the potential to contribute to the improvement process should be promoted. Similar to his unwillingness to single out one specific sector of wealth creation as more important than the others, he insisted that all useful knowledge was valuable and that the more people knew about one part of nature the more they would understand about the rest. He noted, "[i]n as much as all sciences have human happiness as their ultimate end, they also have their mutual serviceability to each other in common." Indeed, he added, "every branch of science is more or less dependent on the assistance of the others."[29]

In the realm of natural knowledge, the broadest and most immediately useful epistemic sphere was *natural history*.[30] By advancing knowledge about objects in nature and by exploring their usefulness to humanity, this branch was absolutely crucial. Natural history mainly focused on nature's external, visible characteristics. As long as all useful properties could be ascertained by such an examination, there was no need to go beyond natural history. However, nature often hides, its essence and keeps its usefulness to humanity a secret. To discover nature's innermost qualities, people therefore had to turn to *chemistry* for further assistance.[31] Chemistry offered insights into nature's hidden realms, revealing the composition and inner structure of matter. To find out how nature's powers could be harnessed, it was necessary to engage in *physics*.[32] "Nature will not be forced," Berch argued, "so anyone who wants to use nature, must adjust to her, follow in her tracks, and figure out how she gives birth to everything around her."[33] Physics provided guidance as to what specific elements can achieve, either on their own or when combined with others, and what happens to bodies in nature when elements are altered. Physics had many different subfields, including *mechanics, statics, pneumatics,* and *hydraulics*, each of which provided practical guidance in multiple spheres.[34] Moreover, all of the wealth-generating sectors employed *mathematics* on a daily basis, from merchants using accounting techniques to manage their operations to manufacturers using geometry in the design of mechanical devices.[35]

Berch described in detail how the aforementioned fields of knowledge were employed in agriculture, mining, manufacturing, and trade. It was impossible to turn nature into useful raw materials and edible foods without a profound understanding of how nature works. Chemistry and physics were thus absolutely central to agriculture. He also noted that it was useful to agriculture to grasp the behavior of water particles in the atmosphere. The ability to understand and predict cloud formations and precipitation through the science of *meteorology* was therefore of great benefit. No longer based on prophecies and folklore, the analysis of weather patterns was now considered a scientific pursuit. In addition to knowing more about the weather, advanced agricultural practices also required a deep understanding of the overall climate. In particular, to engage in botanical transmutations of the kind that Linnaeus advocated, it was necessary to know how plants reacted to different climates and especially how plants could be seasoned to grow in unfamiliar environments.[36] Moreover, agriculture required farmers to have a basic command of mechanics, without which they would not be able to utilize complex technologies such as mills, plows, and seeding machines.

Mining also required a great deal of scientific expertise. To successfully extract silver, iron, copper, and other metals and minerals from deep underneath the earth's surface, a number of intricate technological solutions were required. Engineers had to be able to construct and maintain complex drilling devices, hoisting mechanisms, and pumping systems. Berch noted that such technological accomplishments relied on a deep understanding of *subterranean architecture*, mechanics, pneumatics, and hydraulics.[37] Once miners brought ore to the surface, expertise in physics, chemistry, and metallurgy was necessary to properly separate and purify the metals and minerals.[38] Next, the metals had to be properly assayed and refined through various involved procedures.[39]

The next step in the nation's enrichment process was to turn raw materials derived from agriculture and mining into useful commodities. This process could be small-scale, as in handicraft operations, or large-scale, as in manufacturing, but it was clear to Berch that both cases demanded a firm grasp of the raw materials and an expertise in the use of tools, equipment, and machines. The greater the producers' command of physics and mechanics, the more successful they would be in producing commodities of high quality that could be sold at competitive prices. Although the advancement of mechanical devices and machines was still in its relative infancy, Berch nevertheless recognized their vast potential. With the aid of mechanical knowledge, producers would be able to harness nature's hidden powers and expand production to levels previously unimaginable. Indeed, the development and implementation of new mechanical devices were so important that they had to be protected by patents, providing innovators with guaranteed rewards. Although patents limited people's economic liberty, Berch reasoned that this was a small price to pay to ensure that the knowledge-based economy remained vibrant.

The final source of riches—trade—was not directly dependent on scientific advancement to the same extent as the other sources. The role of trade was not to transform nature, but rather to "unite, enliven, and set the other three in motion."[40] In addition to providing momentum to agriculture, mining, and manufacturing and thus promoting material abundance, Berch insisted that trade was a catalyst for the promotion of "society's ease and comfort, the advancement of sciences, enhanced friendliness between nations, the discovery of secret conspiracies between nations, and yes, even refinement of religion and the improvement of morality."[41] Yet, there were certain scientific pursuits that were immediately beneficial to trade. In addition to meteorology providing indispensable information to pilots and captains navigating oceangoing vessels, *astronomy* and *geography* were also useful for navigational purposes, and hydraulics and mechanics were essential to the construction and operation of ships—early modern Europe's most complex and expensive technological machinery.

While Berch focused primarily on the promotion of the practical sciences, he never disregarded the importance of theory. He wanted to see a productive balance between the two. He acknowledged, "*praxis Oeconomia* gathers considerable assistance from *Theory*." He continued, "it is impossible to improve any art or technique if the causes of the phenomena cannot be explained."[42] However, given that the benefits of œconomie are ultimately realized in its practical adaptation, œconomie must first and foremost be considered a practical science. People pursuing advancements in the fields of "physics, mathematics, or any other spheres of ingenuity," should, therefore, pay careful attention to the potential practical applications of their innovations.[43] He also pointed out that because of humanity's intrinsic intellectual shortcomings and the brevity of human life, it was impossible for any one person to command all, or even the majority of, available knowledge. It was, therefore, necessary for the knowledge creation process to be a collaborative and public enterprise.

In as much as savants should strive to make advances in both theory and practice, the educational curriculum should reflect this duality. Educational facilities should not be allowed to remain exclusively concerned with speculative, abstract, or purely theoretical knowledge. Instead, students should depart from school equipped with knowledge useful to the challenges and obstacles they were likely to encounter in their efforts to improve their own lot, as well as that of the nation. Students should be taught by skillful and vigorous instructors and should have access to "public *libraries, astronomical observatories, anatomical theaters, botanical gardens, Theatro Machinarum* in *Physics* as well as *Oeconomie, Architecture, Navigation,* and *Fortification,* and *Curiosa-* and *Coin-Cabinets.*"[44] By exposing students to a world of complex technologies, Berch intended to pique the interest and curiosity of the younger generation. Even people who were already engaged in handicraft or manufacturing should have access to such sites of learning and be given opportunities to acquire knowledge and skills that would enable them to make "improvements in arts and techniques."[45]

For Berch, demonstration was a powerful pedagogical tool. He suggested that if each educational institution were equipped with an *Apparatus Œconomieo Mechanicus,* in which all useful "tools and machines" were collected and displayed, political economic knowledge would be disseminated and take root much more effectively.[46] Because most students had not come in contact with advanced technologies before, it was difficult for teachers to adequately describe them with words, or even with illustrations. Explaining the dynamic parts of machines proved particularly challenging. It would, therefore, be of great benefit to the students to be able to observe these devices firsthand. Berch believed that students exposed to advanced technologies would be inspired to learn more about the underlying mechanisms and thus turn their attention away from traditional academic subjects. If such a shift were to happen, he proclaimed in an understated manner, "little damage would be done."[47] It should be noted that Berch certainly did not dismiss the importance of book learning. There were some people who were better equipped for book learning and others who were more inclined toward mechanical knowledge. "Both are necessary," he argued, and society must, therefore, provide adequate instruction in both academic and practical fields. However, in reading Berch, one clearly senses that he thought more people ought to be encouraged to pursue the technical and mechanical arts.[48]

Theatrum Œconomicum

As soon as Berch accepted the professorship at Uppsala University, he started building a collection of essential materials and technological devices and began to search for a space in which they could be housed and displayed. He was not the first member of the university to embark on such a project. Olof Rudbeck had assembled an impressive collection of natural history specimens, all of which were lost in the devastating Uppsala fire of 1702. Christopher Polhem also recognized the value of teaching mechanical knowledge through demonstration and included plans for a permanent exhibition of mechanical devices in his Laboratorium Mechanicum in Stockholm.[49] Berch's collection, however, was far more extensive than these earlier efforts. He succeeded in convincing the university to provide him with considerable resources for the purpose of building up his collection. He also relied on donations, of money as well as exhibition items, from individuals, in particular merchants and industrialists, throughout Sweden. After some time, he was also successful in his quest to find a place to house the collection. In 1754, the university provided him with a sizeable stone building, located at *The Old Square* (*Gamla Torget*)—see Picture 2.

On the ground floor, the building housed the collection and a lecture hall. Berch kept an office and his living quarters on the second floor, next to a few rooms that he rented in order to pay for the upkeep of the building and the expansion of his collection. His *Theatrum Œconomicum* soon became a much-talked-about sensation. In addition to attracting more students to his lectures, it became an attraction that visitors to Uppsala did not want to miss.[50] When the royal family came to Uppsala in 1759, they visited Linnaeus's botanical garden and Berch's *Theatrum Œconomicum.*[51] While the relationship between the two Uppsala professors was often contentious, after Berch retired from his professorship, Linnaeus praised his pedagogical achievements. He insisted on the importance of finding a worthy successor who would remain dedicated to Berch's project, established with "so much toil and labour." To allow Berch's collection to "fall into decay and altogether disappear," Linnaeus wrote, would be a massive "loss to this University."[52]

Berch's collection contained an impressive number of items.[53] In the spirit of Linnaean classification, Berch conscientiously labeled every item and recorded its most essential characteristic. The collection included a number of "models for agriculture," such as plows, seeding machines, and threshing machines.[54] These miniature models were carefully reproduced copies of the originals, including all parts and functions. Most were models of Swedish agricultural machines, but there were also examples of foreign technologies, such as the Swiss seeding machine depicted in Picture 3. In addition to agricultural machines, the collection also included "Models for Manufactures." Although none of these models have survived, the inventory suggests that there were nineteen such models, mostly weaving looms. The majority of the collection, however, was listed under the rubric "Manufacturing and Commercial Cabinet." It contained more than 1600 textile samples, some 350 paper samples, hundreds of wood samples, approximately 150 samples of different types of stones, numerous samples of fur and leather, as well as playing cards, pins and needles, various dyes, pottery and faience, and various types of tea. There was also a small number of scissors, anchors, mirrors, and eyeglasses.[55]

© Jenny Svennås-Gillner, SLU

Berch wanted to be able to show his students materials from all the different phases of the production process. He, therefore, included raw materials in different stages of preparation and completion, as well as samples of finished goods. His collection of textiles was particularly impressive, containing different types of fabrics, cloths, and weaves.

Of the many kinds of yarn included, wool was particularly well represented. Reflecting contemporary efforts to experiment with the quality of Swedish wool, Berch's collection included wool from indigenous Swedish sheep and from imported sheep and goats, as well as wool from crossbred sheep. In addition to different samples of yarn, the collection contained a dizzying array of differently colored silk, cotton, wool, hemp, and linen in different weaving structures, including tabby, warp rep structures, rose path, twill, five-end warp satin, damask, lampas, gauze, velvet, and droguets.[56] Samples came from all over the world, including England, France, Holland, and Denmark, as well as from China, most likely brought to Sweden by the Swedish East India Company. A selection of raw materials, half-finished cloth, and woven samples is depicted in Picture 4.

Collecting valuable objects, raw materials, and commodities was far from a new phenomenon. Princes and wealthy noblemen famously collected objects and artifacts from around the world in Curiosa

Cabinets or Kunstkammers.[57] These collections symbolized the collectors' worldly and imperial power. For example, Swedish aristocrat Carl Gustav Wrangel's collection, housed in his castle Skokloster on Lake Mälaren, contained artifacts from all over the world, including taxidermic animals from Africa, tomahawks from America, and a sealskin kayak from Greenland.[58] The more sensational, rare, exotic, fascinating, and awe-inspiring the objects, the more splendor was conferred on the collector. Berch's collection, on the other hand, was not designed to marvel or awe the audience. Instead, it was designed to highlight the mundane, to demystify the creation of useful everyday commodities. Although the collection contained raw materials and commodities from abroad, Berch focused on domestic resources and commodities that were produced, or could be produced, in Sweden. If the Curiosa Cabinet showcased the owner's imperial command, *Theatrum Œconomicum* highlighted humanity's Promethean power to turn nature into something useful.

In addition to its status as a collection, *Theatrum Œconomicum* was also a space for teaching students how to use knowledge to transform nature. As noted above, Berch insisted in his writings that knowledge was best transmitted via demonstration. He inscribed the following words from Horace above his collection:

> Less vividly is the mind stirred by what finds entrance through the ears than by what is brought before the trusty eyes, and what the spectator can see for himself.[59]

While empiricism and experimentalism were already well established as the preferred methods for investigating nature and society, Berch sought to incorporate his students into a spectacle of learning.[60] He hoped to familiarize his students with different ways to transform nature into useful objects. Put differently, he wanted to show his students that they too had the power to shape nature and harness its power for personal, societal, and national benefit. Whether the students were bound for lives managing farms, mines, or mechanical workshops, or whether they were destined to serve on the Board of Trade or Board of Mines, their experiences at *Theatrum Œconomicum* were designed to provide them with a deep understanding of how nature could be turned into economic wealth.

The pedagogy of the *Theatrum Œconomicum* shared certain commonalities with the epistemological spectacles that took place a stone's throw away in Rudbeck's anatomical theater and in the forests surrounding Uppsala, where Linnaeus conducted his famous *Herbationes Upsalienses* every spring.[61] Anatomical theaters had become popular in Europe as a pedagogical tool ever since its first introduction in Padua and Leiden. These theaters, with their steep tiers, enabled spectators to get a close look of the dissection of human or animal cadavers. The audience was treated to performances in which the physician put his knowledge on display, accompanied by his ongoing commentary. There was a clear purpose to the performance, and it followed a carefully designed script. Each performance had a lesson plan, with a certain set of learning goals. Students were shown a specific feature of the human body and were told how it contributed to the overall functioning of the human body. The audience, as long as it did not succumb to lightheadedness from the odors and gruesome sights, departed the theater with a better understanding.

Similarly, *Theatrum Œconomicum* incorporated the audience in a performance of useful knowledge. Instead of dissected corpses playing the protagonist, the commodities at the center of the economic improvement process constituted the main dramatic plot. Berch staged performances emphasizing the interaction between knowledge and matter, dramatizing the genealogy of commodities. Although the students were not treated to an actual, real time, transformation of nature, Berch used samples from different moments of the production process to show how knowledge was employed at critical junctures. Berch hoped that the experience in his *Theatrum Œconomicum* would inspire and empower his students to embark on their own quest for profitable knowledge and instill in them a sense of the importance and productive potential of new ideas.

Berch also used a metascript to show his students how natural knowledge served as the foundation for economic prosperity and the improvement of the nation more broadly. Berch's commentary on how the commodity fits into the broader project of enriching the body politic echoed the dissecting physician's explanation of how the specific function under examination contributed to the overall health of the human body. In the same way that Rudbeck's anatomical theater was designed not only to promote anatomical knowledge, but also to facilitate the broader aim of health, happiness, and moral refinement, the ambition of Berch's *Theatrum Œconomicum* was to accelerate the enrichment, improvement, and advancement of the nation.[62]

The manner in which Berch instructed students in his *Theatrum Œconomicum* also shared some pedagogical features with Linnaeus's excursions into nature. In addition to his *Herbationes Upsalienses,* the immensely popular public excursions in the forests surrounding Uppsala, Linnaeus brought multiple students along on his many research trips around Sweden. Numbering in the hundreds, these students contributed to Linnaeus's research projects at the same time that they were learning about the flora, as well as local politics, culture, and economy. Linnaeus was always careful to explain the economic rationale behind his botanical projects. In the same way that Berch explained the life cycle of the commodity in the context of Sweden's enrichment, Linnaeus explained nature in terms of the nation's economic affluence and autarky.[63]

By seeing nature in its full complexity, Linneaus's students were able to witness specimens in their natural environment, see plants and flowers at different growth stages, and examine and dissect that which they found of interest. In many ways, these scientific "wanderings" were ideal pedagogical moments. Yet the method had its limitations, in that students could only learn about the plants and flowers with which they came in contact. Clearly, fully trained botanists must also know about plants and flowers that they had not personally encountered. For that purpose, students were encouraged to study illustrations, such as Linnaeus's *Flora Svecica,* natural history collections, and botanical gardens.[64]

Berch could have conducted his pedagogical project in the same spirit as Linnaeus's excursions by bringing his students along on journeys across Sweden, Europe, and the world to witness the sites where commodities were produced. Since this was not a feasible endeavor, he sought to create a teaching environment that enabled him to demonstrate as realistically as possible the process whereby commodities came into being. By bringing the production process to the students, he engaged them in a learning process based on their own observations. While the staging was not entirely realistic, the teaching method was nevertheless superior to pedagogies based solely on books, words, and illustrations. Berch had succeeded in creating a teaching space that embraced demonstration and active learning, and one that was open to any interested student. As such, Berch shaped a particular kind of political economic knowledge that was public, practical, profitable, and performative.

Conclusion

After Berch stepped down from his post in 1770, four years prior to his death, his chair at Uppsala was offered to Pehr Christiernin (1725–1799). The following year when Christiernin moved on to the more prestigious and well-remunerated chair in philosophy, Berch's son Christer was offered the chair. Christer Berch, as well as his successor Gustav Flygare, continued to use Anders Berch's textbook, lecture notes, and *Theatrum Œconomicum,* ensuring that Berch's pedagogical program survived for nearly eight decades.[65] Professor Johan Låstbom (1732–1802) also continued to promote and teach a mix of practical scientific and economic knowledge, with an even greater emphasis on the students' practical facility with different tools and materials. However, by the turn of the nineteenth century, it was clear that the Swedish improvement discourse, with its deep roots in the seventeenth century, was coming to an end, in particular within the universities. Disentangled from science and spirituality, the nature of the political economic discourse changed. Starting in the 1760s, there was a drastic increase in the number of "purely" economic publications, or in what

Eli Heckscher deemed "proper" economic theory.[66] Heckscher scorned Berch for his inability to delineate between nature and the economy and for his lack of theoretical sophistication. He called Berch a run of the mill advocate of "conservative mercantilism," with nothing particularly novel to add. "As a theoretician," Heckscher added, Berch "was unusually weak, far weaker than many of his contemporaries and particularly inferior to his immediate successor, P. N. Christernin."[67] Of course, as this essay has suggested, it was never Berch's intention to theorize "the economy" or anything purely economic. He had no interest in separating the economic from the scientific, or the economic from the natural. Indeed, for him, knowledge about nature was absolutely essential to any project designed to generate material abundance.

Notes

1. Recent scholarship on the relationship between improvement discourses and economic growth in early modern Europe include Joel Mokyr, *The Enlightened Economy: An Economic History of Britain, 1700–1850* (New Haven: Yale University Press, 2012); Paul Slack, *The Invention of Improvement: Information and Material Progress in Seventeenth-Century England* (Oxford: Oxford University Press, 2015); and Steve Pincus, *1688: The First Modern Revolution* (New Haven: Yale University Press, 2009).
2. See, for example, John Robertson, *The Case for the Enlightenment: Scotland and Naples, 1680–1760* (Cambridge: Cambridge University Press, 2005); Sophus A. Reinert, *Translating Empire: Emulation and the Origins of Political Economy* (Cambridge: Harvard University Press, 2011).
3. Eli Heckscher, "Anders Berch och den ekonomiska vetenskapens första steg i Sverige," *Lychnos* (1942): 33–62; Sven Lindroth, *Svensk Lärdomshistoria: Frihetstiden* (Stockholm: Norstedts, 1978); Sven-Eric Liedman, "Utilitarianism and the Economy," in *Science in Sweden: The Royal Swedish Academy of Sciences, 1739–1989*, ed. Tore Frängsmyr (Canton, MA: Science History Publications, 1989); and Lars Magnusson, "Mercantilism and 'reform' Mercantilism: The Rise

of Economic Discourse in Sweden during the Eighteenth Century," *History of Political Economy* 19, no. 3 (1987): 415–33.

4. Johan Nordström, *De Yverbornes Ö* (Stockholm: Bonnier, 1934); Gunnar Eriksson, *The Atlantic Vision: Olaus Rudbeck and Baroque Science* (Canton, MA: Watson, 1994); Tore Frängsmyr, *Svensk Idehistoria: Bildning och vetenskap under tusen år, Del 1: 1000–1809* (Stockholm: Natur och Kultur, 2000); and Sten Lindroth, *Svensk Lärdomshistoria: Stormaktstiden* (Stockholm: Nordstedts, 1975). For a discussion of the connections between members of the Hartlib Circle and the Swedish improvement writers, see Carl Wennerlind, "The Political Economy of Sweden's *Age of Greatness*: Johan Risingh and the Hartlib Circle," in *Economic Growth and the Origins of Modern Political Economy: Economic Reasons of State, 1500–2000*, ed. Philipp Rössner (New York: Routledge, 2016).
5. The agricultural models are currently kept at the Swedish University of Agricultural Sciences. Ragnar Jirlow explores the history and content of this collection in *Plogmodeller Från 1700-talet vid Lantbrukshögskolan* (Uppsala: Jordbrukstekniska Institutet, 1948). The bulk of Berch's collection of materials and commodities is kept at Nordiska Museet. Elisabet Stavenow-Hidemark has examined and reproduced images of the textile collection in *1700-Tals Textil: Anders Berchs Samling i Nordiska Museet/18th Century Textiles: The Anders Berch Collection at the Nordic Museum* (Stockholm: Nordiska Museets Förlag, 1990).
6. For a discussion of recent studies of how historians of science have studied the spatial dimensions of the production and consumption of scientific knowledge, see Hanna Hodacs, "Linnaeans Outdoors: The Transformative Role of Studying Nature 'on the move' and Outside," *British Journal for the History of Science* 22, no. 2 (2010): 183–209.
7. See, for example, Svante Nordin, *Drottningen och Filosofen: Mötet mellan Christina och Descartes* (Stockholm: Atlantis, 2012); Sven Göransson, "Comenius och Sverige, 1642–1648," *Lychnos* (1957–1958): 102–37; Sven Widmalm, "Instituting Science in Sweden," in *The Scientific Revolution in National Context*, ed. Roy Porter and Mikuláš Teich (Cambridge: Cambridge University Press, 1992); Sten Lindroth, *Paracelsismen i Sverige, till 1660-talets mitt* (Stockholm: Almqvist & Wiksell, 1943); and Susanna Åkerman, *Rose Cross Over the Baltic: The Spread of Rosicrucianism in Northern Europe* (Leiden: Brill, 1998).

8. The Swedish ideology of Gothism (Göticism) was based on the notion that Sweden played an exceptional role in God's plan for humanity. Tore Frängsmyr has detailed the interplay between economic improvement, religiosity, and Gothism in the eighteenth century in his article "Den Gudomlige Ekonomin: Religion och Hushållning i 1700-talets Sverige," *Lychnos* (1971–1972): 217–44. See also Håkan Håkansson, *Vid Tidens Ände: Om stormaktstidens vidunderliga drömvärld och en profet vid dess yttersta rand* (Göteborg: Madadem, 2014).
9. For an overview of their ideas, see Stellan Dahlgren and Hans Norman, *The Rise and Fall of New Sweden: Governor Johan Risingh's Journal 1654–1655 in Its Historical Context* (Stockholm: Almqvist & Wiksell, 1988); Hjalmar Fors, *The Limits of Matter: Chemistry, Mining, and the Enlightenment* (Chicago: University of Chicago Press, 2015); and Lisbet Koerner, *Linnaeus: Nature and Nation* (Cambridge: Harvard University Press, 2001).
10. As the Swedish discourse shifted its emphasis away from practical usefulness towards the end of the eighteenth century, natural history fell out of favor and the Swedish improvement discourse lost its coherence and sense of purpose. Karin Johannisson, "Naturvetenskapen på reträtt: En discussion om naturvetenskapens status under svenskt 1700-tal," *Lychnos* (1979–1980): 109–54. See also Widmalm, "Instituting Science in Sweden."
11. For biographical information, see Karl Petander, *Svenskt Biografiskt Lexikon, Tredje Bandet* (Stockholm: Albert Bonniers Förlag, 1922). This essay relies heavily on background information about Berch's life and times presented in Sven-Eric Liedman, *Den Synlige Handen: Anders Berch och ekonomiämnena vid 1700-talets svenska universitet* (Stockholm: Arbetarkultur, 1986).
12. Liedman, *Den Synlige Handen*, 59.
13. Ibid., 59–69.
14. Ibid., 43.
15. Ibid., 66.
16. Quoted in Liedman, *Den Synlige Handen*, 70.
17. The Nordic Museum archive contains a catalogue of Anders Berch's library, titled *Catalog över Berchiska Boksamlingen*. I would like to thank the archivist, Christel Kraft, for generously providing me with a copy.
18. Heckscher, "Anders Berch och den ekonomiska vetenskapens första steg i Sverige," 35.

19. Anders Berch, *Einleitung zur allgemeinen Haushaltung: in sich fassend die Grundsätze der Policey- Oeconomie- und Cameralwissenschaften* (Halle: Johann Jacob Curts, 1763).
20. Anders Berch, *Inledning til almänna hushålningen, innefattande grunden til politie, oeconomie och cameral wetenskaperne* (Stockholm: n.p., 1747), 4–5.
21. Ibid., *Preface.*
22. Ibid., 3, 7.
23. Ibid., 8.
24. Ibid., 10.
25. Ibid., 10–11.
26. Ibid., 11.
27. Ibid. Berch's way of framing the interconnectivity between different spheres shared certain similarities to that of Christopher Polhem, who posited that "a kingdom without *oeconomy, commerce,* and *manufacturing* is like a person without body, feet, and hands; and, these without *mechanics, physics,* and *mathematics* are like a person without life, memory, and understanding." *Twenne betänkande/Det förra angående Oeconomien och Commercen uti Sverige* (Stockholm: n.p., 1721). Emphasis added. There is disagreement in the existing literature on what Berch valued the most. Eli Heckscher and Lars Magnusson suggest that Berch prioritized manufacturing, Sven-Eric Liedman opines that Berch viewed trade as the ultimate goal, and Leif Runefelt argues that Berch primarily advocated agriculture. The above quote seems to suggest that he made it a point to emphasize that all sectors were equally necessary.
28. Ibid., 48. Although Lars Magnusson correctly points out that Berch thought it was a good idea for the government to design the university curriculum with the needs of the nation in mind, adjusting the number of students to the available employments (*Tal om den proportion som de studerande ärfordra till de ledige beställningar i riket* (Uppsala: L. Salvius, 1749)), it should be noted that Berch, in general, was opposed to *Dirigisme.* People should not be told what profession to pursue (48), nor what they should, or should not, consume (100). Magnusson, "Mercantilism and 'reform' Mercantilism," 428.
29. Berch, *Inledning til almänna hushålningen*, 15.
30. Ibid.
31. Berch, *Inledning til almänna hushålningen*, 16.
32. Ibid.

33. Ibid.
34. Ibid.
35. Berch, *Inledning til almänna hushålningen*, 17.
36. Berch noted that botany teaches that "plants that belong to different climates can after some time get used to and grow in unexpected places." Ibid., 155.
37. Ibid., 207–8.
38. Ibid., 210.
39. Ibid., 211.
40. Ibid., 268.
41. Ibid., 270.
42. Ibid., 55.
43. Ibid., 20–21. Linnaeus similarly proclaimed, "No science in the world is more noble, more necessary and useful than Oeconomie, since all people's material well-being is based on it. Hence, this science should be pursued and practiced with the greatest diligence; which means, in effect, that without physics and natural science no oeconomie can survive." Linnaeus, *Doctor Linnaei Tankar om Grunden til Oeconomien genom Naturkunnogheten och Physiquen* (Stockholm: n.p., 1740), 412.
44. Ibid., 53–54.
45. Ibid., 56.
46. Ibid., 22.
47. Ibid.
48. Gösta Berg, "Anders Berch – en forskar- och lärargestalt i 1700-talets Uppsala," in *1700-Tals Textil*, ed. Elisabet Stavenow-Hidemark, 25.
49. Jirlow, *Plogmodeller*, 7. Polhem was provided with a space in the same building as Urban Hiärne's Laboratorium Chymicum in Stockholm, but his planned mechanical laboratory never materialized, as he spent most of his time in the copper mines of Falun during the early years of the 1700s. In 1756, under the guidance of Polhem's son, Gabriel, the *Board of Mines* created a permanent exhibit of Polhem's mechanical devices. It was given the name, *The Royal Model Chamber* (Kongliga Modellkammaren). David Dunér, *Tankemaskinen: Polhems huvudvärk och andra studier i tänkandets historia* (Nora: Nya Doxa, 2012), 183.
50. Liedman, *Den Synlige Handen,* 103.
51. Berg, "Anders Berch," 17–18.
52. Ibid., 18.

53. We know what was included in the collection from two inventories taken in the eighteenth century. A major part of the collection was donated to the Nordic Museum in 1876. Most of the plows and agricultural machines were donated in 1862 to what is now the *Swedish University of Agricultural Sciences.*
54. Jirlow, *Plogmodeller,* 18.
55. Berg, "Anders Berch," 21.
56. See Stavenow-Hidemark, *1700-Tals Textil.*
57. See, for example, Pamela Smith and Laura Findlen, eds., *Merchants and Marvels: Commerce, Science, and Art in Early Modern Europe* (London: Routledge, 2001).
58. Arne Losman, *Carl Gustaf Wrangel och Europa: studier i kulturförbindelser kring en 1600-talsmagnat* (Stockholm: Almqvist & Wiksell, 1980).
59. Horace quoted in Berg, "Anders Berch," 15.
60. In the sixteenth century, *Theatra Machinarum* referred to books containing drawings of various mechanical devices. Some of the most famous examples were authored by Jacques Besson, Agostino Ramelli, and Vittorio Zonca. Berch had a copy of Boecklerus's *Theatrum Movum Machinarum* (undated) and an anonymously published book titled *Theatrum Machinarum Universale* (1734). These books were part of a broader trend disseminating new technical knowledge to anyone interested in their use or advancement. *Catalog över Berchiska Boksamlingen,* Nordic Museum.
61. Hanna Hodacs describes how the participants "arrived in the early morning—as many as two or three hundred students—with horns, banners and drums. The cold May air and dew-damp ground would be offset by the excitement and anticipation of the growing crowd. Even at the last minute, there was much to do: the sharp-shooters tended their guns, someone had to be appointed to write the protocol, others to supervise the crowd—to lead the way and to marshal the stragglers—and in the center of everything was Carolus Linnaeus himself." "In the Field: Exploring Nature with Carolus Linnaeus," *Endeavour* 34, no. 2 (2009): 45.
62. Gunnar Eriksson, *Rudbeck 1630–1702: Liv, Lärdom, Dröm i Barockens Sverige* (Stockholm: Atlantis, 2002), 196.
63. Lisbet Koerner, *Linnaeus: Nation and Nature* (Cambridge: Harvard University Press, 2001).

64. For a discussion of Linnaeus's pedagogy during his excursions, see Hodacs, "Linnaeans outdoors."
65. Liedman, *Den Synlige Handen,* 100.
66. Heckscher and, more recently, Thomas von Vegesack, have documented the powerful surge in political economic publications during the 1760s. In particular, the latter shows that this trend reached its height in 1769, when 138 texts on political economy were published. For a discussion, see Lars Magnusson, *Äran, Korruptionen, och den Borgeliga Ordningen* (Stockholm: Atlantis, 2001), 20.
67. Eli Heckscher, "Anders Berch och den Ekonomiska Vetenskapen i Sverige," 59.

Author Biography

Carl Wennerlind is an Associate Professor of History at Barnard College, Columbia University. Carl is the author of *Casualties of Credit: The English Financial Revolution, 1620–1720* (Harvard, 2011) and coeditor of *David Hume's Political Economy (Routledge, 2008)* and *Mercantilism Reimagined: Political Economy in Early Modern Britain and its Empires* (Oxford, 2013).

Gulliver's Travels, Party Politics, and Empire

Steve Pincus

Jonathan Swift's *Gulliver's Travels* took the reading world by storm in the autumn of 1726. "Gulliver is in everybody's hands," Swift's friend the Tory doctor John Arbuthnot proclaimed in November of that year.[1] This was not the hyperbole of a friend. Recent scholars have estimated that readers purchased over 20,000 copies of the book by December 1726.[2] Swift's contemporaries and his more recent critics have both been drawn to Book IV in which Lemuel Gulliver visits the land of the ultra-rational horse people, the Houyhnhnms. After being forced to leave the land of the horse people and their humanoid antagonists, the yahoos, Swift's protagonist Lemuel Gulliver decides not to provide "a memorial to a Secretary of State" detailing the discoveries he made in his various travels. Such a memorial, Gulliver is well aware, might launch new colonies since "whatever lands are discovered by a subject, belong to the crown." In explaining his decision, Gulliver delivers a stinging critique of the "distributive justice" of those who promoted what he called "a modern colony."[3]

S. Pincus (✉)
Yale University, New Haven, USA
e-mail: steven.pincus@yale.edu

R. Fredona and S.A. Reinert (eds.), *New Perspectives on the History of Political Economy*, https://doi.org/10.1007/978-3-319-58247-4_5

Why did Swift choose to leave his reader with such a powerful condemnation of modern colonies? What was the relationship between Swift's 1726 imaginative pronouncements, and his political-economic writings on Ireland—including the *Drapier's Letters*—of the 1720s? What might Swift have meant by his condemnation of a "modern" as opposed to an ancient colony?

For most scholars, these questions can be easily answered. Those who have focused on Swift have highlighted his consistent and precocious anticolonial attitudes. Scholars of empire, by contrast, have emphasized Swift's intellectual innovations by insisting that the 1720s was a period devoid of debate about empire.

For most of those interested in analyzing Jonathan Swift's intellectual output, Gulliver's outburst at the end of *Gulliver's Travels* was a typical, though pointed, statement of Swift's own anticolonial sentiments.[4] Swift scholarship is not noted for interpretative consensus. Scholars have insisted on seeing Swift as a consistent Whig, a committed Tory, a closet Jacobite. Others have sought to approach his work from a new critical, a psychoanalytic, a historicist, or a postcolonial perspective. Yet most have concurred that Swift's voice was an anticolonial one. For Ian Higgins, "Gulliver's hyperbolic praise of British colonial Christianity is a devastating Swiftian sarcasm against colonialism which also unmasks the rhetoric of Whiggish ecclesiastical imperialism." This, Higgins suggests, is of a piece with "Swift's anti-colonial rhetoric in his imaginative staire and in polemic such as the *Drapier's Letters*."[5] David Nokes agrees that Swift wrote the *Drapier's Letters* "to challenge" the British "colonial system."[6] For Clement Hawes, "*Gulliver's Travels* remains, even today, an effective critique of colonialism in any form."[7] By the end of *Gulliver's Travels*, Carole Fabricant notes, the protagonist "rejects colonialism with a scathing denunciation that substitutes Britain's brutal conquest of overseas territories for its harsh oppressions in Ireland." After editing Swift's Irish writings, Fabricant concluded that Swift was "a critic of colonialism."[8] Such a view accords perfectly with the work of the proponent of the new economic criticism, Sean Moore. In Moore's view, one aspect of Swift's "anti-modernization agenda" is his "unflattering portrait of English imperial power" in *Gulliver's Travels*. For Moore, at least by implication, imperialism is the necessary concomitant of economic modernization, of a transition to capitalism.[9] These literary readings of Swift, of course, fit snugly with an earlier account of the emergence of the ideological origins of Anglo-American republicanism. Caroline Robbins in her classic study of *The Eighteenth-Century Commonwealthman* grouped Swift along with Robert Molesworth, William Molyneux, Samuel Madden, Henry Maxwell, Arthur Dobbs, and George Berkeley as Irishmen who advocated "antimercantilist ideas, and urged reconsideration by the London administration of the Irish situation." "Irish circumstances," Robbins affirms, "stimulated the development and spread of liberal ideas," ideas that would reach their fullest fruition in the radicalism of the age of George III.[10]

Imperial historians, by contrast, have implied that Swift's condemnation of modern colonies was innovative and brilliant precisely because there was, as yet, no coherent discussion of the British Empire. It was only "in the 1740s and 1750s," argued Kathleen Wilson, that "trade and empire, the nature of the national character, and the relationship of all three to Britain's political leadership" became "potent, and related, issues, in and out of parliament."[11] David Armitage agrees that "the British Empire was conceived as a political community incorporating Britain, Ireland and the plantations during the 1730s." Armitage insists that a "pan-Atlantic conception of Empire" could not emerge until the 1730s because of "the failure" of "Walpole and his ministers to square the circle and fashion a suitable theory of empire."[12] Brendan Simms, who is much more alive to the imperial questions of the early eighteenth century than Wilson or Armitage, nevertheless insists that in the 1720s "British politics and foreign policy … were dominated by events in the Holy Roman Empire." Politics in the 1720s "was dominated not by colonial rivalries … but by the old 'imperial' problem of how to prevent the Holy Roman Empire from being used as a base from which to outflank the Barrier [of the Southern Netherlands], and to overturn the European balance of power upon which British security depended."[13] Because there was no British imperial debate in the 1720s, because colonial issues were overshadowed by European ones, Swift's writings in the 1720s must be understood in a narrowly Anglo-Irish context. "Swift," David Oakleaf has insisted, "invariably adopts an Irish perspective on English politics."[14]

Against these views, I suggest that Swift's critique of British imperialism was more complex and more equivocal than most scholars have assumed. By placing Swift's writings in a narrowly Anglo-Irish context, scholars have missed the lively, contentious, and sophisticated discussion of imperial issues taking place right across the British colonies in the second and third decades of the eighteenth century. In every instance, these debates took place in the context of partisan strife, but that partisanship was becoming increasingly complex. In Ireland, but also right across the empire, Walpoleian Whigs, opposition Whigs, and Tories advanced very different visions of empire. These prescriptions, themselves, depended on competing political-economic understandings. Placed in this matrix, Swift's denunciation of "modern" colonies needs to be understood not as an argument against the empire, but as an argument against the competing commercial visions of the different branches of Whiggery. In fact, Swift believed both that Ireland should not be treated as a colony—it was properly one of the three kingdoms—and that colonies that produced precious metals or important raw materials were entirely justifiable.

I

Jonathan Swift wrote *Gulliver's Travels* in an era of imperial crisis and reformulation. In rapid succession, a series of crises shook the British Empire in the second two decades of the eighteenth century. Spain threatened the Bahamas, South Carolina, and Gibraltar, while Britain's Whig government drew up plans to attack Havana during the War of the Quadruple Alliance (1718–1720). These developments, thought Edward Synge, Archbishop of Tuam and longtime friend of William Wake, were of "the greatest importance" in which "we and indeed all Europe is concerned."[15] Swift's friend John Arbuthnot thought it amusing to see the Jacobite Duke of Berwick, as an officer in the French army at war with Spain, joining forces with Britain "to reduce the exorbitant power of Spain."[16]

Meanwhile, a wide range of Britons were alarmed at the French government's renewed interest in colonial affairs. Most understood that the French Mississippi Company was much more than a financial boondoggle; it represented a real effort to consolidate its colonial power. "The French have but one general government and aim," Joseph Boone explained to the Board of Trade in August 1720, and if they prove successful in establishing the new Mississippi territory, they will be able in alliance with their native allies to "harass the scattered plantations of the English and either wholly dispossess them or make them of no use to Great Britain."[17] The new French imperialism was no state secret. Many Britons invested in the Mississippi Company, while at the same time pamphlets alerted Britons to the new threat to their colonies. The widely circulated *St. James's Journal* reported on "the formidable settlement of Louisiana, which for some years past has been carried on by the French with great expense and with the utmost vigour and application." This new French colonial enterprise, warned this newspaperman, would allow them "to draw a line from the borders of Cape Breton to the westernmost part of Carolina. And who can think of this without being in pain for the fate of our provinces in future times?"[18]

Britons knew that the Habsburgs as well as the Bourbons posed a significant threat to the British Empire in the 1720s. The British press quickly drew attention to the new Austrian East India Company based at Ostend. One political observer noted in 1723 that the Ostend Company was "all that embroils us now." The following year one Anglo-Irishman eagerly circulated proposals to destroy the new company. Soon Lord Townshend and William Stanhope were signaling to the international diplomatic community that George I was willing to go to war to defend British imperial trade in the East Indies.[19]

Internal conflict as well as international competition threatened Britain's colonies in the early eighteenth century. In South Carolina, the "Revolutioners" of 1719 overthrew the proprietary government in part because of their failure to defend against Bourbon encroachments and in part because they had failed to live up to Revolution Principles.[20] In Jamaica, a Whig faction committed to exporting British manufactured goods to Spanish America had long been fighting a losing, but often violent battle against a Tory group of powerful sugar planters. In Virginia, there were "great heats" between the supporters of Governor Alexander Spotswood, who sought to develop Virginia's manufacturing sector at the expense of the great tobacco planters, who ultimately forced his ouster.[21]

The bursting of the South Sea Bubble in late 1720 provoked a pan-imperial economic crisis. In Ireland, as is well known, "the miseries" were "truly deplorable." The English-born Timothy Godwin, Bishop of Kilmore, claimed that the South Sea disaster has "put a stop to all trade." On this, if on little else, the Archbishop of Dublin William King agreed: The bursting of the bubble "has surely made us miserable to the high degree, if starving be a misery."[22] What is less well known is that similar dislocations were felt throughout the empire. As in Ireland, local projectors, colonial governors, and the Board of Trade experimented with currency manipulation and a variety of Bank schemes. Swift was well aware, for example, that William Wood "had tried his faculty in New-England."[23] In New England, as in Ireland, the monetary crisis touched off a lively pamphlet debate.[24] In Jamaica, "Carolina and other countries" within the empire, the Jamaican Whig James Knight recalled, governors attempted "injurious" financial experiments.[25] In Massachusetts, as in Ireland, powerful local merchants floated the idea of a bank. There, too, the bank was rejected in part because some believed "that the projectors had calculated it only for their own private advantage."[26]

When Jonathan Swift turned his thoughts to empire in the mid-1720s, he was writing in the midst of a pan-imperial crisis. He knew, as did most of his contemporaries in Ireland, Britain, and in the wider empire, that the Anglo-Irish dispute generated by the Declaratory Act (1720), the failed Bank schemes (1721–1722), and Wood's halfpence (1723–1725) was part of a larger discussion of the redefinition of the British Empire. The great Swift scholar Irvin Ehrenpreis was thinking on too narrow a scale when he proclaimed that "*Gulliver's Travels* does not finally stand within a specific context of public events."[27] Swift was writing with a very specifically defined imperial context, a context that Charles Forman defined as "the Critical Moment for the honour and grandeur of Britain."[28]

II

Britons throughout the empire responded to the imperial crisis of the first two decades of the eighteenth century in a party political context. The rage of the party did not come to an end after the Jacobite rebellion of 1715, the South Sea Bubble of 1720, the Jacobite Atterbury Plot of 1722, or even as a consequence of the struggle over the imposition of William Wood's halfpence. In Ireland, as in Britain, politics remained partisan and bitterly divisive well into the 1720s.[29]

Jonathan Swift, of course, frequently denied the persistence of party divisions in Ireland and that his own work was at all partisan. "It is certain," Swift proclaimed in the wake of the success of his *Drapier's Letters*, "that all the regular seeds of party and faction among us are entirely rooted out."[30] He told his former patron the Tory earl of Oxford that "a silly accident of brass money hath more united [the Irish] than it ever could have been imagined."[31] His own literary contributions in the 1720s, Swift claimed, were strictly nonpartisan. While one critic immediately claimed that the Dean of St. Patrick's 1720 pamphlet *A Proposal for the Universal Use of Irish Manufacture* was penned by "a Tory doctor of divinity," Swift insisted that "there was nothing in the pamphlet either Whig or Tory."[32] The issue of Wood's halfpence Swift maintained "is neither Whig nor Tory, neither of Town nor Country party."[33] Similarly, Swift's hero Lemuel Gulliver asserted that "I meddle not the least with any party, but write without passion, prejudice, or ill-will against any man or number of men whatsoever."[34]

Despite Swift's aspiration to move beyond party, aspirations that would be later echoed by his great friend Viscount Bolingbroke, Irish politics remained fiercely partisan. M. B. Drapier's calls to unity had achieved but momentary success. In Ireland, Swift lamented in the summer of 1725 that "faction has been so outrageous above anything in England."[35] "I tell you there is hardly a Whig in Ireland, who would allow a potato and butter-milk to a reputed Tory," Swift moaned to the Tory Reverend Thomas Sheridan.[36] Several years later, Swift publicly blamed Ireland's poverty on "party rage."[37]

Just about everyone else in the 1720s agreed that Ireland remained fiercely partisan. A wide variety of observers commented on the persistence of fierce tensions between Whigs and Tories. "The people here are possessed with such implacable spirits and such a humour for parties," wrote Philip Percival from Dublin in 1724, "that a poor fiddler can hardly put up a bill for a benefit, but immediately a party is formed for or against him."[38] The partisanship of successive Irish administrations in the second decade of the eighteenth century had left an indelible mark. In 1722, the Bishop of Kilmore tallied ecclesiastical appointments: "Our Lord Lieutenant has made one Whig Dean. Those of Down, Limerick, and Cork are Atterburian Tories."[39] Several years later, Hugh Boulter, Archbishop of Armagh, opposed the appointment of Swift's friend Patrick Delany to a parish church in Dublin because he was "a great Tory."[40] So deeply ingrained were Irish party divisions, "faction upon faction among ourselves" in the view of the Bishop of Meath John Evans, that when John Carteret, as Lord Lieutenant of Ireland, appeared "to court both parties" it was clear that "neither party" was pleased.[41]

Just as in England, Irish party politics became more complex in the 1720s because of deep divisions among the Whigs. Just as in England former Whig allies fell out after the Hanoverian succession. William Conolly, soon after 1715, displaced Alan Brodrick Viscount Midleton as leader of the Castle Party, the Whig group working most closely with the British ministry. In the 1720s, Conolly became the leading establishment Whig politician in Ireland. He and Robert Walpole were, in the view of Conolly's political biographer, "kindred spirits."[42] There can be no doubting the intensity of the intra-party conflict between the Conolly faction and the Brodrick grouping. Personally, there was "not much love between them." "The feud is so great between these two Great Men," Conolly and Midleton, "and the followers of each (who have so often been of a side)" wrote Philip Percival to his brother in the midst of the controversy over Wood's halfpence, "that it is not likely we shall ever see them united." In January 1724, so many "scurrilous ballads" had appeared raising the political temperature between the two groups that a "bloody fray" was narrowly avoided at the Dublin playhouse.[43]

While there was no doubt a certain amount of personal rivalry behind the split among the Irish Whigs, there were also deep divisions over political-economic issues. At the outset of the halfpence controversy, Midleton characterized the differences between the two groups in general terms. Their disagreements had, in Midleton's view, "cemented a body of men in a common interest to preserve the liberties of the country against the attempts of them who would sacrifice everything to their ambition."[44] Later Midleton made clear that at the heart of the differences between the two Whig factions were their respective attitudes toward political-economic projects. "My judgement is that the Bank or Wood's copper money would have effectually taken the whole gold and silver out of the kingdom, and I chose to declare my sense to be so, when those matters came under consideration in Parliament," Midleton recalled. It was "by these steps I fell into the high displeasure of a great man [William Conolly], who would not have been a loser if either of those destructive schemes had succeeded."[45] Contemporaries agreed in highlighting the differences between the Whig groupings over the Bank and Wood's halfpence. And, it is clear that both the Brodricks and the Conolly faction were deeply interested in political-economic issues.[46]

Viscount Midleton's decision to adopt the patriotic mantle in opposition to Conolly's Castle Party led to a strategic but not an ideological rapprochement with the Tories in Ireland. Both Hugh Boulter, Archbishop of Armagh, and Thomas Godwin, Bishop of Kilmore, noted in 1725 that "the Tories have pushed very unanimously with the discontented Whigs."[47] But Midleton could not have made more clear the ideological distance he still perceived between himself and the Tories. When Swift proposed to dedicate his collected Drapier letters to the opposition Whig leader in 1725, Midleton responded by declaring that "I could not by any means consent to the dedication of the Drapier to me, and if done, would complain of the printer [in court]."[48]

Jonathan Swift wrote *Gulliver's Travels* in a deeply partisan atmosphere. Ireland, Britain, and Britain's colonies were deeply divided over a range of issues in the 1720s. Not only did Whigs and Tories disagree bitterly, but Whigs had fallen out among themselves over how to respond to the political-economic crises of the day. While Swift and other Tories, both in Britain and in Ireland, successfully made alliances with opposition Whigs, these alliances were strategic rather than ideological. To understand these ideological disputes that separated Walpoleian Whigs (the Castle party in Ireland), opposition Whigs, and Tories, to come to terms with political-economic issues that divided Irishmen and Britons more generally, it is necessary to place these controversies in a wider imperial context.

III

What then was the Walpoleian Whig and Irish Castle Party approach to imperial questions? What was the establishment Whig approach to empire? Did the Walpoleians and Irish Whigs share a similar outlook?

From Jonathan Swift's perspective, these were non-questions. Walpole's views of Ireland were narrow, insular, and determined by greed. "We are at a great distance from the King's court, and have no body there to solicit for us," Swift complained publicly in 1724. As a result, he surmised, the Englishman William Wood was able to exercise an undue influence over British policy because of his "great friends" and his knowledge of "where to give money."[49] Later, when Swift had a chance to discuss Ireland with Walpole face to face, Swift left disgusted. "Sir Robert Walpole was pleased to enlarge very much upon the subject of Ireland, in a manner so alien from what I conceived to be rights and privileges of a subject of England," Swift informed the earl of Peterborough in 1726. The first Lord of the Treasury "had conceived opinions" about Ireland "which I could not reconcile to the notions I had of liberty."[50] Walpole's notions must have come as no surprise to Swift. He had long been convinced that "the people of England are utterly ignorant of our case, which however is no wonder since it is a point they do not in the least concern themselves about." "As to Ireland," Swift averred, the people of England "know little more than they do of Mexico." The English thought of Ireland as a place "full of bogs, inhabited by wild Irish papists."[51] Swift could not imagine a coherent Walpoleian policy, much less a coordinated approach between Walpole and Conolly's castle group, because the English people and the British ministry were wholly ignorant about Ireland.

Despite his public and private assertions that Robert Walpole and his political allies in Britain and Ireland knew little and cared less about Ireland, Swift provided a hint that he knew otherwise. In July 1726, he refused to allow Thomas Tickell, the editor of Joseph Addison's works and a close friend of the Castle Party leader William Conolly, from previewing *Gulliver's Travels*. After exploring a litany of excuses, Swift admitted that he did not want to show the manuscripts to Tickell "chiefly because they wholly disagree with your notions of persons and things."[52]

In fact, both the English public and Robert Walpole himself were remarkably well informed about Ireland.[53] John Trenchard, who had himself been educated at Trinity College, Dublin, famously denounced British governmental policy in Ireland in his wildly popular *Cato's Letters* in December 1722.[54] "At present the affairs of Ireland make more noise than anything," Viscount Percival reported from England in December 1723.[55] "You cannot imagine what a noise your affair has made on this side the water, nor how 'tis resented by almost all sorts of people" Lord Midleton's son St. John reported from London in the midst of the halfpence controversy.[56] Midleton's brother Thomas was sure that the intrinsic value of Wood's coin was being openly debated in English "coffee houses."[57] And, of course, each stage of the Irish controversy was set off by reports first disseminated in the English periodical press.[58] Walpole himself received a wide range of information about Irish affairs. When St. John Brodrick met with Walpole to discuss Wood's halfpence, he found that Britain's first minister listened "with great attention" for over two hours, afterward telling him that "he had been informed of most of the particulars" already.[59] Not only had Walpole kept abreast of Irish developments with reports from successive Irish Lord Lieutenants, and the Brodricks suspected by William Conolly himself, but also he had his own direct contacts among the Irish and Anglo-Irish. Archibald Hutcheson and Arthur Dobbs from County Antrim, Henry Maxwell from County Down, and Martin Bladen who though English sat in the Irish House of Commons from 1715 to 1727 all corresponded with Robert Walpole. It is perhaps not coincidental that all four of these men also had significant interests in the West Indies and North America.

What then were Walpole's notions of Irish and imperial affairs? What were the ideological assumptions that undergirded Walpole's imperial and Irish policies in the 1720s? While no single memorandum survives in print or among Walpole's papers outlining the assumptions of Walpole's branch of the Whig Party or the Castle Party's ideological prescriptions in the early 1720s, two documents do shed light on the making of Walpoleian imperial and Irish policy.

Martin Bladen, the most influential member of the Board of Trade in the 1720s, had long been one of Walpole's intimates. When in Dublin in 1716, he expressed an eager willingness to support Walpole's "measures" because of their well-established political "friendship."[60] Bladen allied himself with the Conolly faction in Irish politics and bore "a most implacable hatred" to Viscount Midleton.[61] So it was with the confidence of Walpole's support that Bladen took the lead in writing the Board of Trade's 1721 Report on the Plantation Trade, a copy of which is still among Walpole's papers. In that long and detailed analysis, Bladen, like William Wood of Jamaica before him, began from Whiggish political-economic principles. Like John Locke he emphasized the productive importance of labor. However, whereas more radical Whigs like Henry Martin had highlighted the productive interplay between production and consumption, for Bladen labor was only valuable because of its productive capacity. Because Bladen believed that productivity alone was in question, he naturally believed that the imperial center could best determine what goods should be produced for the entire empire. Colonies, in his view, should be entirely subservient to the metropole. Colonial governments, Bladen and the Board of Trade lamented in 1721, "have shown too great an inclination to be independent of their Mother Kingdom and have carried on a trade destructive to that of Great Britain." The British economy would grow more quickly if all of the colonies were placed under the crown's "immediate government and were by proper laws compelled to follow the commands sent them" from Whitehall. This, Bladen and his colleagues concluded, "hath ever been the wisdom not only of Great Britain but likewise of all other states to secure by all possible means the *entire absolute and immediate dependency of their colonies.*" Bladen and the Board of Trade made clear that they understood "the planters, whatever governments they may live under," were subjects of the British crown and should be allowed to do all "reasonable things" provided they were not "*prejudicial to the interest of Great Britain.*"[62] Colonists, in the view of Bladen and the Board of Trade, were conceptually distinct from British subjects, and their local interests should necessarily be secondary to the greater good of Britain.

The Irishman Henry Maxwell reinforced Bladen's imperial blueprint, which focused mostly on the Atlantic, with a broader call for imperial expansion. Maxwell, a lifelong Whig, had associated himself with William Conolly's Castle Party in Ireland as early as 1715. Perhaps as a result of that association, Maxwell increasingly distanced himself from the dissident Whig faction in Ireland led by Viscount Midleton.[63] Like Bladen, Maxwell had made himself known to Robert Walpole long before the South Sea Bubble launched his long career as a chief minister.[64]

In 1723, Henry Maxwell published a much overlooked essay insisting that "Britain by being a free monarchy, is greatly made for increase, and conquest, too, if she pleases."[65] Maxwell made his case in a pamphlet insisting that Britain retains control of Gibraltar and Minorca, precisely the foreign policy issue that had so divided Robert Walpole and his allies from the policies pursued by the earl of Sunderland and James Stanhope. When the Whig ministry floated a rumor that Gibraltar was to be "delivered up" at the conclusion of the War of the Quadruple Alliance, it was opposed vociferously in the House of Commons by "Walpole and the discontented Whigs."[66] Maxwell, long known as a prolific pamphleteer on Irish questions, had devoted his considerable energies and talents to the defense of Walpole's imperial policy.

Maxwell prescribed an empire defined along Whiggish principles. Like Bladen, Wood, and Locke before him, Maxwell insisted that "power is not to be measured by extent of territory, but by the multitude of subjects."[67] But, again like others writing in defense of Walpole's policies, Maxwell emphasized production at the expense of consumption. Whereas more radical Whig political-economic writers like Bernard Mandeville, Joseph Addison and Henry Martin had emphasized that luxurious tastes could spur growth, Maxwell more conventionally thought that "because luxury [made] the body feeble, and effeminate, and corrupting the mind … wise lawgivers have rather thought fit to restrain, than provide for it."[68]

Maxwell also imagined an empire committed to political liberty. Free monarchies based on islands, Maxwell insisted, could create and sustain liberal empires. This was because "free monarchies in an island" were "freed from the necessity of engaging in frequent wars by land."[69] Athens, Sparta, and "afterwards the Lord of Nations, the Romans (all of them great and free governments)" had established great empires. In each and every case, those empires had declined, in part because their geographical situation had compelled them to engage in politically corrosive land wars. But, Athens and Rome were also weakened because they had been mixed commonwealths rather than mixed monarchies. "For the commonwealth consisting but of two orders wants a third to balance both," Maxwell explained, "and then, like Rome, she ends in civil wars and tyranny."[70]

Maxwell advised a new kind of commercial empire, based on islands. "It is plain," Maxwell said, "that the British Empire consisting of large and fruitful islands, her natural power is in the command of the seas."[71] In making this claim, Maxwell defined the proper contours of British imperial power. Jamaica, Ireland, Minorca, Gibraltar (a virtual island)—but presumably not continental North America—were proper subjects of British imperial rule. But, whereas Maxwell had once famously advocated Anglo-Irish union, he now believed that the status of Ireland and all the other islands must be dependent on Britain. "It is the indispensible duty of all island governments to increase and enlarge their commerce and navigation, as much as possible," Maxwell explained, "because they neither can invade, nor be invaded, hurt or be hurt, but by a maritime power." Maxwell knew well that not all islands were capable of such activity. "All islands that are not of sufficient extent, fruitfulness, and industry, as may enable them to carry on an extended commerce and navigation, and to maintain sufficient fleets of war" he insisted, "must be content to become, at one time or other, *provinces* to the Master of the Sea."[72] Gibraltar and Minorca—and presumably Ireland—should have "a good government and constitution"; however in Maxwell's view they could not "subsist but by their daily dependence on Britain."[73]

Maxwell left his readers in no doubt that his imperial precepts applied to Ireland. He dedicated his pamphlet to the Duke of Grafton, then Lord Lieutenant of Ireland. Maxwell hoped his pamphlet would "inspire" Grafton to employ his principles.[74] Maxwell's insistence that Britain's other islands should have provincial status, dependent on Britain, echoes the language with which he began his first polemical work in defense of an Irish bank. There he argued that the Irish should accept their "dependance" on Britain and make the best of it.[75] And, it was surely no coincidence that Maxwell advised that the erection of a bank was "absolutely necessary to the prosperity" of Gibraltar.[76] Maxwell's willingness to endorse "a simple act of violence" to convert the natives of Gibraltar and Minorca so that thereafter the British Empire might be "firmly founded in justice, liberty, equal laws, and a communication of British privileges" might have been written with Ireland in mind as well.[77]

Bladen and Maxwell were eloquent and sophisticated defenders of Walpoleian imperial policy. But they were by no means unique. William Nicolson, the Whig Bishop of Londonderry, praised the Castle Party leader William Conolly as a "person of wonderful parts and temper." Like Maxwell, he emphasized the economic dependence of Ireland's island economy on British prosperity. He also advocated that the Irish parliament should institute "a new Test, requiring all officers civil and military solemnly to recognize the dependence of this kingdom on the imperial crown of Great Britain."[78] Francis Hutchinson, Bishop of Down and Connor, was a great admirer of Henry Maxwell's economic writings, and like Maxwell emphasized his "desire of dependence on England."[79] Another important member of the Castle Party, Arthur Dobbs, later dedicated a manuscript treatise entitled "A Scheme to Increase the Colonies and Commerce of Great Britain" to Robert Walpole. The goal of that work, almost certainly penned around 1730, was to "enlarge our commerce, add to our colonies, [and to] secure their dependence on their Mother Country."[80]

Robert Walpole and his allies in both Britain and Ireland were developing a coherent and sophisticated blueprint for a British Empire in the early 1720s. Empire in the 1720s should not be understood in a narrowly Anglo-Irish context. Walpole's ideological allies on both sides of St. George's channel understood Ireland in a broader imperial context. Britons did not have to wait until the later 1730s and 1740s to be treated to sophisticated new theorizing about empire. The Walpoleian state was to be a new kind of commercial empire. Henry Maxwell was conscious that his "maxims of provincial government" were "widely different from all modern practice."[81] Dobbs, too, expected that Walpole would "not only preserve the extended acquisitions of Great Britain but enlarge and improve them." Narrowing the ideological scope of imperial theorizing, as some scholars have done, to commentary on classical models is to miss the innovative ideological work being done in the Walpoleian age. Before the modern age, Dobbs made clear, states sought colonies either because of their "too great apparent numbers or thirst of dominion." "The increase of commerce or navigation," he believed, "had very little share in it."[82]

IV

Dissident Whigs challenged Sir Robert Walpole's political ascendancy in Britain, Ireland, and across the empire. Right across the empire, dissident Whigs enunciated an alternative version of Britain's proper role in the world. Whereas Walpole and his supporters placed an emphasis on colonial production and colonial dependence, their Whig opponents stressed the interplay of production and consumption, and advocated an integrated imperial relationship.

Opposition Whigs, like their Walpoleian opponents, believed that labor rather than land was the basis of wealth. However, they differed from establishment Whigs in two fundamental respects. Whereas establishment Whigs valued labor primarily within Britain, opposition Whigs like John Trenchard believed that "in many instances, men add more to the public stock by being out of their country than in it."[83] Just as the Dutch "esteem the wealth of their subjects abroad as their own riches," reasoned the Massachusetts agent and distinguished Harvard graduate Jeremiah Dummer in 1721, so should "Great Britain form the same judgment."[84] For opposition Whigs, there was no conceptual distinction between Britons and colonists. In addition, opposition or patriot Whigs valued consumption as well as production in the colonies. They did not follow Henry Maxwell in his condemnation of luxury. "Nothing can free mankind" from the drudgery of a subsistence agrarian life, noted John Trenchard, other than "the invention of arts and sciences." Since it was only consumer demand that could induce people to believe "that other things are necessary to their happiness besides those which nature has made necessary," he reasoned, "the luxury of the rich becomes the bread of the poor."[85] "It is an undoubted truth, that in the multitude of inhabitants consists the welfare, riches and power of any people," Hugh Jones of Virginia intoned in typically Whiggish fashion. This was because—and here Alexander Spotswood defender differed from Walpoleian orthodoxy—after they "improved their manufactures," then "the greater consumption will be made of such things as tend to the public good."[86] Should Virginia develop its own manufactures, Jones elaborated, "our inferior people that are now clothed with rags, being promoted to circumstances that would afford it, would yearly expend vast sums in good apparel, household goods etc. which they must be supplied with from Great Britain."[87]

Whereas Walpole and his supporters sought to extend the empire, opposition Whigs argued that Britain should focus on colonial development. In Jamaica, the court party of the second decade of the eighteenth century espoused political-economic principles remarkably similar to Viscount Midleton's group in Ireland. This was hardly surprising since one of their leaders was Midleton's brother, William Brodrick. Brodrick's commitment to radical Whiggery was not in dispute. His supporters, according to one of his great critics, were the "spawn of Oliver's gang and professedly of the king-killing principles," while Brodrick himself had "come over from Holland with the Prince of Orange" and entertained "the same anti-monarchical principles."[88] In political-economic terms, these Jamaicans advocated the development of manufactures in Jamaica rather "than seeking after settlements in Spanish Dominions" as the South Sea Company demanded.[89] Trenchard objected to colonial conquest on moral and economic grounds. "Force is often dangerous; and when employed to acquire what is not ours, is always unjust," he maintained. "It does not import who they are that have conquered, or inhabit the countries where silver and gold are natives," Trenchard argued similarly, "since they will be the possessors of the coin, who can purchase it afterwards with the goods and manufactures, which the proprietors of the mine and their people want."[90]

Opposition Whigs were more optimistic about the value of plantations to the British economy, than were their Walpoleian opponents. Whereas Walpole and his strategists were constantly devising ways to siphon more wealth from the colonies, opposition Whigs insisted that colonies were already the most dynamic sector of the British economy. "It is evident to all who are conversant in trade," wrote James Knight who was a member of William Brodrick's party in Jamaica and served as the colony's agent in the 1720s, that Jamaica "is of greater consequence to the crown of Great Britain, than all the other sugar colonies belonging to His Majesty."[91] "It were no difficult task to prove that London has risen out of the plantations, and not out of England," insisted Jeremiah Dummer, "'tis to them we owe our vast fleets of merchants ships, and consequently the increase of our seamen, and improvement of our navigation."[92] "The extent, the wealth, the numerous inhabitants, the hands employed, the goods consumed, the duties and customs occasioned by the plantations," chimed in Hugh Jones, are "at present one of the chiefest causes and main supports of our trade and [bring] as much money into the treasury, and the purses of merchants, and other people, as most other parts of the world to which we trade."[93]

The opposition Whigs offered a range of prescriptions for colonial development, prescriptions that catered to the various endowments of each individual colony. But these prescriptions invariably privileged manufacturing over the development of raw materials. John Trenchard followed the radical Whig Henry Martin in urging the development of manufactures in the Northern Colonies of North America, precisely those colonies which Maxwell implied must be jettisoned.[94] Alexander Spotswood and his allies wanted to put a halt to the development of slavery in Virginia by employing the poor from Britain and elsewhere in new industries. In this, Hugh Jones thought the Virginians should follow the Dutch "whose riches and grandeur arose from the increase of their inhabitants, from their industrious improvement of projects, inventions and manufactures at home and abroad."[95] James Knight and the Whigs in Jamaica whom Walpole's ministry deemed were guilty of "faction and sedition," similarly wanted to reorient the colony away from slavery and sugar plantations toward penetrating Spanish American markets with manufactured goods. Trade with Spanish America was once "the chief support of the island of Jamaica," Knight maintained, "nor can it otherwise subsist, without being a very considerable expense to Great Britain, in maintaining a number of regular forces to secure it."[96] Whatever the colonial context, the central point remained the same. "The only interest of the people" in the colonies, insisted Jeremiah Dummer, "is to thrive and flourish in their trade, which is the true interest of the crown and nation, because they reap the profit of it."[97]

Patriot Whigs in Ireland adopted precisely this vision of an integrated imperial economy. Just as Whigs in Jamaica, Virginia, Massachusetts, and South Carolina had argued for the mutual economic dependence of Britain and the colonies, so Patriot Whigs in Ireland argued that what was good for Ireland's economy was good for Britain as a whole. "The Kingdom of Ireland is unalterably annexed to the crown of Great Britain," argued Edward Synge Archbishop of Tuam, "and the chief stream of what little wealth we have amongst us unavoidably runs into that kingdom." So, he reasoned, "the stronger and richer we become, the greater will be the strength and riches of Great Britain."[98] "I can never suppose," chimed in David Bindon who was at the time aligning himself with Midleton's group in Ireland, "but the interest of England and that of Ireland, as now established should be so united" that all would agree "that Ireland can never be destroyed without bringing a most sensible damage to the affairs of England."[99] The Archbishop of Dublin William King made the same point when he asserted that "the taking away our woollen trade has been and will prove a fatal blow to Great Britain" and new plans to harm the linen industry would not only devastate Ireland "but be most mischievous to England."[100]

Some opposition Whigs tied the explosion of piracy in the Caribbean and North American waters to the failure of Whig ministers to support manufactures and private trade with Spanish America. There was, James Knight claimed, not a single "English pirate known in the

West Indies till the latter end of 1716." It was from that moment that Spanish guardacostas began attacking British private traders from the Caribbean islands to Spanish America. These developments coincided with the consolidation of a Walpoleian economic strategy to privilege the production of staple crops at the expense of manufactures. From the 1690s, the Caribbean had attracted "seamen from all parts." In times of peace, these men "went cheerfully into the merchants service, and were well contented with their employment." It was the decline of the export trade as a result of ministerial policies that was "certainly the motive to a course of life, which I am of opinion, most or many of them would not have taken up" had their trading way of life remained an option.[101]

Patriot Whigs from all across the empire in the 1720s blamed the adoption of iniquitous economic policies on a political failure. Whole swathes of the empire, regions that were an increasingly important and dynamic part of the British economy, could not make their needs known. Jamaica, James Knight complained, "has but few friends in England, and those very backward in using their interest and endeavours for its service." Jamaica had no "general representation," no means of making its interests known to the ministry.[102] Jeremiah Dummer made a similar point about Massachusetts, bemoaning that his colony "had no representative in Parliament."[103] Irish patriots advanced a similar case. They complained, John Evans explained to the Archbishop of Canterbury, that "they had no representatives" of their interests. Whereas Manchester had no trouble making its economic interests known in Westminster, William King observed, the Irish had no "agent who understood the circumstances" from an Irish perspective.[104] It was perhaps this sentiment that the English-born bishop of Londonderry, William Nicolson, caught wind of when he spoke of patriot support for "an incorporation into the United Kingdom of Great Britain."[105] While Nicolson thought in terms of the Anglo-Scottish Union, opposition Whigs may have had something grander in mind. John Trenchard wrote in 1722 of a "proposition more honourable to the crown, more advantageous to each kingdom, and to the particular members of them, and vastly more conducive to the power of the whole British Empire, than the doubtful state which they are now in."[106]

In the 1720s, Patriot Whigs right across the empire proposed a very different blueprint for British rule than that advanced by Robert Walpole and his political allies. The starting point of that Whig imperial vision was the belief that colonists benefited the British economy both in their capacity as producers and that of consumers. Colonial consumption, in the view of these dissident Whigs, was the engine that could drive a more dynamic economy. Whereas Walpole and his spokesmen imagined a hierarchical relationship between Britain and its colonies, these dissident Whigs imagined a more integrated economy. These self-proclaimed patriots believed that economic integration required more direct political integration. They may well have come to these beliefs as a consequence of recent political developments—ranging from the suppression of the private trade to Spanish America to the Declaratory Act. In effect, patriots in Ireland, Jamaica, Massachusetts, and in Britain itself demanded the evisceration of the concept of the colony. Subjects of the crown wherever they happened to live and work were all Britons. A British ministry that recognized this point would create a more prosperous and consequently more powerful state.

V

Jonathan Swift did write *Gulliver's Travels* in the midst of a lively contemporary controversy about the proper organization of the British Empire. Postcolonial critics like Clement Hawes are right to situate Swift's masterpiece in the context of a "key turning point in the history of British colonialism."[107] Unlike the postcolonialists, I argue Swift was responding less to the fact of the Assiento—granted over a decade previous to the publication of *Gulliver's Travels*—than to the lively debates provoked by Robert Walpole's new departure in imperial governance. Swift was staking out a Tory alternative to both the Walpoleian empire outlined by Martin Bladen and Henry Maxwell, and the opposition Whig program outlined by a wide range of Britons. Swift understood, as did many of his allies and critics, that the political struggles in the Ireland of the 1720s were part of a larger debate over defining the contours and direction of the British Empire.

No one doubted Swift's political impact in George I's Ireland. Even before the furore over the Declaratory Act, the Bishop of Londonderry wrote derisively that "The Angel of St. Patrick's is now the guardian of the kingdom."[108] After the passage of that Act, Swift "invented" a new popular health "to the immortal memory of Queen Anne who never hurt Ireland."[109] Later that year, Swift's "virulent pamphlet" recommending that the Irish boycott British woolen manufactures was thought "to keep" party divisions.[110] "No one has a greater hand in these heats" than Jonathan Swift, wrote John Evans at the outset of the controversy over Wood's halfpence.[111] At the end of that controversy, the new Archbishop of Armagh, Hugh Boulter, described Swift as "the great fomenter" of Ireland's disturbances.[112]

During this period, Swift often made common cause with Ireland's dissident Whigs. Many grouped Swift with Archbishop William King, Archbishop Edward Synge, and Viscount Midleton as the fiercest critics of Walpoleian and Castle Party policies. Swift himself claimed, in this period, that he was "conversing with the writings" of Robert Molesworth, "Mr. Locke, Mr. Molineaux, Colonel Sidney"—a galaxy of Whig heroes—in formulating his position.[113] He claimed that "the best Whigs in England" had opposed English attempts to control Irish legislation.[114] Had he, in fact, abandoned his earlier Tory views in favor of a more modulated ideological position? Only by placing Swift's writings in an imperial context, is it possible to recover the ideological significance of his work in this period.

Despite Swift's famous proclamations against modern colonies in Book IV of *Gulliver's Travels*, the Dean of Saint Patrick's was no longtime critic of empire. He had been an early supporter of "Oxford's brat," the South Sea Company.[115] At its inception, the South Sea Company had been designed as the commercial arm of Oxford's new territorial empire in South America, with planned bases in Valdivia, Buenos Aires, and the Tierra del Fuego. Swift not only wrote in support of the company, he invested heavily in South Sea stock.[116] Swift counted the Tory financier John Drummond, an early supporter of the South Sea Company and later an advocate for territorial empire in India, among his friends.[117] While Swift and his friends distanced themselves from the South Sea Company after it lost its territorial aspirations, and became a Whig company, after 1713, they quickly rushed to support John Law's new French imperial venture. John Arbuthnot bragged to Swift about his intimacy with "the great Mr. Law." Swift congratulated Bolingbroke for "growing rich" through his Mississippi investments.[118] Modern scholars tend to view Law's Mississippi scheme as a financial boondoggle. Contemporaries knew better. The Mississippi scheme, as Law later explained to Robert Walpole, was based on a "real foundation" in imperial trade and possession to such places as Louisiana, "all the Indies, South Sea" as well as "Senegal, Canada, and Cape Niger."[119] Britons feared the territorial ambitions of Law's new French Empire as much they loathed the destabilizing implications of his financial machinations.[120]

Swift remained committed to the Tory political economy that he had espoused during his period as propagandist-in-chief for Oxford's Tory administration.[121] Whereas both Walpoleian Whigs and opposition Whigs began their political-economic analyses with the assumption that labor created value, Swift insisted that land was the basis of all wealth. In one of his squibs against the Irish Bank proposed by Castle Party members, Swift denounced the proposal as not being supported by those who owned Irish land.[122] "It is the landed-men that maintains the merchant, and shop-keeper, and handicraftsman," Swift insisted in the first of his *Drapier's Letters*.[123] Later that year, he defined law to mean "the will of the majority of those who have the property in land."[124] Swift contrasted "politicians" with all their projects, clearly training his guns on the Whigs William Conolly and Henry Maxwell, with the "honest farmer," concluding that the former were not "half so useful."[125] Later in the 1720s, Swift published an economic treatise that made his assumptions crystal clear. "The first cause of a Kingdom's thriving," he began, "is the fruitfulness of the soil to produce the necessaries and conveniences of life." "The first cause of a nation's riches," Swift reiterated, was "the fertility of the soil, as well as the temperature of climate."[126] This view, of course, perfectly accorded with the opinions of his Tory friends. Like Swift, Francis Atterbury decried "the wars abroad," which he thought were promoted by "the Whigs," because they had done so much to destroy "the landed interest."[127] John Law's Mississippi Company that had attracted so much investment from

Swift's Tory friends was designed to restore "the nobility that was ruined by the long wars."[128]

Given these economic assumptions, it was inevitable that Swift would condemn modern commercial colonial projects. Swift saved his most vitriolic attacks on the integrated commercial empire proposed by the opposition Whigs. It was the Patriot Whigs, Whigs associated with Viscount Midleton in Ireland, his Brodrick cousins in Jamaica, and his political allies like John Trenchard in England, who had advocated illegally trading with Spanish America. It was this project that Swift was most obviously condemning in Book IV of *Gulliver's Travels*. Captain Lemuel Gulliver's trip to the land of the horse people had begun when his crew, recruited "out of Barbados, and the Leeward Islands" turned out to be "Buccaneers," mutinied and abandoned him. "Their design," Gulliver recalled, "was to turn pirates, and plunder the Spaniards."[129] Where Hugh Jones, Jeremiah Dummer, and James Knight had celebrated the economic potential of bringing the British poor to work in colonial manufactures, Swift had Captain Gulliver denounce these men in the West Indies as "fellows of desperate fortunes, forced to fly from the places of their birth, on the account of their poverty or their crimes." These crimes Gulliver happily cataloged as including "drinking, whoring, and gaming," "treason," "murder, theft, poisoning, robbery, perjury, forgery, coining false money," "rapes or sodomy," "flying from their colours or deserting to the enemy." "None of these," Gulliver tells his readers, "durst return to their native countries for fear of being hanged, or of starving in a jail."[130] These, in Swift's view, were clearly not the sort of folks to construct a just and noble empire. It was, however, just these sorts of individuals who populated modern colonies. These colonies were founded, Gulliver noted making clear reference to the origins of English Jamaica, when "a crew of pirates" were "driven by a storm they knew not whither" and then went "on shore to rob and plunder."[131]

Swift denounced modern commercial empires, but he did not denounce empire. Whereas opposition Whigs had celebrated luxury as driving economic growth, Swift had Lemuel Gulliver denounce the deleterious social effects generated by imports catering to tastes for "luxury" and "vanity" in England.[132] Swift, as he had, during the

Oxford/Bolingbroke ministry, defended colonies that generated precious metals and raw materials. After his denunciation of modern colonialism, Lemuel Gulliver explained that there was no point in conquering the various regions he had his visited in his travels because they did not "abound either in gold, silver, sugar or tobacco."[133] Imperial extension, Swift implied, only made sense to gain control of those commodities. This, Swift made clear, had not been the aims of modern (Whig) colonizers in Britain.

Swift, then, was a proponent of colonialism and a critic of Whig modern colonization schemes. What should one make, then, of Swift's bitter denunciations of British policies in Ireland? Ireland, in Swift's view, should be treated as a separate kingdom, not as a colony peopled by pirates. He was furious that the British "look down upon this kingdom as if it had been one of their colonies of out-casts in America."[134] He objected to William Wood's patent for coining, in part, because as a free kingdom the Irish "deserved the liberty of coining for our selves."[135] "We are a free people, in the common acceptance of the word applied to a subject under a limited monarch," Swift repeatedly explained. "Whatever justice a free people can claim we have at least an equal title to it with our brethren of England," Swift made clear.[136] Swift claimed he had studied the English and Irish statute books "without finding any law that makes Ireland depend upon England, any more than England does upon Ireland." This meant only "that we have indeed obliged ourselves to have the same King with them, and consequently they are obliged to have the same king with us." To think otherwise, to claim that Ireland was a "depending kingdom," thundered Swift in a telling phrase, was to deploy "a *Modern* term of art, unknown … to all ancient civilians and writers upon government."[137]

Swift was no anti-imperialist. He had long endorsed extractive colonial projects. He continued to support such ventures in *Gulliver's Travels*. Swift did, however, detest modern colonial projects, by which he meant commercial empires. Swift deployed his sharpest wit, his most pointed rebarbative comments, in his attacks on Patriot Whig integrative empire. Patriot aspirations to develop manufactures in the colonies and sell some of them to Spanish America were, in Swift's mind, merely an endorsement of piracy. Swift's disagreement with the Walpoleian imperial regime lay not so much in its treatment of colonies, but in its insistence on treating Ireland like a colony. Swift was no critic of colonialism. He simply insisted that Ireland was a kingdom not a colony.

VI

Swift's *Gulliver's Travels* was, in part, an engagement with a sophisticated and wide-ranging party political debate about empire. But Swift was no anti-imperialist. He knew well that his fellow Irishmen Martin Bladen and Henry Maxwell were developing an intellectually sophisticated defense of a Walpoleian British commercial empire based on island colonies. He also knew that their Whig opponents were arguing for a commercially and politically integrated commercial empire in which British manufactured goods, wherever produced, would successfully penetrate Spanish American markets. Swift abhorred these modern projects. Instead, he defended a Tory empire in which Britain would only acquire colonies that were rich in gold, silver, tobacco, or sugar.

What is the larger significance of this interpretation of Swift's classic tale? What have we gained by placing Swift in dialogue with the varieties of Whig imperial projects?

First, by recovering Swift's engagement with empire, it becomes easier to understand Jonathan Swift's political commitments. Scholars have long debated with increasing sophistication the exact nature of Swift's politics. They have done so, however, on the terrain established, perhaps mischievously, by Swift himself. "I am weary of being among ministers whom I cannot govern, who are all rank Tories in government and worse than Whigs in Church," he famously complained to the Whig Thomas Tickell, "whereas I was the first man who taught and practices the direct contrary principle."[138] By describing politics narrowly along the two axes of religion and politics, Swift was able to insist on the complexity of his own views. However, politics in the first decades of the eighteenth century was not, as Swift well knew, narrowly about politics and religion. Political economy in general and the political economy of empire in particular had become prominent issues determining party allegiance. Swift's imperial politics were decidedly Tory.

Second, Swift's political interventions of the 1720s need to be understood as part of a wider and vigorous debate about empire that had begun with the Hanoverian Succession. Scholars have rightly emphasized the new central European perspective that the Hanoverians brought to British politics. But in following later Tory criticisms that Walpole had narrowly pursued the German agenda of his royal masters, these scholars have missed the wide-ranging imperial crisis of the later 1710s and 1720s. Walpole responded to this crisis not with "salutary neglect" and "the delegation of oversight, or even policy, to local authorities and agents" as Jeremy Black has claimed, but with a concerted revamping of Britain's colonial agenda.[139] Walpole followed the advice of Martin Bladen and Henry Maxwell in designing an empire that would emphasize colonial production in such places as Virginia and Jamaica, maritime supremacy, and above all colonial dependence. Richard Johnson is right to see this period as one in which "a coherent, London-directed British Empire" took shape. This was as much true for British America, Johnson's focus, as it was for Ireland.[140] It was Walpole's attempt to create a distinctively British modern colonialism that sparked widespread opposition both among the Patriots and among defenders of Tory territorial imperialism like Swift.

Third, it now becomes clear that dissident Whigs or Patriots developed a clear imperial agenda in the immediate aftermath of the Hanoverian Succession. Patriots across the empire, including James Knight of Jamaica, Hugh Jones of Virginia, Jeremiah Dummer of Massachusetts, and John Trenchard, developed a self-consciously oppositional blueprint for a commercially and politically integrated empire. Their agenda did not draw narrowly on the commonwealth tradition. In fact, it was the Castle Party Whig and Walpoleian propagandist Henry Maxwell who drew most heavily on that tradition. Instead, the Patriot Whigs argued for developing a manufacturing empire, one that embraced the value of colonies both as producers and as consumers. These modern colonies, fully integrated into a global British imperial economy and polity, would allow British manufactures to penetrate Spanish American markets. While these Dissident

Whigs did not seek territorial aggrandizement, they were not shy about defending Britain and its commerce from French and Spanish encroachments. Patriot Whigs in Virginia, Jamaica, Massachusetts, and Britain itself understood that French and Spanish imperial ambitions in North America and the East and West Indies needed to be opposed with force. These Patriot Whigs knew well that a narrowly maritime strategy, one that focused only on sea power and diplomacy would not be sufficient. When the Earl of Stair came to describe the rise of the Patriot opposition, he noted how many of the Patriots had "been employed abroad in the most important negotiations of their country." This gave them occasion "to meet frequently together, and to confer freely upon the change of measures of our court." In particular, they lamented that Sir Robert Walpole had taken "the counter-pied of what had been done by King William and Queen Anne in the beginning of her reign," meaning that Walpole had abandoned their aims, the true Whig aims, in which they had "endeavoured to humble France, and to establish a balance of power in Europe." Of course, Stair's vision from the first had been an imperial one. It had been Stair who had sounded the clarion call to arms against John Law's Mississippi Company as it threatened to encircle British colonial possessions in North America and the West Indies. Stair and the Patriots had always bemoaned that Walpole had sacrificed "our trade and manufactures" to his own political ambition.[141]

In the 1720s, Swift did very much engage with colonial issues. Postcolonial critics are right to surmise that empire was at issue in this period. However, their lack of precision has led them to mischaracterize the nature of Swift's contribution. The Treaty of Utrecht did mark the beginning of a new era in the formation of the British Empire. During the War of the Spanish Succession, Whigs and Tories had vigorously debated differing political-economic agendas for the empire. Tories, including Swift, had advocated territorial expansion principally in the Southern Cone of Latin America. Whigs, by contrast, had demanded commercial penetration of Spanish American markets. With the Hanoverian succession, the Whig agenda had split. The Walpoleian wing of the party argued for the consolidation of a raw material producing empire. For Walpole and his political allies, large continental territorial holdings made little sense. They saw no reason to be alarmed at the territorial ambitions of John Law's French projects. Instead, they emphasized the value of Britain's slave-based sugar islands and tobacco colonies. Walpole's Patriot critics imagined an empire in which New England, Virginia, and Jamaica all took advantage of colonial labor markets and shorter distances to develop manufactures that could supply the various European empires with British-made goods. Swift bitterly satirized both Whig agendas. Swift denounced the modern colonial policy of the Patriots as indistinguishable from piracy. Walpole's Whigs, Swift believed, had created the modern category of the dependent kingdom. Swift's disagreement with Walpole was that the great Whig minister failed to understand that Ireland was a kingdom not a colony.

Notes

1. John Arbuthnot (London) to Swift, in *The Correspondence of Jonathan Swift*, 6 vols., ed. F. Elrington Ball (London: G. Bell & Sons, 1910–1914), vol. III, 357.
2. J. Paul Hunter, "*Gulliver's Travels* and the Later Writings," in *The Cambridge Companion to Jonathan Swift*, ed. Christopher Fox (Cambridge: Cambridge University Press, 2003), 216.
3. Jonathan Swift, *Gulliver's Travels*, ed. Claude Rawson (Oxford: Oxford University Press, 2008), 275. All subsequent quotations from the Rawson edition.
4. The exception is Claude Rawson's, *God, Gulliver and Genocide* (Oxford: Oxford University Press, 2001). Rawson sees Swift's attitude toward colonialism as complex: A view I share. But unlike Rawson, I here emphasize that complexity with relationship to the imperial discussions of the 1720s, rather than in dialogue with Michel de Montaigne and Nazi propagandists.
5. Ian Higgins, "Jonathan's Swift's Political Confession," in *Politics and Literature in the Age of Swift*, ed. Claude Rawson (Cambridge: Cambridge University Press, 2010), 15–16.
6. David Nokes, *Jonathan Swift, a Hypocrite Reversed* (Oxford: Oxford University Press, 1985), 286.

7. Clement Hawes, "Three Times Round the Globe: Gulliver and Colonial Discourse," *Cultural Critique*, no. 18 (Spring 1991), 189. I am grateful to Ian McBride for drawing my attention to this essay.
8. Carole Fabricant, "Swift the Irishman," in Fox, 67; Carole Fabricant, Letter, *Times Literary Supplement*, 16 February 2011.
9. Sean D. Moore, *Swift, the Book and the Irish Financial Revolution* (Baltimore: Johns Hopkins University Press, 2010), 124, 132; Sean Moore, "Swift's Financial Satires and the Bank of Ireland Controversy of 1720–1721," *Eighteenth-Century Ireland* 17 (2002): 55–56.
10. Caroline Robbins, *The Eighteenth-Century Commonwealthman* (Boston: Atheneum, 1959), 135–36.
11. Kathleen Wilson, *A Sense of the People* (Cambridge: Cambridge University Press, 1995), 139.
12. David Armitage, *Ideological Origins of the British Empire* (Cambridge: Cambridge University Press, 2000), 173–76. Armitage has missed the ideological significance of Maden's Board of Trade report which he cites and Henry Maxwell's imperial pamphleteering, which he does not.
13. Brendan Simms, *Three Victories and a Defeat* (New York: Penguin, 2007), 159–60. As will become clear, my disagreements with Simms are really ones of emphasis.
14. David Oakleaf, "Politics and History," in Fox, 33.
15. Edward Synge Archbishop of Tuam (Dublin) to William Wake, 11 December 1718, Christ Church Library, 246/31; P. D. Giers (Paris) to Wake, 26 August 1719, CCL, 262/35.
16. John Arbuthnot (London) to Swift, 11 December 1718, *Correspondence*, Bell, vol. III, 24.
17. Joseph Boone, "Answers to the Queries from Board of Trade," [August 1720], CCL, 257/25; Memorandum, ca. 1720, CCL, 257/23.
18. *Some Considerations of the Consequences of the French Settling Colonies on the Mississippi* (London: J. Roberts, 1720); Jeremiah Dummer, *A Defence of the New England Charters* (London: W. Wilkins, 1721), 65–66; *St. James's Journal*, December 1, 1722, no. 32, 190.
19. *Post Boy*, 1 December 1722, no. 5205, 1; ? (London) to Francis Nicholson, 1723, Rhodes House Library, SPG X 182 d, f. 263r; M. Renard (Amsterdam) to Bothmer, 7 July 1724, Cambridge University Library, CH(H) Correspondence, 1147; Charles Foreman (Amsterdam) to Robert Walpole, 27 July 1724, CUL, CH(H),

Correspondence 1152; William Stanhope (Madrid) to Horatio Walpole, 14 October 1726, NS, BL, Add 73922, unfoliated; Townshend (Whitehall) to William Finch, 1 November 1726, BL, Add 73783, f. 28.

20. Nicholas Trott (South Carolina) to William Wake, 25 March 1725, CCL, 257/22; Francis Yonge, *A Narrative of the Proceedings of the People of South Carolina, in the Year 1719* (London, 1726).
21. James Blair (Williamsburg) to William Wake, 19 December 1722, CCL, 257/73; Hugh Jones, *The Present State of Virginia* (London: J. Clarke, 1724).
22. Timothy Godwin Bishop of Kilmore (Kilmore) to Wake, 5 November 1720, CCL, 246/203; William King Archbishop of Dublin (Dublin) to Wake, 23 March 1721, CCL, 246/240; William Nicholson Bishop of Derry (Londonderry) to Wake, 30 April 1721, CCL, 246/245. This is but a small sample of the widespread evidence for discontent.
23. Swift, *Some Observations*, August 1724, in *The Drapier's Letters*, ed. Herbert Davis (Oxford: Clarendon Press, 1935), 57.
24. For a small sample: *Reflections on the Present State of the Province of Massachusett-Bay* (Boston: Daniel Henchman and Benjamin Eliot, 1720); Thomas Paine, *A Discourse* (Boston: J. Franklin, 1721); and John Wise, *The Freeholder's Address* (Boston: J. Franklin, 1721).
25. James Knight, *The State of the Island of Jamaica* (London: H. Whitridge, 1726), 35; Nicholas Trott (South Carolina) to Wake, 25 March 1725, CCL, 257/22.
26. Samuel Shute (Governor of Massachusetts) to Robert Walpole, ca. August 1724, CUL, CH(H) Correspondence 1156.
27. Irvin Ehrenpreis, *Swift: The Man, His Works and the Age* (London: Methuen, 1983), vol. III, 452. Irish readers would have been particularly attuned to Atlantic events as many Irish men and women were migrating to North America and the West Indies at this time: John Evans Bishop of Meath to Wake, 25 October 1718, CCL, 246/20; William King Archbishop of Dublin (Dublin) to Wake, 16 February 1718, CCL, 246/11; Ian McBride, *Eighteenth Century Ireland* (Dublin: Gill and Macmillan, 2009), 11–12.
28. Charles Forman (Amsterdam) to Robert Walpole, 3 July 1724, CUL, CH(H) Correspondence 1145.
29. I will make the case for British party divisions elsewhere. For now, see William King Archbishop of Dublin (Dublin) to Wake, 11 January

1718, CCL, 246/4; William Wotton (Bath) to Wake, 26 March 1722, CCL, 255/119.
30. Swift, *Humble Address to Both Houses of Parliament*, 1724, Davis, 161.
31. Swift to Oxford, 14 August 1725, *Correspondence*, Ball, vol. III, 262.
32. Jonathan Swift, *A Proposal for the Universal Use of Irish Manufacture* (Dublin: E. Waters, 1720); *An Answer to the Proposal* (Dublin, 1720), 2; Swift (Dublin) to Sir Thomas Hanmer, 1 October 1720, *Correspondence*, Ball, vol. III, 64–65.
33. Swift, *Letter to the Whole People of Ireland*, October 1724, Davis, 75.
34. Swift, *GT*, 1726, Rawson, 273.
35. Swift to Oxford, 14 August 1725, *Correspondence*, Ball, vol. III, 262.
36. Swift (Quilca) to Rev. Thomas Sheridan, 11 September 1725, *Correspondence*, Ball, vol. III, 267.
37. Swift, *An Answer to a Paper* (Dublin: S. Harding, 1728), 13.
38. Philip Percival (Dublin) to Viscount Percival, 30 January 1724, BL, Add 47030, f. 57v. My view in this paragraph echoes that of Ian McBride, *Eighteenth Century Ireland*, 296–98.
39. Timothy Godwin Bishop of Kilmore (Dublin) to Wake, 14 April 1722, CCL, 247/4.
40. Hugh Boulter to Newcastle, 12 October 1725, CCL, 172, unfoliated. On Delany's Tory commitments, see Ehrenpreis, *Swift*, vol. III, 86–88.
41. John Evans Bishop of Meath, to Wake, 7 February 1723, CCL, 247/54; John Pocklington (Collinstown) to Wake, 19 August 1725, CCL, 247/280.
42. Patrick Walsh, *The Making of the Irish Protestant Ascendancy: The Life of William Conolly, 1662–1729* (Woodbridge: Boydell Press, 2010), 158–59, 179; D. W. Hayton, "'Paltry Underlings of State'?," in *Politics and Literature*, ed. Rawson, 223.
43. "A Brief Account of Some Proceedings," 16 July 1719, CCL, 246/90; Philip Percival (Dublin) to Viscount Percival, 30 January 1724, BL, Add 47030, f. 57; Henry Downes Bishop of Elphin (Dublin) to Wake, 4 February 1724, CCL, 247/158; Philip Percival (Dublin) to Viscount Percival, 24 April 1724, BL, Add 47030, f. 64r; Henry Downes Bishop of Meath (Dublin) to Wake, 16 November 1725, CCL, 247/304; Philip Percival (Dublin) to Viscount Percival, 27 June 1727, BL, Add 47032, f. 25r.

44. Lord Midleton (Dublin) to Thomas Brodrick, 21 October 1723, Surrey History Centre, Midleton Papers 1248/5/323–324. I am grateful to David Hayton for allowing me access to the transcriptions of this material. The transcriptions on which I have relied are the work of Michael Page of the Surrey History Centre.
45. Midleton (Dublin) to Thomas Brodrick, 8 December 1723, SHC, Midleton Papers, 1248/5/339–340 (Page Transcription).
46. J. Pocklington to Wake, 21 October 1721, CCL, 246/290; Timothy Godwin Bishop of Kilmore (Dublin) to Wake, 24 January 1724, CCL, 247/152; Hayton, "Paltry Underlings of State," 232, 234–43; Walsh, *Making*, 170–77. Interestingly, David Bindon, who would later be counted among Conolly's supporters, championed Viscount Midleton as "the patriot" who "always consulted the good of the commonwealth" during the halfpence controversy. David Bindon, *Some Reasons Showing the Necessity the People of Ireland Are Under for Continuing to Refuse Mr. Wood's Coinage* (Dublin, 1724), 2.
47. Hugh Boulter to Newcastle, 28 October 1725, CCL, 172, unfoliated; Timothy Godwin (Dublin) to Wake, 28 October 1725, CCL, 247/297.
48. Quoted in, Davis, *The Drapier's Letters*, xc.
49. Swift, *A Letter to the Shop-Keepers*, March 1724, Davis, 5. Paul Langford devotes little space to Walpole's interest in Ireland in his otherwise illuminating essay, "Swift and Walpole," in *Politics and Literature*, ed. Rawson, 52–74.
50. Swift to Earl of Peterborough, 28 April 1726, *Correspondence*, Ball, vol. III, 308–9.
51. Swift, *Letter to the Whole People of Ireland*, October 1724, Davis, 81; Swift, *Letter to Lord Chancellor Middleton*, October 1724, Davis, 128.
52. Swift (London) to Thomas Tickell, 7 July 1726, *Correspondence*, Ball, vol. III, 314; Walsh, *Making*, 164; Toby Barnard, "A Tale of Three Sisters: Katherine Conolly of Castletown," in *Irish Protestant Descents and Ascents*, ed. Barnard (Dublin: Four Courts, 2004), 279–80. I am grateful to David Womersley for calling my attention to this letter.
53. James concluded that throughout the eighteenth century, British ministers were very well informed about Ireland: Francis Godwin James, *Ireland in the Empire, 1688–1770* (Cambridge: Harvard University Press, 1973), 295.

54. Trenchard, *Cato's Letters*, 8 December 1722, No. 106, 1748, vol. IV, 11–12.
55. Viscount Percival (Charlton) to Philip Percival, 8 December 1723, BL, Add 47030, f. 44v.
56. St. John Brodrick (London) to Midleton, 12–13 January 1724, SHC, Midleton Papers, 1248/5/356–357 (Page Transcript).
57. Thomas Brodrick to Midleton, 16 November 1723, SHC, Midleton Papers, 1248/5/335–336 (Page Transcript).
58. See, for example, Viscount Percival (Charlton) to Philip Percival, 28 July 1724, BL, Add 47030, f. 74v.
59. St. John Brodrick (London) to Midleton, 17 January 1724, SHC, Midleton Papers, 1248/5/360–361 (Page Transcript).
60. Martin Bladen (Dublin Castle) to Robert Walpole, 19 April 1716, CUL, CH(H) Correspondence 734. Bladen continued to correspond with Walpole throughout his time in office.
61. D. W. Hayton, "British Whig Ministers and the Irish Question 1714–1725," in *Hanoverian Britain and Empire*, ed. Stephen Taylor, Richard Connors, and Clyve Jones (Woodbridge: Boydell Press, 1998), 47; Walsh, *The Making*, 158.
62. Board of Trade, Report on the Plantation Trade, 8 September 1721, CUL, CH(H) 84/11.
63. D. W. Hayton, "Henry Maxwell, M.P.," *Eighteenth Century Ireland* 22 (2007): 35–37, 40; Walsh, *Making*, 123, 157.
64. Henry Maxwell (Dublin) to Robert Walpole, 3 April 1716, CUL, CH(H) Correspondence 724.
65. Henry Maxwell, *Proposals to Render the Possession of Gibraltar and Minorca more Useful to the Commerce of Britain*, 1723, 10.
66. Edward Harley to Abigail Harley, 3 March 1720, in Stephen Taylor and Clive Jones, eds., *Tory and Whig* (Woodbridge: Boydell Press, 1998), 227.
67. Maxwell, *Gibraltar and Minorca*, 1723, 11.
68. Ibid., 8.
69. Ibid., 10.
70. Ibid., 7, 11.
71. Ibid., 13.
72. Ibid., 9.
73. Ibid., 15.
74. Ibid., 23.

75. Henry Maxwell, *Reasons Offered for Erecting a Bank in Ireland*, 2nd ed. (Dublin: Aaron Rhames, 1721), 4.
76. Maxwell, *Gibraltar and Minorca*, 1723, Part II, 12.
77. Maxwell, *Gibraltar and Minorca*, 1723, 22. Hayton has emphasized that Maxwell's Irish situation made him less tolerant of dissent than British Whigs. Equally, he seems to have been rather more intolerant of Catholics than some. Hayton, "Maxwell," 32. See Maxwell (Dublin) to Walpole, 3 April 1716, CH(H) Correspondence 724.
78. William Nicolson (Dublin) to Wake, 1 September 1719, CCL, 246/104; Nicolson (Dublin) to Wake, 31 October 1719, CCL, 246/119; Nicolson to Wake, 21 October 1720, CCL, 246/288.
79. Hayton, "Paltry Underlings of State?," 235; Francis Hutchinson to Wake, June 1721, CCL, 246/251.
80. Arthur Dobbs, "A Scheme to Increase the Colonies and Commerce of Britain," n.d., CUL, CH(H) 84/68, dedication.
81. Maxwell, *Gibraltar and Minorca*, 1723, 23.
82. Arthur Dobbs, "A Scheme to Increase," CUL, CH(H) Papers 84/68, dedication, 4–5. Dobbs argued that Portugal was the first to seek a commercial empire.
83. John Trenchard and Thomas Gordon, *Cato's Letters*, 5th ed. (London: T. Woodward et al., 1748), 8 December 1722, No. 106, vol. IV, 4; 24 February 1722, No. 67, vol. II, 310. All subsequent references to *Cato's Letters* are to the 1748 edition. While Ian Higgins may be right to say that Swift was "parodying" Trenchard's imperialism, Trenchard was certainly not a "loyal" Whig in 1722: Higgins notes in *GT*, Rawson, 361.
84. Dummer, *A Defence*, 1721, 64.
85. Trenchard, *Cato's Letters*, 24 February 1722, No. 67, 1748, 307; 8 December 1722, No. 106, 1748, vol. IV, 6.
86. Jones, *The Present State of Virginia*, 1724, 112–13.
87. Ibid., 142.
88. Roderick Mackenzie (Spanish Town, Jamaica) to Captain Alex Gawne, 18 June 1712, Bodleian, Rawl. A312, ff. 82–83; Peter Beckford (Jamaica) to ?, 25 October 1713, Bodleian, Rawl A312, f. 105r.
89. *The Trade Granted to the South Sea Company* (London: Samuel Crouch, 1714), 8.

90. Trenchard, *Cato's Letters*, 24 February 1722, No. 67, 1748, vol. II, 306, 309–10.
91. James Knight, *The State of the Island of Jamaica* (London: H. Whitridge, 1726), 1. Knight was a great opponent of the Walpoleian South Sea Company in Jamaica: James Knight (London) to ?, 18 March 1726, BL, Add 22677, f. 1.
92. Dummer, *A Defence*. 1721, 64; *St. James's Journal*, December 1, 1722, No. 32, 190.
93. Jones, *The Present State of Virginia*, 1724, 145–46.
94. Trenchard, *Cato's Letters*, 8 December 1722, No. 106, 1748, vol. IV, 6, 10.
95. Memorandum Regarding Virginia, ca. 1720, Rhode House Library, SPG X182b, ff. 38–39; Jones, *Present State of Virginia*, 1724, 113.
96. James Knight (London) to ?, 18 March 1726, BL, Add 22677, f. 2r; Knight, *The State of the Island of Jamaica*, 1726, 28–29. This was also Yonge's argument for South Carolina.
97. Dummer, *A Defence*, 1721, 68.
98. Edward Synge (Dublin) to Wake, 21 October 1723, CCL, 247/106. See also Synge to Wake, 4 November 1723, CCL, 247/114.
99. Bindon, *Some Reasons*, 1724, 25.
100. William King (Dublin) to Wake, 18 January 1723, CCL, 247/49.
101. Knight, *State of the Island of Jamaica*, 1726, 8, 13. For the explosion of piracy after the War of Spanish Succession, see, for example, London Newsletter to Earl of Wigtown, 9 January 1722, Bodleian, MS Eng. Hist. c.1041/1, f. 4r.
102. James Knight (London) to ?, 18 March 1726, BL, Add 22677, f. 2r; Knight, *The State of the Island*, 1726, 4.
103. Dummer, *A Defence*, 1721, 78.
104. John Evan Bishop of Meath to Wake, 31 October 1719, CCL, 246/120; William King (Dublin) to Wake, 28 January 1724, CCL, 247/153.
105. William Nicolson (Londonderry) to Wake, 30 April 1721, CCL, 246/245; Nicolson (Dublin) to Wake, 28 October 1721, CCL, 246/292.
106. Trenchard, *Cato's Letters*, 8 December 1722, No. 106, 1748, vol. IV, 5. I am sceptical of the arguments advanced by James Kelly that there was no unionist sentiment in the early 1720s. His arguments seem to me to depend on a static, unchanging model of what union might

mean: see Kelly, "Public and Political Opinion in Ireland and the Idea of Anglo-Irish Union," in *Political Discourse in Seventeenth and Eighteenth-Century Ireland*, ed. D. George Boyce, Robert Eccleshall, and Vincent Geoghegan (Basingstoke: Palgrave, 2001), 120.

107. Hawes, "Three Times Round the Globe," 188.
108. William Nicolson (Dublin) to Wake, 31 October 1719, CCL, 246/119.
109. John Evans Bishop of Meath to Wake, 23 April 1720, CCL, 246/170.
110. J. Pocklington to Wake, 4 June 1720, CCL, 246/177; John Evans to Wake, 19 June 1720, CCL, 246/182.
111. John Evans to Wake, 28 May 1723, CCL, 247/77.
112. Hugh Boulter (Dublin) to Newcastle, 10 February 1726, CCL, 172, unfoliated.
113. Swift, *A Letter to ... Viscount Molesworth*, December 1724, Davis, 108.
114. Swift, *Letter to the Whole People of Ireland*, October 1724, Davis, 79.
115. Duchess of Ormond to Swift, 18 April 1720, *Correspondence*, Ball, vol. III, 49.
116. Paul V. Thompson and Dorothy Jay Thompson, eds., *The Account Books of Jonathan Swift* (Newark: University of Delaware Press, 1984), cxxi.
117. Thompson and Thompson, eds., *Account Books of Jonathan Swift*, 96.
118. John Arbuthnot (London) to Swift, 14 October 1718, *Correspondence*, Ball, vol. III, 17; Swift to Bolingbroke, 19 December 1719, *Correspondence*, Ball, vol. III, 40.
119. John Law, Vindication, ca. 1726, CUL, CH(H) Papers 82/3.
120. *Some Considerations of the Consequences of the French Settling Colonies on the Mississippi* (London: J. Roberts, 1720); Dummer, *A Defence*, 1721.
121. See also Swift's comments on the debt in his *History of the Last Four Years of the Queen* (London, 1753 [1713]).
122. [Jonathan Swift], *Subscribers to the Bank* (Dublin, John Harding, [1721]).
123. Swift, *A Letter to the Shop-Keepers*, March 1724, Davis 9.
124. Swift, *Humble Address to Both Houses of Parliament*, 1724, Davis, 164.
125. Swift, *Humble Address to Both Houses of Parliament*, 1724, Davis, 172. In case anyone missed the point of his ire, Swift had earlier poked fun at "squire Conolly": *A Letter to the Shop-Keepers*, March 1724, Davis, 8.

126. Jonathan Swift, *A Short View of the State of Ireland* (Dublin: S. Harding, 1727–1728), 4, 7.
127. Francis Atterbury, *English Advice to the Freeholders of England* (London, 1714), 4.
128. John Law, Vindication, ca. 1726, CUL, CH(H) Papers 52/3. Law also argued that for France's economic superiority on the basis that "France has the advantage over England by its climate, by its produce and by its situation." Based on this rigorously agrarian calculation, Law concluded that France's comparative advantage could be "reckoned to be as three to one."
129. Swift, *GT*, 1726, *GT*, Rawson, 207–8.
130. Swift, *GT*, 1726, *GT,* Rawson, 226.
131. Ibid., 275.
132. Ibid., 235.
133. See note 131 above.
134. Jonathan Swift, *A Proposal for the Universal Use of Irish Manufacture* (Dublin: E. Waters, 1720), 13.
135. Swift, *A Letter to Mr. Harding*, August 1724, Davis, 20; Swift, *Some Observations*, August 1724, Davis, 44; Swift, *A Short View of the State of Ireland*, 1728, 10.
136. Swift, *A Letter to Lord Chancellor Middleton*, October 1724, Davis, 124; Swift, *Some Observations*, August 1724, Davis, 40, 45, 51.
137. Swift, *Letter to the Whole People of Ireland*, October 1724, 78. My understanding of Swift's formulation of Anglo-Irish relations is close to that developed by Fabricant, "Swift the Irishman," 59–60. Our differences are over his attitude toward empire.
138. Swift (London) to Thomas Tickell, 7 July 1726, *Correspondence*, Ball, vol. III, 314.
139. Jeremy Black, *Crisis of Empire* (London: Continuum, 2008), 42.
140. Richard R. Johnson, "British North America, 1690–1748," in *The Eighteenth Century: Oxford History of the British Empire*, ed. P. J. Marshall (Oxford: Oxford University Press, 1998), 295. I am less happy with Johnson's insistence on "institutional stability" (p. 297) which seems to me only sustainable with a very narrow definition of institutions.
141. Stair to Duchess of Marlborough, November 1737, BL, Add 61467, ff. 3131–3134; Stair to Duchess of Marlborough, 11 March 1738, BL, Add 61467, f. 69–70. Stair had been ambassador to France 1715–1720.

Author Biography

Steve Pincus is Bradford Durfee Professor of History at Yale. Steve has published widely on seventeenth and eighteenth century British and British Imperial history, including *1688: The First Modern Revolution* and *The Heart of the Declaration: The Founders Case for Activist Government.* He is currently working on a history of the British Empire in the seventeenth and eighteenth centuries.

Commerce, not Conquest: Political Economic Thought in the French Indies Company, 1719–1769

John Shovlin

Late in 1752, the royal commissioner of the Compagnie des Indes, Étienne de Silhouette, wrote to the company's chief servant in India, Governor-General Joseph-François Dupleix, to tell him that the directors were impatient for peace. In the preceding years, Dupleix had led the company's forces in regional power struggles as an auxiliary of Indian rulers—wars in which Britain's East India Company (EIC) had taken the opposing side. In so doing, he had significantly expanded the territories and population the company controlled in India, but at the expense of its commerce and profits. This trade-off was not welcome in Paris. "Here," Silhouette wrote, "peace is generally preferred to conquests." Speaking for the directorate as a whole, he wrote: "We do not wish to become a political power in India; we want only a few establishments to aid and protect trade." So, he told Dupleix, "No more victories; no more conquests; plenty of merchandize, and some increase of the dividend."[1] These demands were, to some degree, a function of the particular circumstances in which the company found itself in the

J. Shovlin (✉)
New York University, New York, USA
e-mail: john.shovlin@nyu.edu

R. Fredona and S.A. Reinert (eds.), *New Perspectives on the History of Political Economy*, https://doi.org/10.1007/978-3-319-58247-4_6

early 1750s, but they were also the expression of a distinctive tradition of political economy prevalent in the company since its foundation in 1719 stressing the value of commerce over conquests.

That the Compagnie des Indes should have fostered the development of particular forms of political economic thought is unsurprising. Its rival, the English East India Company (EIC), was the site of innovative political speculation and argument throughout the seventeenth and eighteenth centuries.[2] Corporations, such as the EIC, could make claims to the loyalty of "subjects" and develop languages and practices of governance in ways analogous to states. Indeed, given the many sovereign functions the company exercised east of the Cape of Good Hope, it is to be expected that it would behave and be seen in political terms. The argument I make here concerning the French company is different. It was less like a state than its English rival, more fully subordinate to its home government, and less the object of potential political allegiance. Where it was most fully analogous to the EIC was in its international presence and personality: it sustained a regular body of troops and its own navy (something the EIC lacked); it built and garrisoned fortresses; fought wars; and conducted regular diplomatic relations with Asian powers and with competing companies. It was thus an international actor in its own right, if a minor one, and constantly exposed to the pressures and pulls of global politics. It was against this background that its distinctive tradition of political economic and strategic thinking developed.

This tradition was a species of a broader genus of political economic argument emphasizing that an age of conquest was giving way to an age of commerce, that the foundations of power were increasingly economic, and that economic capacity might be to some degree incompatible with the military spirit. If the power of states had once been based on military virtue and expressed through the extension of control over territory and populations, it was increasingly founded on trade and on the ability to master the "arts of peace." In the words of Daniel Defoe, "Peace and Trade have so far got the Start of War and the Sword that the *Trading Nations* of the World are now become infinitely superior in Wealth and Power, to those who might properly be call'd the *Fighting Nations*, and whose Grandure [sic] depended on the Extent of their Dominions, and number of conquer'd Countries."[3] Claims of this sort were ubiquitous in European political economy during the age of Enlightenment. In a seventeenth-century context, they can be read as a reflex of the Dutch Republic's success in throwing off the dominion of the Spanish Empire and emerging as a great power in its own right. In the eighteenth century, such pronouncements also reflected the perceived failure of Louis XIV to extend his "universal monarchy" in the face of Dutch and English resistance, and the sudden emergence of commercial Britain as a major factor in European power politics.

Of course, there were deep ambiguities in this perspective, as almost every commentator recognized. Was the rise of the Dutch only based on commerce, or did it follow from a kind of bastard of trade and war, as the Asian and American conquests of the Dutch East and West India companies might suggest? Did not England's commercial success follow, to some degree, from its role as a conqueror in Ireland and the New World, and from its dominance of the high seas, which secured its commercial access to the Spanish Empire at the Treaty of Utrecht (1713)? Even Louis XIV, on reflection, was an ambiguous case. If the Sun King's lust for conquest had been his undoing, in more lucid moments he "saw plainly that the way to make the *French* Nation the Terror of the World, was not so much by the Success of his Arms, and his Conquests upon his Neighbours, as by encouraging the Commerce of his own Country." This design his able finance minister Jean-Baptiste Colbert went a long way toward realizing.[4] Even perfectly peaceful economic development might eventually threaten the security and independence of other states if this process produced an economic hegemon capable of "giving the law" to weaker competitors.[5] What was at issue, then, was a wide consensus on the notion that commerce had displaced conquest, territoriality, and war, and an equally broad disagreement on the precise content and practical implications of such a proposition.

The variant of this line of thinking fostered within the Compagnie des Indes was composed of two distinct strands, a dualism which followed from the bifurcated character of the company itself—part commercial and colonial venture, part pillar of Paris finance. One strand emphasized that the company's interests were best served by a climate of international stability and the avoidance of war and territorial expansion in India. To be sure, this perspective was always contested, at times by some of the company's servants in Asia and at other moments by metropolitan interests, yet it remained the dominant perspective within the organization, especially among the directors and shareholders. The second strand emanated from John Law, the founder of the company, and while it cannot be seen as an official position of the organization any time after his disgrace in 1720, it was a line of thinking to which many directors and major shareholders were sympathetic. This version of the commerce not conquest theme delineated a strategy for peaceful French aggrandizement through the adoption of modernized techniques of public credit. The land, population, and labor of the national territory were to be set in motion by a reorganization of public credit which would create a new money, or monetary equivalent, to supplement the existing money supply. Monetary stimulus would be the herald of prosperity and rapid economic growth.

The striking feature of both strands is the ambivalence about empire they express. War, conquest, and territorial control were seen to be incompatible, to some degree, with commerce. They ate up profit or fostered conditions of instability in which trade could not thrive. The French company was grappling with a distinctive feature of all the great chartered trading companies and arguably the hallmark of early modern European colonialism *tout court*: the bundling of commercial functions with sovereign agency, especially the provision of security. The Compagnie des Indes repeatedly ran up against the limits of this strategy, the potential incompatibility between profit making and the provision of a political framework in which trade could be safely continued. Leaders of the company thought creatively about how this problem could be solved outside the framework of formal empire, on the one hand, or free trade on the other. Its preferred solution in the early 1750s was a security cartel with the EIC, though this proved unattainable. What the company was groping toward by the end of the 1760s, when its trade was suspended, was a functional separation of politics and economics, with sovereign functions to be hived off to the French state.

The second strand of thinking, derived from John Law, with its emphasis on using monetary stimulus to set underutilized labor and land into productive use, was even more reluctant in its embrace of empire. It was the national territory and population, principally, which were to be set in motion; colonies were to play only a modest role in this ambitious scheme for economic development, and, in theory, they could be dispensed with altogether. This strand should be read as an effort to grapple with the problem of French geopolitical disadvantage faced with a British rival enjoying both naval superiority and a significant edge in the organization of its public finances. The Law strategy met the latter problem head-on by offering to bring about in France the kind of financial revolution that had installed a modern system of public credit in Britain in the decades after 1688.[6] The monetary expansion that would accompany the establishment of modern public credit would make it possible to take advantage for the first time of France's huge advantage over Britain in population and territory. Once its unexploited domestic resources were mobilized and thrown into the power-political scale, imperial competition would become a sideshow, and Britain's naval advantage would be neutralized.

The essay begins with a discussion of the geopolitical vision of John Law, the source of the company's distinctive tradition of thinking about public credit. The following section explores political economic perspectives nurtured within, or on the margins of, the company in the 1720s and 1730s, after Law's fall. Here, the focus is on the political economy of Jean-François Melon, Law's former secretary and the author of the most successful and influential work of French political economy published in the 1730s, the *Essai politique sur le commerce*. The next section deals with the geopolitical outlook of the company from the 1720s through the 1750s, focusing on an effort in 1753 to create a treaty committing the Compagnie des Indes and the East India Company to ending their military struggles in Asia and neutralizing the whole zone east of the Cape of Good Hope in the case of a future European war. The final section explores the place of commerce, not conquest thinking in the 1760s, a decade which saw a brief renaissance of the company, and then the suspension of its exclusive privilege in 1769.

Ideological Foundations: John Law's Geopolitics

The geopolitical and political economic vision of John Law was critical to the subsequent ideological trajectory of the company. From him came the idea of mounting a financial revolution to emulate and surpass Britain's public credit; the creation of a new monetary medium to bring underutilized economic resources into productive use; and the notion that a stable and peaceable international order would best foster French aggrandizement, with a special imperative to reach accommodation with the British rival. The son of an Edinburgh banker, Law fled England in 1694 after killing a man in a duel and for most of the next two decades resided abroad, making a living as a speculator and developing theories about the power of paper money to stimulate economic growth. In the aftermath of the War of the Spanish Succession, he convinced the Duke of Orléans, regent for the minor Louis XV, that he could solve France's problems of public insolvency and economic depression by transforming the system of public credit and introducing paper currency. Orléans authorized Law to establish a joint-stock bank in 1716 to discount commercial paper and to issue notes backed by specie. In 1717, Law founded the Compagnie d'Occident (familiarly known as the Mississippi Company) to revivify a failing French Louisiana. Modeled on Britain's South Sea Company, it doubled as a scheme to restore public credit by absorbing unfunded royal debt in exchange for shares. Law merged this enterprise with the other chartered trading companies, the royal mint, the tax farms, and his bank in 1719, naming the new combine the Compagnie des Indes, and moving to absorb the whole public debt in a debt for equity swap.[7]

Law's System was intended to renew France as a great power, indeed to make France hegemonic in Europe. Commerce, not conquests, would be the basis of French revival. "It is on an extensive trade, on the number and wealth of inhabitants," Law argued, "that the power of France must be based." He claimed that the new monetary and public finance system he was establishing would allow France to supplant Britain as Europe's premier economic power. "This great kingdom, well governed," he claimed, "would be the arbiter of Europe without having to use force." Other powers would shrink from forming coalitions against it; instead, they would look to France for their own security.[8] While Law envisioned the complete overthrow of the balance of power, this was not Louis XIV's universal monarchy by another name, he insisted. France would "command other nations without dominating them and give them the law without usurping anything of their rights ... qualities ... much more glorious than the vain title of a universal monarchy."[9] A Europe of independent states would persist, stabilized by the overwhelming predominance of France.

The basis for this transformation lay in increasing the size and altering the composition of the French money supply. The paper currency issued by Law's bank, together with the shares of his companies, which he regarded as functional equivalents of money, would augment the existing circulation of money and drive down interest rates. Law held that unemployment and an underutilization of economic resources were caused by an inadequate supply of money, and that increasing the size of the money supply in conditions of economic depression would set underutilized resources in motion and stimulate prosperity.[10] An abundance of money "would put France in a position to do all the trade of Europe, and would render this great kingdom cultivated like Holland, full of towns, villages and people; it would restore navigation and the navy. Millions of people who are currently a charge to the state would find work and would earn a living agreeably; they would come here from every country in Europe, and the lands of France would be brought to produce double what they produce at present. This product would be manufactured in the country and transported abroad on French vessels."[11]

Law claimed that an earlier transformation of international order brought about by the exploitation of the Indies was being superseded in his own day by a second geopolitical revolution associated with the adoption of modern institutions of public credit. In the sixteenth and seventeenth centuries, the expansion of European trade had brought about a radical redistribution of power by increasing the relative weight of commercial states. But this earlier shift was overshadowed by the recent development of British public credit. Credit was more powerful than trade as a stimulus to prosperity, Law claimed.[12] The introduction of new forms of paper credit in France "would augment the quantity of money more in a year that an advantageous commerce could in ten."[13] What Law meant is that while a positive balance of trade could, over time, draw specie into a country, and augment the money stock, the same effect could be achieved much more rapidly by the adoption of substitutes such as paper money or by company shares which could function as money.

Law's political economic vision—his version of the commerce, not conquest thesis—can be contrasted with others available in the same period. The idea that territorial acquisitions should be avoided and the full exploitation of economic resources pursued instead was a precept of the leading French critic of Louis XIV's foreign policy, Archbishop François Fénelon. Fénelon distinguished power based on territory and military resources from power based on economic foundations, arguing that "one cannot too much seek out this latter superiority, nor more avoid the former kind, which has only a false brilliance."[14] Unlike Law, however, he believed that only a balance of power could serve as a legitimate foundation for European international politics. Moreover, he criticized the policies of Colbert which, he argued, had engendered conflict abroad and luxury at home. Law's vision of French economic flourishing based on thriving manufacturing and trade, by contrast, was firmly in the tradition of Colbert, as was the deeply agonistic conception of commerce and finance that was at the heart of his vision. Law's position diverged even further from that of the abbé de Saint-Pierre, whose *Projet pour rendre la paix perpétuelle en Europe* caused such a stir when it was first published in 1713. While Saint-Pierre was a critic of the balance of power, which he believed produced endless wars, he saw European confederation, not French hegemony, as the means to stabilize European politics.[15]

Law's position can also be contrasted with those of Sir William Petty and Charles Davenant; indeed, his vision should be seen, in some respects, as a critique of theirs. Both Petty and Davenant offered versions of the commerce not conquest thesis. Petty claimed it was "a mistake, that the greatness and glory of a Prince lyeth rather in the extent of his Territory, then [sic] in the number, art, and industry of his people, well united and governed."[16] Davenant warned "what ill consequence it is to grasp at an extended but a barren dominion," suggesting it might be worthwhile to contract Britain's American population into a handful of the most productive provinces, abandoning the rest.[17] Both argued that the ability to undersell foreign rivals was the key to augmenting the wealth and increasing the power of the nation. Both also claimed—and here Law sharply disagreed—that France was incapable of challenging Britain and Holland economically. The central thrust of Petty's *Political Arithmetick* was that a small country, like Holland, could by its situation, trade, and policy be equivalent in wealth and strength to a far larger people living on a much larger territory.[18] Davenant concurred. Drawing on Petty, he argued that "neither the genius of the [French] nation, their site nor ports will allow them the same success ... as has attended the English and the Dutch, more skilful [sic] in trade and in sea-matters."[19] By contrast, Law argued that the French kingdom's abundance of land and population advantaged it in the struggle for wealth and power. With an adequate money supply, and better economic direction, there was no reason why France should not be "cultivated like Holland," and, if it were, it would overshadow Holland and England.

Exactly what role empire was to play in this vision of the French future was ambiguous. On the other hand, Law's Compagnie des Indes was one of the greatest colonial ventures of its day and made a serious bid to reinvigorate France's flagging commercial empire. Millions were spent buying or fitting out ships for colonial and international trade, sending specie and merchandise to Asia, reorganizing factories in Bengal, and sending colonists to Mauritius and Louisiana.[20] Yet, in his own writings, Law said little about colonies. Public credit and paper money rather than empire were at the heart of his thinking. The initiative to revivify Louisiana did not come from Law but from French financial circles, and it was only Law's grandiose claims for the potential of the enterprise to soak up unfunded debt which won him leadership of the group that launched the so-called Mississippi Company in 1717.[21] Law always saw the metropolitan assets of his company—its control of the mint and the tobacco farm, for example—as much more valuable in financial terms than its more speculative colonial assets.[22] He flatly rejected the conception of informal empire in Spanish America associated with Louis XIV's foreign policy. The Spanish Empire was irrelevant to France's future as a great power, he argued.[23] Once silver and gold currencies were supplemented or replaced by paper money, France's dependence on Spanish silver would be greatly reduced.

Given the accent on domestic economic development rather than colonies, the rejection of Louis XIV's foreign policy, and the devaluing of Spain's empire, Law's political economy was conducive to a more amicable Franco-British relationship. Law also believed that a Franco-British political entente would create the best framework to foster his ambitious projects of commercial and financial regeneration. He was persistently concerned that British or Dutch competitors would launch a financial attack on his System in its early vulnerable stages, and he hoped a close political relationship with Britain would ward off such a threat. For these reasons, he became a key supporter of the French alliance with Britain, negotiated by his ally the abbé Guillaume Dubois in 1716–1717. "I know how much he was concerned in the treaty that was to affirm our union," Lord Stanhope later remarked to Dubois, "and that he regarded the union of the two crowns as the foundation of his schemes."[24]

There is no doubt that Law continued to see Britain as the great rival of France, but the terrain on which he envisioned his adoptive country successfully fighting and beating the British was economic. A key dimension of this struggle would be a battle between Law's Compagnie des Indes and Britain's South Sea Company. Law interpreted the South Sea bubble in Britain as an effort to destroy his System by draining mobile international capital away from Paris where it was needed to sustain share prices. British diplomats became convinced that Law intended to strike back by mounting a raid on London capital markets intended to spark a market panic and discredit British financial institutions.[25] In the event, no such attack materialized and both the South Sea bubble and Law's System collapsed under their own weight in the latter half of 1720, but the legacy of Law's thinking in France, and especially within the Compagnie des Indes, would be significant.[26]

Law's Ideological Legacy

After Law was disgraced and exiled late in 1720, his System, including the Compagnie des Indes, was taken over and reorganized by his political enemies. Yet many associated with the company continued to be sympathetic to Law's ideas.[27] The principal shareholders of the company from the 1720s through the 1740s were mostly great "Mississippians," who had made fortunes in Law's System and who might be disposed to appreciate its virtues. In the overlapping social circles of Abraham Peyrenc de Moras and the comtesse de Verrue, memoranda written by Law were preserved and circulated, while new schemes for the reform of public credit, and its use as an instrument of geopolitical struggle, were devised and shared. A singular advantage of the Compagnie des Indes' organization as a joint-stock enterprise, wrote an anonymous memorialist in 1724, was that its shares functioned to augment the money supply, stimulating prosperity. With an adequate monetary medium, France would be far wealthier than the English or the Dutch who did not enjoy the same natural advantages and whose wealth was based in part on a credit that was overextended.[28] A memorandum composed in 1726 went further: the artificial prosperity of the Dutch and British economies would collapse once a revived Compagnie des Indes undermined their East India trades and discredited the shares of the EIC and the Dutch East India Company (VOC), which functioned as money there. "Is there a war, be it ever so successful," asked the writer, "which could be so advantageous to us, and do so much harm to them, without shedding so much as a drop of blood?"[29] Another scheme for aggrandizing France via financial means was elaborated by Arnaud de Silhouette, father of the future royal commissioner of the company and himself a major shareholder. Silhouette *père* proposed that the company be recapitalized and expanded, and that it be given the privileges of a General Bank. "It is evident," he wrote, "that this public credit will give us a superiority over our neighbors which will make them shudder."[30]

The most sophisticated and influential articulation of this line of thinking was developed by Jean-François Melon, a former employee of the Compagnie des Indes and Law's one-time secretary. Melon had worked unsuccessfully to bring his former employer back to France in the early 1720s. He was active in the internal politics of the Compagnie des Indes in this period and made an unsuccessful bid to become a director.[31] He was also closely tied to the social circle of one of the great Mississippians, Madame de Verrue. Melon developed his political economic perspective in a series of unpublished memoranda dating to the mid-1720s and systematized his thinking in the *Essai politique sur le commerce* (1734). Like Law, he viewed a modernized public credit as critical to the restoration of French power. He was consulted in 1723 on a scheme to have the Compagnie des Indes issue 150 million livres worth of circulating credit instruments intended to supplement the money supply.[32] In memoranda composed in the mid-1720s, he represented shares of the company as playing the role of credit currency without entailing the dangers or inconveniences of a true paper money backed by the Crown.[33] In the *Essai* he was more bold, arguing that public debts if they took the form of a circulating medium could function as money, and that the best way to cause such paper money to circulate in private transactions was to make it the medium of payment for taxes. For Melon, as for Law, the function of such additions to the money supply was to stimulate the real economy, to bring underutilized labor and assets into production by pushing down interest rates.[34]

In addition to such monetary stimulus, Melon's strategy for French economic regeneration entailed fostering agricultural prosperity by liberalizing the grain trade, encouraging manufacturing, especially by promoting mechanization, and expanding the consumption of ordinary people. This strategy had a place for colonies and international trade, but a relatively modest one. Melon rejected the Spanish model of territorial conquest and subjection of subordinate peoples, which he believed had weakened Spain. Russia owed its recent increase in power not to the subjection of Siberia and Tartary but to the progress of commerce. Melon favored what he regarded as the Dutch imperial model: the establishment of *comptoirs* with a small garrison force; no working of the land; and minimal transfer of European populations. Yet, he recognized the benefits of plantation colonies, praised the pattern on which the British colonies in America had evolved, and saw great potential in the French territory of Louisiana. In the end, however, his development strategy, like Law's, was focused on the potential of economic assets closer to home. It is striking that he finished his short chapter on colonies with an exhortation to steer national energies into domestic projects of improvement: "To clear new land is to conquer new countries without causing misery," he argued. "The Landes between Bordeaux and Bayonne are twenty leagues across. The legislator who would people them would render a greater service to the state than he who by a murderous war would seize the same extent of territory; but he would not have such a brilliant glory in the eyes of the vulgar, because it would be acquired without military peril, without losing a citizen, and without attracting the jealousy of one's neighbors."[35]

As this last quotation suggests, Melon echoed Law's view that peace not war best served French interests, and that the means to French security and power lay in peaceful economic growth. Melon had participated in the abbé Dubois's pacific diplomacy before joining Law in the Compagnie des Indes. He published the *Essai politique sur le commerce* on the cusp of French entry into the War of Polish Succession, most likely as a warning against any return to the adventurous foreign policy of Louis XIV. He famously claimed that "the spirit of conquest and the spirit of commerce are mutually exclusive in a nation," a remark that has been interpreted to mean that trade naturally functions to pacify international relations through the civilizing action of "le doux commerce."[36] In fact, as John Robertson points out, "Melon's point was that commerce was a better instrument of national aggrandizement than war and conquest."[37] Another former employee of the Compagnie des Indes, and lieutenant of Law, Nicolas Dutot, put the idea in a more forceful and aggressive way when he wrote: "To make peace in order to reap all the advantages of a great trade is to make war on our enemies .... An end to those victories won by ruinous efforts.... France, superior by the advantages of her trade will make known to neighboring states that she is as capable of increasing her power by peace as by war."[38] Dutot believed that a reform of public credit to augment the size of the money supply was critical to the economic regeneration of the kingdom. He wrote perhaps the most influential eighteenth-century apology for Law's System, noting that Law's bank stimulated economic activity of all sorts and regenerated the country to the point that it "alarmed our neighbors."[39]

Dutot's emphasis on commerce rather than conquest convinced Étienne de Silhouette, who would later serve as commissioner of the Indies Company. Shortly after the publication of Dutot's book, Silhouette wrote to cardinal Fleury promoting the geostrategy outlined there, telling the cardinal that the English feared the pacific projects of the French more than their military ones because "it is in fact more by the arts of peace than by those of war that France is in a state to ruin this rival and enemy nation." British trade, the foundation of its power, could not be destroyed by war—their navy was too powerful—but it could be ruined by peaceful competition. Referring to the branches of trade in which Britain was dominant, Silhouette stated: "There, my lord, are the kingdoms and the provinces it would be necessary to conquer from these islanders; each branch of trade is for them a fort, a citadel, impregnable by force and by armies, easy to take by industry and economy."[40] Silhouette restated this position in a celebrated memorandum written in 1747 which won him a position in the French ministry as an expert on Britain and on Anglo-French relations.[41] A few years later, he was to put the theory into practice in attempting to check Dupleix's expansionary policy in India.

Yet Silhouette's views mark a departure from the political economy represented by Dutot, Melon, and Law. He placed colonies, especially France's American colonies, at the center of his vision of French economic renewal. His views on public credit were ambiguous. When he was appointed Controller-General in March 1759, it was widely expected that he would introduce some kind of paper money scheme.[42] He was the son of a projector in the mold of John Law, and he was also close to François Véron de Forbonnais, the most influential exponent of a modernized public credit in the 1750s.[43] Forbonnais proposed to establish an institution in France analogous to the Bank of England, which would expand the money supply by issuing notes, lend money to the Crown at a moderate rate of interest, and consolidate the existing debt in whole or in part. Stimulated by an expanding money supply, economic activity would thrive, easing the burdens of taxation. Forbonnais expressly conceived of this scheme as a means to destroy the foundations of British public credit: foreigners would withdraw their funds from Britain and Holland, striking "a furious blow at the credit and trade of these two states."[44] But if Forbonnais was an advocate of paper money, his ally Silhouette resisted it as Controller-General, believing that, in the economic and political conditions of 1759, it would fall into discredit.[45] On the other hand, Silhouette enacted a scheme to sell shares in the future profits of the *Fermiers Généraux* and planned an operation to consolidate unfunded debt with echoes of the South Sea Company.[46]

Both Silhouette and Forbonnais were anxious to avert the war that broke out between France and Britain in 1755. Silhouette was the central figure in French diplomatic efforts to achieve an accommodation with Britain over tensions in India and America in the 1750s. As royal commissioner of the Indies Company, he led efforts to negotiate a treaty with the British company to end the military struggles between the two entities in India—a topic to which we will return in the following section. He was simultaneously one of the two French commissioners appointed to resolve frictions in North America over French and British territorial claims there. While Silhouette's tactics were often counterproductive in this role, there can be no doubt of his desire to avoid a war.[47] This perspective was shared by Forbonnais. While recognizing the economic value of France's colonies, he argued that war with Britain must be avoided even at the cost of national honor. In his view, the kingdom was not prepared economically or financially for a conflict and to enter a war in this situation would be reckless.[48]

The Geopolitics of the Compagnie des Indes

This preference for peace resonated with the dominant geopolitical outlook in the Compagnie des Indes in the 1750s, indeed, in almost the whole post-Law era. In the early 1720s, the company had conducted brief and costly military campaigns to eject Dutch interlopers from its holdings in West Africa and to establish a pepper factory at Mahé in India, but it settled subsequently into more or less peaceful and stable relations with the VOC and the EIC.[49] Its ties with the English company might even be described as cooperative at points in the 1730s.[50] The long Franco-British peace of the 1720s and 1730s was good for the company: the volume of its shipping and trade greatly expanded; profits and share prices rose. But this progress came to a halt with the War of Austrian Succession (1741–1748). The company suffered major shipping losses; its trade largely dried up; shareholders had to recapitalize the company; and dividends went unpaid, leading to a revolt of the shareholders in 1745 and a reorganization of the direction.[51] Such events powerfully reinforced the dominant perception in the company that war had to be avoided in India and in Europe. Only in conditions of international stability—and particularly of peace with Britain—could the company be run profitably.

Alas for the shareholders and directors, the 1748 Peace of Aix-la-Chapelle did not end the tensions and military clashes between the two companies in India. While the French returned Madras, seized in the course of the war, elsewhere on the Coromandel Coast and in the Deccan, both companies became embroiled in Indian succession struggles as auxiliaries of competing factions. The French Governor-General, Joseph-François Dupleix, had come to see matters very differently than the men in Paris. Struggling since the early 1740s to meet the challenges of managing the company's operations in India in the face of local political instability, global war, and conflict with the English company, he developed a radical alternative to the mainstream geopolitics of the company. No company could expect to be able to finance its operations in the long run on the basis of trade alone, he argued. The key to commercial success was to secure control over a tax base in India, which a small number of soldiers would be adequate to secure, and which could be used to buy Indian goods for shipment to Europe. This territorial strategy would have the additional benefit of ending the outflow of precious metals from France used to purchase East India goods.[52] To secure the necessary concessions from Indian powers, Dupleix entered more completely than any of his predecessors into South Asian politics, committing the forces and the money of the company to building the political support necessary for the realization of his politico-fiscal schemes.[53]

From 1751, however, there was growing disquiet among shareholders in Paris at the direction Dupleix was taking the company.

Representative was the complaint of syndic Joseph-Philippe Narcis that the bullion sent to India to purchase merchandize was being diverted to military spending. He estimated that the policies of Dupleix had already cost the shareholders 100 million livres. Following a couple of good postwar years, the customary dividend of 150 livres had for several years been canceled or reduced.[54] The travails of the company could be read in the decline of share values. After a sharp rise in the value of company stock in the three years following the War of Austrian Succession, erosion followed from 1751. In the prevailing conditions of uncertainty, rumors of developments in India, whether founded or unfounded, could lead to sharp fluctuations in the share price. Hostilities in India might even lead to war in Europe, a war for which France was unprepared, and which would be devastating for the company. Could Dupleix be unaware, asked one director, of "the public outcry against a company of merchants which dares ... to abandon its trade to give itself over to a spirit of conquest, and does not fear to provoke a rupture with our neighbors?"[55]

Even more than the fortunes of the shareholders, those of the directors were tied to conditions of international stability. In addition to their perquisites and dividends, the directors profited from the company as a platform to facilitate a lucrative private trade. François Castanier shipped merchandize to Spanish America and sent the piasters he earned to Acapulco and from thence to China where they were converted into gold and shipped back to Europe using company vessels.[56] The profits Castanier realized from these arbitrage operations contributed to making him one of the richest merchants in Europe (at his death in 1759, he left a fortune of 40 million livres). There is some evidence that Pierre Duvelaer and Gabriel Michel engaged in similar dealings, on occasion using connections in the English company to move specie back to Europe.[57] Taking advantage of rights the Compagnie des Indes held to exploit the slave trade, a number of the directors, syndics, and royal commissioners were also involved in the two largest French slaving ventures of the period, the Angola Company and the Guinea Company.[58] War was not conducive to the profitability of any of these enterprises.

These pressures gave rise to creative thinking within the company on the means to reconcile commerce and security in the long run. One of the syndics, Pierre-Claude Delaître, suggested in the summer of 1752 that a treaty be made with the English company to recast the relationship between the two entities. Delaître called for an end to the war between the companies; it imposed crushing financial burdens on the Compagnie des Indes and had ruined its trade. The division between the French and the English exposed both to harassment by Indian rulers. Their cooperation with these princes risked disseminating European military discipline and technology in India, which, in time, could prove dangerous. Moreover, the disunion of the companies favored the establishment of other European enterprises in India and exposed both companies to being exploited by their own servants, who pursued their political and financial ambitions at company expense.

Delaître proposed to resolve these problems by an accord between the two companies. They should agree to a permanent division of settlements in India and then guarantee the possessions of the rival company. They should disengage from the wars of Indian rulers. If war broke out in Europe, the two companies should remain neutral, and their possessions should be exempt from attack. Both should enjoy freedom to trade in all parts of India not directly the possession or jurisdiction of the other.[59]

This position found favor with Étienne de Silhouette.[60] Appointed in 1751 to represent the Crown's interest in the company, Silhouette quickly placed himself at the head of the anti-Dupleix faction. As already noted, he was already disposed toward avoiding war in the interest of fostering the long-term aggrandizement of French power. His political superior, Controller-General Jean-Baptiste Machault d'Arnouville, also ardently wanted peace. His policy was one of financial reform and retrenchment, and for this, the avoidance of war was essential. Moreover, Silhouette was alarmed at the company's financial state. It would need huge new loans if it was to be placed on a stable footing, and these would be difficult to raise while dividends and share prices were sinking. Thus, Silhouette and Machault responded enthusiastically when, in February 1753, the chairman of the EIC, William Baker, approached the Compagnie des Indes in search of an accommodation in India.[61] "One cannot desire too much the end of the troubles in India," the Controller-General wrote, "All the Company is of the same sentiment, and if that of England thinks likewise, I hope that these first overtures will be followed by a happy success."[62]

One of the directors, Pierre Duvelaer, was sent to London to open negotiations with the EIC.[63] The proposals of Delaître were to form the basis for the company's negotiating position. The talks turned on two central issues: fixing the recognized rights and jurisdictions of the two companies in India and creating a neutrality agreement in the event of a future European war. Both issues proved thorny. While the English company favored the idea of neutralizing the Indian Ocean in case of future Franco-British wars, the British government was very reluctant to tie its hands in this fashion.[64] Reaching agreement on a permanent division of rights and territories in India was even more difficult. Ultimately, after eighteen months of talks, the best that could be achieved was an anodyne declaration on the part of the two companies that they were "commercial" organizations, not "warlike or conquering" ones.[65] A more substantive agreement was reached in India, at least in the short run. The French company sent director Charles Godeheu to Pondichéry to replace Dupleix and to negotiate a truce with the servants of the English company. When he arrived late in 1754, he quickly made a treaty embodying much of the substance of Delaître's proposals. Under the agreement, troops of the two companies agreed not to act against one another either as principals or as auxiliaries of country powers. Trade was declared "free throughout the Karnatick and in all the Countries to the Northward of the Choromandel Coast for the two contracting Nations, they may fetch Merchandizes from all the Places in the dependence of each other and transport them freely without any Restraint through the respective Jageers and Territories." The two companies entered into a defensive alliance to repel all potential enemies, and they promised to guarantee each other's possessions.[66] The agreement, however, quickly became a dead letter. France and Britain were moving toward war in America, and with the failure of the company talks in London, the local agreement in India could not be expected to last.

With limited capacity to reinforce its position in North America, the French government decided to launch a diversionary attack on the British in India, and, to this end, a new force was sent to the

Indian Ocean under the leadership of Thomas Arthur Lally, comte de Tollendal, with orders to defend the settlements of the Compagnie des Indes and attack those of the English. Despite this aggressive mission, Lally-Tollendal's expedition should not be regarded as a complete reversal of policy for the company, much less a return to the strategy of Dupleix. The general was expressly ordered not to pursue the same kind of expansionism as the former governor-general but to limit his conquests "to commercial establishments on the coast and to a circumscribed territory around these establishments." Under no circumstances was he to hold onto the factories taken from the English, but rather to evacuate and destroy them. He was ordered to abstain entirely from Indian political struggles and was placed on his guard against the former lieutenants of Dupleix still serving in India who might try to drag him into local struggles.[67] In the event, these warnings were to no avail. The appearance of an English squadron off Madras in February 1759 broke Lally-Tollendal's siege of the city. Reinforced by EIC forces fresh from victories in Bengal, the English attacked Pondichéry late in 1760 and the French were forced to capitulate after a five-month siege. The Indian theater of the Seven Years' War ended in a complete English triumph.

Commerce and Conquest in the Final Years of the Company

At the end of the Seven Years' War, the future of the company was in doubt. The peace settlement in 1763 left open the possibility of a renewal of trade. The gains of Dupleix were forfeited, but all territories the French had held at the beginning of 1749 were restored to the company, though with restrictions on fortification and garrisoning in the Bengal *comptoirs*. Yet the war years had been devastating physically and financially. The fortifications of Pondichéry had been demolished; trade had ceased for several years; and the company had run up huge new debts. There was a debate in 1763 and 1764 about the future of the enterprise, with one faction pushing for liquidation on reasonable terms and another, led by Jacques Necker, calling for a recapitalization of the company, the preservation of its monopoly, and a renewal of its trade.

In the short term, Necker prevailed. But beginning in 1767 a new financial and political crisis began to develop which would ultimately be resolved in 1769 with the suspension of the company's privilege and the opening of Asian trade to all French merchants. These tumultuous years saw the recrudescence of the Law–Melon–Dutot line of thinking in the form of a proposal to abandon the company's trade monopoly and reorganize it as a discount bank (*caisse d'escompte*), to issue notes, lower interest rates, and to catalyze commercial and agricultural prosperity. More immediately, the postwar period produced fresh thinking on the means to balance the security needs of the company with the imperative of profitability.

The failure or rejection of the various political strategies pursued by the company in the 1750s and 1760s to meet the challenges of Indian politics and British geopolitical competition left open the question of what formula would best serve the company and France in the future. The uncertainties of the moment are expressed in *Le politique indien*, the work of the abbé Roubaud, a leading comparative student of empire and physiocratic sympathizer. Roubaud was highly critical of the company's efforts to negotiate with the EIC in the 1750s. It was absurd to think that such agreements could hold, even if made in good faith. Roubaud was especially critical of Godeheu whom he blamed for conceding too much to the British in his search for an accommodation. Lally-Tollendal came off even worse, savaged for his insouciance and his ignorance of Indian politics. In Roubaud's view, successful negotiation with Indian powers was the key to commercial success. Dupleix had been right to insinuate himself into the diplomatic and courtly culture of India, to take on Indian titles, and adopt Indian splendor—as his rival Robert Clive of the EIC would do in Bengal. But companies were ill-designed to bear the burdens of conquest and sovereignty, in Roubaud's view. In the business of profit making, they could not patiently await the outcome of a war with no means to pay dividends or service debts. In effect, Roubaud was suggesting that the business of carving out a territorial empire in India was an activity for states not companies. Companies were better off without fortifications and troops, which ate up the profits of trade, and which inevitably drew mercantile enterprises into local political struggles. Moreover, it was possible to conduct commerce in India without such establishments, as the Swedes had shown.[68]

Some of these arguments had been anticipated by Necker, the leading figure in the postwar politics of the company. A Genevan who had come to Paris in 1750 to serve as a clerk in the banking house of Vernet and Thellusson, by the early 1760s Necker was a partner in the bank and an influential shareholder in the Compagnie des Indes.[69] He argued that the company's difficulties followed from being forced to bear costs of sovereignty and being run to suit political dictates rather than on mercantile principles. What he wanted was the separation of these functions in so far as was practical. He proposed a reorganization to make the company answerable only to shareholder interests, not to the Crown. In so far as possible, the burdens and the costs of sovereignty should be passed off to the state.[70] The 1764 settlement reflected these preferences, with a significant deterritorialization of the company: it retroceded to the Crown the port of Lorient in Brittany, which it had built and governed, along with its jurisdiction on the western coasts of Africa, and sovereignty over the islands of Bourbon (Réunion) and France (Mauritius) in the Indian Ocean. The Crown disinvested from the company, giving up the 12,000 shares of company stock held by the king.[71] The company would no longer have to answer to royal commissioners, though the Controller-General would still have significant influence in its decision making.

The call for a separation of sovereignty from trade reemerged in the debate over the suspension of the company's monopoly in 1769. Necker defended the new status quo established in 1764, while the abbé André Morellet, writing on behalf of Controller-General Étienne Maynon d'Invault, called for the revocation of the company's exclusive privilege and the opening of Asian trade.[72] The many divergences between Necker's views and Morellet's obscured a key area of agreement. Both believed that the travails of the company followed from mixing political and economic functions, and the challenges of a regional and geopolitical context in which war was a permanent threat. In Necker's words, "the trade was always profitable," while "the losses were derived from the expenses of war and sovereignty."[73] For Morellet, the solution to this problem was to abrogate the company's privilege and throw

Asian commerce open to all French merchants. Not having to bear the burden of exercising political functions, the costs of free traders would be lower, and they would be able to respond more flexibly to war, suspending commercial operations for the duration. Ultimately, both Necker and Morellet envisioned the Crown taking over the functions of sovereignty long sustained by the company in Asia. For Necker, this would make possible the commercial success of the company, while for Morellet it would follow from the liberalization of the trade.

A third interest group in 1769, led by the banker Isaac Panchaud, championed the opening up of the Indies trade and the transformation and recapitalization of the company as a discount bank (*caisse d'escompte*). Panchaud was a London-born financier of Vaudois origins who had established a banking partnership with a cousin in Paris. He was one of the several bankers in the 1760s who controlled large blocks of Compagnie des Indes shares held on behalf of clients, many of them foreign.[74] Panchaud had been instrumental in catalyzing the final crisis of the company, publishing a pamphlet in 1767 in which he criticized the reorganization of 1764 and claimed that the company's reports hid a brewing financial crisis.[75] He was closely linked to a group of major shareholders who became successful free traders after the company's privilege was abrogated, and he was heavily engaged in financing this trade in the 1770s.[76] Panchaud's proposal to turn the company into a *caisse d'escompte* drew on the intellectual traditions in the company going back to Law and Melon.[77] The bank he envisioned would discount commercial and other paper and thereby augment circulation, stimulate trade, lower interest rates, and, by issuing its own notes, augment the money supply. This plan initially had the backing of Maynon d'Invault, but though it had support from an influential minority of major shareholders, it failed to win the assent of the majority and had to be abandoned.[78]

Foiled in 1769, Panchaud would get a second chance in 1776 when a new Controller-General, Jacques Turgot, permitted him to establish a discount bank on a modest scale. The new *caisse d'escompte* shared the same premises as the Compagnie des Indes and also the same treasurer, Pierre de Mory.[79] Panchaud presented the bank as a means to lower interest rates and to stimulate agricultural and commercial prosperity.[80] For him, the *caisse d'escompte* was part of a strategy for financial revolution in France. Together with the establishment of a new sinking fund, it would place French credit on a healthier foundation than that of its British rival. Like Law before him, Panchaud saw French and British public credit as having a directly competitive relationship. As a financial advisor to the Controller-General, Jean-François Joly de Fleury, he guided a French strategy of redirecting Dutch capital away from investment in the British public debt, which he represented as an unstable and declining investment, and into French public credit.[81] By the eve of the French Revolution, Paris had replaced London as the dominant destination for new Dutch investment in foreign public debt.[82]

Conclusion: The Compagnie des Indes in the History of Political Economy

It should be clear at this point that the Compagnie des Indes fostered a rich tradition of political economic speculation and argument from its foundation by John Law in 1719 to the abrogation of its monopoly in 1769. As we have seen, this tradition had two principal strands, one continuing and developing Law's ideas about regenerating French power by creating monetary abundance and reforming the institutions of public credit, and the other grappling with problems of balancing the need for security with the imperatives of profit in the East India trade. If the company has not hitherto been recognized as a hotbed of French political economic debate, this is because a series of preconceptions have profoundly shaped, and to some degree distorted, our understanding of political economy in the age of Enlightenment. Traditionally, the most important such bias has been in favor of texts with a strong theoretical orientation, those which go furthest toward offering an abstract conceptualization of economic processes or an anticipation of later theoretical discoveries. By this teleological standard, the political economy of the Compagnie des Indes hardly even qualifies as such.

A second key bias has been a focus on the emergence of economic liberalism as the most important story to be told. In this reading, of the texts analyzed here, only the abbé Morellet's *Mémoire sur la situation actuelle de la Compagnie des Indes* of 1769 counts as a truly important intervention because of the way it mobilizes and develops liberal precepts to mount a decisive challenge to monopoly, and a ringing call for tree trade. To be sure, Melon also attracts some attention for his advocacy of free trade in grain, while he is misread as an apostle of "doux commerce" and ripped from his context as the most important French advocate of Law's political economic vision. The persistent myth that Law's ideas aroused only horror in France during the two generations that followed his disgrace in 1720 has also tended to occlude the intellectual history of the company he founded.

A reading of French political economy as a form of reflection on international competition and geopolitics has only recently emerged as a key strand of historical analysis, and it is principally within such a setting that the debates within and about the Compagnie des Indes are significant.[83] The ideas analyzed here, with few exceptions, had no place in the great domestic debates on the deregulation of the grain trade and the abolition of the guilds which have traditionally been the focus in histories of eighteenth-century political economy.[84] In recent decades, the public sphere has been privileged as the critical site for political economic debate, implicitly occluding the other spaces in which political argument could be articulated and perhaps entailing an unconscious bias against manuscript sources which circulated only within the narrow confines of the administrative milieu or intellectual circles. We need a history of political economy sensitive to the full diversity of political economic sources and ideas, attentive to political economy as a conversation about international relations as well as domestic economic organization, and alive to ideas which did not have a future as well as to those which laid the ideological foundations of our own age. In such a history, the French Indies Company will have an important place.

Notes

1. Bibliothèque Nationale de France (BNF), nouvelle acquisitions française (naf) 9150 fols. 266–67.
2. Philip J. Stern, *The Company-State: Corporate Sovereignty & the Early Modern Foundations of the British Empire in India* (Oxford: Oxford University Press, 2011).
3. Daniel Defoe, *The Advantages of Peace and Commerce, with Some Remarks on the East-India Trade* (London, 1729), 3. On Defoe's political thought, see Lawrence Dickey, "Power, Commerce and Natural Law in Daniel Defoe's Political Writings 1698–1707," in *A Union for Empire: Political Thought and the British Union of 1707*, ed. John Robertson (Cambridge: Cambridge University Press, 1995).
4. Defoe, *Advantages of Peace and Commerce*, 7.
5. On this theme, see Sophus A. Reinert, *Translating Empire: Emulation and the Origins of Political Economy* (Cambridge, MA: Harvard University Press, 2011).
6. See P. G. M. Dickson, *The Financial Revolution in England: A Study in the Development of Public Credit, 1688–1756* (London: Macmillan, 1967); Larry Neal, *The Rise of Financial Capitalism: International Capital Markets in the Age of Reason* (Cambridge: Cambridge University Press, 1990); Henry Roseveare, *The Financial Revolution 1660–1750* (London: Taylor & Francis, 1991); Bruce G. Carruthers, *City of Capital: Politics and Markets in the English Financial Revolution* (Princeton: Princeton University Press, 1996); David Stasavage, *Public Debt and the Birth of the Democratic State: France and Great Britain, 1688–1789* (Cambridge: Cambridge University Press, 2003); and Carl Wennerlind, *Casualties of Credit: The English Financial Revolution, 1620–1720* (Cambridge, MA: Harvard University Press, 2011).
7. The key work on Law's System is Antoin E. Murphy, *John Law: Economic Theorist and Policy-Maker* (Oxford: Oxford University Press, 1997). Also useful are Edgar Faure, *La banqueroute de Law, 17 juillet 1720* (Paris: Gallimard, 1977); Claude Frédéric Lévy, *Capitalistes et pouvoir au siècle des Lumières*, 3 vols. (Paris: Mouton, 1969–1980), vols. 2–3; Peter M. Garber, *Famous First Bubbles: The Fundamentals of Early Manias* (Cambridge, MA: The MIT Press, 2000), 91–107; and François R. Velde, "Government Equity and Money: John Law's System in 1720 France" (Federal Reserve Bank of Chicago working

paper no. 2003–31, December 2003), accessed June 30, 2014, http://ssrn.com/abstract=486983.

8. John Law to Philippe d'Orléans, December 1715, in *Œuvres complètes*, ed. Paul Harsin, 3 vols. (Paris: Sirey, 1934), ii, 262–67.
9. John Law, "Idée générale du nouveau système des finances," in *Œuvres complètes*, iii, 89n.
10. Law's monetary ideas no longer appear as original as they once did. See Wennerlind, *Casualties of Credit*.
11. John Law, "Mémoire sur les banques," in *Œuvres complètes*, ii, 307–8.
12. Law to Orléans, December 1715, in *Œuvres complètes*, ii, 262–67.
13. Law, "Mémoire sur les banques," ii, 305. See also John Law, "Effets que le Système de M. Law a produit sur les espèces dans plusieurs Etats de l'Europe," *Œuvres complètes*, iii, 170; idem, "Mémoire pour démontrer 1° qu'il est nécessaire d'établir le crédit; 2° qu'il est practicable de l'établir en France quoyque cet établissement aye déja été entreprise et qu'il aye manqué," *Œuvres complètes*, iii, 184.
14. François de Salignac de la Mothe Fénelon, "Examen de conscience sur les devoirs de la royauté. Supplément," in *Œuvres*, ed. Jacques Le Brun, 2 vols. (Paris: Gallimard, 1983–1997), i, 1009. Probably composed between 1708 and 1711, this work was not published until 1734, and most of the edition was suppressed. However, it circulated in manuscript, and an English translation was published as "Sentiments on the Balance of Europe," in *Two Essays on the Balance of Europe* (London, 1720). See also Michael Sonenscher, *Before the Deluge: Public Debt, Inequality, and the Intellectual Origins of the French Revolution* (Princeton: Princeton University Press, 2007), 109–12.
15. Charles Irenée Castel de Saint-Pierre, *Projet pour rendre la paix perpétuelle en Europe* (Utrecht, 1713).
16. William Petty, *A Treatise of Taxes and Contributions* (London, 1662), 5.
17. Charles Davenant, "On the Plantation Trade," in *Political and Commercial Works of that Celebrated Writer Charles D'avenant*, ed. Charles Whitworth, 5 vols. (London, 1771), ii, 28.
18. William Petty, *Political Arithmetick* (London, 1690).
19. Charles Davenant, "Discourses on the Publick Revenues, and on the Trade of England, Part II," in *Political and Commercial Works*, i, 116.
20. See Holden Furber, *Rival Empires of Trade in the Orient 1600–1800* (Minneapolis: University of Minnesota Press, 1976), 136–37; Philippe Haudrère, *La Compagnie française des Indes au XVIIIe siècle*, 2nd ed., 2 vols. (Paris: Les Indes Savantes, 2005), i, 52–54; and Marcel Giraud,

Histoire de la Louisiane française, vol. 3, *L'époque de John Law (1717–1720)* (Paris: Presses Universitaires de France, 1966), 101–5.

21. Jacob M. Price, *France and the Chesapeake: A History of the French Tobacco Monopoly, 1674–1791*, 2 vols. (Ann Arbor: University of Michigan Press, 1973), i, 197–212.
22. John Law, "Réponse aux deux lettres, sur le Nouveau Système des Finances," in *Œuvres complètes*, iii, 115–16. See also the memorandum by Law at Cholmondeley (Houghton) Papers, Cambridge University Library, 82/1/16 fols. 36–40.
23. Law to Orléans, December 1715, in *Œuvres complètes*, ii, 266–67.
24. Archives du Ministère des Affaires Etrangères (AAE), Correspondance politique (CP), Angleterre (Ang) 327 fols. 209–10, James Stanhope to Guillaume Dubois, 18/29 December 1719.
25. The National Archives (TNA), SP 78/166 fols. 191–92, Daniel Pulteney to James Craggs, 10 April 1720; fol. 198, Pulteney to Craggs, 29 April 1720; SP 78/167 fols. 271–72, John Dalrymple, Earl of Stair to Craggs, 12 April 1720.
26. For a fuller discussion of these themes, see John Shovlin, "Jealousy of Credit: John Law's 'System' and the Geopolitics of Financial Revolution," *Journal of Modern History* 88 (2016): 275–305.
27. On the continuing appeal of Law's ideas generally during the decades after his fall, see Paul Harsin, *Crédit public et banque d'état en France du XVIe au XVIIIe siècle* (Paris: Droz, 1933).
28. Anon., "Mémoire fait en May 1724," Bibliothèque de I'Arsenal, Paris, MS 4500 fols. 137–64. See also AAE Mémoires et Documents (MD) France 1258 fols. 8–18; Archives Nationales (AN), Paris, K 1230.
29. Anon., "Mémoire pour la compagnie des Indes en décembre 1726," Arsenal MS 4500 fols. 167–232.
30. Arnaud de Silhouette, "Mémoire pour le rétablissement de la confiance," AAE MD France 1268 fols. 133–44. See also Silhouette's covering letter dated 1 January 1734 at AAE MD France 1289 fol. 7.
31. Simone Meyssonnier, *La balance et l'horloge: La genèse de la pensée libérale en France au XVIIIe siècle* (Montreuil: Éditions de la Passion, 1989), 62.
32. See Joseph Fleuriau d'Armenonville to Jean-François Melon, 23 November 1723, with accompanying draft decree at Arsenal MS 3857 fols. 312–20.
33. Jean-François Melon, "Mémoire pour examiner quels sont les contradicteurs de la Compagnie des Indes, pourquoi ils en demandent la

suppression, et de quelle utilité cette Compagnie est à l'Etat," Arsenal MS 3857 fols. 351–80.

34. Jean-François Melon, *Essai politique sur le commerce* (n.p., 1734), 243–59.
35. Melon, *Essai politique sur le commerce*, 51–60, 105, quotation on 59–60.
36. Albert O. Hirschman, *The Passions and the Interests: Political Arguments for Capitalism before its Triumph*, 2nd ed. (Princeton: Princeton University Press, 1997), 79–80.
37. John Robertson, *The Case for the Enlightenment: Scotland and Naples 1680–1760* (Cambridge: Cambridge University Press, 2005), 343. See also Istvan Hont, "The 'Rich Country–Poor Country' Debate Revisited: The Irish Origins and French Reception of the Hume Paradox," in *David Hume's Political Economy*, ed. Margaret Schabas and Carl Wennerlind (London: Routledge, 2008), 261.
38. Nicolas Dutot, *Rēflexions politiques sur les finances, et le commerce*, 2 vols. (The Hague, 1738), ii, 403–4. Dutot criticized Melon for advocating currency revaluations, but in many other respects their views were similar. Dutot had been a cashier of the Compagnie des Indes under the System. See François Velde, "The Life and Times of Nicolas Dutot," *Journal of the History of Economic Thought* 34 (2012): 67–107.
39. Dutot, *Rēflexions politiques*, ii, 338–39, 356–57.
40. AAE CP Ang 405 fols. 394–99, Étienne de Silhouette to André-Hércule de Fleury, 31 December 1739.
41. Étienne de Silhouette, "Observations sur les finances, la navigation & le commerce de l'Angleterre," AAE MD Ang 46 fols. 45–88.
42. Joël Félix, "Comprendre l'opposition parlementaire: Le parlement de Paris face aux réformes de Silhouette (1759)," *Parlement(s), Revue d'Histoire Politique*, no. 15 (2011): 31–43.
43. Arnaud Orain, "Soutenir la guerre et réformer la fiscalité: Silhouette et Forbonnais au Contrôle général des finances (1759)," *French Historical Studies* 36, no. 3 (2013), 417–47.
44. François Véron de Forbonnais, "Abrégé des mémoires pour l'établissement du crédit public," Arsenal MS 4591.
45. Étienne de Silhouette, *Réponse de M. le Contrôleur général à M. le Premier President de la Chambre des Comptes, lorsqu'il y est venu prêter serment* (n.p., n.d.), 2; AN H 713, unfoliated, Silhouette to Antoine-Louis Lefebvre de Caumartin, 31 August 1759.

46. François Véron de Forbonnais, *Lettre d'un banquier à son correspondant de province* (n.p., 1759), 45.
47. See, for example, "Mémoire sur les moyens de prévenir la guerre et de parvenir à une conciliation avec l'Angleterre," AAE CP Ang, Supplément 11 fols. 165–90. An earlier draft by Silhouette exists at AN Marine B^4 47 fols. 214–32.
48. François Véron de Forbonnais, "Réflexions sur la nécessité de comprendre l'étude du commerce et des finances dans celle de la poltique," in *Considérations sur les finances d'Espagne*, 2nd ed. (Dresden, 1755), 60, 64.
49. Haudrère, *Compagnie française des Indes*, i, 95–96.
50. For evidence of the relatively good relations between the two companies in the 1730s, see British Library (BL), India Office Records (IOR) E/1/22 fols. 160–61; E/1/24 fol. 157; E/1/25 fols. 94, 163–64; H/74 fols. 172–76, 233–34, 579–80.
51. Haudrère, *Compagnie française des Indes*, i, 126–27.
52. BNF naf 9335 fols. 343–47; AAE MD Asie 4 fols. 44–62; AN Col C^2 84 fols. 18–25.
53. Haudrère, *Compagnie française des Indes*, ii, 730–37.
54. AN Col C^2 44 fols. 48–60.
55. BNF naf 9150 fols. 22–23, Gabriel Michel to Dupleix, 21 January 1754.
56. AN Col C^2 32 fols. 72–85.
57. In 1739, for example, Duvelaer transported gold aboard the East Indiaman *Winchester*. Robert Knight (former cashier of the South Sea Company) and Alexander Hume (former director of the Ostend Co. in Bengal, and subsequently a director of the EIC) played some role as intermediaries. See BL IOR B/65, Court Book, 22 August 1739. For Gabriel Michel, see "Projet d'une Expédition pour la Mer du Sud" (1743), Maurepas Collection, 4614, Division of Rare and Manuscript Collections, Cornell University Library, Ithaca, New York, Box 13, folder 11.
58. Herbert Lüthy, *La banque protestante en France de la révocation de l'Édit de Nantes à la Révolution*, 2 vols. (Paris: S.E.V.P.E.N., 1959–1961), ii, 168–72.
59. "Mémoire sur les inconvénients pour les trois Compagnies françoise, angloise et hollandoise de leur mésintelligence dans l'Inde, sur les avantages communs à ces trois Comp.[es] qui resulteroient de leur Union. Projet pour l'Etablissement et le maintien de cette Union," 30 July 1752, AN Col C^2 38 fols. 74–81.

60. Étienne de Silhouette, "Mémoire sur les affaires de l'Inde," AN Col C^2 39 fols. 88–102.
61. On the English approach, see AAE CP Ang 435 fol. 350, Gaston-Pierre de Lévis, duc de Mirepoix to François-Dominique de Barberie, marquis de Saint-Contest, 10 February 1753.
62. AAE CP Ang 436 fol. 7, Jean-Baptiste Machault d'Arnouville to Saint-Contest, 1 March 1753.
63. BL IOR/I/1/4 Secret committee of the Compagnie des Indes to the Secret committee of the East India Company, 21 March 1753.
64. BL Egerton MS 3484 fol. 17, Minute of a meeting at Newcastle House, 30 May 1753.
65. Haudrère, *Compagnie française des Indes*, ii, 743.
66. BL Add MS 32856 fol. 279–89.
67. Haudrère, *Compagnie française des Indes*, ii, 746–47.
68. Pierre-Joseph-André Roubaud, *Le politique indien, ou considérations sur les colonies des Indes orientales* (Amsterdam, 1768).
69. Robert D. Harris, *Necker: Reform Statesman of the Ancien Régime* (Berkeley: University of California Press, 1979), 5–6.
70. "Discours de M. Necker Banquier," AN Col C^2 47 fols. 53–60.
71. Kenneth Margerison, "The Shareholders' Revolt at the Compagnie des Indes: Commerce and Political Culture in Old Regime France," *French History* 22, no. 1 (2006): 25–51.
72. André Morellet, *Mémoire sur la situation actuelle de la Compagnie des Indes* (n.p., 1769).
73. Jacques Necker, *Réponse au mémoire de l'abbé Morellet sur la Compagnie des Indes* (Paris, 1769), 27–28.
74. Panchaud was said to have 4000 shares on deposit in 1767. Haudrère, *Compagnie française des Indes*, i, 121.
75. [Isaac Panchaud], *Lettre d'un actionnaire de la Compagnie des Indes, à Messieurs les commissaires nommés à l'Assemblée du 4 Avril 1767* (1767), AN Col. C^2 105 fols. 349–51.
76. L. M. Cullen, "Luthy's La Banque Protestante: A Reassessment," *Bulletin du Centre d'Histoire des Espaces Atlantiques*, new series, 5 (1990): 229–63.
77. One of his supporters, the comte de Lauraguais, republished Dutot's apology for Law's System. See Louis-Léon-Félicité, comte de Lauraguais, *Mémoire sur la Compagnie des Indes, dans lequel on établit les droits & les intérêts des actionnaires. En réponse aux compilations de M. l'Abbé Morellet* (n.p., 1770), 114–33.

78. Lüthy, *La banque protestante*, ii, 393.
79. Ibid., ii, 436.
80. BNF Joly de Fleury 1434 fol. 131.
81. [Isaac Panchaud], *Réflexions sur l'état actuel du crédit public de l'Angleterre et de la France* (n.p., 1781). For his comments on the Sinking Fund and the Caisse see pp. 45–47.
82. J. C. Riley, "Dutch Investment in France, 1781–1787," *Journal of Economic History* 33 (1973): 732–60; idem, *International Government Finance and the Amsterdam Capital Market, 1740–1815* (Cambridge: Cambridge University Press, 1980), 95, 107, 174–75.
83. See, for example, Antonella Alimento, "Entre animosité nationale et rivalité d'émulation: la position de Véron de Forbonnais face à la competition anglaise," in *Governare il mondo: l'economia come linguaggio della politica nell'Europa del Settecento*, ed. Manuela Albertone (Milan: Feltrinelli, 2009); Paul Cheney, *Revolutionary Commerce: Globalization and the French Monarchy* (Cambridge, MA: Harvard University Press, 2010); and Hont, "The 'Rich Country–Poor Country' Debate Revisited."
84. Steven L. Kaplan, *Bread, Politics and Political Economy in the Reign of Louis XV*, 2 vols. (The Hague: Martinus Nijhoff, 1976); idem, *La fin des corporations* (Paris: Fayard, 2001).

Author Biography

John Shovlin is an Associate Professor of History at New York University where he lectures in early modern and modern European history. John's research focuses on the history of political economy in eighteenth-century Europe. He is the author of *The Political Economy of Virtue: Luxury, Patriotism, and the Origins of the French Revolution* (2006), and editor of *The Bordeaux–Dublin Letters, 1757: Correspondence of an Irish Community Abroad* (2013), along with Thomas M. Truxes and Louis M. Cullen. Supported by the National Endowment for the Humanities, he is currently writing a book on capitalism and international order in eighteenth-century Europe with a focus on the Franco-British global rivalry.

The Economics of the Antipodes: French Naval Exploration, Trade, and Empire in the Eighteenth Century

Arnaud Orain

The pioneering work of scholars like David Armitage has, over the last decade, engaged intellectual history in an "international turn," profoundly affecting the history of empires.[1] One aspect of this influence is a growing awareness among historians that it is now necessary to write the prehistory of reflections on globalization, i.e., of the emergence of a consciousness, and then of an analysis, albeit fleeting, of the relationship among peoples, goods, and ideas across continents. Numerous moments and junctures over the last five centuries could provide a backdrop for this, but there is likely none better than "[t]he period between the end of the Seven Year's War and the defeat of Napoleon," which Armitage has described as "a heyday both for imperial historiography and for a renewed attention to the importance of sea power in history."[2] Much of the interest of earlier historians in this period has focused on the colonial encyclopedia of the Enlightenment, the *Histoire des deux Indes*, published by Abbé Raynal.[3] So, rather than examining its great philosophical metanarrative one more time, this article tries to reframe

A. Orain (✉)
University of Paris 8, Paris, France
e-mail: arnaud.orain@univ-paris8.fr

R. Fredona and S.A. Reinert (eds.), *New Perspectives on the History of Political Economy*, https://doi.org/10.1007/978-3-319-58247-4_7

the issue. In the 1750s, the colonial debate inherited from previous centuries came to be reconfigured by economists into two competing visions no longer as focused on the "Colony for Trade"/"Colony for Empire" dichotomy. Using 1765–1789 exploration accounts, I present two case studies to test the influence of the new colonial models developed by economists on the navigators of the period, always keeping in mind that though they do pass judgments of their own on the colonial past, just as in the *Histoire des deux Indes*, the navigator—authors of these accounts are first and foremost sailors—commissioned to produce knowledge, often for commercial purposes.

Inspired by the approaches of Emma Rothschild and Paul Cheney, I first survey how the terms of the debate were set by the economists, before beginning to consider how it was received by navigators.[4] Ocean exploration, at least with respect to the great eighteenth-century figures, has spawned a staggering amount of historical work.[5] No connection is made in this literature between exploration and the emergence in the 1750s of a "science of commerce" around the Gournay circle and, to a lesser extent, the physiocrat. Or, to be more precise, though a few historians have looked back on one crucial book for the exploration of the South Seas, the *Histoire des navigations aux terres australes* of Charles de Brosses, none seems to have noticed that it was an almost complete—and explicit—presentation of the Gournay circle's ideas on colonial trade.[6]

Following Melon and Montesquieu, economists in the Gournay group believed that England had finally managed to reach and maintain an equilibrium between *libertas* and *imperium*, energies long deemed irreconcilable.[7] The ancient trading "republics," like Athens, had been traditionally opposed to Rome, the cruel conqueror of what would become an "empire." Additionally, "colonies for trade," relatively peaceful and relatively free, were opposed to "colonies for conquest," dependent tributaries rather than partners in exchange, signifying the invasion and subjugation of entire peoples. For the Gournay circle, then, England was thought to rule over a "republican" empire, using its naval power to create colonies in the spirit of liberty and trade, not conquest, even when resorting to force might sometimes be necessary. As Talleyrand would note at the very end of the century, France was therefore meant to emulate the colonial policy of its remarkable rival.[8] The Gournay circle's point of view was not shared by the other rising group among Pre-Revolutionary French political economists, the physiocrats. Adopting the example of China, François Quesnay and the explorer-administrator Pierre Poivre promoted instead the establishment of settlements intended not for trade but for grain. The physiocrats tried to overturn the traditional history, replacing received notions of English and Dutch *doux commerce* with bloody (Spanish-style) territorial conquests in their narrative of colonial expansion. Quesnay and Poivre rejected both the "colony for trade" and "colony for conquest" concepts, envisaging instead territories no longer subject to the metropole, but part of a kingdom's provinces, and with the same goals (achieving a greater net agricultural product) and the same rights (the right to totally free trade, even with foreign merchants).

Listening for echoes of the economists' models in accounts of explorations around the Southern Ocean, both of my case studies set Enlightenment economic theory side by side with the objectives that colonial navigators were contemplating, or were required to aim for, during their expeditions. The first case study reexamines the issue of *doux commerce* and free trade. Sophus A. Reinert has noted that "the '*doux-commerce* thesis' has proven rewarding in recent years and become nothing less than a 'mantra of modernity.'"[9] Through the accounts of Bougainville and especially Lapérouse, both deeply influenced by De Brosses, I will call attention to the relevance of *doux commerce* as a "mantra" even at the dawn of modernity. Lapérouse is constantly invoking free trade and the benefits of peaceful trade in the pages of the diary he intended to publish. At the time he was keeping secret memoirs, and in these he speaks of conquering trading posts by force and appropriating the exclusive benefits of whole trading areas. The second case study focuses on the implementation of the physiocrats' program in the Indian Ocean by the intendant Pierre Poivre. My goal is not to present a summary of his actions in favor or against cereal grain farming in the French Mascarene Islands, but to see how he was instrumental to expeditions in the South Seas to benefit the physiocratic colonial ideal before ultimately deviating from it.

Antipodean Economics: The Two Models

It was only after attending a reading of Maupertuis's *Lettre sur le Progrès des Sciences* (1752), in which the famous scientist explained the usefulness of recent discoveries in the south, that Charles de Brosses (1709–1777) decided to set down on paper his long meditations on the subject, which soon became the two-volume *Histoire des navigations aux terres australes* first published in Paris in 1756.[10]

De Brosses begins by dividing the ocean lying below the known lands and above the mythical Austral continent into three seas: "the Magellanic, Polynesia, and Australasia." The first lies to the south of the *Tierra del fuego*, at the extreme south of the Americas; the second south of Japan and west of the Philippines, and the third somewhere below the Indian Ocean and Africa. He invited navigators to seek, in the latter two, the great conjectured continent where they should find "whole branches of new trade." Indeed, "Polynesia," so close to Dutch trading posts, could not but be rich in "spices"; and "Australasia," not far from the *Île Bourbon* (now called Réunion) and the *Île de France* (now Mauritius) as well as India, would facilitate trade with all these regions. The purpose of such discoveries is set down openly from the very first pages of the book—what is at stake is trade. De Brosses is full of enthusiasm and certainty about the success of such an undertaking: "So many branches of trade—in furs, silk, spices, medicines, dye woods, gold and precious stones! So many ways to produce our colored glass grains, our small pieces of fabric, our paper, spirits, iron tools, our hardware, our small seven *sols*, a dozen mirrors, with as much profit as the revenue brought back from the first voyages to the West Indies!"[11] The trading economy that must prevail in the French southern lands colonies is fundamental and will distinguish them from the "mistakes, greed and cruelty" of the Spanish:

> We know from experience that in those distant climes trading must prevail & not conquest. It is not a question of owning imaginary kingdoms beyond the equator; it will suffice to have a few well-placed colonies, a few strong fortresses supporting them, intelligent traders, and well-supplied stores; that any trade & every colony shall prioritize the benefits

of the metropolis, and that the surest way to keep the savages in useful dependence.[12]

An overall vision of the Southern adventure is laid out in the clearest terms by De Brosses. The French had to remain wary of the greed for gold and silver, of subjecting peoples, destroying indigenous civilizations, and even of stealing trading posts from other European nations. Their colonies should have but one purpose: expanding trade in favor of the metropolis, thereby providing a living for ever more sailors, farmers, and factory workers. To enrich the metropolis, it would first be necessary to find a place to install a "settlement." Exactly where would be left up to the captain of the exploratory mission, but it had to be south of Japan, and near Guam.[13] Then, to avoid depopulating the mainland, which was already short on labor, De Brosses proposes to use convicts and female offenders as what amounts to slave labor in the colonies, at least until the settlers get rich enough to import black slaves from the African coast. These slaves would work in "trade warehouses" and in land cultivation, always to complement and never to replace the output of the metropolis. Tests would be made to determine the qualities of the soil, and "it will soon be found that all the hopes raised by compatible temperatures & climates were not in vain, and that those precious commodities, *épiceries* (spices), herbs, dyes, &c, thought to be exclusive to some countries, can also grow in others." Land cultivation, far superior to mining for gold and silver, enhances trade and enables settlers to buy more products made in the metropolis, which is why large slave plantations would be needed to yield exotic produce rather than basic food crops.[14] Finally, in order to foster emulative trade between France and its "Australasian" colonies, fully free trade would have to be organized among domestic traders. De Brosses has harsh words for the greed of exclusive companies, especially the Dutch East India Company (VOC), and he would prefer instead the kind of "competition" that "a great modern writer" has established "as the core & active ingredient for Trade," but allowing foreign merchants to trade in the French Southern colonies remains out of the question.[15]

De Brosses explicitly admits drawing his inspiration for this model of colonial relations from "the reflections of an already quoted writer

(M. de F…) who has explained in so great detail everything that concerns colonies, their laws & their results."[16] The *Élémens du Commerce* (1754) by François Véron de Forbonnais (1722–1800) is indeed mentioned many times in the *Histoire des Navigations* and if anything it is a euphemism to say that the author was only "inspired" in these matters by the famous Gournay circle economist. It was indeed Forbonnais who formalized trade settlement patterns in the early 1750s. In his article "Colonie," written for the *Encyclopédie* and included in the second volume of the *Élémens*, he describes nothing less than a complete typology and periodization of colonization. Colonies, he argues, would have to be fully designed for the benefit of the metropolis insofar as they would provide it busier trade and greater consumption and production. Given the high cost of cultivation without them, slaves would be indispensable and their use would also keep the metropolis from being deprived of its own inhabitants. Since "the driving force behind that cultivation is trade," export commodities (Forbonnais lists sugar, indigo, coffee, and tobacco) would be required from the colonies:

> 1° This is a law enacted in accordance with the very nature of colonies: they should have no culture, no art that could be in competition with the arts & culture of the metropolis.
>
> 2° It would be a crime for colonies to consume foreign goods, which the metropolis agrees to provide them the equivalent of, or sell to foreigners commodities granted access to its ports by the metropolis.[17]

Unable to grow cereals already produced in the metropolis, the colonies would have to acquire them from the metropolis while their plantations were exploited for what the metropolis did not produce. Moreover, though "trade is only possible in the context of competing traders" and though it is therefore necessary to remove those "tolls, duties and easements—in short, regulations" that impede trade, this applies only to nationals, since foreigners should be banned from the colonial trade.[18] Colonial trade requires ships capable, among other things, of reaching nearby continents likely to provide what the metropolis cannot and undertaking trade with them. In Forbonnais's scheme, these tasks would have to be performed "by vessels of the countries of domination."

This would require restricting the number and size of ships stationed in the colonies in order to prevent them from trading with each other and eventually being so empowered. It would also require powerful war fleets capable of protecting the connections between metropolis and colony.[19]

"The Physiocrats responded to Forbonnais's typology and its implicit colonial ideology with their own scheme."[20] Their ideas are clearly expressed by a tireless traveler and botanist who, like De Brosses, albeit in different ways, played an important role in the discovery of Southern Seas: the physiocrat Pierre Poivre (1719–1786). After several visits to China, Cochin, India, the Moluccas, and the Mascarene Islands on behalf of the French East India Company, and especially after becoming acquainted with François Quesnay, Poivre became *commissaire général faisant fonction d'Intendant* over the islands of France and Bourbon (July 1767–October 1772). Upon his arrival, he delivered two important speeches. The first was addressed to "the inhabitants of the colony assembled in government" and the second to the "new Board of Governors of the Island of France." Both clearly present his plans for the French possessions in the Indian Ocean and more generally for all future colonial enterprises. From the outset, he objects to the idea that these should solely be designed to trade with and enrich the metropolis. "Let all cultivations be replaced by grain food crops for a time. The state no longer demands coffee or cotton of you":

> Let us start by storing up the greatest possible abundance of food: the time will come when you will be able to indulge in the cultivation of some objects of wealth; then, your well-established abundance will enable you to enjoy them; then will you be rich and powerful.
>
> Otherwise, your wealth would be uncertain and insecure, because you would remain powerless. They would only attract enemy forces against you, as they would consider this colony as nothing more than an easy prey.[21]

At the foundation of colonies must stand "the noblest of all arts," namely "nurturing agriculture." Against the luxury of merchants enriched by export products and slave plantations, Poivre opposed the ideal of a farming society united by the virtues of frugality and patriotism. All the language of classical republicanism is deployed in these speeches. From now on, let "every Frenchman here be a farmer and soldier." And let that "inhuman exploitation" of slavery—unfortunately introduced into the Mascarene—be as small and gentle as possible.[22]

An analysis of the fragility of commercial colonies, pointing to the desirability of agricultural colonies made up of militiamen, had already been developed by Roubaud and the Mirabeau brothers for Canada and the French West Indies.[23] Quesnay himself had laid the foundations for this in an article published in the *Journal de l'Agriculture, du Commerce et des Finances* in April 1766, entitled "Remarques sur l'opinion de l'auteur de l'*Esprit des Loix* concernant les colonies." The repeated objections made by the founder of Physiocracy against Montesquieu may be encapsulated in the idea that trade expansion should not be the ultimate goal of establishing colonies. Castigating colonies made up of trading posts belonging to merchants and companies as well as those established to cultivate export goods only, he praised the contrary, those "cultivators' colonies that had never been intended mainly [...] for trade to the benefit of the metropolis." Even while paying "the state a proportionate contribution from the net product of their lands, for defending their properties and for other government spending," and of course even while offering refuge to the Navy at the time of war, they must be self-sufficient. In order to accomplish this, full ownership of the land must be given to the settlers who must also be granted full freedom of trade in these distant lands—even the freedom to trade with foreigners, without reciprocity. No distinction should exist any longer between "colonies" and the "metropolis," since the former are provinces in their own right, just like any other, even if located a little further away.[24] Free trade and competitions circumvent war because war only results from monopolistic arrangements. The idea that the *doux commerce* of nations with trade colonies (like England and Holland) was less harmful than those with conquered ones (like Spain) was, for the physiocrats generally and for Roubaud in particular, a chimera: "It is an error to believe as Montesquieu does that those nations which treated America as an object of commerce were wiser than those [who treated it as an object] of conquest."[25]

Unlike Poivre, De Brosses, Forbonnais, and Quesnay were theorists discoursing on the colonies from the comfort of their studies. Their ideas, however, were to permeate the projects to discover southern lands and lead explorers in these areas, if not to judge, then at least to test the applicability of that twofold "Antipodean economics." From this point of view, we will see that even merely confronting the supposed facts of the competing colonial models, without undertaking any serious analysis, becomes complicated if not contorted to the point of falsity.

Free Trade or Aggression? Bougainville and Lapérouse in Asia

The *Histoire des navigations aux terres australes* by De Brosses was a phenomenal success in France and abroad. This is especially true in England, where it became the major inspiration for Darlymple's *An Account of the Discoveries made in the South Pacific*.[26] Both books also serve the same historical function: to be the starting point for southern expeditions planned or carried out by the two countries, since their respective ministers (in their instructions) and sailors (in their accounts) all refer in some way to De Brosses's work.

A personal friend of Bougainville's, De Brosses supervised the preparation of the 1766–1769 expedition. Even the king's instructions were written by Bougainville and largely drew their inspiration from the *Histoire des navigations*.[27] The journey had three goals: return the Falklands to the Spaniards; a reconnaissance mission in the Southern Pacific islands to find "their rich metals and spices"; and to find an island near China that could accommodate a French colony to compete with the Spanish and Dutch trading posts.

The second objective was directly related to the *Île de France*, since Bougainville was commissioned to bring back spice tree seedlings to acclimatize them to the Mascarene Islands. On that count, the expedition was a failure. During his short stays in the Pacific Islands, Bougainville checked one of De Brosses's hypotheses: The natives are eager to get iron tools.[28] But he, for his part, never found what he sought, neither in Tahiti (where tobacco and spices repelled inhabitants) nor in New Britain. In the Maluku Islands archipelago, where the VOC ruled, he looked for small islands the Dutch had possibly not settled, but again, he did not get his way: No spices were to be found in Boero (Buru, an island near Amboyna) or in the Button Straits. He added, however, that exclusive trade would not last long, because the English were trying at all costs to establish trade in the region. This point is related to the voyage's third objective of finding an occupant-free harbor capable of accommodating a French colony. Despite Bougainville's great efforts, he did not find what he wanted because the Dutch occupied all the right places in the Moluccas, even those they did not operate, in order to prevent other nations from setting up there. He then deemed there was no other way to accomplish the third goal of his mission without resorting to force. In his logbook, he kept assessing the Dutch military power and one passage even mentioned how one might bombard one of their Forts to take it.[29] Yet, as he noted in the margins of an unpublished passage of his diary:

> If I may, I would add that the Dutch have few naval forces in these waters. One frigate in Ternate, a 14-gun senault here, a few boats there, are these obstacles too hard to overcome? In truth, governors in Ambon and Banda do sail around their possessions every year with a fairly large number of carawres. But we know how long this cruise takes and, besides, an army of these carawres would not much harm warships, would they?[30]

Indirectly, this was actually a way to contradict the optimism of his friend De Brosses, who believed Southern lands were large enough for the French nation to establish a colony there without attacking their rivals.[31] But Bougainville never found such immense wealth, or, more importantly, those spices everyone made such a fuss about. So, he planned offensive action: why not seize a Dutch settlement and establish a trading station there? Though he never gives advice on how later to manage it, Bougainville is very appreciative of the VOC's practices and organization. It can therefore be suggested that he rather imagined a company monopoly rather than free trade, domestically. The navigator's empirical findings thus led him to depart from De Brosses's views and advocate a more mercantilist policy in the strictest sense of the term, not even close to Forbonnais's (who did not promote launching an offensive against European trading posts).

Free trade was apparently one of the leitmotifs of the other great French expedition in the Enlightenment period, Lapérouse's (1785–1788), but we will again see that things seldom are as simple as they sound. Prepared with great care and outstanding human and material means, Lapérouse's adventure ended tragically in June 1788 with the demise of the entire crew after a tropical storm in the archipelago of the Solomon Islands. Yet, thanks to Lapérouse's decision to forward copies of his diary and sporadic letters, we know much about the journey.[32] His writings were compiled, rewritten, and published in 1797 by Brigadier General Milet-Mureau, pursuant to the April 22, 1791 National Assembly Decree. The unpublished manuscripts by Lapérouse and Milet-Mureau, in turn, give us quite another picture of the trade issue than what is depicted in the published version.

Lapérouse had of course read De Brosses's work with the utmost attention, and with a view to competing with England: he "realised how right De Brosses was in urging his compatriots to explore the Pacific and not leave it all to the British."[33] The second part of the king's instructions to Lapérouse, "Matters relating to the Trade Policy," made no reference to the *Histoire des navigations*, but they had the same goals: to get information about spice cultivation in the Pacific, New Zealand, and the Moluccas. The king also wanted to know about Spanish, Dutch, and—if they existed—British trading posts in these regions. The explorer was not explicitly asked to find locations for commercial ports on behalf of France but rather to assess naval and land forces in each of these regions. No offensive plans were made, and, on the contrary, Lapérouse's mission was to show the greatest deference to friendly nations, especially Spain, and behave with the utmost respect toward neutral or potentially hostile nations. In the Moluccas, "he shall take great care to understand the benefits derived by England's trade from the freedom that power has obtained thanks to the latest peace treaty with Holland, to navigate and traffic throughout the Asian Seas." The French government was therefore interested in the effects of free trade on its rivals, and it is worth remembering that the Eden Agreement (1786), meant to lower tariffs between France and England, was being prepared during this time.[34]

At first glance, Lapérouse is in step with his times in this respect. His diary is full of references to the benefits of free trade. He denounces exclusive companies and their trading privileges in South America and concludes that "if Spain does not change its system, if free trade is not allowed and if the various duties on foreign consumption are not moderated [...], the kingdom of Chile will never achieve the level of growth that can be expected from this country's situation." In Manila, Lapérouse also writes at length about Spain's carelessness:

> All sorts of edibles are there to be found in the greatest abundance and at the cheapest price, but European raiment, hardware and furniture are sold at excessive prices. Lack of emulation, prohibitions, hindrances of all kinds trammeling trade make production and sale of goods at least as expensive as in Europe.[35]

Time and again, Lapérouse highlighted the profits to be gained if the Spaniards would only scrap exclusive companies in favor of free trade. He also imagined these benefits would be shared both with the colony (as he previously had written on the development of Chile) and the metropolis. From this perspective, he is close to the Poivre-Quesnay model, especially since he was very interested in food crops and laments the low cereal production. However, next to that "official" narrative found in Lapérouse's papers at the national archives, there is also a "Mémoire sur Manille" in which the navigator leaves aside the benefits of free trade to return to a more bellicose design for commercial relationships:

> In the chapter about Manila, I have presented all my ideas about the new Company just established in Spain, but I did not deem I ought to talk – in a book likely to become public – about how easy it would be for a nation to seize this Colony. Spanish possessions in the Philippines are confined to Luzon only, which in truth is very considerable, and contains nine hundred thousand inhabitants capable of exercising all trades, and tend all cultivations. These people hate the Spaniards, who terribly upset them and despise them so much, and I am convinced that a nation that provided them with weapons would trigger, with very small means, an insurrection in this island. [...]

> Manila Bay is open to all vessels and can be defended only by warships: therefore, launching an attack on this Colony implies boasting superior naval forces. The island's fortifications, though regular and well-maintained would delay only by a few days the fall of this town, which has no support to expect from Europe, or any other country for that matter.[36]

He sounds almost frightened by his own ideas, when he adds: "Yet, we must consider the Spaniards as good and faithful allies rather than enemies." Even so, he cannot help but alluding to it again a few lines further down, imagining the benefits of capturing that island in terms of turning it into an outlet for French trade and a base for its warships. In addition to his diary, he also penned another offensive plan, this time against Formosa (present day Taiwan). Conquest would be easy and should not be left to the English, who were highly dependent on trade with China due to England's high tea consumption. Once again, this is not quite *doux commerce*.

These ideas do not line up entirely or neatly with the thought of the physiocrats, for even when "enlightened" explorers such as Lapérouse favored a form of free trade, and were attentive to agricultural developments, etc., as one would expect from physiocratic doctrine, they nonetheless undoubtedly meant to restrict access to domestic traders or, at most, those of allied nations only, a view quite similar to that of Forbonnais. Moreover, and quite importantly, these men had no qualms about considering offensive conquests to set up commercial establishments—not settlements. Nevertheless, the problem could be tackled in another way: like Bougainville, Lapérouse was painfully aware of how difficult it was to install a French settlement in Asia (he deemed this possible only in North America, though for other purposes). On the other hand, he witnessed the British operations in China and feared they would seize Manila and Formosa before the French did. Although he ideally rejects trade prohibitions and does not envisage military offensives, "imperial" considerations necessarily lead him to speculations that partly disagree with his views on trade relations among European nations.

An Export Colony or a Subsistence Colony? Poivre and Expeditions to the South Seas

On landing on the *Île de France*, Poivre is brimming with physiocratic ideas about subsistence colonies, but he is also the man who once worked for the East India Company to settle the Mascarene Islands in search of spices. Furthermore, he is an administrator with specific orders, which he has agreed to implement:

> The Île de France and Bourbon can become, like our other colonies, a means to increase trade in the Kingdom, as these islands provide us an outlet for our foodstuffs and goods, and could also give us in exchange what trade goods we are short of, and which we can now get only from abroad, such as spice plantations.[37]

The government's language is quite different from Poivre's when he talks to residents on his arrival in the Indian Ocean. Indeed, the king seems to have intended to set up an export colony, subject to the metropolis, quite remote from the ideal of a grain colony on an equal footing with all other provinces in the kingdom. This reference to spices is crucial, suggested by Poivre, it was a way for him to reconcile his colonial ideal with the government's perspective. To do this, he took liberties with Quesnay's ideas on the issue and proceeded by intermediate steps: To turn the Mascarene into cereal and autonomous islands, one first had to encourage exploration for commercial purposes.

In a brief justification written after leaving the Mascarene Islands, Poivre explained in greater detail his particular idea of introducing spice trees, in addition to food crops. Recalling that he wanted to make the islands a "*colonie de subsistance,*" he explained that:

> there remained very little agricultural land – hardly 100,000 acres, to be used to foster grain cultivation […] Based on this observation, it was obvious that the Île de France, after completing its main destination, had no more land to cultivate luxury goods […]

> The whole Île de France, if entirely dedicated to the cultivation of coffee, indigo, and sugar cane, would result in a colony being very dependent on the state. In a time of war, it would be of no use to the king's troops and wings, and the enemy would always succeed in famishing it into submission. In peacetime, all this produce could hardly suffice to levy a tax as compensation to the State [...]
>
> It is from the bulk of these widely checked and verified truths (in the eyes of every wise observer) that we had planned to establish the cultivation of spices in the Île de France, as the only one that is suitable without causing any harm in any way to the main object of its purpose. This cultivation needs very little land, very few slaves.[38]

Poivre was therefore quite consistent with Quesnay's ideas, the objectives he had been assigned, and his own study interests. He wanted to extend cereal crops, and to destroy traditional export crops (in particular coffee), which took up too much surface area. However, since the colony had to pay tax and be useful for the metropolis, he proposed to introduce rare, lucrative crops instead of indigo, sugar, coffee, etc.: spices, and in particular nutmeg and clove, which did not require large land holdings. The Intendant explicitly presented these plants being introduced as a condition for the success of a food colony. The question, however, remained where to find these much vaunted spice trees.

Rather than resorting to force, as Bougainville suggested, Poivre sought by ruse to circumvent the Dutch's exclusive trade. To do this, he sent several secret expeditions to the Moluccas in order to convince the natives to sell spice trees to French rulers. Some failed, but others succeeded, and he managed to introduce their cultivation to the *Île de France*.[39] Aside from these expeditions, which he supervised directly, three other major explorations emerged in 1769–1772. They all had a priori commercial objectives, and this time Poivre took no part in their launch. Nevertheless, he tried to influence their course so they might positively affect his initial project to settle a grain colony.

The first expedition was led by the St. Malo-born Marc-Joseph Marion Dufresne, who died in New Zealand in June 1772. In the late 1760s, he had left the city and moved to the *Île de France*. He had become a landowner, like his uncle René Magon, another native of St. Malo, who was himself Maupertuis's nephew.[40] Marion led, at that time, many trading voyages (including slave trade,) in Cape Town and Madagascar. He was reportedly one of these profit-driven men, greedy for luxury, the type Poivre blasted upon his arrival. But Marion and Magon were important characters of the island, and Poivre saw them regularly. When Marion Dufresne intended to undertake the exploration of the Seychelles archipelago at his own expense, with a ship belonging to the king (*La Digue*), Poivre agreed, hesitantly, and presented his conditions. Marion wanted to find cowries to do business in the slave trade, fisheries and land turtles to exploit, and safe harbor to cabotage all the way to India.[41] But he fell ill, and the navigator had to let his second in command, Duchemin, make the trip in his stead. Poivre therefore dictated instructions for Duchemin to Marion Dufresne. He had explicit plans to plant spice trees in the Seychelles, both to increase production and restrict the land use of these export commodities in the Mascarene, in perfect harmony with his initial goal of establishing cereal production there. It should be noted, however, that parts of his intermediate aims for planting spices aligned very poorly with the colonial model advocated by Quesnay. On July 16, 1770, Governor Desroches and Intendant Poivre enacted an ordinance that forbade "all people of color, whether free, slave or freedman to carry off this island any plant or fruit likely to sprout."[42] This decision triggered the physiocrat Dupont's wrath, who pitied Poivre for having to accept the practice of "exclusive privileges" that was so repugnant in his eyes.

> [If] these settlers' avid prejudices had become so violent that they might manage to wrench from some Leaders of the Colony some Ordinance consistent with their views of exclusion, these directors should be pitied […] and the most to be pitied would be Mr. Poivre, whose highfaluting notions on economics would make it even more painful to experience an operation so contrary to justice & well-informed interest, and that would of course so severely curtail the service rendered to the Colonies under his administration.[43]

The physiocrat hoped that the king's State Council would break this ordinance in favor of "Guyana, our Caribbean, the Nation & finally

Europe." Yet, the reality was quite different. Poivre was not forced to sign the order, apparently, as he can be alleged instead to have been its instigator. He did everything he could to delay sending the plants to Cayenne, all the while Controller-General Terray insistently requested him to do so.[44] Therefore, in a letter to his friend Jean-Nicolas Céré dated February 4, 1780, he wrote: "Pepper trees would be especially appropriate to that hot and rainy colony [...] It was the right thing for Cayenne, and we ought to restrict precious spices to the Île de France, as I have always recommended we do."[45] Poivre added no argument to this judgment, so we are left to our own guesswork. Did he sincerely believe this type of spice grew better in *Île de France*? That would be odd, as he repeatedly referred to the latitudes appropriate for the spice in question and deemed the Seychelles more suited to that type of cultivation. Objectively, he should have favored Guyana for these reasons. Did his passion for this type of spices overtake his principles—the nation's interest—in that he wanted to see his work in the Mascarene universally recognized? Did he get carried away by his thirst for recognition and become oblivious to good political-economic principles? This is an open question, which marks a very interesting departure from the theoretical concepts of the physiocrats' colonial model.

The second voyage again resulted from Marion Dufresne and his uncle Magon's speculations. "The desire to make our own contribution to the success of your administration can only be exercised on new branches of trade," they wrote to Poivre on February 22, 1771. The two men then asked the Mascarene colonial government for an advance on exploration expenses to the South Seas, an advance secured against their personal properties. The objectives were to (1) take on board, and bring to his homeland, the Tahitian man who had made the return trip with Bougainville; (2) explore Polynesia for other islands "similar to those whose productions are the most valuable"; and (3) "make a reconnaissance trip to the southern lands from 30 up to 45 degrees of latitude," because "although these climates seem little promising, the Navy can derive great benefits from them and fishing can be as abundant as on the banks of Newfoundland." This was, unmistakably, the way De Brosses would speak. While the Malo citizen, always on the lookout for adventure and profit, wants to find "new areas of trade," he nevertheless wants to please his Intendant—who may have changed his principles, as has already been seen—while claiming at the end of his letter that he "has never asked privilege [monopoly] on his discoveries [...], as this would amount to putting chains on industry."[46] Indeed, Poivre himself had given Marion Dufresne precise instructions, though the documents in question unfortunately disappeared when he and 30 of his sailors were killed by New Zealand natives. Though it remains a mystery what the Intendant asked Marion, the latter's second in command on the *Mascarin*, Julien Crozet, left us some manuscripts alongside his *Nouveau voyage la mer du sud* (1783). From them, we learn that while Poivre hoped once again to find spice plants in Tahiti and the Moluccas,[47] he was also most interested in wood and other natural resources for the Navy:

> There was talk of moving far enough southwards, to try and discover the islands – or even the continent – that had got to lie there, in the southern part of the globe. From the islands of France and Bourbon the Intendant [Poivre] especially wanted to explore the northernmost part, as it was the nearest of these colonies, & in more temperate climes. There, he hoped to find trees suited to be turned into masts, and an infinity of relief, which these islands, too far from the metropolis, cannot exploit without great pains & very great expense.[48]

Poivre emphasized a form of empowerment for the Mascarene: The State and metropolitan merchants (the former for budgetary reasons, the latter out of concerns with profitability) were not always able to adequately supply the settlements, which consequently had to find resources on their own.[49] This was also a tribute paid to the physiocrats' colonial ideal: The Mascarene should no longer be regarded as islands of commerce, but as places of settlement and subsistence. Therefore, they had to do so without help from the metropolis. Unfortunately for Poivre, Crozet's report, which survived the massacre in New Zealand, is very disappointing on this point: "These islands' barren aspect seems to indicate there is nothing much to expect from them." The expedition failed to go further south, because one of the two ships dismasted.

Crozet, however, reported that they had seen the islands spotted by another famous navigator, Kerguelen, several days before him, and so this discovery should be credited to deceased captain Marion. Such fierce competition—between two expeditions that had sailed out almost simultaneously in search of the southern continent—brings us back very directly to our subject, namely the performativity of the explorers' economic discourses.[50]

The third expedition Poivre assisted, though not on his own initiative, was in fact Kerguelen's. He left *Île de France* on January 16, 1772, with two ships: the *Fortune*, under his command, and the *Gros-Ventre,* under the command of François Aleno de St. Alouarn's (1737–1772). In mid-February, the expedition spotted several lands (soon to be called the Kerguelen Islands). Without landing, without reconnoitering the coast, and abandoning the *Gros-Ventre* in terrible weather conditions, Kerguelen returned to *Île de France* to proclaim, on 16 March, that he had discovered the southern continent. This was the beginning of an incredible and tragic adventure. He was accused of lying about his discoveries, of trading in trinkets in Madagascar and Cape Town, of having abandoned some of his crew, and of having stowed his young mistress; Kerguelen was prosecuted before the war council and imprisoned from 1775 to 1778. He again joined the Navy during the American War of Independence and, in 1782, published an account of both his trips to the Southern Ocean in an attempt to vindicate himself.

The instructions given by the king and by the Controller-General of Finances for his expedition in 1771 were crystal clear and fully echoed De Brosses's ideas. His goal was to be nothing less than "trying to achieve one of the most important discoveries yet to be made," namely finding the "southern continent [*continent austral*]" once and for all. Poivre gave his support to the project.[51] His instructions were unfortunately lost, but we do have a letter from the Intendant on Kerguelen's return which clearly indicates the expedition had nothing to do with looking for spice trees in these regions.

Convinced—or rather desperately trying to persuade himself—he had indeed accomplished his mission, Kerguelen, on his return to *Île de France*, wrote a "Reflections on the potential advantages France might derive from its southern possessions." This document, as well as many of his letters and memoirs, is currently preserved in the national archives. They are of crucial importance for understanding his ideas, though he understandably watered them down in his 1782 book. Full of incredible enthusiasm, he had no qualms to write, in March 1772, that:

> [t]he latitude where the sea lies is very promising: there can be grown all crops found in the metropolis which the islands is to far away from to be easily supplied with them. *France Australe* will provide specific grains, suited to human consumption, timber and mast-trees, which are excessively priced across India, breeches, tar of various kinds, hemp, seeds and fruit suited to yield oil; animal hides and livestock of all sorts, to be transported around our isles, either alive or salted. [...] The soil of *France Australe*, the same as in the metropolis, will provide settlers, transplanted from Europe into the torrid zone, products they are accustomed to in their natural environment and which they cannot do without.

In addition to these elements, he then resumed the usual enumerations about mining and precious stones to be found—the term was directly taken from De Brosses—in "Australasia." Poivre was, at first, excited by this account. On March 21, 1772, he wrote to the Minister that Kerguelen "has found a new world for France." While the goal was to engage in "beneficial exchanges," the difference from De Brosses and Forbonnais's colonial model was noticeable: Poivre empowered *Île de France* in its trade and took initiatives that would tend to reduce exchanges with the mainland.[52] His enthusiasm was all the more understandable as what Kerguelen proposed, which well may have been influenced by their previous discussions, was not to establish a trading post but rather a colony of settlement based on the cultivation of cereals. In fact, it was a new Canada that the explorer was so keen to discover, if only to avenge the disasters of the Seven Years' War:

> Our establishment requires all kinds of tools and workers, especially laborers and plowmen, as well as growers. Nothing better can be done than establish our new colony on tillage and agriculture and grant it to a few selected families among poor Acadians now living in different corners of France in the most frightful state of misery.

The project looked like Noah's ark. Kerguelen stressed sending animals, grain, and agricultural tools. One would then have to give the colony:

> time to settle down, build barns, sow and harvest; but before 6 years have passed, I'm sure it will pay with interest for the services we have bestowed it, and that far from needing assistance from our islands [of France and Bourbon], it will begin to provide them in its turn many forms of relief, to enrich their business, and eventually will stand for them as their metropolis.[53]

Kerguelen returned to France in late 1772. He sailed from Brest in March 1773, after successfully setting up a second expedition which actually brought Acadian settlers and farming resources on board. The adventure ended in total failure: Kerguelen barely managed to land and bitterly concluded in May 1774 that "the southern lands we traveled do not seem to offer any resources; they are covered in snow almost everywhere."

In both these tragic events, two crucial elements are particularly relevant for our purposes. The first is that Kerguelen relied more on the imaginations stirred by southern lands—and probably more on De Brosses's—than on his own observations. The performativity of economics of the Antipodes is here complete: The explorer has no doubt about Australasia's agricultural and commercial resources, even if he saw nothing to suggest it. The second relates to the final aims of this new colonial enterprise: Although De Brosses's work forms the backdrop of the belief, Kerguelen and Poivre subverted the project. This had nothing to do with trade, but rather with establishing the Poivre-Quesnay model, i.e., a farming colony that might become a new "metropolis" to the Mascarene Islands. By empowering them away from France, the southern Utopia turned into a Mascarene-Australasian complex, no longer meant to work for the benefit of French traders at all.

Despite his posturing and admiration for physiocratic ideas, however, could Poivre have been blinded by his greed for spices and expeditions, ultimately neglecting farming? This is what his successor, Maillard du Meslé, would like us to believe, in a letter to the Secretary of State for Marine in October 8, 1772:

> All those expeditions, my lord, that were meant to support discoveries of any kind or transporting *épiceries*, have cost enormously to the king, and the colony is also short of everything, of bread even. I will never understand the calculations leading to trying to rely on the outside and spend great wherewithal for that purpose, while one's own ground is not even exploited and funds are not forthcoming to do what is necessary: to me, this is most extravagant.
>
> Everything here seems to be related to subsistence [...]; if we are to achieve this, we must encourage and support agriculture [...].
>
> At the end of the day, discoveries are only an accessory, no doubt a useful one, but only insofar as the main purpose has been achieved and solidly established, so as not to be frequently exposed to shortages of every sort and to starvation. This is what I staunchly believe.[54]

Obviously, the debts left by the various expeditions—especially Marion Dufresne's—may partially explain such acrimony. Above all, two hurricanes had just damaged crops and warehouses, and food was in short supply. That was not the case from 1768 to 1771 when Poivre tried to follow the colonial model that he had described with such emphasis and conviction upon his arrival in 1767. Yet, what is more likely is that the difficult circumstances surrounding the arrival of the new Intendant masked some of Poivre's real achievements. Another assumption might also be made. Spices were seen as a way to get cereal crops to flourish, eventually replacing export crops (indigo, coffee, etc.) that were deemed exceedingly farmland-consuming. Most likely, similarly to what happened to another colonial physiocrat, namely Lemercier de la Rivière in the West Indies, Poivre managed only to partially implement his reformist program, because of the lack of resources he faced there.[55] Settlers could only be favorable to importing spice plants, as they must have been quite profitable for them. But did they follow Poivre's recommendations of rooting out their plantations of exotic products to grow wheat instead? Did they actually abandon trade and "luxury" goods? Yes, and for a while the island of France became a food crop colony, but due to lack of storage, rivalries and natural catastrophes, the program eventually failed. In a letter dated January 26, 1771, by Poivre to his friend Bernardin de Saint-Pierre, the Intendant wrote: "I am disgusted with the country and especially from my place, to a point that I cannot fully convey to you."[56] Later, the famous author of *Paul et Virginie* described Poivre as "one of the most attractive men I have ever known. However, due to his so many qualities, he made many enemies [...] I regretted it, and looked to him as a true philosopher, and a man who could bring happiness to the colony, if he had not so often been put off by the greatly hostile passions fermenting against him on the island." As such, the story seems to vindicate Charles and Cheney's findings on the limited resources available to colonial administrators, again demonstrating the tension between knowledge and zeal on the one hand, and practical achievements on the other, at least when it was a matter of implementing radical changes to French colonial practices.[57]

Conclusion

I have reified two models in this study. The first one is related to the Gournay circle and specifically codified in the work of De Brosses and Forbonnais, a model of colonies for trade, dedicated to the exclusive benefit of the metropolis. The second one is a physiocratic model of settlement and subsistence, where the aim of a colony is everything *except* trade. Emma Rothschild recently qualified the colonial economic theories of the period 1760–1770 as "unsuccessful ideas." To a certain degree, this is true: These ideas were never to be carried out, at least in their "pure" form. But if we look at the fates of these models, the specificity of this "lack of success" is worth exploring.[58]

This article shows that if the De Brosses's model is the most commonly used and repeated, it was also subverted both by the explorers (against free trade) and by Poivre (for the sake of his own model). Of course, this model seems never to have been formally implemented and Bougainville, for instance, questions the naivety and ignorance of his close friend in his *Voyage*. On the one hand, De Brosse's book became the basis for the explorations of the South Seas, leading a generation of Navy officers to reflect on questions of trade and empire. On the other, it became an intermediary target in favor of Poivre's ideal. In this sense, these models were not "unsuccessful" but rather inflected by their interaction with other interests during their implementations.

Furthermore, the notion of a "mantra" concerning free trade must be kept. Superficially, the doctrines of the Gournay circle and the physiocrats were completely successful: Lapérouse and Poivre profess free trade all throughout their printed works. But there is here a performativity of language that must be circumvented by historians, especially concerning the *doux-commerce* thesis. As we have seen, Bougainville or Lapérouse speak the language of prohibitions, of conquest, and exclusive companies in their manuscripts. The objectives of the government, its policy of "Empire," and conflicting passions, including Poivre's for spices, ultimately outweighed the supposedly well-balanced interests of theoretical political economy. In this sense, we can still describe our time as "Laperousian"; if the official discourse of international institutions and governments long has been that of free trade, rather, real economic policies remain based on aggressive conquests, depending on force, deceit, and even war.

Secondly, the failure of the colonial ideas of the physiocrats should be questioned in another way. If Poivre seems not to have achieved his objectives concerning the creation of a colony of subsistence, and if he seems to have abandoned some of his ideas, he did try to exploit commercial explorations in order to implement Quesnay's model. The quest for spices was *the* means to increase grain production and eventually create a new French Canada in the Southern Hemisphere. Yet, he was faced with competing passions and interests, including those of Marion Dufresne and Kerguelen, their hopes and dreams, not to mention those of the colonists. If the successes anticipated by the models of De Brosses and Forbonnais, or of Quesnay and Poivre, were not forthcoming, the attempts and experiences they generated were not in vain.

Notes

1. See in particular David Armitage, *Foundations of Modern International Thought* (Cambridge: Cambridge University Press, 2013); David Armitage, *The Ideological Origins of the British Empire* (Cambridge: Cambridge University Press, 2000); Susan Manning and Francis D. Cogliano, eds., *The Atlantic Enlightenment* (Aldershot and Burlington:

Ashgate, 2008); Sankar Muthu, *Enlightenment against Empire* (Princeton: Princeton University Press, 2003); Sankar Muthu, ed., *Empire and Modern Political Thought* (Cambridge: Cambridge University Press, 2012); Sophus A. Reinert, *Translating Empire. Emulation and the Origins of Political Economy* (Cambridge and London: Harvard University Press, 2011); Emma Rothschild, "Global Commerce and the Question of Sovereignty in the Eighteenth Century," *Modern Intellectual History* 1, no. 1 (2004): 3–25; Emma Rothschild, "Language and Empire, *c.* 1800," *Historical Research* 78 (2005): 208–29; and Emma Rothschild, *The Inner Life of Empires. An Eighteenth-Century History* (Princeton and Oxford: Princeton University Press, 2011).

2. Armitage, *Foundations*, 54.
3. See Anthony Pagden, *Lords of All the World. Ideologies of Empire in Spain, Britain, and France c. 1500–c. 1800* (New Haven and London: Yale University Press, 1995); Muthu, *Enlightenment*; Rothschild, "Global Commerce"; and Armitage, *Foundations*.
4. Rothschild, "Global Commerce"; Paul Cheney, *Revolutionary Commerce. Globalization and the French Monarchy* (Cambridge and London: Harvard University Press, 2010).
5. See Edward Duyker, *Marc-Joseph Marion Dufresne. Un marin malouin à la découverte des mers australes* (Rennes: Les Portes du Large, 2010); Catherine Gaziello, *L'expédition de Lapérouse (1785–1788). Réplique française aux voyages de Cook* (Paris: CTHS, 1984); and Etienne Taillemite, *Bougainville* (Paris: Perrin, 2011).
6. Madeleine Ly-Tio-Fane, "Pierre Poivre et l'expansion française dans l'Indo-Pacifique," *Bulletin de l'École française d'Extrême-Orient* 52, no. 2 (1967): 453–512; Philippe Despoix, *Le monde mesuré. Dispositifs de l'exploration à l'âge des Lumières* (Genève: Droz, 2005); and John Dunmore, *Where Fate Beckons. The Life of Jean-François de Lapérouse* (Fairbanks: University of Alaska Press, 2007). In France in the 1750s, the *Intendant du Commerce* Jacques Vincent de Gournay (1712–1759) brought together young learned men around a reformist economic program. Concerning the Gournay circle in general, see Loïc Charles, Frédéric Lefebvre, and Christine Théré, eds., *Le cercle de Vincent de Gournay. Savoirs économiques et pratiques administratives en France au milieu du XVIIIe siècle* (Paris: Institut National d'Études Démographiques, 2011).
7. Reinert, *Translating Empire;* Michael Mosher, "Montesquieu on Empire and Enlightenment," in *Empire and Modern Political Thought*, ed. S. Muthu (Cambridge: Cambridge University Press, 2012), 112–54.

8. See Armitage, *Ideological Origins*, 155; Pagden, *Lords of all the World*, 126–27.
9. Reinert, *Translating Empire*, 7.
10. Despoix, *Monde mesuré*, 28–29; Charles de Brosses, *Histoire des navigations aux terres australes*, 2 vols. (Paris: Durand, 1756), I: i.
11. De Brosses, *Histoire des navigations*, I: ij; I: 4, and I: 16. One must create a need among these peoples: "Whatever the attachment of these raw peoples for their old manners, it is impossible that they cannot be caught in the long run by the example of a more gentle and convenient life." (ibid., II: 320). See also François Véron de Forbonnais, *Élémens du commerce*, 2 vols. (Leyde et Paris: Briasson, David, Le Breton & Durand, 1754), II: 14–15.
12. De Brosses, *Histoire des navigations*, 18.
13. Ibid., II: 345; I: 28; II: 346.
14. Ibid., I: 40–42.
15. Ibid., I: 26; II: 372.
16. Ibid., I: 42.
17. Forbonnais, *Élémens du commerce,* II: 21–32. De Brosses quotes several passages from these pages.
18. Ibid., II: 32; II: 41. Except during periods of war, when traders from neutral countries should be allowed to trade with the French colonies in order to support them. See François Véron de Forbonnais, *Essai sur l'admission des navires neutres dans nos Colonies* (Paris, 1756). On this question, see Antonella Alimento, "Competition, True Patriotism, and Colonial Interest: Forbonnais' Vision of Neutrality and Trade," in *Trade and War: The Neutrality of Commerce in the Inter-State System*, ed. K. Stapelbroek (Helsinki: Helsinki Collegium for Advanced Studies, 2011), 61–94.
19. Forbonnais, *Élémens*, II: 25–26; II: 10–11. "It is therefore obvious that between two peoples who make war, the one with a better Navy [...] increases its trade, while the other has lost its own." (ibid., II: 10–11).
20. Cheney, *Revolutionary Commerce*, 160.
21. Pierre Poivre, "Discours Prononcé par P. Poivre, à son arrivée a l'Île de France, aux habitans de la Colonie assemblés au Gouvernement," in *Œuvres Complettes* [sic] *de P. Poivre, Intendant des Île de France et de Bourbon, Correspondant de l'académie des sciences,* etc.*; Précédées de sa vie, et accompagnées de notes* [by Du Pont de Nemours] (Paris: Fuchs, 1797 [1767]), 199–232. See also Pierre Poivre, "Discours Prononcé à

la première assemblée publique du nouveau conseil supérieur de l'Île de France, le 3 août 1767," ibid., 233–52.
22. Poivre, "Discours Prononcé," 200–223.
23. Cheney, *Revolutionary Commerce*, 161–62.
24. François Quesnay, "Remarques sur l'opinion de l'auteur de l'*Esprit des Loix* concernant les colonies," in *François Quesnay. Œuvres économiques complètes et autres textes*, ed. Ch. Théré, L. Charles et J.-C. Perrot (Paris : INED, 2005 [1766]), II: 869–79, 873–77. See also Pierre-Joseph Roubaud, *Histoire générale de l'Asie, de l'Afrique et de l'Amérique*, 15 vols. (Paris: Des Ventes de la Doué, 1770); Cheney, *Revolutionary Commerce*, chap. 6.
25. See in particular Cheney, *Revolutionary Commerce*, 157. It is that very view of commercial relationships Forbonnais severely criticized in 1767 in his *Principes et observations économiques*: "The conclusion of the system [the Physiocrats'] is that we must not make offensive war; however, a checks and balance system is assumed; now, to support it, the need arises to protect & help it offensively: & a state that were never offensive would be perpetually busy defending itself." (François Véron de Forbonnais, *Principes et observations œconomiques* (Amsterdam: Rey, 1767), 294).
26. Odile Gannier, "La compilation et l'usage des journaux de bord dans l'histoire des idées et des sciences," in *Relations savantes. Voyages et discours scientifiques*, ed. S. Linon-Chipon and D. Vaj (Paris: Presses Universitaires de la Sorbonne, 2006), 70; Despoix, *Monde mesuré*, 30.
27. Constant, "Introduction," xv. One should add that the Bougainville brothers at the time had relations with a future member of the Gournay circle, G.-M. Butel-Dumont (1725–1789). See the correspondence of P.-M. Hennin, *Bibliothèque de l'Institut de France*, Ms. 1266 and Ms. 1254.
28. Constant, "Introduction," xi; Louis-Antoine de Bougainville, *Voyage autour du monde, par la frégate du roi la* Boudeuse *et la flûte l'*Étoile, *en 1766, 1767, 1768 et 1769*, 2nd édition (Paris: La Découverte 2006 [1772]), 129–30. He questions the advance knowledge of such a metal by these peoples.
29. Ibid., 152, 210, 239, 252, 273–75.
30. Archives Nationales, Marine, B/4/314, f°123.
31. De Brosses, *Histoire des navigations*, II: 345.
32. First, when he authorizes the naturalist Dufresne to return to France from Macao in January 1787, then in September 1787 when he leaves

the officer de Lesseps in the Kamchatka (who travels through Russia and Europe before returning to Paris), finally on February 7, 1788, at Botany Bay where Lapérouse leaves a few letters to an English squadron, which will then transmit it to the French government.

33. Dunmore, *Where Fate*, 43.
34. Louis-Marie-Antoine Milet-Mureau, *Voyage de La Pérouse autour du monde, publié conformément au décret du 22 avril 1791,* 4 vols. (Paris: Imprimerie de la République, 1797-An V), I: 30–42.
35. Ibid., II: 34–35; II: 61–62; II: 346–47.
36. "Mémoire sur Manille," Archives Nationales, Marine, B/4/320/n°1.
37. "Mémoire du Roy pour servir d'instruction aux Srs Dumas et Poivre, 28 novembre 1766," Archives Nationales, Marine, C/4/17/f°3–4.
38. "Observations sur l'introduction et la culture des epiceries aux îles de France, de Bourbon et de Séchelles, 12 septembre 1773," Archives Nationales, Marine, C/4/30, f°345.
39. Ly-Tio-Fane, "Pierre Poivre."
40. Duyker, *Marc-Joseph Marion Dufresne*, 215.
41. Poivre is completely in line with physiocracy on fisheries: "Mirabeau, for example, described the 'primary, immense utility and surprising facility' of fisheries, in contrast to the 'secondary, limited utility and dependent character' of the fur business." (Rothschild, "Global commerce," 11). See also Archives Nationales, Marine, B/4/317/n°1.
42. Archives Nationales, Marine, B/4/317/n°2 and n°10; C/4/3/f°307; C/4/27.
43. *Éphémérides du Citoyen*, 1770, tome 8, 159–60.
44. Archives Nationales, Marine, C/4/29, f°55–56; Colonies, B/202.
45. "Lettress inédites de Poivre et de Céré," *Revue historique et littéraire de l'île Maurice* 1890, 337.
46. Archives Nationales, Marine, B/4/317/n°16 and B/4/317/n°16.
47. "There is suspicion that the clove tree and the nutmeg can be found in New Guinea, as well as in Moluccas: but one may be certain to be able to buy plants of these precious trees in the adjacent islands; and in this regard, the secret instructions of the intendant Poivre, will put the Captain Marion in the right attitude in order to achieve a significant part of his mission in a useful way to the colony of the île de France." (Alexis-Marie de Rochon, *Voyages à Madagascar, à Maroc et aux Indes Orientales*, 3 vols. (Paris: Prault et Levrault, 1802), III: 315).

48. Julien Crozet, *Nouveau voyage a la mer du sud* (Paris: Barrois, 1783), 3–4.
49. Concerning the Mascarenes during the War of American Independence, see Arnaud Orain, "Les contraintes d'approvisionnement pendant la guerre d'indépendance américaine: une étude de cas dans l'océan Indien," in *Enquêtes et Documents. Échanges, relations internationales et histoire du monde atlantique*, ed. D. Plouviez (Rennes: Presses Universitaires de Rennes, 2013).
50. Archives Nationales, Marine, B/4/317/n°42. See also Crozet, *Nouveau voyage*, 21–22.
51. Kerguelen "will look to the productions of the land, its culture, its Manufactures, if there are, & how to make best use of it for the Kingdom trade." (Yves-Joseph de Kerguelen, *Relation de deux voyages Dans les mers Australes & des Indes faits en 1771, 1772, 1773, & 1774* (Paris: Knapen & Fils, 1782), 5); Archives Nationales, Colonies, C/4/30, f°261.
52. Archives Nationales, Marine, B/4/317/n°108 and B/4/317/n°68.
53. "Mémoire pour l'établissement d'une colonie dans la France Australe" (Archives Nationales, Marine, B/4/317/n°109).
54. Archives Nationales, Marine, B/4/317/n°163 and B/4/317/n°101.
55. Loïc Charles and Paul Cheney, "The Colonial Machine Dismantled: Knowledge and Empire in the French Atlantic," *Past and Present* 219, no. 1 (2013): 127–63.
56. Archives Municipales du Havre, Ms. 671, 5^1.
57. Maurice Souriau, *Une aventure de Bernardin de Saint-Pierre à l'Île de France* (Paris: Société française d'imprimerie et de librairie, 1901), 397; Charles and Cheney, "The Colonial Machine."
58. Rothschild, "Global Commerce," 24.

Author Biography

Arnaud Orain is Professor of Economics at the University of Paris 8 (France) and was David Fellow of the History Department of Princeton University in 2015–2016. Arnaud specializes in the history of economic thought of the French Enlightenment, with a particular emphasis on anti-physiocracy on the one hand, and the links between religion (Jansenism), literature, and economics, on the other hand. He is currently completing a cultural history of John Law's financial system in France from 1717 to the Revolution.

A "Surreptitious Introduction": Opium Smuggling and Colonial State Formation in Late Nineteenth-Century Bengal and Burma

Diana Kim

It began as a petty dispute over the modest sum of two rupees. In November 1870, opium cost twenty-two rupees in the Bengali port city of Chittagong, but only twenty rupees in the neighboring enclave of Akyab in Burma. At the time, both locations were administered under the Government of India and colonial bureaucrats of Bengal asked their counterparts in Burma to "equalize" the difference of two rupees.[1] When refused, the former marshaled evidence to demonstrate first, "the existence of a widespread system of smuggling," and second, "the fact that the responsibility of the present state of things rest[ed] with the authorities of British Burma."[2]

On one level, this was a dispute over the proper fiscal role of a government toward an overseas dependency during the late nineteenth century. The seemingly small price difference reflected a large gap between established approaches to opium revenue extraction in Bengal and Burma. "Whilst both are portions of the Empire, a wide difference exists between the two," one official explained.[3] In Bengal, independent

D. Kim (✉)
Edmund A. Walsh School of Foreign Service,
Georgetown University, Washington, USA
e-mail: Diana.Kim@georgetown.edu

R. Fredona and S.A. Reinert (eds.), *New Perspectives on the History of Political Economy*, https://doi.org/10.1007/978-3-319-58247-4_8

merchants ordered a competitive opium market where top-down restrictions upon the commodity's sale, distribution, and consumption were minimal. In British Burma by contrast, the government farmed out the right to tax opium to a few wealthy entrepreneurs, dividing the market into and controlling it through local monopolies.

At another level, this dispute was about illicit colonial markets. Involved administrators disagreed, not simply about who was at fault but over how to make sense of secretive economic activities. Allegedly, there was a steady flow of contraband traveling between Chittagong and Akyab, where Bengali free markets and Burmese tax farms were brought into close proximity. Purportedly, merchants and tax farmers were working together in ways that upset the commodity's value in one place, while rewarding its "surreptitious introduction" into another.[4] And, lamented another official, it appeared that there was "no exaggerated picture of lawlessness" that could be portrayed as resulting from such opium smuggling in the colonies.[5] Yet, the existence and dynamics of this hidden trade, let alone its causes and consequences, were difficult to establish because the local administrators of these two British-ruled provinces made competing arguments, espoused different types of evidence, and held conflicting stakes toward observing an unobservable economic activity. Thus, the dispute about two rupees was also a dispute over the epistemological basis of colonial knowledge concerned with the commercial life of opium and its hidden operations.

How and with what significance did this dispute emerge? This chapter traces the administrative struggles that gave rise to the 1870 Chittagong-Akyab episode in the context of late nineteenth-century developments in colonial state formation. At the time, dealing with opium smuggling was at once a challenge to and opportunity for legitimating European control over non-European markets. Local disagreements over how to understand contraband in the colonies and how to regulate it also reflected important debates that preoccupied the imperial world, including whether empires should defend commerce in opiates as productive or worry about its dangerous influences; and what constituted a proper relationship between government and commerce in unfamiliar settings.[6]

My emphasis lies in the capricious nature of regulatory controls over opium, which I argue reflects the instabilities of colonial state interests and reveals the tenuous basis upon which seemingly authoritative claims to govern were made. As Eric Tagliacozzo has astutely shown of British and Dutch rulers in Southeast Asia during this time period, "there was, in fact, no ontology whatsoever to the category of contraband… [it] was whatever those in power said it was, and these designations sometimes changed very quickly."[7] The episode of opium smuggling that I explore yields insight into the conceptual and discursive resources involved in such designations and the swiftness with which they changed. In doing so, it underscores the extent to which what appears as self-evident antagonisms between state and illicit economic activities are context specific and indebted to particular historical and structural conditions.

This chapter as such suggests a new direction for scholarship on the coevolution of states and illegal markets. Current research on this topic has long moved away from identifying smuggling and other illicit activities as constant threats to state capacity and authority.[8] Historians and political scientists alike are more attentive to the myriad sociopolitical linkages that blur distinctions between state and non-state actors, legal and illegal acts, as well as legitimate and illegitimate forms of violence.[9] Recent studies in this vein show, for example, the malleable meanings of crime and corruption in seventeenth-century transatlantic piracy and privateering; the fuzzy boundaries of underground economies in alcohol and salt in eighteenth-century France; as well as the diverse incentives, shifting interests, and overlapping roles of participants in contemporary trafficking networks in drugs across present-day Southeast Asia's "Golden Triangle" region.[10] Such thoughtful works see more to illegal markets and smuggling in particular than "mere" subversion or a natural obverse of state control.[11] They elucidate not only how non-state, illegal, and illegitimate activities have putatively contributed to the making of key features of modern states, but also how states partake in the creation of illegal markets by labeling certain economic acts as crimes. Most often, this recursive relationship has been examined from the vantage point of the smuggler's complicated regard of an entity called the state.[12] This chapter considers another perspective: the state's complex understanding of entities known as smugglers.

Specifically, I present two conflicting accounts by colonial administrators caught in an indecisive moment in 1870. Of course, there were likely many more public and private narratives at work, and the bureaucratic departments considered in this chapter capture but one of many sites that comprised the British colonial state in India and Burma. In this regard, the history of opium's regulation I recount is necessarily partial and underrepresents the multiplicity of perspectives. Nonetheless, a close look at the Chittagong-Akyab dispute offers an unparalleled glimpse into a state's unstable and shifting regard of opium smuggling. For what happened in November 1870 was a failed seizure in which no amount of contraband, small or large, was actually discovered, or at least, reported officially. There were only many suspicions and conflicting diagnoses that divided administrative agents of the state regarding the same provincial border, traversed by a common invisible movement, of the same commodity. The following narrative, therefore, is a story of smuggling told by the colonial state on the ground.

Imperial Opium and Excise Taxation

Although Bengali Chittagong and Burma's Akyab embraced different types of administrative frameworks by the 1870s, these two port cities also hosted opium markets that shared some similarities. In addition to their involvement in India's great opium trade to China, Chittagong and Akyab had local consumer bases for the commodity, and thus, provincial governments raised revenue, not only from duties on exportation but also from an excise tax collected on the retail sale of opium for internal or "home" consumption.[13] The capacity of local administrations to levy taxes on opium within their territorial jurisdictions (while seemingly straightforward in retrospect) was the product of a long controversy over how the British in India should deal with opium as a market commodity.

Since the late eighteenth century—after the British East India Company (EIC) conquered Bengal (1757), centralized control over opium production and sale (1775), and consolidated a direct monopoly over the export trade from the Bay of Bengal toward the east (1797)—there had been disagreement over whether Bengal opium should be treated as a domestic good of territorial revenue or a foreign article of commercial investment.[14] Politically, this distinction was significant as it meant a difference between whether the locus of opium law and policy making would lie with the EIC Board of Directors (because for foreign articles of commercial investment, the charter of the EIC exercised a trade monopoly) or the Legislature of Britain (because the EIC's charter also acknowledged and yielded purely domestic articles of territorial revenue in the Indian subcontinent as the property of the King of England). Administratively, there was a difference over whether customs officers would primarily enforce those rules or whether the jurisdictional authority of excise officers would take precedence. And socially, the different regulatory status accorded to opium entailed competing understandings of whether it represented an indigenous intoxicant, consumed popularly by the people of India or not. As a foreign good, opium was presumed a commodity in demand among only a small and wealthy portion of the Indian population, but highly coveted in China and beyond. By contrast, opium as a domestic good implied its nested place within the everyday Indian economic and social life.[15]

Initially, the former regard of opium and its profit as a commercial rather than territorial return prevailed. The mercantilist EIC successfully embraced the idea that:

> "[I]t was undesirable to increase the production of any article not necessary to life, and that opium was 'not a necessary of life but a pernicious article of luxury which ought not to be permitted but for the purposes of foreign commerce only, and which the wisdom of Government should carefully refrain from internal consumption.'"[16]

The key significance of opium's treatment as an *Article of Luxury* was that even when its commercial life generated revenue within the subcontinent through cultivation across the poppy fields of Bihar and Benares, manufacture in the opium factories of Patna and Ghazipur, as well as distribution through the bazaars of India, the mechanisms for taxing domestic sales were lax, compared to the elaborate system of export duties, purchase certificates, and Calcutta auction for opium moving outside of India. Over time, the EIC's arbitrary distinction became controversial, however, in part as the weakness of top-down regulatory control over inland opium markets gave an extraordinary amount of autonomy to local power holders and provided numerous opportunities for the EIC's own underpaid employees to supplement their meager salaries through graft and other administrative malfeasances. Independent merchants contracted with the EIC were also able to circumspectly exact more privileges than their formal agreements stipulated.[17]

Moreover, it eventually became difficult for the EIC to plausibly uphold—to a growing audience of moral critics—that opium was a little-consumed luxury good, given growing domestic demands and mounting evidence of popular consumption throughout Bengal.[18] In 1823, the EIC sought to recategorize opium as a domestic good, subject to the control of local revenue boards. The Bengal Board of Revenue, for instance, was a regulatory institution that oversaw matters pertaining to revenue produced within territorial jurisdictions of the province and began to categorize opium along with other provincial articles of excise including salt, spirituous liquors, and intoxicating drugs such as hemp (instead of export-centered items of luxury such as spices and silks).[19]

On the one hand, the inclusion of opium within the excise is important to understand because it illustrates a dynamic of British colonial rule in India common to both Bengal and Burma during this time period. The collapsing of distinctions believed as indigenous to extant inhabitants under an encompassing English label was a conventional way that the British in London and India sought to overcome their vast ignorance about the nature of the subcontinent's history, political economy, religious and social orders as well as legal structure.[20] For example, since the beginning of Company rule, the Persian word *abkaree* (*abkari*), literally translated into English as "strong waters," had been used to label legal rules for the manufacture and sale of stimulants understood as uniquely consumed by the people of India. Although at first *abkaree* regulations only included alcoholic liquors (such as *tari,* a type of palm wine), its schedule grew over time to extend to any intoxicants produced within India (such as toddy and distilled whiskey). Opium was first specifically mentioned as an intoxicating drug under the Bengal Regulation X of 1813; by 1823 when opium became subject to inland taxes, the terms *abkaree* and excise were used interchangeably. *Abkaree*, came both to refer to a British fiscal understanding of excise and to confer an official understanding of native intoxicant upon opium. In 1870, both British Burma and Bengal, as provinces of British India were subject to the 1856 *Abkaree* Act XXI, which had codified the regulatory power accorded to excise officials regarding matters concerning opium. As a result, "excise" as a label used by colonial officials in Bengal and Burma during this time period referred simultaneously to the market value of a commodity as well as the social meaning of a good.[21]

On the other hand and given these two intertwined meanings of excise, the inclusion of opium within this legal administrative category helps explain a key difference between Bengal and Burma's approach to opium that emerged over time. After the establishment of opium as an excise/*abkaree* good, both areas began auctioning off the privilege of extracting revenue to willing individuals with the necessary means. This decentralized arrangement for control accorded a great deal of autonomy to local power holders who at once drew upon and reconfigured their hold upon existing social and economic ties within specific areas, generating and extracting profit from local systems of production. It was a type of tax-farming system under which an individual or collective exercised a quasi-monopoly over provincial distribution and retail sales. Although generally a cost-effective arrangement for the government, one drawback to this arrangement was the expanding prowess of the tax farmer, who could and often did engage in undertrading.[22]

The responses of Bengal and Burma's administrators to illicit traffic, however, differed. Smuggling, Bengal decided, provided good reason to abolish the farming system. In 1857, the closed opium market was opened as the local government introduced a new regulatory system. Instead of protected sub-monopolies, free licenses were liberally granted to anyone deemed a "respectable and responsible" person wanting to enter the competitive market.[23] The only duty levied on opium was the fee that licensed vendors paid to obtain it from a government factory.

The market price of opium became cheaper as vendors were simultaneously less capable of passing on the costs to buyers (because there were many other competitors) and less inclined to increase the sales costs of their goods (because the fixed price of the excise opium was minimal). Enthusiastic supporters spoke of it as a successful fiscal arrangement that fostered competition and was thought to have "effectually remove (d) any inducement to smuggle."[24] Bengal's bureaucrats called it the "free trade" system for opium.

In contrast, Burma did not abolish opium farming. Or more precisely, the local administration briefly experimented with the same opium licensing system in the same year as Bengal, but quickly chose to revert back to tax farming.[25] The state of the colonial market appeared differently from their perspective, as colonial bureaucrats in Burma claimed to see the opposite of what their Bengali counterparts regarded as reality. Hardly a deterrent to illicit flows of opium, the former spoke of the competitive opium market as a catalyst to contraband and the "free market" system as a failure that brought "deplorable and disastrous results."[26] In Burma, many argued that loosening controls over opium and making it more readily available had created "a new and insatiable demand" that overwhelmed what the colonial administration could supply. From their vantage point, opium tax farms served a necessary role in both curtailing growing demand for opium and preventing local merchants from smuggling.[27] Thus, two contradictory arrangements for opium—the free-trade system in Bengal and the tax-farming system in Burma—came to exist conterminously and in some places, in provincial border areas for example, alongside each other. It was the juxtaposition of these two different systems that portended a clash among local bureaucrats over the proper administrative approach to the colonial opium market and its contraband elements.

What Causes Contraband (in Bengal)

The dispute began on November 10, 1870, when the Bengal Board of Revenue noted something odd happening in Chittagong. Although there was reportedly only a modest taste for opium within the port city's local bazaars, sales had increased exponentially over the past five years. At a fixed price of twenty-two rupees per mound, local merchants were competitively supplying more and more opium, despite an apparent absence of commensurate growth in consumption.[28]

Puzzled by this phantom demand, the bureaucrats of Bengal looked east beyond the provincial border and found their answer. On the other side of a narrow body of water, known as the Naf Estuary, was Akyab, the main seaport of British Burma's northwestern coast. Here, opium was sold to farmers for only twenty rupees, two rupees less than the price set for merchants on the Bengali side of the Naf. The actual market price for opium, however, was much higher in Akyab, a price far beyond that in Chittagong. It was, according to the Revenue Collector of Chittagong, "raised to 30 rupees, nay, even alleged [as] 40 rupees."[29] It seemed that Burmese tax farmers were able to manipulate the value of opium in ways that merchants competing within Bengal's market could not.[30] Particularly in the case of Akyab, explained the Collector, farmers were doing so by limiting the supply of opium while raising its selling price "so as to obtain a larger rate on a small quantity and thus obtain larger returns on a smaller capital," exercising a prerogative included in their contracts with the local administration.[31] In turn, merchants in Chittagong were buying more opium and secretly sending it across the Naf, capitalizing on the scarcity of supply in Akyab. These were what revenue officers in Bengal called "powerful inducements to smuggle" linking the two British Indian provinces.[32]

Bengal considered the flow of contraband from Chittagong to Akyab a political-economic anomaly that British Burma was responsible for. From their perspective, the illicit opium market spanning across the Naf stemmed from external interruptions to a competitive market. More precisely, clarified the Bengal Board of Revenue, smuggling was caused by distortionary administrative practices in British Burma, which since 1862—by reinstituting and protecting the sales monopoly of the Akyab tax farmer—effectively established an extravagant set of restrictions that disrupted the normal and natural workings of the local market.[33] Such restrictions included limits on the yearly quantity of opium that could be sold in a locale, licensing fees for opium farmers, and jurisdictional parameters around opium shops.

In this respect, a local complaint about different opium prices in Chittagong and Akyab more broadly articulated Bengal's principled objection to the continuance of tax farming that was "a remnant of the old mode of selling opium and…should be abolished." As the Bengal Board of Revenue called upon Burma to equalize prices, it was effectively pressing for institutional reforms that would assimilate the latter's approach to the former by limiting intervention into the colonial opium market. "(F)ree trade in both parts of the empire is all that is needed," insisted the bureaucrats of Bengal.[34]

What Causes Contraband (in Burma)

British Burma saw the matter differently. The connection between Chittagong and Akyab was a matter of alleged smuggling, countered members of its Excise Department.[35] They asked: What evidence did Bengal have to prove that a so-called widespread system of opium smuggling existed between Chittagong and Akyab? On what basis could they establish this as a fact, let alone attribute responsibility to the neighboring administration? For "in spite of the strong incentive to smuggling offered by the very much higher cost of licit opium in Burma than in India, very little smuggling ha[d] taken place."[36] In so doubting what those in Bengal took for granted, colonial administrators stationed in Burma were voicing at least three broader points of disagreement.

For one, they were denying that the tax-farming system was accountable for the growth of opium smuggling. There are many motivations for one group of administrators to defend themselves against the criticisms of another group that include personal rivalries, status anxieties, and worries of reputation and policing resources. And indeed these are some reasons why the issue of who was at fault for causing illicit trade was at stake. This was an accusation that would not only embarrass the Excise Department (relatively young and understaffed compared with the large number of pedigreed personnel that Bengal enjoyed) but also potentially carry practical repercussions for a nascent administration in Burma by reflecting poorly upon its management capacities. Yet, these were extant and latent tensions in place. Why did the matter of opium smuggling become particularly contentious in the fall of 1870?

For Albert Fytche, Chief Commissioner of British Burma, disagreements with his counterpart in Bengal stemmed from how differently they theorized the causes of contraband. For unlike the Collector of Chittagong who spoke of smuggling as an anomaly, Chief Commissioner Fytche regarded such exchanges as a natural accompaniment to the excise market. In the case of Chittagong and Akyab, he elaborated, the emergence of an illicit opium trade represented a trend coeval to the rise of opium's licit and legal trade between Bengal and Burma. To the extent that these flows were in place prior to the latter's reintroduction of the farming system, the complainants were, in Fytche's opinion, embarrassingly mistaken in their historical knowledge of the matter and guilty of reversing the causes and consequences of British Burma's so-called interferences.[37]

It was not Burma's opium tax farming but rather the free-trade system that had catalyzed trans-Naf exchanges in illicit opium, Fytche declared. He dated the precise origins of the smuggling that so alarmed Bengal to July 1857 when Bengal's *Abkaree* rules had first come into force in Burma. According to Fytche, during the few years that the free-trade system so lauded by Bengal was put in place, "drinking spirits and smoking opium had become almost universal among the young men of Arakan; and in Akyab alone...upwards of ninety [new] shops had been established for the sale of intoxicating liquors and drugs." He explained how, in response, Burma's colonial Excise Department had been forced to revert back to tax farming in order to curtail the growth of this public demand.[38]

From the Chief Commissioner of British Burma's perspective, smuggling only appeared to be quantitatively growing, but this was actually reflecting a qualitative change to the nature of opium's consumption pattern in places like Akyab. Put simply, according to Fytche, the complaints of the Chittagong Collector were based on the greater visibility of public demands for opium rather than the new emergence or exceptional growth of contraband flows per se. The ranking authority of British Burma acerbically pointed out that the only reason why "much of [this] smuggling has been brought under notice by the authorities of Chittagong [was] in some measure attributable to the unhappy tastes which were spread...by the facilities furnished...between 1857 and 1862."[39]

A second disagreement concerned varying understandings of the proper role of colonial administration. Fytche interpreted the overarching British Indian legal framework for excise in general and opium, specifically, the 1856 *Abkaree* Act XXI, as "founded upon two distinct principles:

> [F]irst, to raise as large an amount of revenue from intoxicating liquors and drugs as is compatible with the greatest possible discouragement of their use, and second, to avoid raising the tax on opium or checking its sales beyond certain limits as experience teaches that, under such circumstances, the people will procure the drug by surreptitious means."[40]

While Bengal had embraced the second principle, in British Burma, Fytche argued, "it [had] been found absolutely necessary to give prominence to the first principle, namely that of *raising for the public benefit the greatest amount of revenue with the smallest possible consumption* [emphasis added]." The difference between the two, he claimed, was the end to which the means of opium taxation would serve the colony. In his own words, what constituted the "public benefit" in Burma concerning opium was distinct from that for Bengal, because "other races…might be contented with a moderate enjoyment of such a stimulant but the Burmese were uniquely vulnerable," in suffering an "unfortunate craving" for opium and "could not resist indulging in excess." Fytche attested to the unusual circumstances for which he considered excise taxes on opium as not only appropriate, but also a necessary check on the colonial market. His administration and the contracted tax farmers had thus aligned to impose prohibitively high prices on opium, effectively imposing an unforgiving sumptuary tax upon consumers.[41]

Of course, Fytche's call for protectionism echoes old and familiar defenses of excise taxation that originated outside of British Burma. The administrative phrases he used directly borrowed from a utilitarian language in vogue among influential European thinkers and learned bureaucrats and judicial officials in India at the time. For example, amid debates over the 1856 *Abkaree* Act, the Chief Justice of Bengal framed his objections to the new legal rules by reminding the Legislative Council of Samuel Johnson's definition of excise from the *Dictionary of the English Language* (1776): "a hateful tax levied upon commodities and adjudged, not by the common judges of property but wretches hired by those to whom excise is paid."[42] The influence of utilitarian discourse is further demonstrated by how administrative manuals circulated by the Government of India drew directly from John Stuart Mill's *Principles of Political Economy* to define the objective of excise administration in Bengal (as well as other provinces). According to Mill, regarding the "Comparison between Direct and Indirect Taxes":

> No tax ought to be kept so high as to furnish a motive for its evasion, too strong to be counteracted by ordinary means of prevention; and especially no commodity should be taxed so highly as to raise up a class of lawless characters, smugglers, illicit distillers, and the like.[43]

What is distinctive, however, about the Chief Commissioner's pronouncement is an expressed sentiment that the opium market in Burma worked differently from elsewhere in the British Indian Empire. He reasoned that the colonial bazaar was not a simple replica of metropolitan markets because of the peculiar nature of opium consumption and its observed demand, perceived failures of a free-trade system in Burma unlike its success in Bengal, as well as an understanding that practical variations to general principles of excise were an administrative necessity.

Relatedly and finally, a third disagreement concerned competing perspectives over how a political economy of excise worked within an overseas colony. The British in Bengal presumed similarities between European and non-European contexts as they looked at price differentials and abrupt increases in sales volumes to explain incentives prompting actors to hide and hoard opium. "Doubtless," claimed the Collector of Chittagong, individuals were seeking profit and seizing opportunities for contraband.[44] He marshaled descriptive statistics showing that tax farmers, merchants, and traders were colluding to supply opium sparingly in Akyab and its environs in order to manipulate the value of a scarce good, while inundating the bazaars near and in Chittagong with unwanted opium, generating an arbitrary surplus. These activities disrupted the Bengal free market that was already distorted due to the British Burmese farming system. Contraband flows existed and were growing, argued the Collector. The more burgeoning the business of opium shops in Chittagong and the larger the gap between the fixed price of opium and that reported by officers touring local bazaars, the more insistently the Collector reported that an already widespread system of smugglers was spreading more widely.[45]

But, protested Chief Commissioner Fytche "exact statistics as regards illicit trade are scarcely attainable."[46] His doubt about the availability and accuracy of numbers was also a skepticism toward the evidence that Bengal relied upon. Rather, to understand the "fact of smuggling," the Chief Commissioner invited those outside of the colony to literally look within "sea ports towns…where there is generally a considerable foreign population already accustomed to the use of stimulants."[47] In Akyab, the oldest of such locations, a divided market had emerged around this foreign population.[48] Some were foreign because they originated outside of the land of Burma and established only a fleeting presence, such as the sailors and occasional *laskars* docking at the piers of Akyab, while others like the migrant workers who took up residence in the port were foreign because their recently established status within Burma derived from other countries. Regardless, foreign populations constituted a remarkably sturdy type of opium consumer, one accustomed to consuming extensive quantities of opium with little bodily ill-effect.[49] Then, there were extant inhabitants of Akyab who "could not resist indulging to excess whenever opium was placed before them."[50] Not all of the indigenous population experienced these effects in the same way, Fytche made clear; the "most deteriorating effect" primarily affected the younger generation of Akyab.[51]

In addition to specifying a comparative imbalance to consumer capabilities by pointing to the more unhappy taste for opium among Akyab's inhabitants, the Chief Commissioner spoke of power asymmetries as he emphasized the influence of foreign populations, namely migrants coming from places outside of British Burma, such as Bengali Chittagong. Fytche explained: The indigenous opium consumer of Burma encountered foreigners in a precarious manner.[52] And while foreign providers of opium established one type of tie with other foreigners impervious to the effect of opium, the foreign-indigenous relationship over the same commodity took on a more insidious nature, not least because it placed a vulnerable consumer in a position of dependency upon the powerful provider. The illicit trade from Chittagong into Akyab exemplified this dynamic at work, identifying as foreign the source of opium that fed a growing domestic consumption in British Burma.

Chief Commissioner Fytche's description of smuggling as such discounted the power of numbers favored by the Collector of Chittagong. What the former referred to as "statistics" fell short of capturing what the latter conceived of as a defining feature of colonial political economy: the extent to which market ties at once drew upon and reconfigured myriad extra-market relationships. Fytche believed that in British Burma, incentives to profit were only tangentially related to the existence of smuggling, let alone a factor motivating its growth. What this official referred to as the "fact" of smuggling was grounded in the sensual nature of consumption, the physical dependencies, and predatory ties mediated through opium that were unique to this colonial setting, which were revealed through its exchange as a commodity in local bazaars. If, by smuggling, one meant the quantitative growth in contraband traveling across provincial borders, then "very little smuggling has taken place," opined the Chief Commissioner.[53] However, if by smuggling, one considered a qualitative change to the social dynamics underlying Burma's opium market, then there was indeed an upward trend because a vulnerable consumer base was increasingly at the mercy of powerful providers. By focusing on who provided, who consumed, and what distinguishing attributes these actors might share, this local official made sense of illicit opium in terms of a marketplace that instantiated a microcosm of colonial society and its power struggles. Thus told, the fact of smuggling offered an alternative way of knowing, one that dealt with an invisible activity as if it were visible.

The Chittagong-Akyab dispute endured for nearly two decades as bureaucrats on either side of the Naf struggled (and failed) to convince each other of the accuracy, validity, and superiority of their respective positions. To be sure, there were small concessions that occurred, such as in April 1871, when British Burma formally abolished its opium farming system.[54] However, this hardly represented a definitive victory or defeat for either side. While new *de jure* arrangements replicated the licensed vendor system of Bengal, the Excise Department of British

Burma de facto institutionalized sub-monopoly privileges again by placing prohibitively high costs on sales licenses that only past farmers or the occasional rich entrepreneur could afford (unlike the free licenses distributed to any willing merchant in Bengal). Likewise, an 1873 proposal for Bengal to yield jurisdiction over the contentious strip of land around the Naf Estuary over to British Burma did not resolve the extent to which bureaucrats saw Chittagong and Akyab differently nor absolve the political, economic, and symbolic link between the two locales of its controversial nature.[55] Rather, two opposing perspectives with myriad underlying points of contention would continue stubbornly over time.

Notes

1. Bengal Board of Revenue to Government of Bengal, November 10, 1870, no. 499B, P/2780, India Office Records (IOR).
2. Albert Fytche, Chief Commissioner, British Burma to Government of India, March 31, 1870, no. 118–119, P/2780, IOR.
3. Ibid.
4. Commissioner of Arakan to Herbert Thirkell White, Secretary to the Chief Commissioner, British Burma, February 26, 1886, no. 321, P/2780, IOR.
5. C. A. Samuells, Officiating Secretary to the Board of Revenue, Lower Provinces to Government of Bengal, Revenue Department, 1885, P/2780, IOR.
6. I am indebted to Jennifer Pitts for this formulation.
7. Eric Tagliacozzo, *Secret Trades, Porous Borders: Smuggling and States Along a Southeast Asian Frontier, 1865–1915* (New Haven, CN: Yale University Press, 2009), 364.
8. See Josiah Heyman and Alan Smart, "States and Illegal Practices: An Overview," in *States and Illegal Practices*, ed. Josiah Heyman (Oxford, UK: Berg Publishers, 1999), 1–24; Donatella Della Porta and Alberto Vannucci, *The Hidden Order of Corruption: An Institutional Approach* (Farnham and Burlington: Ashgate, 2012), 1–15.
9. For an influential formulation, see Charles Tilly, "War Making and State Making as Organized Crime," in *Bringing the State Back In*, ed. Peter Evans et al. (Cambridge, MA: Cambridge University Press, 1985).

Exemplary works specifically on smuggling and contraband include Janice Thomson, *Mercenaries, Pirates, and Sovereigns: State-Building and Extraterritorial Violence in Early Modern Europe* (Princeton, NJ: Princeton University Press, 1996); William Ashworth, *Customs and Excise: Trade, Production, and Consumption in England, 1640–1845* (New York, NY: Oxford University Press, 2003).

10. On seventeenth-century piracy, see Douglas Burgess Jr., *The Politics of Piracy: Crime and Civil Disobedience in Colonial America* (Lebanon, NH: University Press of New England, 2014). On eighteenth-century underground economics, see Michael Kwass, "Court Capitalism, Illicit Markets, and Political Legitimacy in Eighteenth Century France: The Example of the Salt and Tobacco Monopolies," in *Questioning Credible Commitment: Perspectives on the Rise of Financial Capitalism*, ed. D'Maris Coffman et al. (New York, NY: Cambridge University Press, 2013), 228–50. On opium in Southeast Asia, see Pierre-Arnaud Chouvy, *Opium: Uncovering the Politics of the Poppy* (Cambridge, MA: Harvard University Press, 2010).
11. I echo Tagliacozzo, *Secret Trades*, 373.
12. See Renate Bridenthal, ed., *The Hidden History of Crime, Corruption, and States* (New York and Oxford: Berghahn Books, 2013); Michael Kwass, *Contraband: Louis Mandrin and the Making of a Global Underground* (Cambridge, MA: Harvard University Press, 2014).
13. A. Eden, Junior Secretary to Board of Revenue to Secretary to the Government of Bengal, November 21, 1859, no. 405, in "Report from the Select Committee on East India Finance" (1871), 521–26.
14. R. M. Dane, "Historical Memorandum," August 9, 1894, in *First Report of the Royal Opium Commission with Minutes of Evidence and Appendices* (ROC), vol. 6, 28–63. Also see John Richard, "The Opium Industry in British India," *Indian Economic & Social History Review* 39 (2002): 153. Two general schemes divided British India's management of opium: the eastern Bengal system and the Bombay system in the west. My discussion here is limited to the former, which was managed by the Bihar agency in Patna and the Benares agency in Ghazipur. On the latter, see Amar Farooqui, "Opium Enterprise and Colonial Intervention in Malwa and Western India, 1800–1824," *Indian Economic & Social History Review* 32 (1995): 447–73.
15. Dane, "Historical Memorandum," 38–45; House of Commons, February 14, 1859, vol. 152, 351–61; Nancy Cassels Gardner, *Social*

Legislation of the East India Company: Public Justice versus Public Instruction (New Delhi and Thousand Oaks, CA: 2010), especially chap. 5, "Abkarry and Pilgrim Taxes: Excise as a Regulating Instrument." Especially salient socioeconomic concerns included the exploitation and hardship of opium cultivating peasants (*ryots*) in India. See John Richards, "Indian Empire and Peasant Production of Opium in the Nineteenth Century," *Modern Asian Studies* 15 (1981): 59–82.

16. Dane, "Historical Memorandum" quoting Warren Hastings (1773) in App. 59 to the 9th Report of the Select Committee (1783).
17. Ibid.
18. There were also important counterargument to this notion of increasing opium consumption and its harms, which endured well into the 1870s. For example, see George Smith, Witness on May 19, 1871, Question 5120, *Report from the Select Committee on East India Finance* (London: Parliament, House of Commons Reports and Papers 363, 1871), 237.
19. Dane, "Historical Memorandum"; James Lyall, "Note on the History of Opium in India and of the Trade in it with China," February 15, 1894, ROC, vol. 6: 9–13, 23–28.
20. See Bernard Cohn, "From Indian Status to British Contract," *Journal of Economic History* 21 (1961): 613–28.
21. Cassels, *Social Legislation,* 298 and 301; Dane, "Historical Memorandum"; Act XXI to consolidate and amend the Law relating to the *Abkaree* Revenue in the Presidency of Fort William in Bengal, November 22, 1856, V/8/35, IOR.
22. *Annual Report of the Excise Administration, British Burma* (AREABB), 1868–1869. On other types of tax farming in colonial South and Southeast Asia, see Ian Copland and Michael Godley, "Revenue Farming in Comparative Perspective: Reflections on Taxation, Social Structure, and Development in the Early Modern Period," in *The Rise and Fall of Revenue Farming: Business Elites and the Emergence of the Modern State in Southeast Asia,* ed. John Butcher and Howard Dick (New York, NY: St. Martin's Press, 1993), 45–68.
23. Thomas Brassey, "Final Report," ROC, vol. 6, April 16, 1895, 75.
24. Bengal Board of Revenue, November 10, 1870.
25. *AREABB*, 1869–1870: 12–16.
26. Fytche, March 31, 1870.

27. Ibid.
28. Bengal Board of Revenue, November 10, 1870.
29. David Robert Lyall, Collector of Chittagong. "Consultation with Board of Revenue, Undated," P/2780, IOR.
30. AREABB, 1870–1871.
31. Bengal Board of Revenue, November 10, 1870.
32. Ibid.
33. Ibid.
34. Ibid.
35. AREABB, 1868–1869: 5.
36. Fytche, March 31, 1870.
37. Ibid.
38. Ibid.
39. Ibid.
40. Ibid.
41. Ibid.
42. Quoted in Cassels, *Social Legislation*, 298.
43. John Stuart Mill, "Principles of Political Economy with Some of their Applications to Social Philosophy," Book 5, chap. 6 in *The Collected Works of John Stuart Mill*, vol. 3 (Toronto: University of Toronto Press, 1965), 871.
44. A. L. Clay, Collector of Chittagong to Sir Ashley Eden, Chief Commissioner, British Burma, September 20, 1872, No. 935, P/2780, IOR.
45. Ibid.
46. Fytche, March 31, 1870.
47. AREABB, 1867–1868: 3–4.
48. Commissioner of Arakan to Albert Fytche, Chief Commissioner, British Burma, AREABB, 1867–1868: 20–21.
49. Ibid.
50. Fytche March 31, 1870.
51. Ibid.
52. Ibid.
53. AREABB, 1868–1869: 1–2.
54. Ibid.
55. Secretary to the Chief Commissioner, British Burma to the Government of Bengal, June 27, 1873, P/2780, IOR.

Author Biography

Diana Kim is Assistant Professor in the Edmund A. Walsh School of Foreign Service at Georgetown University and a core faculty member of the Asian Studies Program. Diana received her Ph.D. in political science from the University of Chicago (2013) and held a Postdoctoral Prize Fellowship in Economics, History, and Politics at Harvard University (2013–2016). Diana's research and teaching focuses on the transnational politics and history of markets across Southeast and East Asia, with particular interest in the regulation of vice, illicit economies, and legacies of empire and colonialism. Her first book, entitled *Empires of Vice*, develops a comparative study of the rise of opium prohibition in British Burma, Malaya, and French Indochina since the late nineteenth century.

A Place in the Sun: Rethinking the Political Economy of German Overseas Expansion and Navalism Before the Great War

Erik Grimmer-Solem

It has long been tempting to see the political economy of German imperialism as little more than a handmaiden to disaster. This perspective is supported by the fact that many of the economists active in this prewar *Weltpolitik* were later also involved in wartime administration, wartime strategy, and defining German war aims. Indeed, it is striking just how many of the younger students of prominent economists of the period would play significant roles in German imperialist politics and in the war. Among those worth mentioning is Karl Helfferich, a student of Georg Friedrich Knapp and director of the Deutsche Bank, who oversaw the prewar construction of the Berlin-Bagdad Railway, was named State Secretary of the Reich Treasury in 1915 and in that capacity

This is a revised version of a paper first given at the conference "New Perspectives on the History of Political Economy" held at Harvard Business School, November 1–2, 2013. I would like to thank David Armitage for his insightful critiques of this paper. Phil Pomper, Michael Trautwein and Gerhard Wegner gave valuable feedback on earlier drafts, for which I am also very grateful. The author takes sole responsibility for any remaining errors or omissions.

E. Grimmer-Solem (✉)
Wesleyan University, Middletown, USA
e-mail: egrimmer@wesleyan.edu

R. Fredona and S.A. Reinert (eds.), *New Perspectives on the History of Political Economy*, https://doi.org/10.1007/978-3-319-58247-4_9

was responsible for financing the war. Max Sering, a student of both Gustav Schmoller and Knapp and professor at the Landwirtschaftliche Hochschule Berlin, became chairman of a commission in the Ministry of War to prepare the economy for a wartime footing. He was also charged by the Foreign Office to study the occupied territories to the east to advise on future annexations. Hermann Schumacher, another of Schmoller's students, was professor at the University of Bonn and during the war active as an expert advisor to the Essen Chamber of Commerce, where he helped work out the war aims of German heavy industry in Belgium and France. Ernst Levy von Halle, a student of Sering and Schmoller and professor at the University of Berlin, became an influential expert advisor to the Imperial Navy and spearheaded the prewar naval propaganda campaign.

The historian Fritz Fischer saw this fateful amalgamation of economic scholarship and policy—which predated the war and which Max Weber had already sharply criticized—as responsible for Germany's uniquely aggressive war aims and wartime strategy. Fischer also saw in these war aims important precursors for a second attempt to seize world power under Hitler.[1] Historians of the Bielefeld School have since built a solid footing for this view of the Great War by emphasizing that Germany's aggressive prewar diplomacy and policy was an outgrowth of a crisis of domestic politics that resulted from the contradictions of Germany's modern industrial economy and bourgeois society retaining an antiquated, authoritarian government, which allowed its foreign policy to be led astray by unenlightened "Neomercantilist" views in order to keep the German public distracted.[2] Years before the outbreak of the war this "social imperialism" was focused on building a high seas fleet, the creation of a central European customs union, and gaining colonial concessions in the Near East, Africa, and South America.[3]

Economists and economic historians have long known a similar interpretation of the war. In a famous essay written shortly after the end of the First World War, Joseph Schumpeter emphasized the peaceful and anti-imperial tendencies of capitalism, highlighting the irrationality of the aggressive imperialism of the prewar period, which he blamed on the egoistic interests of a small minority and the atavistic habits of a disappearing feudal caste.[4] Had Europe's and—above all Germany's—elite and political leadership had a more enlightened grasp of self-interest and had the commercial bourgeoisie enjoyed more influence on politics, then the enormous advantages of free trade enabled by the British Empire would have been grasped, and the senseless construction of battleships and the aggressive *Weltpolitik* of the prewar period might have been avoided. One could add: Had the German elite read more Smith, Ricardo, and Marshall rather than List, Roscher, and Schmoller while at university, peace might have prevailed in 1914.

The same year that Schumpeter's essay on imperialism appeared, Karl Helfferich published his three-volume book *Der Weltkrieg*.[5] In the first volume, he analyzed the prehistory of the Great War, complaining in one passage of the diplomatic mistakes that resulted from speeches that "expressed the German desire for peace by underscoring all too clearly our readiness for war."[6] As an economist, he nevertheless emphasized the structural forces behind the tensions of the prewar period which restricted the political room for maneuver.[7] While Helfferich's explanation was undoubtedly self-exculpatory given his role during the war, his insights cannot be dismissed out of hand. The driving structural forces that gave rise to prewar tensions were geopolitical, economic, and demographic, and these were reflected in many areas of prewar German economic thought and policy. It is mistaken to see these primarily as an outgrowth of a crisis of domestic politics or as the expression of "unenlightened" Neomercantilist views. Indeed, perception of these driving forces was often a product of close study of other countries and the international economy following lengthy travels abroad. It is notable, for example, that Helfferich, Sering, Schumacher, and von Halle had all spent much time abroad before the war and devoted their scholarship to various aspects of the international economy, notably Asia and North America.[8] If one adds one other German economist of the prewar period active in German *Weltpolitik*, such as the first Rector of Hamburg University, Karl Rathgen—a student of Schmoller—the outward orientation of these economists is quite remarkable.[9] Indeed, there is strong evidence that *Weltpolitik* as articulated by these and other German economists was a product of experiences and exposure to ideas abroad, notably in the USA, the other rapidly developing world economic power of the time.

What were the assumptions of this new perspective and upon what specific set of observations was it based? Addressing this question afresh from a transnational and comparative perspective promises new insights because it allows recovery of a strand of transatlantic economic discourse that has been obscured by more national perspectives, a strand also largely neglected by the history of economic thought. It also offers an opportunity to reorient the history of political economy toward those ideas that have been particularly influential to economic policy since the beginnings of modern economic thought. In order to do this, it will first be necessary to sketch out the political economy of German *Weltpolitik* around 1900. This will be followed by a discussion of the role of the USA in the evolution of these ideas to offer a reorientation of the history of political economy that can highlight a common transatlantic discourse traceable to seventeenth-century England.

The Political Economy of *Weltpolitik* Around 1900

The economic war aims of Imperial Germany in the First World War were in many respects nothing new but rather a radicalized version of specific desires and demands that had emerged from the experiences of the prewar period, which had highlighted the precarious geopolitical and economic circumstances of Germany. Already in the 1890s, a consensus had emerged among influential German economists that Germany's industrialization and the heightened competition with other industrial powers justified a new orientation in foreign policy. This new orientation involved securing Germany's maritime interests, which had grown as a consequence both of increased industrial exports and rising imports of raw materials and foodstuffs, and were threatened by growing international protectionism. Prominent in this development was the American Tariff Act of 1890 (McKinley Tariff), which had raised average import tariffs to nearly 50%. Another challenge to which the Germans were responding was Britain's formalization of a two-power standard in naval arms through the Naval Defence Act of 1889, which sought to expand the number of battleships in the Royal Navy to at least the size of the next two largest navies combined (at the time, those of France and Russia). Intended as a deterrent to rival powers, the Act of 1889 sparked an international arms race that would involve both the USA and Germany. It is neither possible nor necessary to discuss the expansion of Germany's High Seas Fleet after 1897 in this essay in any detail, much less to assess the strategic calculus of the energetic architect of the German Navy, Alfred von Tirpitz. It is enough to mention that in addition to trade and colonial interests, as well as the interests of German heavy industry, a range of factors played a role in the passage of the German naval bills, notably the influence of the American naval strategist Alfred Thayer Mahan within naval circles and the educated German public, the international tensions of the 1890s (the Venezuela Crisis of 1895, the Sino-Japanese War of 1894–1895, and the Jameson Raid 1895–1896), Tirpitz's own departmental zeal and hunger for power, and, not least, Kaiser Wilhelm's naval enthusiasm. In any case, Volker Berghahn's familiar thesis that this naval legislation was devised to shore up Germany's monarchical authoritarian regime has been thrown into serious doubt by recent research.[10]

What were the arguments deployed by German economists on behalf of an expanded navy? A letter written by Gustav Schmoller to Alfred Tirpitz in late July 1897 illuminates some of these motivations:

> I am very pleased if those conducting German trade policy grasp the enormous dangers of Panamericanism, the English agitation for Greater Britain, and Russian plans for world power. ...And naturally all our plans for the fleet are tied in the closest possible way to future German trade policy. I only fear the penetration of agrarian interests will hinder a keen policy oriented toward the future. If a system of high tariffs in the Bismarck-Kardorffian[11] sense were to be introduced then one cannot pursue export and naval policy.
>
> Naturally I still have hopes for Hohenlohe,[12] who as an old free trader will not be had easily for excessive protective tariffs. But we must also not neglect our trade treaties if we do not want to destroy our industry and exports.[13]

Such views were shared in particular by economists of a progressive liberal persuasion, notably Lujo Brentano:

> Every policy that effectively works toward raising our exports is assured my support. For—whether one may view it as a fortune or misfortune—it is nevertheless a fact that Germany is now an industrial state. Since this is how things are, the most important concern is to find sales markets for its products, and particularly the export of its industrial products. On this the sales will now depend, namely even the domestic sales market of our agricultural products. For our domestic sales market is dependent upon whether we have a solvent working population. The solvency of the industrial working population has replaced the old: "if the farmer has money, so does everybody." The future of agriculture lies in the purchasing power of our industrial working population, in the development of its necessities, the increase of its efficiency and the adjustment of agricultural production to its needs. Yet the solvency of our working population has as a precondition the development of our exports
>
> The future of our exports is, however, currently very threatened. The development of the relationship between England and its colonies could become very detrimental to us. Similarly, our senseless bounty policy has given us the American Dingley Bill,[14] whose horrors will likely be felt even sooner. Decades of work of our businesspeople could be endangered by it. Under such conditions it is natural that one looks about for alternatives. To expect this from our colonies would be childish. But in Asia and South America there may still be very much to be had. From this viewpoint an increase in the German fleet appears justified.[15]

What clearly stands out in these letters as a justification for a larger fleet among economists was the growing dependence of German industry on exports and rising protectionism abroad, especially in the USA. What also emerges from these letters is growing disappointment with German colonies and the importance instead of promising future markets in South America and Asia. The Spanish-American War that broke out only a few months later and gave the USA the status of an overseas colonial power for the first time—simultaneously in the Caribbean and Pacific—would only serve to reinforce these fears, just as would German disputes with the Americans and the British over the colonial administration of Samoa in 1899. Highly provocative around this time were also the views of the British Secretary of State for Colonies, Joseph Chamberlain, who was noted in Germany for his fiery jingoism during the Second Boer War (1899–1902) and who began to speak out openly in support of a protectionist British Imperial Customs Union.

Not surprisingly, very similar views to those of Schmoller and Brentano would spread among the ranks of other German economists by the year 1900, many of whom would involve themselves willingly in advocating for naval bills. Of the 270 so-called fleet professors from all branches of the arts and sciences, some 38 were economists, among them (and supplemental to those already mentioned above) Heinrich Dietzel, Richard Ehrenberg, Wilhelm Hasbach, Wilhem Lexis, Sartorius von Waltershausen, Gustav Schönberg, Albert Schäffle, Werner Sombart, Adolph Wagner, and Max Weber.[16] The arguments that were mobilized were multifarious but are very neatly illustrated by a lecture given by Gustav Schmoller in 1900.[17]

In addition to the already discussed problems of growing international protectionism, Germany's increasing export dependence, the importance of promising export markets in South America and Asia, as well as trade treaties to keep the door to trade open, Schmoller's speech was concerned with strong German population growth, which he estimated would leave Germany with 104 million people by 1965 and which a French demographer cited by him estimated would reach 200 million by the year 2000.[18] The growing population density, the limited possibilities for productivity increases in agriculture, and the challenges posed to increasing exports made German settlement of areas outside of Europe along the lines of Britain's settler colonies on the African Cape, Canada, and Australia a necessity. This would secure Germany a place alongside the great peoples of the earth but would only be possible with a larger navy.[19] Among the promising areas for such a settler colony, southern Brazil was mentioned, where it was hoped an autonomous German territory with 20–30 million Germans would emerge in the twentieth century, a project that would be impossible without an enhanced German naval presence.[20]

A question posed in the speech was whether under current conditions in Britain and the US, trade policy could be conducted in the future without power politics and the instruments of power offered by an enhanced navy. The contrast between the liberal British era of Cobden and Gladstone could not be starker to the one ushered in by Disraeli, which made increasing use of blockades, searches, and seizures of neutral shipping, as well as restrictions on the use of coaling stations and undersea telegraph cables, and in the case of the South African Boers, included naked aggression. Schmoller noted that between 1866 and 1899, the territory of the British Empire had expanded from 12.6 to 27 million square kilometers.[21] Likewise, the Russian Empire had expanded into East Asia and the USA westward on the North American continent and into the former colonies of Spain in Cuba and the Philippines. As a medium-sized power, Germany had to defend itself against these "three great conquering and colonizing empires" with a stronger fleet in order to have a place at the table in the future division of Africa and China, the future of the South Pacific and in assuring access to the North and South American markets.[22] Germany had not created these conditions, but it could not evade the bitter struggle for economic survival:

> The turnaround of world conditions, the necessary liquidation of dying empires, the necessary division of the earth between *Kulturnationen* [cultured nations], which alone rule [and] can create advanced economic conditions and institutions, [and] the heightened competition in the world economy have created the new state of affairs from which today's tensions, envy of trade, and conflicts of all kinds came into being. We must not forget that it was precisely in the freest states, in England and North America, that popular and mass instinct fed conquering tendencies, imperialist plans, and hatred of up-and-coming economic competitors, where their leaders emerged from the ranks of great speculators with manners half those of pirates, half of stock brokers, possess billions and at the same time serve as party leaders and ministers.[23]

Only a larger fleet could countervail this "overstrung robber-mercantilism" everywhere and the division of the earth by these three world powers who sought to exclude all other states and to destroy their trade.[24]

A protective tariff wall of the kind erected by Russia, France, and the USA was strictly rejected due to the dangers it posed to Germany's relations with Britain and due to the significance of the export trade for German industry. Instead, Schmoller hoped that an enlarged High Seas Fleet could protect Germany and the other European medium and smaller states with the expectation that Germany's neighboring states (Austria, Switzerland, the Scandinavian states, and the Netherlands) would come to see the logic of a trade, customs, and colonial union with the German Empire.[25]

If one overlooks the somewhat overheated rhetoric of this speech, written as it was in the shadow of the Second Anglo-Boer War, it encapsulates the key components of *Weltpolitik* embraced by most German economists in the prewar era: (1) worldwide free trade through the open door and trade agreements; (2) a central European customs union; and (3) German settler colonies. This was the mainstream position of those German economists who fully embraced Germany's industrial future and for which an expanded fleet was seen as the natural tool.

Perhaps less appreciated today is the extent to which these aims were shaped by direct observations of, and comparisons with, the USA at the time. Research over the last several years has highlighted just how entangled the USA and Germany were in the late nineteenth century, an entanglement shaped by an unparalleled flow of people and ideas between the two countries, the coincidence of their simultaneous industrialization and urbanization, the influence of American enterprise and technology, and, conversely, German models in higher education, social reform, and administration.[26] As recent scholarship has shown, those strong connections also extended to German understandings of colonial empire and naval power.[27] Indeed, it could be argued that the USA was an even more influential point of reference in these areas than the British Empire. An important point to make here is that globalization and the encounter with both the USA and British Empire around 1900 did not dissolve German national identity but rather served as a catalyst for the assertion of German national claims elsewhere in the world.

Lessons from Venezuela and the Philippines

Ernst Levy von Halle would play a key role as a close observer of the USA and mediator of ideas that evolved over the course of the 1890s to influence the German government and wider public, in this case to shape German perceptions of the challenges posed by the USA and the necessity of an expanded German High Seas Fleet. Von Halle, who was from Hamburg and had close ties to the city's merchant interests, had studied political economy in Leipzig and Berlin. He was living in Chicago and attending the World's Columbian Exposition in May 1893 when he received a commission from the Verein für Sozialpolitik (Association for Social Policy) to compile a major report on industrial trusts in the USA.[28] Over his time in the USA during 1893–1895 and then on an excursion to the West Indies and Venezuela from January–March 1896, von Halle also became an expert on cotton cultivation, which he had the opportunity to study directly by travelling through the American South in 1894.[29] These materials were used to write a major study on the history of cotton production in the American South,[30] which together with his work on American trusts and syndicates, firmly established von Halle as one of the leading specialists on the American economy in Wilhelmine Germany.

Shortly after his return from Venezuela and the West Indies in 1896, von Halle published an article in Schmoller's *Jahrbuch* which distilled his impressions of the USA in the shadow of the Venezuela crisis of 1895, during which the USA came to the brink of declaring war on Great Britain for allegedly violating the Monroe Doctrine in a border dispute between British Guyana and Venezuela.[31] The threat of war and the expanded American naval forces which made the threat credible led to an uncharacteristic withdrawal of British claims—despite their validity—and submission to American arbitration.[32] Von Halle was deeply concerned in his article about the growth of jingoistic and belligerent public opinion in the USA that he himself witnessed during the Venezuela crisis. He was also worried that the new more muscular Monroe Doctrine together with America's very high protective tariffs and powerful trusts would eventually exclude German exporters from the Western Hemisphere.[33] He urged the German government to purchase the Danish island of Saint Thomas before it fell into American hands to assure German traders a tariff-free port to Central and South American markets.[34] He also proposed coordinating retaliatory tariffs between Germany and the countries of continental Europe in a customs union in order to force the American market open to European trade.[35] Finally, von Halle proposed shifting German immigration away from the USA toward South America and developing alternative sources of cotton in German colonies with the aid of Texas German planters as additional leverage over the Americans.[36]

It is almost certain that von Halle had by this time steeped himself in the writings of the American naval officer Alfred Thayer Mahan, whose *Influence of Sea Power upon History, 1660–1783* (1890) and *Influence of Sea Power upon the French Revolution and Empire, 1783–1812* (1892), had been published shortly before von Halle's travels in the USA and quickly became influential in naval policy circles in both the USA and Germany.[37] In any case, von Halle's writings on the history of American cotton production as well as his subsequent writings on the role of the Union blockade in the defeat of the Confederacy demonstrate that he drew parallel conclusions from this more recent episode of history: "Nearly half of the German people is directly or indirectly dependent upon industries reliant on the import of raw materials and semi-manufactured goods and export of semi-manufactured and manufactured goods. If these suffered restrictions limiting the possibilities of work and commerce, a terrible crisis would doubtless ensue."[38]

The lessons learned for German trade from his American experiences won von Halle admiration from German naval circles, and shortly after Alfred von Tirpitz was named State Secretary of the Reich Navy Office in 1897, von Halle was appointed as press secretary of the Navy Office's Information Bureau, where he worked vigorously and very effectively to propagandize for expansion of the German High Seas Fleet in various publications, often under the pseudonym "Nauticus."[39] The Spanish-American War, which followed closely on the heels of von Halle's appointment to the Navy Office, seemed only to confirm the wisdom of a modernized and expanded navy, a conflict in which naval power proved decisive in America's victory and subsequent territorial claims. During the war, Germany contemplated seizing the Caroline Islands, the Sulu Archipelago and the Philippine islands of Mindanao and Palwan and intervened very provocatively by sending the Cruiser Division's flagship and three other cruisers to Manila in June 1898 to make the German presence known, inspecting various prospective islands and in the process repeatedly violating American blockade rules and refusing to cooperate with the US Navy inspecting ships for contraband.[40] These German vessels also violated their neutrality during their reconnaissance of Subic Bay in July 1898, nearly leading to conflict with the American Navy commanded by Admiral George Dewey.[41] With the arrival of American naval reinforcements, the Germans were nevertheless forced to beat a hasty retreat, giving up any hope of territorial gains. It was only following negotiations with the Americans, Spanish, and British that Germany was permitted to purchase the Caroline, Palau, and Marianna Islands (excepting Guam) from Spain in February 1899, a rather modest prize given earlier ambitions in the Philippines.[42] As von Halle concluded in an assessment of the new North American imperialism, "Mahan's expanded idea of the significance of sea power had found among them [the Americans] receptive students."[43]

The British were long accustomed to using their maritime hegemony to search and seize shipping, impose blockades, and, *in extremis*, to destroy rival navies without consideration of international treaties like the Paris Declaration of 1856. Jackie Fisher and the rest of the British Admiralty made no secret of this intention, which was the cornerstone of British prewar deterrence maintaining freedom of the seas.[44] This was confirmed during the Boer War, when in December 1899 and January 1900, the German postal and merchant steamers *Bundesrath, Herzog,* and *Hans Wagner* were seized by the Royal Navy in Delagoa Bay in Portuguese East Africa (a neutral port) and taken to South Africa on suspicion of carrying contraband.[45] Shortly thereafter the German postal steamer *General* was stopped and boarded at Aden for similar reasons. No contraband was ever found. During the Boer War, similar violations of ships under neutral flags or neutral harbors occurred, and before the First World War, Great Britain refused to offer neutral ships greater protections or constrain its unilateral right to impose blockades—the London Declaration of 1909, for example, was never ratified by the House of Lords.[46] A common refrain heard at the time was "Britannia rules the waves because she waives the rules." This reinforced the logic of German maritime power. As was noted at the time in a newspaper widely read by the German educated *Bürgertum*:

> The organs of the British government are accustomed to the fact that they can act freely on the open sees. It is now obvious that the only states which can hope to deter such pretentions are those with the validity offered by possessing a fleet that England respects. All games with big words have no practical value and thus the only proper raison d'être to be learned from this incident is strengthening the fleet in the form of legal commitments for a "giant step" which we feel compelled to take and carry out as quickly as possible.[47]

Tirpitz's program for an expanded German fleet was of course later shown to have been based on faulty premises (coastal blockade, risk theory, and enhanced German alliance potential) and took on a dangerous dynamic of its own with devastating consequences for German public finances, Anglo-German relations, and the strategic position of the Reich in Europe. The expanded navy was nevertheless supported enthusiastically by the German bourgeoisie, which saw in the showcase technology of the fleet a confirmation of progress, modernity, and Germany's equal status as a great power.[48] For liberals and moderate conservatives, the fleet had the additional appeal that it could be deployed as a deterrent and thus could be justified as a peace-preserving tool of power to assure freedom of the seas. Indeed, recent research has highlighted the very strong affinities between German and American "maritime militarism" in the years preceding the First World War.[49] As aspiring world powers challenging British maritime predominance, where the two countries truly diverged was that Germany's reliance on foreign trade was so much greater. What made Germany's naval militarism so much more dangerous was thus much less its premises or its brash manner, but rather Germany's location so near the British Isles.

Farmers and Frontiers

As was made clear in Brentano's correspondence with Schmoller and from Schmoller's hopes for a German settler colony in Southern Brazil discussed earlier, by 1900, Germany's overseas colonies had become a major economic disappointment. It was true that many economists still supported the colonial effort in the years before the war, notably during the colonial crisis years 1906–1907 sparked by native rebellions in German Southwest and East Africa and their brutal suppression by German troops.[50] One such example was the formation of the Kolonialpolitisches Aktionskomité by Schmoller and Max Sering in late 1906, which supported Chancellor Bernhard von Bülow and the new State Secretary of the Colonial Office Bernhard Dernburg's colonial reforms in the 1907 Reichstag election campaign.[51] Shortly before the First World War, the Verein für Sozialpolitik took up a comprehensive study of the European settler experience in tropical colonies and came to rather sobering conclusions which dashed any lingering hopes for an autonomous German settler colony in southern Brazil and elsewhere in the tropics.[52] By 1910, there were only 15,420 German settlers in German colonies, the majority (9283) in arid and inhospitable German Southwest Africa.[53] With the exception of tiny Togo, none of the German colonies could bear its own administrative costs, and all German colonies together accounted for only a tiny fraction of German trade.[54] Not even massive investments in colonial railways after 1907, a more professional colonial administration trained in the new Hamburg Colonial Institute (founded 1908), or modern development strategies such as systematic cotton cultivation in Togo and East Africa could change these basic facts.[55]

In assessing the German colonial endeavor, it is frequently overlooked that German expectations for settler colonies were often measured against westward expansion in the USA. With the growth of American agricultural exports to Germany in the early 1880s putting severe competitive pressure on German farming, Max Sering had been sent by the Prussian Ministry of Agriculture to investigate North American agricultural conditions, the Homstead Act, and westward settlement in 1883. In a remarkable letter written to Schmoller from a farm in Minnesota in July 1883, Sering wrote about his very positive impressions of the tidy settlements of this newly cultivated territory:

> The week that I spent in St. Paul and Minneapolis is among my most pleasant travel memories. The Germans here are still aware of the advantages of their nationality and eager to preserve it. The main topic of

discussion is German instruction in primary school which the Americans sought to displace. I am convinced that German nationality cannot be maintained in this land for many generations, and as a result I have become, mainly for this reason, an enthusiastic supporter of the idea of German colonies. It is my most fervent desire to later visit South America, to study the sources about this land and to eventually bring German emigrants to these territories where a dying European population resides who are of no threat to the unique qualities of our compatriots. I am ever more convinced that we do have many advantages over the Yankee and that it is a shame if our compatriots, forced by the external circumstances of making a living, are compelled to assimilate and subordinate themselves to him. All of the great economic and psychological processes which a wide and untapped territory offers a nation would become ours through colonies, [and] much damage to our national life would be healed.[56]

Like so many other German liberals going back to the Revolutions of 1848 and earlier, Sering was animated by the role that settler communities had allegedly played in the USA and white British settler colonies in preventing political radicalism and in securing a liberal constitutional political order, a future he hoped to reproduce for Germany.[57] Frederick Jackson Turner would himself later accurately quip: "American colonization has become the mother of German colonial policy."[58]

The work that Sering eventually completed on North American farming in the years after his return established him as the leading authority on American agriculture and the Homestead Act,[59] yet remarkably and very tellingly, soon after his return to Germany, Sering devoted his efforts in focusing German colonization not in Brazil but in internal colonization of the Prussian East, which he began to conceive as an eastern frontier invested with much of the Jeffersonian promise and the contiguous advantages of the American West. It was hoped that land-hungry German peasants could thus be retained for Germany rather than be lost to the inexorable "Yankee" assimilationist pressures; in the east, they would also shore up "Germandom" against the demographically expanding Prussian Poles and Russian Polish migrants.

This colonization activity first took on practical form through the initiative of the Bromberg Government President Christoph von

Tiedemann, who helped establish the Royal Prussian Settlement Commission in 1886.[60] After 1894, Sering was also active in the Land Economy Collegium in developing the laws and statutes governing *Rentengüter*, the homestead parcels created by dividing large defunct grain estates in the predominantly Polish-speaking parts of Prussia. Yet this work, too, brought Sering many disappointments due to the very modest resources the Prussian state devoted to it and the many legal hurdles that prevented parceling these lands, such as entail. By comparison to the massive expansion of small- and medium-sized farm holdings in the USA, the British Empire, Russia as well as the much more active cultivation of small and medium peasant holdings in Scandinavia by 1912, the German efforts were a clear disappointment.[61] Sering thus cofounded the Society for Fostering Inner Colonization in 1912 in order to spread greater awareness in the German public about the opportunities offered by a more expansively funded and executed policy.

More promising avenues then opened up during the war, when Sering served as an expert advisor to the German Foreign Office to study the conquered eastern territories of Lithuania and Courland. Here plans were afoot to nationalize Russian noble estates and to parcel out these lands to western German farmers and some of the two million uprooted ethnic German peasants of Tsarist Russia in a new area that Sering and others came to call "Neu-Ostland" (New Eastland) and "Neu-Deutschland" (New Germany.)[62] It is thus striking how visions for the German and European East as an area of colonial activity were shaped quite directly by a desire to emulate North American conditions. This "colonial gaze" eastward would take on even greater importance with the formal loss of Germany's overseas colonies in 1919.

Hamilton, List and the Heritage of "Whig" Political Economy

The transnational and comparative perspective of German *Weltpolitik* before the First World War emerging from the discussion so far questions a German "Neomercantilist" special path. This is supported further with a glance at average tariff rates. By comparison with the other continental European states such as Austria-Hungary, France, Italy, Russia, Spain, or Sweden, Germany's import tariffs on industrial products were low, and in comparison with the protectionism of the other two rising economic powers of the time—the USA and Japan—the British Dominions (Australia, Canada, and New Zealand) and Latin America, Germany almost appears as a free-trading outlier.[63] This free trade nevertheless relied upon the power politics and naval hegemony of the British Empire—that is, a sovereign economic order—whose reality, while often taken for granted, could be felt very immediately in case of tensions or war, as shown during the Boer War.

The involvement of the USA and Germany in tensions with the British Empire was a direct result of the rapid industrialization of these two countries, which clearly also generated its share of tensions between the USA and Germany. At its core, the big economic question facing Germany before 1914 was how, with its modern, export-oriented industry and growing population, it could continue to grow against a rising tide of protectionism abroad and without the convenience of productive overseas or contiguous territories of the kind enjoyed by Britain and the USA. This perspective was shaped by yet another area of German-American entanglement, namely in political economy. German and American economic thinkers of the nineteenth century shared a critique of classical political economy that was less a rejection of its assumptions and methods than a rejection of British imperial economic policy, policies often justified with the aid of classical political economy.

Alexander Hamilton was one of the first to subject the British colonial division of labor to a systematic, empirical critique in his brilliant and far-sighted "Report of the Subject of Manufactures" of 1791, which would later be popularized by Daniel Raymond and Henry Clay and others into the program of the "American System." In his report, Hamilton relied on the insights of Adam Smith and David Hume in order to question the logic of the imperial division of labor of the Atlantic world in which the former British North American colonies had been born and integrated, a division of labor in which classical political economy only foresaw an agricultural future for the new republic. In doing so, Hamilton questioned Adam Smith's physiocratic privileging of agriculture particularly sharply, though his most pointed barbs were clearly aimed at his Democratic-Republican opponents in the southern states, above all Thomas Jefferson and James Madison, who had been very strongly influenced by François Quesnay:

> It has been maintained, that Agriculture is, not only, the most productive, but the only productive species of industry. The reality of this suggestion in either aspect, has, however, not been verified by any accurate detail of facts and calculations, and the general arguments, which are adduced to prove it, are rather subtil and paradoxical, than solid or convincing.[64]

Hamilton then enumerated the many ways in which nonagricultural industry made positive contributions to the national product and income:

> 1. The division of labor.
> 2. An extension of the use of Machinery.
> 3. Additional employment to classes of the community not ordinarily engaged in the business.
> 4. The promotion of emigration from foreign Countries.
> 5. The furnishing greater scope for the diversity of talents and dispositions which discriminate men from each other.
> 6. The affording a more ample and various field of enterprise.
> 7. The creating in some instances a new, and securing in all, a more certain and steady demand for the surplus produce of the soil.[65]

Hamilton praised as an example the development of the cotton industry in England, which by applying machinery to a high degree increased the natural productivity of labor to an even higher degree than was possible in agriculture.[66] Later in his report, Hamilton noted that those European states with simultaneously flourishing industry and agriculture achieved higher levels of welfare and a positive balance of trade as compared with purely agricultural states.[67] Some of the sharpest of Hamilton's insights and most relevant for the arguments of this essay were those that related to trade, notably the insight that the Smithian system was hardly reflected in the realities of European and British trade:

> If the system of perfect liberty to industry and commerce were the prevailing system of nations—the arguments which dissuade a country in the predicament of the United States, from the zealous pursuits of manufactures would doubtless have great force. ...In such a state of things, each country would have the full benefit of its peculiar advantages to compensate for its deficiencies or disadvantages. If one nation were in condition to supply manufactured articles on better terms than another, that other might find an abundant indemnification in a superior capacity to furnish the produce of the soil... though the circumstances which have been mentioned and others... render it probable, that nations merely Agricultural would not enjoy the same degree of opulence, in proportion to their numbers, as those which united manufactures with agriculture. ...
>
> But the system which has been mentioned, is far from characterizing the general policy of Nations. The prevalent one has been regulated by an opposite spirit.
>
> The consequence of it is, that the United States are to a certain extent in a situation of a country precluded from foreign Commerce. They can indeed, without difficulty obtain from abroad the manufactured supplies, of which they are in want; but they experience numerous and very injurious impediments to the emission and vent of their own commodities. ... The regulations of several countries, with which we have the most extensive intercourse, throw serious obstructions in the way of the principle staples of the United States.
>
> In such a position of things, the United States cannot exchange with Europe on equal terms; and the want of reciprocity would render them the victim of a system, which should induce them to confine their views to Agriculture and refrain from Manufactures.[68]

As is well known, for these very reasons Hamilton justified promoting domestic industry with the aid of protective tariffs. The consolidation and securitization of the national debt, the Bank of the USA (1791), investments to improve infrastructure, and good diplomatic relations with Great Britain were also part of the economic program of the first Treasury Secretary, which shaped the economic policy of the American republic until 1837.[69] As the War of 1812 and the British Blockade of the years 1812–1814 would show, the sovereign economic and trade policy of the USA, despite efforts to cultivate good relations with Britain, was a challenge to the British Empire that threatened the viability of the Atlantic colonial division of labor upon which the empire had been built. Indeed, the war and blockade very nearly snuffed out the early USA, but because the republic could now arm and clothe itself having developed a more national economy, it prevailed without foreign assistance despite overwhelming British naval might.[70]

At root, what Hamilton had argued for and helped create was what Schmoller later dubbed "*Staats- und Volkswirtschaftsbildung*" (cultivating a state and national economy) and the German economist Walter Eucken later more accurately described as "*Gestaltung der Ordnungsformen der Wirtschaft*" (constructing the legal-constitutional order of an economy).[71] This is the act of legally defining both the spatial dimensions and legal and institutional foundations of the economy of a sovereign state. In the American case, the Civil War and Reconstruction Era saw the expansion of a federal state, which, if often less visible than European bureaucratic states, did not govern any less and became particularly active in the area of trade and commerce.[72]

Friedrich List's *National System of Political Economy* of 1841 was influenced to an overwhelming degree by Alexander Hamilton and Daniel Raymond's ideas during List's many years in the USA—indeed, Keith Tribe is surely right in arguing that List's piece is, in fact, an American economic tract, and not just because of List's naturalization as a US citizen in 1830.[73] Despite List's unsystematic journalistic style, the in part unjustified accusations leveled against Adam Smith, and his overheated anti-English polemics, his conclusions mesh with those of Hamilton and Raymond. At the annual conference of the German Economic Association in 1907, Gustav Schmoller honored his Swabian compatriot for having introduced German economists to stadial economic thinking, the National *Standort* (location) of the economy, as well as the productive power of political and economic institutions.[74] If this is true, German economists spoke with an American accent long before the twenty-first century. Put another way, very early on German political economy became part of an anti-imperial Atlantic World which invented catch-up industrialization—the USA and Germany became the world's first two developing economies.

As is known to anyone with some familiarity with the history of economic thought, thinkers such as Hamilton, Raymond, and List, if they are treated at all, fit uncomfortably into the existing categories of thinking that define this field. The search for forebears to classical political economy has resulted in their neglect or pejorative classification as "Mercantlists" or "Nationalists." Instead, much effort has gone into identifying and studying the influences on Adam Smith, and for that reason, much space has usually been given to the French physiocrats, despite the fact that their various projects were almost without exception practical failures.

As Steve Pincus has reminded us recently, "Mercantilism" is a notorious term largely invented in the twentieth century to give artificial unity to a variety of economic thought and policy for which there was never clear consensus but which can be differentiated into two broader positions: Whig and Tory.[75] "Whig Mercantilism" drew from the writings and ideas of a number of English explorers, politicians, merchants, and writers including John Smith, Carew Reynell, Richard Blome, William Carter, John Lowther, John Cary, John Locke, Daniel Defoe, Roger Coke, Nicholas Barbon, and Henry Martin.[76] Measured by his contemporaneous influence on English economic policy and by the number of editions and translations of his writings, the Bristol merchant John Cary (born 1649) may have had the biggest impact on the economic thinking of Hamilton and List.[77] After his death, Cary became one of the most influential economic writers of the eighteenth and nineteenth centuries. His "Essay on the State of England in Relation to its Trade" (1695) was much appreciated by contemporaries such as John Locke, and his strong support of Parliament, domestic commercial freedom, modern state finance through the Bank of England, abolition of trading monopolies, and active promotion of textile manufacturing are very much part of the political economy of the Enlightenment.[78] What particularly stands out in Cary's thought is his early—indeed, revolutionary—appreciation of the advantages of the inventive spirit in the mechanization of many trades, which not only gave England competitive advantages but also increased its productivity and wages:

> Manufacturers… may be carried on to Advantage, without running down the Labour of the Poor; …Refiners of Sugars go through that operation by easier methods, and in less Time, than their Predecessors did: Thus the Distillers draw more Spirits from the Things they work on, than those formerly did who taught them the Art. The Glass-Maker hath found a quicker way of making it out of Things which cost him little. Silk stockings are wove; Tobacco is cut by Engines: Books are printed; Deal Boards are sawn with Mills; Lead is smelted by Wind-Furnaces; all of which save the Labour of many Hands, so the Wages of those employed need not be fallen. …
>
> New Projections are every Day set on Foot to render the making our Woolen Manufactures easy, which should be rendered cheaper by the Contrivance of the Manufacturers, not by falling the Price of Labour: Cheapness creates Expense, and gives fresh Employments, whereby the Poor will still be kept at Work.[79]

These passages have uncanny affinities with those of Alexander Hamilton quoted above. That said, Cary also advocated a ruthless trade policy with foreigners and the English colonies in order to secure the predominance of English-manufactured exports and the restriction of English imports to raw materials.[80] The 1699 trade treaty with Ireland, which reduced Irish exports to raw wool monopolized by England, as well as the two Calico Laws of 1701 and 1721, which banned Indian cotton fabrics but allowed the importation of raw cotton, leaned on Cary's ideas, just as did the export bounties that were passed for silk (1722), gunpowder (1731), sail cloth (1731), and sugar (1733) to strengthen English manufacturing.[81]

Cary's association with such active trade and industrial policy almost assured him future obscurity within the history of economic thought, written as it often has been by neoclassical economists who were prone to categorize ideas which they did not fully comprehend or agree with as "unenlightened" and therefore "Mercantilist."[82] Schumpeter would himself dismiss Cary's work as lacking any analytical value.[83] It has been no better in influential dictionaries of economics: While the first edition of the *Palgrave Dictionary of Economics* (1910) still contained a biographical entry for Cary, in the 1987 *New Palgrave* he had disappeared without a trace.[84] Beyond the obvious glorification of free trade as a litmus test for what counts as economic thought, there are other reasons for these biases and the underestimation of "Mercantilism." They are, in fact, the result of a curious blind spot that has been part of classical political economy since its inception.

In several very suggestive passages in his book *Location and Space-Economy* (1956), Walter Isard bemoaned the "spacelessness" of neoclassical economic theory, which he attributed to specific biases of classical economics that were the product of England's unique geography and early colonial empire:

> The classical school and their followers were too prone to overlook the local differences within the English economy. England's dominant international position and the dynamic aspects of her industrial development further helped to cloud their vision. It was in international trade theory that the spatial structure of the domestic economy was most explicitly assumed away or relegated to the background.[85]

An important point to add here is that the "spaceless" economy conceived by classical political economy was also situated in a colonial world without rival sovereignties. After the publication of *The Wealth of Nations* (1776), the British national and colonial divisions of labor were such obvious "facts" that few if any English economic thinkers ever gave their creation any systematic thought. It is hardly coincidental that the economics of space and geography was left to Germans to invent (Heinrich von Thünen, Alfred Weber, and Wilhelm Launhardt), where a national division of labor was created by wars and treaties between rival sovereignties and by the legal and institutional framework of a new national state. By contrast, England's island location, the woolen industry, the textile trade, and the enormous growth of London had turned England's provinces into a London-oriented hinterland well before Adam Smith. Shortly after his death in 1790, the worldwide monopoly position of British manufacturing became yet another "fact" whose creation few English economists ever pondered other than to attribute to the same "natural" forces that had created a national and colonial division of labor. In the metropole-centered world of classical political economy, it was quite natural to measure general welfare by consumption, while production and the role of merchants, entrepreneurs, traders, and the crown in creating and encouraging that production were neglected or ignored. Smith himself bears some responsibility for this blind spot and the dismissive attitudes toward "Mercantilism" it generated, *The Wealth of Nations* itself being something of a jeremiad against the "Mercantile System," with little appreciation of its role in creating the very division of labor Smith became so famous for identifying.[86]

To make the previous points clearer, it is necessary to briefly touch upon another problem tied closely to the neglectful and dismissive "treatment of mercantilism" within the history of economic thought. This is the fact that British economic history has often been written with classical and neoclassical economic biases that have tended to stress "natural" endogenous economic development, political gradualism, a limited state, low taxes, and laissez-faire economic policies as keys to British prosperity and to attribute the Industrial Revolution to the ideas of the Enlightenment and classical political economy.[87]

It is today more commonly accepted that the 1688 Revolution was a genuinely violent event which ushered in profound political, institutional, and economic changes comparable in many ways to the French Revolution.[88] An unusually dynamic royal state emerged that became very active in economic and trade policy. The new liberal constitutional order enabled significantly higher taxes than in absolutist states such as France and Spain and the construction of an unrivaled navy.[89] The Bank of England was founded in 1694 to help finance this navy and shore up royal finances in war which enabled England to displace the Netherlands as the premier world trading power by 1700 and to prevail in four wars against France that led to seizure of much of the French overseas empire between 1702 and 1814.[90] As mentioned, between 1701 and 1733 numerous protective tariffs and export bounties were passed to encourage domestic manufacture which inadvertently and unexpectedly offered infant industry protection to domestic cotton spinning and calico production.[91] The later mechanization of cotton and iron production was itself a product of unusually high wages produced by the growth of London as a major colonial entrepôt and the early adoption of coal due to rapid population growth, urbanization, and deforestation.[92]

As early as 1784–1786, nearly 60% of British cotton exports went to the Americas, Africa, and Asia.[93] At the same time, import duties on colonial raw materials were abolished, just as metal and textile industries were prohibited in the colonies or hindered by prohibitive duties.[94] From this newer perspective, the British state, the Royal Navy, colonies, and the colonial division of labor played a decisive role in the development of capitalism and the Industrial Revolution in Britain.

Research over the last several years has also come to question the influence of classical political economy upon British economic policy in the nineteenth century. In reality, no clear break can be seen with "Whig Mercantilist" views after 1815, and many features of "Mercantilist" economic policy can be traced well into the nineteenth century.[95] In the 1820s, British protective tariffs on manufactured imports were by far the highest in Europe and on average even 10% higher than in the unusually protectionist USA.[96] The long list of naval conquests and blockades of the eighteenth century and Napoleonic era cannot be meaningfully differentiated from the two Opium Wars against China (1840–1842, 1856–1860), the blockade of Russia during the Crimean War (1854–1856), the blockades of Istanbul (1897) and Venezuela (1902–1903), or the violation of neutral harbors and shipping during the Boer War (1899–1902). Moreover, in the transition to free trade, the arguments of David Ricardo were of only very minor influence. Much more important instead were the widespread evangelical Christian views of the middle classes after the parliamentary reform of 1832, which tended to see in free trade the salvation of the nation.[97] One of the politicians most associated with free trade, President of the Board of Trade William Huskisson, was in the first instance motivated by the desire to secure Britain's position as "workshop of the world" through bilateral trade agreements before other European states closed their markets; indeed, it was widely hoped that free trade would prevent the spread of industrial machinery abroad and assure the continuation of British trade and naval supremacy.[98] It was not until 1849 and 1854 that the last provisions of the Navigation Acts were abolished, and it is a fact that Britain still had higher average tariffs than France until the end of the 1870s.[99] Yet even this relatively late free trade came to be questioned in the 1890s with rising competition from the USA and Germany, as well as growing protectionism in the USA and British Dominions. Britain reimposed protective tariffs in 1915 and introduced an imperial customs union in 1932. The era of British free trade thus lasted only some forty years. If there was ever a "Neomercantilist" special path, it may well have been British.

From this perspective, it is easy to see Hamilton, Raymond, and List's ideas as a continuation of the "Whig" strand of seventeenth-century English political economy in a noncolonial setting. This developed in the late eighteenth and early nineteenth century into a transatlantic critique not only of the colonial and neocolonial division of labor of the British Empire, but also of classical political economy's neglect of sovereignty, economic policy, industrial production, and the economics of space. Seen this way, the difficulties reconciling the two countries with British naval hegemony in the late nineteenth and early twentieth century make much more sense. This may also serve to better explain the striking similarities between American and German naval militarism before the First World War, American protectionism, and, conversely, Germany's quest for its own settler colonies and desire for access to international trade without the looming threat of Royal Navy seizures or blockades.

Conclusion

The transnational perspective of German *Weltpolitik* before the First World War has highlighted the entanglement of Germany and the USA linked fundamentally to the anti-imperial logic of both the German and American projects of sovereign political consolidation and economic development. The USA and Germany were the two most successful projects of emulative industrialization in the nineteenth century. This had many causes, but breaking with Britain's formal and informal colonial division of labor was an important enabling step in that direction. It was no coincidence that this anti-imperial logic was articulated in a common line of economic discourse that can be traced to List and Hamilton but which had much deeper roots in English Whig political economy of the seventeenth and eighteenth centuries, revolutionary ideas that transformed England into the leading economic power of the time. These ideas, mediated by American thinkers, became part of the consensus of German political economy which had a subtle but persistent influence on the development of German *Weltpolitik*. This cannot be meaningfully disentangled from the fact that the USA was also one of the most important points of reference in the development of German colonial and naval policy before the First World War. The examples of Ernst Levy von Halle and Max Sering revealed that German navalism and settler colonialism had many American features or were direct responses to American developments.

The comparisons with the USA also suggest that it was not Germany's "Neomercantilist" *Sonderweg* but rather its European geography, its demographic growth, and its heavy reliance upon trade that drove prewar tensions and ultimately gave German *Weltpolitik* its dangerous contours. There is no doubt that Germany's clumsy prewar diplomacy sharpened those contours and later played a fateful role in escalating the July 1914 crisis. The spread of industrialization and the globalization of trade before 1914 did not alone cause the First World War, but they created trade frictions and protectionism which reinforced the logic of blue water navies with the capacity to threaten blockades. Those frictions and demographic growth, in turn, reinforced the logic of contiguous or overseas settler colonies. The Great War itself validated this logic: The Entente powers, and in particular Britain, prevailed because of massive deliveries of foodstuffs, raw materials, war materiel, and soldiers from the formal and informal colonies. And the successful British naval blockade of the Channel and North Sea in the last two years of the war was critically important to the collapse of the Central Powers in November 1918.

Beyond a more differentiated and nuanced understanding of German imperialism, this essay may also offer some insights into contemporary relevance. As Ha-Joon Chang has argued in his critical analysis of economic development strategies, historical amnesia about the path of economic development of industrialized countries has shaped the current discussion over optimal development strategies and policy.[100] Developing countries are today being put under enormous pressure by developed countries and such bodies as the World Bank, the International

Monetary Fund (IMF), and the World Trade Organization (WTO) to eschew active industrial, trade and technology policy, to respect intellectual property rights, and to pursue restrictive fiscal and monetary policies which allegedly represent "best practice" drawn from the lessons of history but which not a single successful industrializer ever practiced in the course of its economic development. The parallels between these development strategies and the colonial division of labor envisioned by the Whig imperialists of eighteenth-century England, the free trade imperialists of nineteenth-century Britain, and the Washington consensus today are suggestive, just as are the parallels between the relationship of Britain and Germany in the early twentieth century and the USA and China today. Whether the current wave of globalization and the movement of the world's economic center of gravity eastward will be any less violent than it was one hundred years ago can only be hoped. As before 1914, it is doubtful that globalization will make conflict any less likely because it is invariably bound up with questions of rival sovereignty and defining the rules of international order that economic integration alone cannot answer.

Notes

1. Fritz Fischer, *Germany's Aims in the First World War.* With an introduction by Hajo Holborn and James Joll (New York: Norton, 1967).
2. See here Hans-Ulrich Wehler, *Deutsche Gesellschaftsgeschichte*, vol. 3 (Munich: C.H. Beck, 1995).
3. Ibid., 1109–52.
4. Joseph Schumpeter, "Zur Soziologie der Imperialismen," *Archiv für Sozialwissenschaft und Sozialpolitik* 46 (1918–1919): 1–39, 275–310.
5. Karl Helfferich, *Der Weltkrieg*, 3 vols. (Berlin: Ullstein, 1919).
6. Ibid., vol. 1: Die Vorgeschichte des Krieges, 37.
7. Ibid., 37.
8. See for example Karl Helfferich, *Das Geld im russisch-japanischen Krieg: Ein Finanzpolitischer Beitrag zur Zeitgeschichte* (Berlin: Mittler, 1906); Max Sering, *Die landwirthschaftliche Konkurrenz Nordamerikas in Gegenwart und Zukunft: Landwirthschaft, Kolonisation und Verkehrswesen in den Vereinigten Staaten und in Britisch-Nordamerika. Auf Grund von Reisen und Studien* (Leipzig: Duncker & Humblot, 1887); Hermann Schumacher,

Die Chinesischen Vertragshäfen, ihre Wirtschaftliche Stellung und Bedeutung (Jena: Fischer, 1899); Ernst von Halle, *Baumwollproduktion und Pflanzungswirtschaft in den Nordamerikanischen Südstaaten*, Staats- und Socialwissenschaftliche Forschungen vol. 15 [1897] and 26 [1906] (Leipzig: Duncker & Humblot, 1897–1906).

9. Karl Rathgen, *Japans Volkswirtschaft und Staatshaushalt* (Leipzig: Duncker & Humblot, 1891).
10. See here Rolf Hobson, *Imperialism at Sea: Naval Strategic Thought, the Ideology of Sea Power, and the Tirpitz Plan, 1875–1914* (Boston: Humanities Press, 2002); Patrick J. Kelly, *Tirpitz and the Imperial German Navy* (Bloomington and Indianapolis, IN: Indiana University Press, 2011); and Dirk Bönker, *Militarism in a Global Age. Naval Ambitions in Germany and the United States before World War I* (Ithaca and London: Cornell University Press, 2012); cf. Volker Berghahn, *Der Tirpitz-Plan: Genesis und Verfall einer innenpolitischen Krisenstrategie unter Wilhelm II* (Düsseldorf: Droste, 1971).
11. Wilhelm von Karforff, confidant of Bismarck, estate owner, and cofounder of the Free Conservative Party (Deutsche Reichspartei). Kardorff was influenced in his protectionism by the American economist Henry Charles Carey and was an early supporter of a German system of protective tariffs. His influence on Bismarck can be seen in the protective tariffs passed in 1879.
12. Prince Chlodwig von Hohenlohe-Schillingfürst, German Chancellor 1894–1900.
13. Bundesarchiv N 253 Nl Alfred Tirpitz, Nr. 40, Bl. 154–155, Schmoller to Tirpitz, Berlin, July 29, 1897.
14. Dingley Act of 1897, the highest and longest-lived American protective tariff which amounted to 52% on average.
15. Geheimes Staatsarchiv Preußischer Kulturbesitz [GStA PK], VI. HA Nl Schmoller, Nr. 114, Bl. 275–276, Brentano to Schmoller, Munich, July 27, 1897.
16. Wolfgang Marienfeld, "Wissenschaft und Schlachtflottenbau in Deutschland 1897–1906," *Marine Rundschau* Beiheft 2 (April 1957): 109–15. The claim that economists and other scholars became engaged for the fleet because they were cleverly manipulated by the Navy Office is a distortion. See here Erik Grimmer-Solem, "Imperialist Socialism of the Chair. Gustav Schmoller and German Weltpolitik, 1897–1905," in *Wilhelminism and Its Legacies: Crisis,*

Continuity, and the Meanings of Reform in Germany, 1890–1930, ed. Geoff Eley and James Retallack (New York and Oxford: Berghahn, 2003), 106–21; and Guenther Roth, "Der politische Kontext von Max Webers Beiträge über die deutsche Wirtschaft in der *Encyclopedia Americana*," *Zeitschrift für Soziologie* 36 (February 2007): 65–77.

17. Gustav Schmoller, "Die wirtschaftliche Zukunft Deutschlands und die Flottenvorlage," in *Zwanzig Jahre Deutscher Politik (1897–1917). Aufsätze und Vorträge,* ed. Lucie Schmoller (Munich and Leipzig: Duncker & Humblot, 1920), 1–20.
18. Ibid., 3.
19. Ibid., 3–9.
20. Ibid., 19.
21. Ibid., 10–13.
22. Ibid.
23. Ibid., 14.
24. Ibid., 18.
25. Ibid., 15, 19.
26. See, for example, Alexander Schmidt, *Reisen in die Moderne: Der Amerika-Diskurs des deutschen Bürgertums vor dem Ersten Weltkrieg im europäischen Vergleich* (Berlin: Akademie Verlag, 1997); Daniel T. Rodgers, *Atlantic Crossings: Social Politics in a Progressive Age* (Cambridge, MA: Belknap Press of Harvard University Press, 1998); Frank Trommler and Elliot Shore, *The German-American Encounter: Conflict and Cooperation Between Two Cultures, 1800–2000* (New York: Berghahn, 2001); Sebastian Conrad and Jürgen Osterhammel, eds., *Das Kaiserreich Transnational: Deutschland in der Welt 1871–1914* (Göttingen: Vandenhoeck & Ruprecht, 2004); Christof Mauch and Kiran Patel, eds., *Wettlauf um die Moderne: Die USA und Deutschland 1890 bis heute* (Munich: Pantheon, 2008).
27. See here among others Andrew Zimmerman, *Alabama in Africa: Booker T. Washington, the German Empire, and the Globalization of the New South* (Princeton: Princeton University Press, 2010); Bönker, *Militarism in a Global Age*; and Jens Uwe Guettel, *German Expansionism, Liberal Imperialism, and the United States, 1776–1945* (Cambridge: Cambridge University Press, 2012).
28. Ernst von Halle, *Trusts or Industrial Combinations and Coalitions in the United States* (New York: Macmillan, 1899 [1895]), xiii.

29. GStA PK VI HA, Nl. Schmoller, Nr. 126, Bl. 15–26, von Halle to Schmoller, Savannah, Georgia, October 22, 1894; Ernst von Halle, *Reisebriefe aus West Indien und Venezuela* (Hamburg: A.G. "Neue Börsen-Halle," 1896).
30. von Halle, *Baumwollproduktion und Pflanzungswirtschaft*.
31. Ernst von Halle, "Das Interesse Deutschlands an der amerikanischen Präsidentenwahl des Jahres 1896," *Jahrbuch für Gesetzgebung, Verwaltung und Volkswirtschaft in Deutschen Reiche* 20 (1896): 1353–86.
32. Von Halle was himself convinced that most of Britain's claims were valid, making the British retreat all the more out of character. See von Halle, *Reisebriefe*, 93.
33. Idem, "Das Interesse Deutschlands," 1359–61, 1371–73.
34. Ibid., 1373–74.
35. Ibid., 1380–81.
36. Ibid., 1382–83.
37. See James R. Holmes, "Mahan, a 'Place in the Sun' and Germany's Quest for Sea Power," *Comparative Strategy* 23 (2004): 27–61.
38. Ernst von Halle, *Die Blockade der nordamerikanischen Südstaaten* (Berlin: Mittler, 1900), 34.
39. See here Wilhelm Deist, *Flottenpolitik und Flottenpropaganda: Das Nachrichtenbureau des Reichsmarineamtes 1897–1914* (Stuttgart: Deutsche Verlagsanstalt, 1976).
40. Heiko Herold, *Reichsgewalt bedeutet Seegewalt: Die Kreuzergeschwader der Kaiserlichen Marine als Instrument der deutschen Kolonial- und Weltpolitik, 1895–1901* (Munich: Oldenbourg Verlag, 2013), 302–13.
41. Ibid., 314–15, 317.
42. Ibid., 321–22.
43. Ernst von Halle, "Die Bedeutung des nordamerikanischen Imperialismus [1901]," in *Volks- und Seewirtschaft: Reden und Aufsätze* (Berlin: Mittler, 1902), 183.
44. Avner Offer, *The First World War. An Agrarian Interpretation* (Oxford: Oxford University Press 1989), 270–99.
45. See here "Aufbringung eines deutschen Dampfers in Südafrika," *Münchener Neueste Nachrichten*, December 30, 1899; "Die Affäre Bundesrath," *Berliner Tageblatt*, January 3, 1900; and "Die Beschlagnahme deutscher Schiffe durch Engländer," *Berliner Lokal-Anzeiger*, January 3, 1900.

46. Lance Davis und Stanley Engerman, *Naval Blockades in Peace and War. An Economic History Since 1750* (Cambridge: Cambridge University Press, 2006), 13.
47. "Deutsches Reich: Eine bittere Lehre," *Allgemeine Zeitung*, January 3, 1900.
48. Jan Rüger, *The Great Naval Game. Britain and Germany in the Age of Empire* (Cambridge: Cambridge University Press, 2007), 50–92.
49. Bönker, *Militarism in a Global Age*, 23–46.
50. On the genocidal colonial war in German Southwest Africa, see Isabel V. Hull, *Absolute Destruction: Military Culture and the Practices of War in Imperial Germany* (Ithaca and London: Cornell University Press, 2005), 7–90.
51. Schmoller, Dernburg, Delbrück, Schäfer, Sering, Schillings, Brunner, Jastrow, Penck, *Kahl über Reichstagsauflösung und Kolonialpolitik: Offizieller stenographischer Bericht über die Versammlung in der Berliner Hochschule für Musik am 8. Januar 1907*, ed. Kolonialpolitischen Aktionskomité (Berlin: Wedekind, 1907); Erik Grimmer-Solem, "The Professors' Africa: Economists, the Elections of 1907, and the Legitimation of German Imperialism," *German History* 25 (2007): 312–47.
52. Ständiger Ausschuss des Vereins für Sozialpolitik, "Die Ansiedlung von Europäern in den Tropen," *Schriften des Vereins für Sozialpolitik* 147 (1912–1915). This study was published in five parts: (1) Deutsch-Ostafrika unter Berücksichtigung Britisch-Ostafrika und Nyassalands (1912); (2) Mittelamerika, Klein Antillen, Niederländisch-West und Ostindien (1912); (3) Natal, Rhodesien, Britisch-Ostafrika (1913); (4) Britisch-Kaffraria und seinen deutschen Siedlungen (1914); and (5) Die deutschen Kolonisten im brasilianischen Staate Espirito Santo (1915).
53. *Statistisches Jahrbuch für das Deutsche Reich, 1910*, ed. Kaiserliches Statistischen Amt (Berlin: Puttkammer & Mühlbrecht, 1911), 396.
54. See here Horst Gründer, *Geschichte der deutschen Kolonien*, 5th ed. (Paderborn: Schöningh, 2004). Even the most productive colony, Southwest Africa, generated exports worth only 70 million marks in 1913, the lion's shares from diamonds and copper. Ibid., 126.
55. On the Hamburg Kolonialinstitut, see Jens Ruppenthal, *Kolonialismus als "Wissenschaft und Technik": Das Hamburgische Kolonialinstitut 1908 bis 1919* (Stuttgart: Steiner, 2007). On German cotton cultivation initiatives in East Africa and Togo, see Thaddeus Sunseri,

"The Baumwollfrage: Cotton Colonialism in German East Africa," *Central European History* 34, no. 1 (2001): 31–51; and Sven Beckert, "From Tuskegee to Togo: The Problem of Freedom in the Empire of Cotton," *The Journal of American History* 92, no. 2 (September 2005): 498–526.

56. GStA PK, VI. HA Nl Schmoller, Nr. 141, Bl. 185–192, Max Sering to Gustav Schmoller, Ramsey's Farm near Warren, Minnesota, July 16, 1883.
57. See especially Guettel, *German Expansionism*, 126–27.
58. Quoted in ibid., 2.
59. Max Sering, "Die Landpolitik der Vereinigten Staaten von Nordamerika," *Jahrbuch für Gesetzgebung, Verwaltung und Volkswirtschaft im Deutschen Reiche* 8 (1884): 441–95; idem, *Die landwirthschaftliche Konkurrenz Nordamerikas in Gegenwart und Zukunft: Landwirthschaft, Kolonisation und Verkehrswesen in den Vereinigten Staaten und in Britisch-Nordamerika. Auf Grund von Reisen und Studien* (Leipzig: Duncker & Humblot, 1887).
60. See Robert L. Nelson, "From Manitoba to Memel. Max Sering, Inner Colonization and the German East," *Social History* 35, no. 4 (November 2010): 439–57.
61. Max Sering, *Verhandlungen des Landes-Oekonomie-Kollegiums am 9. Februar 1912 über die Politik der Grundbesitzverteilung in den grossen Reichen* (Berlin: Paul Parey, 1912).
62. Idem, ed., *Westrussland in seiner Bedeutung für die Entwicklung Mitteleuropas* (Leipzig and Berlin: B.G. Teubner 1917), xxix–xxx.
63. Donald Findlay and Kevin O'Rourke, *Power and Plenty: Trade, War and the World Economy in the Second Millenium* (Princeton and Oxford: Princeton University Press, 2007), 403. In 1913, average ad valorem tariffs on imported manufactured goods were 20% in France, 40% in Spain, 25–30% in Japan, 26% in Canada, 44% in USA, 28% in Argentina, 50–70% in Brazil, and 40–50% in Mexico. They were only 13% in Germany.
64. Alexander Hamilton, "Report on the Subject of Manufactures [1791]," in *Writings* (New York: Library of America, 2001), 647–734, here 650.
65. Ibid., 659.
66. Ibid., 660–61.
67. Ibid., 689–90.
68. Ibid., 668.

69. See here Songho Ha, *The Rise and Fall of the American System: Nationalism and the Development of the American Economy, 1790–1837* (London: Pickering & Chatto, 2009); John Lauritz Larson, *Internal Improvement: National Public Works and the Promise of Popular Government in the Early United States* (Chapel Hill and London: University of North Carolina Press, 2001); and John R. Nelson, Jr., *Liberty and Property: Political Economy and Policymaking in the New Nation, 1789–1812* (Baltimore and London: Johns Hopkins University Press, 1987).
70. See above all Richard Buel Jr., *In Irons: Britain's Naval Supremacy and the American Revolutionary Economy* (New Haven and London: Yale University Press, 1998).
71. Gustav Schmoller, *Umrisse und Untersuchungen zur Verfassungs-, Verwaltungs- und Wirtschaftsgeschichte* (Leipzig: Duncker & Humblot, 1898), 37; Walter Eucken, *Grundsätze der Wirtschaftspolitik*, 6th ed. (Tübingen: J.C.B. Mohr, 1990), 336.
72. See here Brian Balogh, *A Government Out of Sight: The Mystery of National Authority in Nineteenth-Century America* (Cambridge: Cambridge University Press, 2009); Richard Franklin Bensel, *Yankee Leviathan: The Origins of Central State Authority in America* (Cambridge: Cambridge University Press, 1990); and Stephen Skowronek, *Building a New American State: The Expansion of National Administrative Capacities, 1877–1920* (Cambridge: Cambridge University Press, 1982).
73. Keith Tribe, *Strategies of Economic Order: German Economic Discourse 1750–1950* (Cambridge: Cambridge University Press, 1995), 32–65.
74. Gustav Schmoller, "Friedrich List als praktischer Volkswirt" [Vortrag 8.12.1907], *Volkswitschaftliche Blätter* 7 (1908): 1–12.
75. Steve Pincus, "Rethinking Mercantilism: Political Economy, the British Empire, and the Atlantic World in the Seventeenth and Eighteenth Centuries," *William and Mary Quarterly*, 3. Ser., 69, no. 1 (January 2012): 3–34.
76. Ibid., 16, 20–23, 26–27; idem, *1688. The First Modern Revolution* (New Haven, CT and London: Yale University Press, 2009), 369–72, 382–83, 386–87, 390, 392, 396.
77. Sophus A. Reinert, *Translating Empire. Emulation and the Origins of Political Economy* (Cambridge, MA and London: Harvard University Press, 2011).
78. Ibid., 73–128.

79. John Cary, *A Discourse on Trade and Other Matters Relative to It* (London: T. Osborne, 1745), 98.
80. David Armitage, *The Ideological Origins of the British Empire* (Cambridge and New York: Cambridge University Press, 2000), 163–65.
81. On British cotton protectionism of the seventeenth and eighteenth centuries, see Sven Beckert, *Empire of Cotton: A Global History* (New York: Alfred A. Knopf, 2014), 47–48.
82. See for example Joseph A. Schumeter, *History of Economic Analysis* (London: Allen & Unwin, 1954), 197–98, 267, 273, 293, 350.
83. Ibid., 197: "... every attempt he [Cary] makes to carry analysis beyond the obvious is a failure."
84. Robert H. I. Palgrave, ed., *Dictionary of Political Economy*, vol. I (London: Macmillan, 1910), 230; John Eatwell, Murry Milgate, and Peter Newman, eds., *The New Palgrave: A Dictionary of Economics*, 4 vols. (London: Macmillan, 1987).
85. Walter Isard, *Location and Space-Economy. A General Theory Relating to Industrial Location, Market Areas, Land Use, Trade and Urban Structure* (New York and London: MIT/Wiley and Chapman & Hall, 1956), 27.
86. See especially Adam Smith, *An Inquiry into the Nature and Causes of the Wealth of Nations*, ed. Edwin Cannan (Chicago: University of Chicago Press, 1976), bk IV, chaps. II–V, VIII.
87. See for example most recently Joel Mokyr, *The Enlightened Economy: An Economic History of Britian, 1700–1850* (New Haven and London: Yale University Press, 2009).
88. On the revolutionary economic consequences, see Pincus, *1688*, 366–99.
89. Philip T. Hoffman and Kathryn Nordberg, eds., *Fiscal Crises, Liberty and Representative Government, 1450–1789* (Stanford: Stanford University Press, 1994), 299–310.
90. See John Brewer, *The Sinews of Power: War, Money and the English State, 1688–1783* (New York: Knopf, 1988).
91. William Bernstein, *A Splendid Exchange. How Trade Shaped the World* (New York: Atlantic Monthly Press, 2008), 261–63.
92. Robert Allen, *The British Industrial Revolution in Global Perspective* (Cambridge: Cambridge University Press, 2009).
93. Findlay and O'Rourke, *Power and Plenty*, 326.
94. Ha-Joon Chang, *Kicking Away the Ladder: Development Strategy in Historical Perspective* (London: Anthem, 2002), 51–53.

95. Patrick K. O'Brien, "Inseparable Connections: Trade, Economy, State, and Empire," in *The Oxford History of the British Empire,* vol. II (Oxford: Oxford University Press, 1998), 52–77.
96. Chang, *Kicking Away the Ladder*, 17.
97. Anthony Howe, "Restoring Free Trade: The British Experience, 1776–1873," in *The Political Economy of British Historical Experience, 1688–1914,* ed. Donald Winch and Patrick O'Brein (Oxford: The British Academy/Oxford University Press, 2002), 193–213.
98. Ibid., 196–99; Bernard Semmel, *The Rise of Free Trade Imperialism* (Cambridge 1970), 203–11.
99. Kenneth Morgan, "Mercantilism and the British Empire, 1688–1815," in *The Political Economy of British Historical Experience*, ed. Winch and O'Brein, 165–91; John V. C. Nye, *War Wine and Taxes: The Political Economy of Anglo-French Trade, 1689–1900* (Princeton/Oxford: Princeton University Press, 2007), 4.
100. See Chang, *Kicking Away the Ladder.*

Author Biography

Erik Grimmer-Solem received his D.Phil. in economic history from Nuffield College, Oxford, and joined Wesleyan University's faculty in 2002. Previously, Erik held appointments at the University of Chicago and Balliol College, Oxford. He has authored *The Rise of Historical Economics and Social Reform in Germany* (OUP 2003) and many articles that have appeared in such journals as the *Leo Baeck Year Book, German History*, the *Journal of World History, History and Theory, Militärgeschichtliche Zeitschrift*, and a number of edited volumes. His research has been discussed by *DER SPIEGEL* and in the German Bundestag, and he has received fellowships from the Fritz Thyssen Foundation and the Leverhulme Trust, as well as distinguished teaching prizes from Wesleyan University. Since 2015, he has served as coeditor of *Schmollers Jahrbuch: Journal of Contextual Economics*. A new book, *Elusive Empire: Globalization, Political Economy, and the German Quest for World Status, 1875–1918*, is forthcoming.

Wesley Mitchell's *Business Cycles* After 100 Years

Walter A. Friedman

Wesley Mitchell's *Business Cycles* (1913) was published just over a century ago. It is a neglected classic that should be recognized, as one contemporary noted, as *the* key economic text between Alfred Marshall's *Principles of Economics* (1890) and John Maynard Keynes's *General Theory* (1936).

Its importance does not come from its being a bestseller, for it was not. Nor is it known for being read cover-to-cover by other academic economists. Instead, the book deserves our attention because it was a great distillation and analysis of economic thought, bringing together a huge range of ideas about economic "cycles," "oscillations," "fluctuations," and "rhythms" that had long occupied the attention of leading economists, such as Clément Juglar and Karl Marx.[1] It was an omnibus, collecting statistics on a range of topics, including production, prices, debt, and bank deposits. It was international in perspective and included comparisons of the economic history of the USA, England, France, and Germany. Moreover, it not only summarized, and gave authority to, a wealth of existing ideas and information, but

W.A. Friedman (✉)
Harvard Business School, Boston, USA
e-mail: wfriedman@hbs.edu

R. Fredona and S.A. Reinert (eds.), *New Perspectives on the History of Political Economy*, https://doi.org/10.1007/978-3-319-58247-4_10

also pointed the way forward for future scholars and analysts, providing them with a new and ambitious research agenda. Its many tables exemplified the vastness of economic data newly available and yet, at the same time, the book had the markings of an unfinished project, ripe for further inquiry.

Most of all, *Business Cycles* helped to popularize a "cyclical" understanding of the economy that became adopted by businesspeople, politicians, and journalists in the decades following its publication. It provided a way to make sense of the whole economic "system" from a deep historical perspective. It described an inherent logic to the workings of capitalist, profit-seeking, business-oriented economies.

The central theme of the book—arguing that cycles of prosperity and of depression had their origins in the behavior of business enterprise—gained popularity in the 1910s and 1920s. For many, the idea that the economy went through discernible "business cycles" provided a comforting transition from an agricultural past. The notion of an industrial or economic cycle, recalling a natural or seasonal one, brought a sense of control, or at least understanding, amid relentless change. It promoted the idea that the trajectories of capitalist economies were not random. Rather, they followed a recognizable pattern. Even more, the book promised the idea that government action could dampen the severity of economic fluctuations and could foster stable economic growth—a new role for public officials that is now deeply entrenched.

The goal of this paper is not to support or criticize Mitchell's *Business Cycles* but rather to explain how the central concept of the book, the phenomenon of business cycles, became of seminal interest to a range of Americans in the early twentieth century. My argument is not that Mitchell's book alone *created* an intense popular fascination with cycles. Rather, it is that Mitchell's book helped to crystallize and give authority to ideas about business cycles that proved widely appealing—and, moreover, helped to shape economic, popular, and public discussions about capitalism. Indeed, the term "business cycles" became a popular shorthand way of describing the boom-and-bust nature of capitalism in the decades before the publication of Keynes's *General Theory* (1937), and the Keynesian Revolution that helped promote the field of macroeconomics.[2]

Why did the idea of business cycles resonate with a diverse group of people in the USA in the early twentieth century? The idea that capitalist economies operated according to the laws of business cycles provided for many businesspeople and politicians useful clues for shaping strategy and public policy. Among those who were inspired by Mitchell's work on business cycles were three groups.

1. Economists and statisticians, including those of the new National Bureau of Economic Research (NBER, an organization that Mitchell co-founded), who saw, in *Business Cycles*, a plan for measuring economic activity and a way to tie together many disparate aspects of economic life. Theoretical economists had long been interested in the idea of cycles, but the effort among quantitative and data-gathering economists was different: They sought to observe cycles and to use them to measure change over time. Indeed, the study of business cycles provided a way to measure all aspects of economic life—construction, production, trade, commodity prices, etc.—as moving either with or against the cycle.

2. Entrepreneurs and businesspeople, who, in a time of frequent economic panics, became infatuated with the idea of "business cycles" and began to make predictions of future ups and downs in output and in the prices of securities and commodities in order to formulate investment and purchasing plans. The entrepreneurs who pushed this idea furthest were the founders of the economic forecasting industry, a nascent business in the early twentieth century that later became well established. Nearly, all of the pioneering forecasters based their predictions on cyclical models—citing Mitchell's work even though they often greatly simplified or even distorted his ideas.

3. Politicians, who saw the idea of "business cycles" as a way to gain rational control over the whole economy—and began to conceive of ways to dampen cyclical swings. In the 1920s, for instance, Herbert Hoover became a major figure in this effort. While head of the Department of Commerce, he courted Mitchell aggressively to serve on his Business Cycle Committee and began the publication of government reports and bulletins on the subject. Hoover's view of government's role in dampening cycles was far more restrained than his successor in the Presidential office, Franklin Roosevelt. But Hoover brought the mandate of controlling economic cycles into the orbit of executive power.

To put this more poetically, the idea of "business cycles," backed by such empirical evidence in Mitchell's book, kindled three dreams in the early twentieth century. The first, of empirical economists and statisticians, was to analyze and measure business cycles; the second, of entrepreneurs and businesspeople, to predict future cycles; and the third, of politicians, to control them.

Not all of the individuals in these three groups—empirical economists, forecasters, and politicians—defined the business cycle in the same way, of course. Some, such as the statistician and economist Warren Persons, saw business cycles as fluctuations stemming from relations between investing, business enterprise, and banking in capitalist economies. Others, such as the popular forecaster Roger Babson, fetishized the idea of the business cycle, seeing in it ties to the natural sciences and even the work of seventeenth-century physicist and mathematician Sir Isaac Newton. Still others, including Herbert Hoover, saw the business cycle as resulting from inefficiencies in the economy that could be reduced with better information and technology and a more enlightened class of business managers.

While few closely followed Mitchell's own nuanced definition of the business cycle, all benefited from the authority he gave to the phenomenon—and all found something deeply appealing in the idea of a cyclical economy. The efforts to pursue these "dreams" had significant social, political, and economic consequences.

The story of this article, then, is not only of *Business Cycles* itself, but also of Mitchell's working out of the promise of the book, with the formation of the NBER and with his service in government. It is also the story of how, in the 1910s and 1920s, the idea of "business cycles," like other economic ideas in other times, inspired disparate audiences with widely varying agendas. In the end, it is the story of how this captivating idea, a description of a measurable economic phenomenon, was popularized, commercialized, and used in the exercise of political power.

Mitchell

Wesley Clair Mitchell was born in 1874 and died in 1948, making him a near contemporary of economists Irving Fisher and John Maynard Keynes. When mentioned at all today, Mitchell is recalled as one of the founders, along with Harvard Business School dean Edwin Gay, of the National Bureau of Economic Research. In the 1910s and 1920s, though, Mitchell was one of the two or three best-known American economists of the time. He was at least as well known as Fisher, and he attracted scores of students to Columbia to study with him—something Fisher, with his heavily mathematical approach, did not do at Yale. Indeed, Mitchell was a highly successful institution builder. In addition to establishing the NBER in 1920, Mitchell was instrumental in the founding of the New School for Social Research in 1919 and the Social Science Research Council in 1922.

Mitchell was regarded as immensely knowledgeable about both economic history and statistics and for being extremely judicious. Herbert Hoover referred to Mitchell as an "umpire" because of his sound judgment in weighing conflicting ideas.[3] The economist Joseph Schumpeter said of Mitchell in a eulogy: "Here was a man who had the courage to say, unlike the rest of us, that he had not all the answers; who went about his task without either haste or rest; who did not care to march along with flags and brass bands; who was full of sympathy with mankind's fate, yet kept aloof from the market place; who taught us, by example and not by phrase, what a scholar should be."[4]

Mitchell was a member of the first class at the University of Chicago in 1890. His teachers included philosopher and educational reformer John Dewey and economist J. Laurence Laughlin, who had come from Cornell to head the Chicago economics department, bringing with him Thorstein Veblen—who had been a fellow in Laughlin's department in Ithaca.[5] Veblen, who had a doctorate in philosophy from Yale University (1884), encouraged Mitchell to take a multidisciplinary approach to understanding how economies functioned, advising him to study psychology, anthropology, and culture. At the time Mitchell arrived, Veblen was undertaking a statistical analysis of commodity prices—similar to the type of work Mitchell produced throughout his career.[6]

For his doctoral dissertation, Mitchell studied the effect on prices of the printing of greenbacks by the federal government during the Civil War. The thesis is nearly 600 pages long, with roughly 150 pages devoted to statistical tables covering gold prices, wages, cotton prices, salaries, and other data from 1860 to 1866. Mitchell used these statistics to dispute the idea, expressed in the Quantity Theory of Money (popularized by Yale's Irving Fisher), that changes in prices occur relatively evenly throughout industries. Instead, he gathered detailed evidence to see what actually happened to prices as new bills were introduced. Mitchell found that in some, but not all, industries, prices increased and that the effects of the new bills were unevenly distributed.

While Veblen moved on from his statistical studies to pioneer his idiosyncratic and satirical approach to economics, Mitchell continued in that vein, a quintessential observer and data gatherer.[7] Still, the two are alike on some levels. While Mitchell was at the University of Chicago, Veblen published *The Theory of the Leisure Class* (1899), his classic text on conspicuous consumption. The book offered a description of capitalist economies as complex phenomena, rife with envy, ornament, and display—worlds away from the rational marketplace of utility maximizers that some economists, like Fisher, were describing in mathematically precise terms.[8] To Mitchell, like Veblen, economics was a science of human behavior rather than of timeless principles of wealth creation. Classical economists, such as Adam Smith and his followers, wrote as if their theories were permanently true. Mitchell thought instead that economic theories evolved over time and that economic "laws" depended on context. He was interested in developing the field of economics as one that took into account what human beings actually did.

Business Cycles

After the turn of the century, Mitchell turned to what would be the main intellectual subject of his lifetime: business cycles. It is perhaps not surprising he took on this subject. Mitchell wrote during a time of financial panic. Financial crisis was followed by severe economic hardship in 1873, 1893, and 1907. Many attributed these downturns to speculation and to schemes by leading business titans and politicians.

The 1907 panic was particularly perplexing, as it seemed to come without warning. Financial writer Alexander D. Noyes noted that part of the reason for the resulting alarm was that, due to the strength of banks and to efficiencies in industry, existing wisdom in financial circles held that panics were a thing of the past: "The opinion then entertained by these practical banking experts … was that 'aggregation of banking resources' and 'coordination of industry' had, between them, created a new economic situation, where old-fashioned financial and commercial panics … would be no longer possibilities."[9]

Before Mitchell's 1913 book on the subject, the term "business cycles" was not in the mainstream. Instead, panics were thought to be man-made events, brought on by the greed of business barons or the machinations of political bosses, or to stem from acts of God, such as massive crop failure or devastating storms. In the nineteenth century, the English economist William Stanley Jevons (1835–1882) enlisted mathematical techniques in one of the earliest statistical analyses of the business cycle. His paper titled "Commercial Crises and Sun-Spots" (1878) linked economic fluctuations to meteorological conditions that affected harvests.[10]

In popular writing, the business cycle, when referred to, was usually meant as a fixed cycle, often of 7 or 10 years, depending on the writer. One mention in 1896, for instance, in a House of Representatives report, described cycles in such terms. "Prosperity, panic, and liquidation … constitute the business cycle, or circle," it read. "Prosperity from 5 to 7 years, panic a few months or a year later, and liquidation a few years, more or less."[11] Moreover, there was far more interest in the periods of crisis than in efforts to link periods of prosperity and periods of depression.[12]

In *Business Cycles,* Mitchell looked at the evolution of thinking about economic fluctuations and how to predict them. He carefully summarized the writings of economic fluctuations from such luminaries as the British economists William Henry Beveridge and John Hobson; the German scholar Arthur Spiethoff; and the economist and sociologist Veblen, and Irving Fisher. By 1913, there were many opinions being advanced about the cause of such ups and downs—some of which Mitchell dismissed quickly. "Each recurring crisis, indeed, produced a fresh crop of ill-considered explanations," he observed.[13]

Mitchell's *book* came out the same year as other volumes on the business cycle, including the French economist Albert Aftalion's *Les crises périodiques de surproduction* [Periodic Crises of Overproduction] and British economist R.G. Hawtrey's *Good and Bad Trade: An Inquiry into the Causes of trade Fluctuations.*[14] But Mitchell's book was distinguished as the authoritative text. "It bids fair, we venture to pronounce, to be regarded as the classical authority for future students," said one reviewer. The book was an oversized volume of 12.5 inches by 10 inches and published in a tiny font. The text was divided into three main sections: the first, on the "problem and its setting," including summaries of existing business-cycle theory; the second, on key comparative statistics from the USA, England, France, and Germany, 1890–1911; and the final section on Mitchell's own observations of "the rhythm of business activity." It was a highly ambitious work that included dozens of statistical tables and detailed explorations of the crises of 1873, 1893, and 1907.

Reviewers praised his "penetrating acumen and the sane persuasive judgment which he displayed with much advantage some years back in his earlier study on the issues of 'greenbacks.'"[15] *Business Cycles* brought Mitchell acclaim. In a review of *Business Cycles* in the *Quarterly Journal of Economics*, the Harvard statistician Warren Persons wrote that the genius of the book lay in "the marshaling of the data, and the clear expositions and the combination of the ideas of various writers into a self-consistent theory of business cycles."[16]

Mitchell's book spawned interest in the topic and a swarm of new studies, including William Franklin Gephart's *Bank Credit and the Business Cycle* (1923); William Charles Schluter's *The Pre-War Business Cycle 1907 to 1914* (1923); Carl Snyder's *The Influence of the Interest Rate on the Business Cycle* (1925); Alvin H. Hansen's *Business-Cycle Theory: Its Development and Present Status* (1927); and Dorothy Swaine Thomas's *Social Aspects of the Business Cycle* (1927).[17]

There was also an awareness that Mitchell's approach, as he intended, would appeal to both academics and practitioners. It would be a work frequently returned to "by statisticians, by economists, and by statesmen and business organizers in every country where the phenomena here defined, investigated, and explained have become normally recurrent."[18]

Mitchell's *Business Cycles* popularized a four-phase description of the business cycle that became common in the late 1910s and the 1920s—of depression, revival, boom, and crises. He wrote that "business cycles" is a "vivid term for this recurrent ebb and flow of business activity ... Depressions pave the way for business revivals, revivals develop into 'booms,' booms breed crises, and crises run out into depressions." He did not treat the ups and downs of the market phenomena as dependent on external events—rather they were inherent to moneymaking economies. Moreover, he used statistical series to reveal these cycles, studying numerous types of economic data to determine how cycles in one sector of the economy could affect fluctuations in another.[19]

Though he regarded cycles as an intrinsic feature of capitalism, he did not believe that they were inalterable. *Business Cycles* embodied Mitchell's commitment to rigorous empiricism and observation, but his approach was based on the pragmatic idea that it was possible to control the extremes of the peaks and troughs of cycles—once enough was known about them.[20] He also argued for the need for measures of national incomes and of national product, two projects he would later pursue at the NBER.

Mitchell did not believe in the perfectibility of knowledge about cycles. He thought that the search would be ongoing. Mitchell likened the task of an economist trying to construct a theory of business cycles to a mechanical engineer trying to improve the design of an existing machine—say, a lamp. The engineer first had to understand the operation of all existing lamps and their flaws and then painstakingly design a new one, testing it over and over again to see that it was efficient. This described how Mitchell worked carefully through existing business-cycle theories. But, Mitchell conceded his own work was more difficult than that of the engineer. "The social sciences give no such guidance to a social engineer as the physical sciences give to a mechanical engineer," he wrote. "Human beings are the most intractable of materials. Nor can an inventor experiment with them at will as he can with alloys and plastics; he has to persuade his fellows to experiment on themselves, which they are generally reluctant to do."[21]

But he also believed that there was no need to wait until more knowledge had been gained before acting. What kinds of things could be tried? Long-range planning of public works, for instance, or a change in the policy of banks regarding credit ratios, and establishing new forms of unemployment insurance.[22] It was important to press ahead to try to curb unemployment during hard times. "Social experimentation, based on clearly thought-out hypotheses and accompanied by careful record-keeping, is one of the essential processes in increasing social knowledge and gaining social control," wrote Mitchell.[23] In this way, his thinking was parallel to that of his former teacher at Chicago, John Dewey, as it pertained to social experimentation and solving social problems. Ideas needed to be tested through social experimentation. This separated economics from the hard sciences.[24]

The Term "Business Cycles"

Mitchell's book was instrumental in increasing the popularity of the phrase "business cycles." Not everyone approved of the term, however. The most prominent critic was the stellar economist Irving Fisher—author of *Our Unstable Dollar and the So-Called Business Cycle* (1925). Fisher called the "business cycle" a "myth."[25] For Fisher, fluctuations in the price level alone explained the rise and fall of trade and hence accounted for what most people referred to as the "business cycle." He called such changes the "dance of the dollar."[26] The idea of a cycle, Fisher wrote, "implies a regular succession of *similar* fluctuations, constituting some sort of *recurrence*, … as in the case of the phases of the moon, the tides of the sea, wave motion, or pendulum swing …"[27]

In 1925, the *New York Times* reported on this claim, writing that Fisher "attempted to explode one of the most favored of economic theories."[28] Observing fluctuations in the economy was not like the tides, he wrote, but like watching the swaying of treetops and branches in a forest. "If, in the woods, we pull a twig and let it snap back, we set up a swaying movement back and forth… In actual experience … twigs or tree-tops seldom oscillate so regularly, even temporarily. They register, instead, chiefly the variations in wind velocity."[29] Similarly, the business world "oscillated" with variations in the "velocity" of money through the economy, in an uneven and irregular pattern.

But, for Wesley Mitchell, the term "business cycle" did not imply the scenario that Fisher described. Mitchell preferred the term "cycle" to other possibilities, such as "rhythm," "oscillation," or "fluctuation." Stock prices could go up and down several times in a day—from 10, say, to 3, and then up to 15. They "fluctuated" but they did not exhibit a secular pattern. Hence "cycle" was not appropriate to frequent changes in securities prices or commodity prices, but seemed a better choice to describe long-term trends in production, unemployment, and trade.[30]

For Mitchell, the term described an "exceedingly complex phenomena" by which "seasons of business prosperity, crisis, depression, and revival come about in the modern world."[31] Both parts of the term "business" and "cycle" were essential. He differentiated the *business* cycle from the "economic cycle," which is as "old as economic records" and from "financial cycles." In neither of these instances, Mitchell wrote, did the causes for crisis emerge from "business sources." The business cycle, instead, dated essentially from the nineteenth century.

The "business cycle," Mitchell believed, was a phenomenon directly linked to the process of moneymaking, profit seeking, and business operations in a modern capitalist economy. Business cycles came gradually into existence as business enterprise grew to dominate the production and distribution of goods and the allocation of resources. This came to some industries faster than others. In some, even in the early twentieth century, craftsmanship was a primary concern and in some professions, such as medicine, the profit motive was not an overriding issue. Mitchell wrote:

> In size, in complexity of organization, in dependence on the money market, in singleness of business aim, the typical farm, small retail store, handicraft shop, and professional office are not equal to the typical corporate enterprises of wholesale trade, transportation, manufacturing, lumbering, mining, and finance. These highly organized enterprises of the latter fields constitute the world of business *par excellence.* In the study of business cycles this uneven development of business organization in different fields is highly important. For it is within the circles of full-fledged business enterprise that the alternations of prosperity and depression appear most clearly, and produce their most striking effects.[32]

Business Cycles criticized the notion that depressions or expansions were aberrations from some "normal" level of economic activity. Instead, Mitchell pointed out that business fluctuation was a constant process, a necessary consequence of a money-pursuing economy.[33] "Business cycles get their economic interest from the changes they produce in the economic well-being of the community," wrote Mitchell. "This well-being depends upon the production and distribution of useful goods. But the industrial and commercial processes by which goods are furnished are conducted by business men in quest of profits."[34]

What caused cycles, however, was not merely individual profit seeking, but the fact that business enterprises were deeply interrelated. "For the accountant's purpose each enterprise may be treated as a separate unit; but for the economist's purpose, all enterprise are so bound to each other by industrial, commercial, and financial ties that none can prosper and none can suffer without affecting the others."[35]

The causes of cycles, then, came when individual businesspeople, managers, and entrepreneurs sought profits within the interdependent network—each business affecting the others through, for instance, credit, the supply of raw materials, consulting, or through distribution. Mitchell's effort to understand the causes of business cycles led him to analyze the vast array of connections between businesses—and how changes introduced by several firms, or by a single large firm in a key industry, could have widespread consequences.

While each business cycle was different, Mitchell believed that enough similarities existed to begin to map out a common sequence of events in the course of a cycle. In a period of depression, Mitchell wrote, giving one such scenario, the level of prices was lower than in comparison to periods of prosperity; there were widespread reductions in the overall cost of doing business; profit margins were narrow; and consumers exhibited cautious buying. Some entrepreneurs, however, took advantage of these relatively inexpensive terms and began making profits, or, perhaps, some external event, such as a generous harvest or increased government spending, occurred, and this increased business activity. Mitchell wrote that such revivals could occur in widening economic circles and feed a feeling of optimism. "This increase in profits, combined with the prevalence of business optimism, leads to a marked expansion of investments," Mitchell wrote. "Of course the heavy orders for machinery, the large contracts for new construction, etc., which result, swell still further the physical volume of business."[36]

Mitchell, that is, did not reduce the story of business cycles to a few variables or to simplified causes. Rather, he saw business cycles as stemming from the formation, and growing dominance, of large business organizations in the national economies of the USA, England, France, and Germany. Moreover, Mitchell thought that the causes and nature of business cycles would continue to evolve as business organizations themselves evolved and therefore required persistent study.

Mitchell's overall exploration of the field of business cycles and his careful analysis of data inspired a strong following. While Mitchell's views of business cycles were cautious and highly informed, many of those who latched on to the idea of "business cycles" sought to apply his ideas—often in highly simplified forms. Among the first group of these were other empirical economists and statisticians.

Economists and Statisticians

Mitchell promoted his longtime interest in business cycle research among empirical economists and statisticians in the early twentieth century, most notably through his role as Research Director of the National Bureau of Economic Research.

The origins of the NBER can be found among the social scientists, including Mitchell, who were engaged in the mobilization effort during World War I. At the time of the USA's entry into World War I in 1917, the federal government had little ability to chart, distribute, and interpret economic data. Statistics available during the war were haphazardly collected and inadequate in their coverage. When President Woodrow Wilson declared war, for instance, there were at least twenty separate data-gathering bureaus in Washington—most of which were narrow in their mission and acted independently of other bureaus.

Accordingly, when war was declared, the government moved to increase its knowledge of gathering economic and population statistics and turned to academics for help. Mobilization bore the unmistakable stamp of American fascination with efficient management systems. Economists and statisticians brought to Washington new ideas about creating statistical portraits of the mobilization effort and increasing the efficiency of labor. They were joined by other scientists, including industrial psychologists. Harvard professor Robert Yerkes persuaded the surgeon general to administer his Alpha and Beta tests, devised to measure general intelligence to 1.75 million army soldiers.

Among the most important efforts in the collection of data were those undertaken by statistician Leonard Ayres for the Council of National Defense and by Harvard Business School's Edwin Gay, who served as chair of the Central Bureau of Planning and Statistics of the War Industries Board. Ayres, for instance, oversaw the creation of about 230 organization charts to help create a sense of order in the chaos of Washington. Edwin Gay promoted the use of cost accounting as a way to improve the economic efficiency of business.

Mitchell headed the Price Bureau of the War Industries Board. After Armistice, Mitchell underlined the war's importance for the field of economic statistics. "The war forced a rapid expansion in the scope of federal statistics and the creation of new statistical agencies," he recalled. "What is more significant, the war led to the use of statistics, not only as a record of what had happened, but also as a vital factor in planning what should be done." The war experience made government officials aware of the value of accurate data to inform decision making—and especially the need for improved government methods of estimation to produce a better understanding of the state of economic activity.

Toward the end of World War I, Mitchell and his friend Edwin Gay conceived of creating a national organization to gather economic statistics, similar to the wartime Central Bureau of Planning and Statistics, which collected similar information as presented in *Business Cycles* (1913). They thus envisioned turning the Central Bureau into a peacetime organization. But Woodrow Wilson was opposed to this and the Bureau came to a close in June 1919.

Mitchell and Gay then decided to pursue the formation of a private bureau. Malcolm Rorty, a statistician from AT&T, joined them and helped secure $20,000 in funding from the Commonwealth Fund, a philanthropy founded by a Standard Oil executive. In February 1921, the NBER was incorporated. Mitchell served as the research director from the Bureau's founding to 1945 and was its intellectual leader. The NBER, now headquartered near the Harvard University campus in Cambridge, Massachusetts, was originally based in New York City.

The idea of a scientific research center was largely new in economics, a field still dominated by nonquantitative methods. The NBER was not the only effort along these lines, however. Other entrepreneurs and academics formed centers for gathering economic data. The Harvard Economic Society, headed by economist C.J. Bullock and statistician Warren Persons, developed economic "observatories" to gather statistics around the world—in England, Italy, France, Germany, and other countries.[37] Irving Fisher also founded a large data-collection operation in the basement of his massive house in New Haven; the Index Number Institute published economic statistics, including on the cost of living, in newspapers on a weekly basis. Neither of these organizations survived the 1930s, however.

Instead, the NBER became the pre-eminent center due to its stellar staff and its close association with the US government. As Director of Research, Mitchell's goal at the NBER was not only tracking historical business cycles but also taking the pulse of the current phase. This, in many ways, was a fulfillment of the outline of research he had described in *Business Cycles* (1913).

The Bureau began developing aggregate statistics to measure different parts of economic life. Under Mitchell's guidance, research at the Bureau had five precepts: Research should "concentrate on determining facts"; the knowledge should be "quantitative in character"; research should follow "scientific principles"; research should be impartial; and the NBER should not engage in making policy.[38] For its first project, the NBER undertook a massive study of national income—including a study of the geographical distribution of income and a study of the rate of savings. Mitchell was clear that such studies should not only serve academic interest but also have contemporary relevance.[39]

In the early 1920s, Mitchell embarked more directly on a study of the business cycle, enlisting now the resources of the Bureau in studies of production, employment, spending, saving, and other phenomenon. In the mid-1930s, his student, Simon Kuznets, developed the concept of Gross National Product, which became the standard measure of economic health. The figure was a major innovation in the history of economics and in business cycle research because it provided an accepted baseline from which to measure change in output over time—in the USA and in other countries. GNP provided a clear way to compare different national economies; the British economist Colin G. Clark was among those who recognized the use of GNP for this purpose.[40]

At the NBER, Mitchell wrote, edited, or coauthored many books on the subject of cycles, including *Business Cycles: The Problem and Its Setting* (1927); *Business Cycles and their Causes* (1941); and *Measuring Business Cycles* (1946). A final project, *What Happens During Business Cycles: A Progress Report* (1951), was published posthumously.

Over the course of the twentieth century, virtually every well-known economist has been associated with the Bureau. Many of the Nobel laureates of the twentieth century were members, including Simon Kuznets, Milton Friedman, George Stigler, Robert Fogel, Robert Merton, Joseph Stiglitz, and Paul Krugman—exploring a wide variety of subjects.

Entrepreneurs and Forecasters

Another group for whom *Business Cycles,* and Mitchell's promotion of the central ideas of the text, played a formative role was businesspeople and investors interested in predicting the economic future.

Mitchell included a section on forecasting in his 1913 book. "The uncertainty attending present forecasts of business conditions arises chiefly from the imperfections of our knowledge concerning these conditions in the immediate past and in the present," Mitchell began. "For, since business cycles result from processes of cumulative change, the main factors in shaping tomorrow are the factors at work yesterday and today."[41] Mitchell wrote of the need for improved business barometers to mark historic trends in business production, distribution, trade, and profitability. Mitchell suggested that while businessmen "of means" had access to substantial data, and to analysts who could decipher it, most business leaders lacked information—on bank clearings, railways earnings, employment, imports and exports, and manufacturing output—to give them a broader sense of current conditions.[42]

Mitchell's book came out at a time when business managers were enamored of finding "systems" (a highly popular word in business journalism in the early twentieth century).[43] *Business Cycles*, for instance, was published around the same time as Frederick Winslow Taylor's *Scientific Management* (1912). While the texts are quite different—Mitchell's is exhaustive and academic, while Taylor's is brief and popular—they shared some similarities. What "Taylorism" was for factory owners—that is, a promise of how to conceptualize and control the administration of factory labor using quantitative metrics—the notion of "business cycles" was to those who sought to understand how the overall economy worked. How could one make sense of the very atmosphere in which business operated—the ups and downs businesspeople faced in prices, demand, and employment? What metrics would be used to measure progress? Could the economic cycles be predicted?

There was a growing demand for answers to such questions among business leaders. The proponents of business cycle forecasting included Isidor and Nathan Strauss at Macy's, paper manufacturer Henry Dennison at Dennison Manufacturing Company, and Clarence Woolley at American Radiator—all of whom instituted business cycle planning at their firms. They and other forward-looking business managers sought information about upcoming fluctuations to help plan future purchases, plant openings, and the hiring of personnel—just as they sought out any information they thought would bring them competitive advantage. Dennison wrote articles on the subject of countercyclical planning, urging, for instance, the need to resist firing salespeople in times of overall depression.[44] In the 1920s, there were several efforts to formalize a relation between business investments and spending and the business cycle, including Joseph H. Barber's *Budgeting to the Business Cycle* (1925) and John Everette Partington's *Railroad Purchasing and the Business Cycle* (1929).

In the early 1920s, Mitchell himself completed a series of forecasts in the *New York Evening Post*, where his friend the economic historian Edwin Gay was working as editor.[45] These writings show Mitchell's somewhat cautious approach to solving economic problems. In his own forecasts, Mitchell avoided a single approach. He looked at a great number of indicators, including factors that would affect demand for crops, and economic conditions overseas. To these, he added his view of the expectations of investors and myriad other statistical and qualitative conditions.[46]

But Mitchell only pursued commercial forecasting briefly. By the mid-1920s, especially, he had grown suspicious of the industry—and of the vast marketing that private forecasters were using to promote their newsletters and build confidence in their predictions. He believed that the entrepreneurs who issued forecasts cultivated a false sense of security among businesspeople and investors, as well as promoted a good deal of "misunderstandings and exaggerations" in popular discussion. "Many a businessman is developing the precipitate zeal of a new convert and talking about cycles as if they came around with the regularity of presidential elections," wrote Mitchell in a 1923 article in the *Journal of Accountancy*. "Not a few forecasting agencies are publishing prophecies as if they had the certainty of history." Mitchell feared that investors and businessmen had begun to have blind faith in entrepreneurial forecasters, who hoped to prosper from boom-and-bust calls. There was a need, wrote Mitchell, for "clear and sober thinking … by men of trained minds."[47]

But despite Mitchell's reservations, the forecasting industry gained great strength in the 1920s, mostly around ideas about cyclical fluctuations. At the start of World War I, there were only about five forecasting agencies operating in the USA. By 1925, Irving Fisher observed, "We now have nearly fourscore forecasting agencies to help the business man."[48]

Many forecasters cited Mitchell's work as proof of the idea that the economy was cyclical in nature.[49] Among those referring to Mitchell as the authority on business cycles were the famous economic graph maker Karl Karsten, economist and writer Carl Snyder, and the Massachusetts-based entrepreneur Roger W. Babson. Babson wrote, "There is … a law under which mechanics, medicine and other sciences move …" and noted Mitchell as first among those who had made "recent scientific contributions to the literature on business cycles …"[50]

Forecasters developed their own theories of how economies worked. For instance, Babson developed the Babsonchart, which used the theories of Isaac Newton to predict the ups and downs of macroeconomic change. He argued that "depressions" and "expansions" would always exactly equal out in severity, just as "equal and opposite reactions" operate in the natural world. Around this time, James H. Brookmire pioneered the Brookmire Economic Service, which also built a business barometer, and often featured Brookmire's "Cycle Chart of Business and Banking."[51] These forecasters were essentially trend analysts who looked through past data hoping to find historical patterns that they thought would recur into the future. They emphasized what today we would call the "real economy"—upcoming changes to production, employment, trade, and services—rather than trends in the stock market.

These early forecasters often distributed their predictions in weekly bulletins that carried relevant business news and economic indexes. They devoted substantial time to sales and marketing and further popularized ideas about a cyclical economy. Some forecasters built sales forces to travel from office to office in lower Manhattan or in Boston and Chicago. Others sent their representatives to Rotary Clubs and churches in smaller cities and towns to give lectures. Nearly all forecasters advertised in the *New York Times*, the *Wall Street Journal*, the *Commercial and Financial Chronicle*, and the *Chicago Tribune.* Many of these advertisements encouraged the "zeal" Mitchell had feared by claiming the future was now predictable.

The forecasting industry thus grew markedly in the decade after 1913, with the industry centered chiefly on predicting phases of the business cycle. In 1938, *Fortune* magazine noted that forecasting had become as required as "breathing" in the operation of a firm: "Business can no more do without forecasting than it can do without capital. From birth to death a business is the moving sum total of its adjustments to the future."[23] While forecasting later went in new theoretical directions and became a site for serious academic work (such as that by Laurence Klein after World War II), its early entrepreneurial phase was greatly influenced by the authority Mitchell's work gave to the idea of business cycles.

Politicians

Finally, a third group that responded to the idea of business cycles, expressed in Mitchell's 1913 book, was politicians. In the 1920s, the term "business cycle" became of great political interest—it was fastened on by members of both political and conservative parties. For conservative politicians, the idea that the economy operated according to cyclical swings supported the policy that government intervention was futile—and that periods of prosperity and depression were merely the working out of the true nature of capitalist economies.

For others, though, the idea that economies had predictable cyclical swings brought the idea that, if properly anticipated, these cycles could be dampened or even flattened entirely. Herbert Hoover, a moderate Republican, played a key role in promoting the latter view. In the 1920s, Hoover and Wesley Mitchell collaborated to develop a government-led program that would provide business leaders and analysts with information that, they hoped, would enable them to improve their ability to forecast economic conditions. They aimed to educate business leaders on economic affairs so that these business leaders would make their companies more efficient and more attuned to economic conditions. Business leaders who recognized whether they were in the midst of a boom or bust cycle, the argument went, would enact countercyclical strategies that, in aggregate, would stabilize the economy.

The two of them came at this work from different angles: Mitchell's interest in the field stemmed from his profound belief in the nature of business cycles; Hoover's desire to combat economic volatility had a more political orientation and stemmed from his experiences in Europe. In the wake of the Bolshevik Revolution in Russia, nations throughout Europe and the Americas saw class revolution as a genuine threat. "We have witnessed in this last 8 years the spread of revolution over one-third of the world," Hoover wrote in the first sentence of his book *American Individualism* (1922).[52] He wanted to eliminate the "hallucinations transported from Europe" of rosy ideas about socialism.[53]

The commerce secretary hoped to establish a uniquely American solution to the problem of economic crises. His overriding idea was that the New World was separated from the Old World by the American sense of "individualism." An earlier generation of pioneers had surveyed and explored the American West; new ones would shape the country's economic and social future. They would explore the "continent" of science. The goal was not to overturn capitalism with a new system but to encourage individuals in ways that would alleviate its cyclical extremes and avoid its bottlenecks.

Mitchell and Hoover promoted the idea that governments should be deeply engaged with combatting cycles—most notably through the indirect methods of spreading objective information and by sharpening theories about why cycles occurred. They developed a plan to modify cycles that depended on the interrelation of three parties: The Department of Commerce, which would circulate ideas and information; economists and statisticians at the NBER, who would provide objective data and analysis; and private philanthropies, which would fund these efforts. The number of philanthropies interested in improving society through expert-led research increased substantially in the early twentieth century; the Carnegie Foundation (1905), the Rosenwald Fund (1917), the Rockefeller Foundation (1913), and many others were formed during this time.

Essential to the plan was a clearer understanding of the nature of the business cycle.[54] To gain knowledge and to draft policy, Hoover believed in holding conferences of experts from diverse backgrounds—and he drafted Mitchell to lead these conferences. The two of them set about creating an extraordinary network of businesspeople, scholars, and philanthropists. Among the experts were Harvard Business School (HBS) dean Edwin Gay; Arch Shaw (1876–1957), a Chicago office supplier and HBS instructor; John J. Raskob (1879–1950), an executive at DuPont and General Motors; and Owen D. Young (1874–1962), an industrialist, lawyer, diplomat, and chairman of General Electric. Several in this group had written on the subject of forecasting and business planning. Dennison, in particular, promoted the idea of business cycle planning.[55]

Hoover and Mitchell held three major business cycle conferences, each of which produced a major report: *Business Cycles and Unemployment* (1923); *Recent Economic Changes in the United States* (1929); and *Recent Society Trends of the United States* (1933). Mitchell, as research director at the NBER, contributed significant essays to each of these reports and supervised the collection of articles for all of them. He wrote four of twenty-one chapters for *Business Cycles and Unemployment* (1923), the report of the first meeting. The book advanced several recommendations to reduce the extremes of business cycles. It emphasized the importance of the dissemination of statistical information and encouraged the active role of the Federal Reserve in moderating cyclical fluctuations. Mitchell also called for "informed action by individual businessmen in periods of rising markets in order that excessive expansion may be prevented and the extent of the decline reduced."[56]

Through their partnership, Mitchell and Hoover promoted the idea that federal policy could stabilize cycles. Even in the early 1930s, when it was clear that their hope that business leaders could revive the economy had failed, their work had lasting effect. Mitchell and Hoover had successfully promoted the idea that it was the government's role to track economic cycles, collect and publish economic data, endorse a standard measure of economic prosperity (which became GNP in the 1930s), and attempt to flatten the extremes of boom-and-bust periods. The federal government continued all of these activities under Franklin D. Roosevelt. That is not to say, of course, that these presidents used the same means to curb economic cycles. President Roosevelt's direct fiscal involvement in the economy was far different than Hoover's ideal, for example. But it was in the 1930s that the president became the one responsible for these activities. The impact of these legacies can hardly be overstated. No president since Roosevelt has failed to make a promise to improve GNP and promote stable economic growth. The effort to do this and the consequences of these efforts have engaged thousands of government personnel, have been the focus of elections, and have been the measure of success of presidential administrations.

Conclusion

The Keynesian Revolution, and the rise of macroeconomics, moved the center of the field of economics away from Mitchell's emphasis on observation and the history of economic institutions toward a formal, mathematical, and policy-oriented approach. The Econometric Society, founded in 1930 by Irving Fisher, Ragnar Frisch, Charles Roos, and others, began to draw the attention of young empirically oriented economists toward model building and higher mathematics. Economics, as a discipline, also moved beyond another pillar of Mitchell's work—the assumption that studies of business cycles could, in some way, encapsulate all aspects of economic activity. One of the last books to treat the subject in such a comprehensive way was by Mitchell's friend, the Harvard economist Joseph Schumpeter, who published a two-volume book entitled *Business Cycles: A Theoretical, Historical, and Statistical Analysis of the Capitalist Process* (1939).[57]

Keynes's insight that market competition did not guarantee full employment and, in times of lasting and severe depression, governments should engage in fiscal and monetary intervention, became the predominant research focus for decades. The Keynesian approach promoted a new way to make sense of business cycles. It flourished in the USA in a mixed economy in which the scale of industry and the size of government spending increased dramatically—as FDR initiated the New Deal and, even more important, increased spending for wartime mobilization. In 1932, total federal government spending was $12.4 billion; in 1952, it had risen to $99.9 billion.

But for the pre-Keynesian period, *Business Cycles* was the key text. For observers and analysts who were uncertain about the scale of economic change, the idea of "business cycles" promised that ups and downs were measurable. For managers in large firms, looking to make purchases or to plan new plant openings, "business cycles" promoted an understanding that the economic atmosphere was also part of a system—a system that, if understood, could yield advantages and efficiencies. For government officials who wanted to control fluctuations, "business cycles" seemed to promise that ups and downs were potentially controllable. The idea of "business cycles" presented a way to encompass all the big questions of the field: What economic activity contributed to growth? What signaled recession? How could statistics be combined? How could change be measured?

In the years after Mitchell's 1913 book on the subject, the idea of business cycles took hold of the American imagination and influenced economic analysis and thought, business strategy, and political policy. Mitchell's book helped promote the idea that economies were best understood through statistical series and empirical observation. It emphasized the idea that the best way to talk about an economic phenomenon was to compare such aggregate series of industrial production, trade, unemployment, or credit. It popularized the idea that economies can largely be thought of as existing in one of four phases (recovery, prosperity, crisis, or depression) that move up or down in this wavelike fashion.[58] A review of the book and of Mitchell's endeavors in promoting his research agenda helps illuminate economic strategies and political policies of the 1910s and 1920s—the growing interest in economic data gathering organizations, the birth of the economic forecasting industry, and the rising involvement of politicians in efforts to promote national economic stability.

Notes

1. Economist Arthur Burns makes this observation, recorded in Lucy Sprague Mitchell, *Two Lives: The Story of Wesley Clair Mitchell and Myself* (New York: Simon and Schuster, 1953), 291.
2. See Clément Juglar, *Des Crises commerciales et leur retour periodique en France, en Angleterre, at aux Etas-Unis* (Paris: Guillaumin, 1862); Karl Marx, *Das Kapital* (Hamburg: Meisner, 1867).
3. David Glasner, ed., *Business Cycles and Depressions: An Encyclopedia* (New York and London: Garland, 1997), iv.
4. Quoted in Mark C. Smith, *Social Science in the Crucible: The American Debate over Objectivity and Purpose, 1918–1941* (Durham: Duke University Press, 1994), 50.
5. Joseph Schumpeter, "Wesley Clair Mitchell (1874–1948)," *Quarterly Journal of Economics* 64, no. 1 (February 1950): 155.
6. John Maurice Clark, "Thorstein Bundy Veblen: 1857–1929," *American Economic Review* 19, no. 4 (December 1929): 742–45.
7. Veblen's quantitative work included "The Price of Wheat since 1867," *Journal of Political Economy* 1, no. 1 (December 1892): 68–103, which included charts of the ups and downs of prices in this commodity, and "The Food Supply and the Price of Wheat," *Journal of Political Economy*

1, no. 3 (June 1893): 365–79, which included some statistics-based forecasts.

8. Mitchell, *Two Lives*, 305.
9. Ibid., 176.
10. Alexander D. Noyes, "A Year after the Panic of 1907," *Quarterly Journal of Economics* 23, no. 2 (February 1909): 186.
11. William Stanley Jevons, "Commercial Crises and Sun-Spots," *Nature* 19 (November 14, 1878): 33–37.
12. House of Representatives, *Hearings and Arguments before the Committee of Banking and Currency* (Washington, DC: Government Printing Office, 1896–1897), 165.
13. See Paul Barnett, *Business-Cycle Theory in the United States, 1860–1900* (Chicago: University of Chicago, 1941).
14. Wesley C. Mitchell, *Business Cycles* (Berkeley: University of California Press, 1913), 3.
15. Albert Aftalion's Les crises périodiques de surproduction [Periodic Crises of Overproduction] (Paris, M. Rivière et cie, 1913); R. G. Hawtrey's *Good and Bad Trade: An Inquiry into the Causes of Trade Fluctuations* (London: Constable & Co., Ltd., 1913).
16. See a review of these three titles: L. L. P., Review: "Les Crises Periodiques de Surproduction by Albert Aftalion: Good and Bad Trade: An Inquiry into the Causes of Trade Fluctuations by R.G. Hawtrey; Business Cycles by Wesley Clair Mitchell," *Journal of the Royal Statistical Society* 77, no. 2 (January 1914): 218.
17. Warren Persons, review of Wesley C. Mitchell, "Business Cycles," *Quarterly Journal of Economics* 28, no. 4 (August 1914): 796.
18. William Charles Schluter, *The Pre-War Business Cycle 1907 to 1914* (New York: Columbia, 1923); William Franklin Gephart, *Bank Credit and the Business Cycle* (St. Louis: First National Bank, 1923); Carl Snyder, *The Influence of the Interest Rate on the Business Cycle* (New Haven: American Economic Association, 1925); Joseph H. Barber, *Budgeting to the Business Cycle* (New York: Roland Press, 1925); Alvin H. Hansen, *Business-Cycle Theory: Its Development and Present Status* (Boston: Ginn, 1927); Dorothy Swaine Thomas, *Social Aspects of the Business Cycle* (New York: Knopf, 1927); and John Everette Partington, *Railroad Purchasing and the Business Cycle* (Washington, DC: The Brookins Institution, 1929).
19. See a review of these three titles: L. L. P., Review: "Les Crises Periodiques de Surproduction by Albert Aftalion: Good and Bad Trade:

An Inquiry into the Causes of Trade Fluctuations by R.G. Hawtrey; Business Cycles by Wesley Clair Mitchell," *Journal of the Royal Statistical Society* 77, no. 2 (January 1914): 218.
20. Daniel Breslau, "Economics Invents the Economy: Mathematics, Statistics, and Models in the Work of Irving Fisher and Wesley Mitchell," *Theory and Society* 32, no. 3 (June 2003): 379–411, discusses the use of the word "economy" by Mitchell and Fisher.
21. Smith, *Social Science in the Crucible*, 124.
22. Mitchell in 1943, quoted by Dorfman, *The Economic Mind in American Civilization* 4:361.
23. Hirsch, "Reconstruction in Economics," 126.
24. Ibid., 126; original source: "Unemployment and Business Fluctuations," 17–18.
25. Ibid., 127.
26. See, for instance, "Review: Recent Books on Business Cycles," *The Quarterly Journal of Economics* 38, no. 1 (November 1923): 153–68. This included reviews of several books including *Business Cycles and Employment* by the Committee of the President's Conference on Unemployment; *The Stabilization of Business* by Wesley Clair Mitchell and Lionel D. Edie; *Business Forecasting* by David F. Jordan; and *The Trade Cycle* by F. Lavington; and others, seven in all.
27. Irving Fisher, "Our Unstable Dollar and the So-Called Business Cycle," *Journal of the American Statistical Association* 20, no. 150 (June 1925): 179. Fisher wrote, "It seems certain, humanly speaking, that wherever the dollar—our yardstick of commerce—suffers wide fluctuations in purchasing power, those fluctuations largely predetermine or, at any rate, precede closely related fluctuations in trade."
28. Irving Fisher, "Our Unstable Dollar and the So-Called Business Cycle," *Journal of the American Statistical Association* 20, no. 150 (June 1925): 192.
29. "Assails, 'Business Cycle,'" *New York Times*, November 8, 1924, 24.
30. Irving Fisher, "Our Unstable Dollar and the So-Called Business Cycle," *Journal of the American Statistical Association* 20, no. 150 (June 1925): 192.
31. For current understandings of the business cycle, see Arnold G. Lutz, *Business Cycle Theory* (New York: Oxford University Press, 2002). This describes Keynesian economics, monetarism, new classical economics, the real business cycles theory, and new Keynesian economics understandings of the cycle.

32. Mitchell, *Business Cycles,* 3, vii.
33. Mitchell, *Business Cycles,* 22–23.
34. See Mitchell, *Business Cycles.*
35. The English economist A.C. Pigou noted this aspect, and included this quote, in his review of Mitchell's book. See A. C. Pigou, "A Review of *Business Cycles* by Wesley Clair Mitchell," *The Economic Journal* 24, no. 93 (March 1914): 78–81.
36. Mitchell, *Business Cycles,* 23.
37. Ibid., 572.
38. Mason, "Harvard Economics Department," 411. Persons also taught a course in the college on statistical theory and analysis; William Trufant Foster, "Warren Milton Persons," *Journal of the American Statistical Association* 34, no. 206 (June 1939): 413. According to one observer, "In that course, as elsewhere, [Persons] held staunchly to the view [that] statistics is much more than a collection of numerical facts; that it is, on the contrary, a method and a logic; that it is an applied science in which, therefore, it is just as necessary to scrutinize the premises as the logic and mathematics." The *Harvard Alumni Bulletin,* of April 8, 1920, contained an article describing the work of the Review.
39. See Solomon Fabricant, "Toward a Firmer Basis of Economic Policy: The Founding of the National Bureau of Economic Research," NBER (1961), 1–6, 14.
40. Simon Kuznets, *National Income and Capital Formation, 1919–1935* (New York: National Bureau of Economic Research, 1937). On the history of GNP, see also Thomas A. Stapleford, *The Cost of Living in America: A Political History of Economic Statistics, 1800–2000* (Cambridge: Cambridge University Press, 2009), 319–24. See also Colin G. Clark, *National Income 1924–1931* (London: Macmillan, 1932).
41. Mitchell, *Business Cycles,* 589.
42. Ibid., 593.
43. See, for instance, *System* magazine.
44. See, for instance, Henry S. Dennison, "Management and the Business Cycle," *Journal of the American Statistical Association* 18, no. 137 (March 1922): 20–31. See also C. H. Crennan, "Business Men and the Business Cycle," *Annals of the American Academy of Political and Social Science* 109 (September 1923): 291–95; J. H. Jones, "Business Forecasting," *The Economic Journal* 8, no. 151 (September 1928): 414–25.

45. See, in the *New York Evening Post,* "The Outlook of 1921 as Seen by Bankers, Business Men and Economists," December 31, 1920, Sect. 3, part I, 2; "Present Facts and Past Experience Indicate Revival Is Now at Hand," October 17, 1921, 1, 13; "Business Revival Expected to Gather Momentum in Immediate Future," October 18, 1921, 1, 10; "Business Making Progress in Positive Phase of Cycle," December 31, 1921, Sect. 2, part I, 1; "Business Revival Shows Signs of Developing into Prosperity," December 30, 1922, Sect. 2, part I, 1, 9; and "Business during 1924 Likely to Be Generally Satisfactory," December 31, 1923, Sect. 2, part I, 1–2. Mitchell also wrote on the subject in "How You Can Use 'The Business Cycle,'" *System* 5, no. 40 (1921): 683–85, 767–68.
46. See Dorfman, *The Economic Mind in American Civilization*, 4:552. Abraham Hirsch, "Reconstruction in Economics: The Work of Wesley Clair Mitchell" (Ph.D. diss., Columbia University, 1958), 121–24. The original source is "Unemployment and Business Fluctuation," *American Economic Review* 5, no. 8 (1923): supplement, 47. See, in the *New York Evening Post,* "The Outlook of 1921"; "Present Facts and Past Experience"; "Business Revival Expected to Gather Momentum in Immediate Future"; "Business Making Progress in Positive Phase of Cycle"; "Business Revival Shows Signs of Developing into Prosperity"; and "Business during 1924 Likely to be Generally Satisfactory."
47. Wesley C. Mitchell, "Accountants and Economics with Reference to the Business Cycle," *Journal of Accountancy* 25, no. 3 (March 1923): 167.
48. Irving Fisher, "Our Unstable Dollar and the So-Called Business Cycle," *Journal of the American Statistical Association* 20, no. 150 (June 1925): 180. Many of these are listed in an unpublished booklet by the Illinois Chamber of Commerce (Research Dept.), Commercial Services (Chicago, 1927), available in the Baker Library, Harvard Business School.
49. See, for instance, Roger W. Babson, "International Cooperation for the Standardization of Statistical Work," *Publications of the American Statistical Association* 14, no. 109 (March 1915): 462–66; Roger W. Babson, "Factors Affecting Commodity Prices," *Annals of the American Academy of Political and Social Science* 38, no. 2 (September 1911): 155–88; Irving Fisher, "'The Equation of Exchange' for 1911, and Forecast," *The American Economic Review* 2, no. 2 (June 1912): 302–19; Irving Fisher, "A Weekly Index Number of Wholesale Price," *Journal of American Statistical Association* 18, no. 143 (September 1923): 835–40; Irving Fisher, "Mathematical Method in the Social

Sciences," *Econometrica* 9, no. 3/4 (July–October, 1941): 185–97; Warren M. Persons, "Statistics and Economic Theory," *The Review of Economics and Statistics* 7, no. 3 (July 1925): 179–97; and Warren M. Persons, "Theories of Business Fluctuations," *The Quarterly Journal of Economics* 41, no. 1 (November 1926): 94–128.

50. See Roger W. Babson, *Business Barometers Used in the Accumulation of Money* (Wellesley Hills, MA: Babson Service Co., 1918), 120; Karl G. Karsten, "The Theory of Quadrature in Economics," *Journal of the American Statistical Association* 19, no. 145 (March 1924): 14–29, see p. 27; and Carl Snyder, "New Measures in the Equation of Exchange," *The American Economic Review* 14, no. 4 (December 1924): 699–713.
51. James H. Brookmire, *The Brookmire Economic Charts: A Graphic Record of Fundamental, Political and Industrial Conditions as a Barometer to the Financial and Business Situation* (St. Louis: Brookmire Economic Chart Co., 1913).
52. Herbert Hoover, *American Individualism* (Garden City, NY: Doubleday, 1922), 1; Guy Alchon, *The Invisible Hand of Planning: Capitalism, Social Science, and the State in the 1920s* (Princeton: Princeton University Press, 1985), 80. In this view, proper forecasting could lessen class conflict: Hoover's argument that both labor and management should receive recognition as actors who can stabilize the economy, and who should be equipped with a rational organizational and informational apparatus to do so, pointed to a different balance between manager-led and worker-led reform than that promoted by (some of) the private forecasters, who were as a body less interested in questions of class conflict. See also Robert Zeigler, "Labor, Progressivism, and Herbert Hoover in the 1920s," *Wisconsin Magazine of History* 58, no. 3 (Spring 1975): 196–208.
53. See Alchon, *The Invisible Hand of Planning*, 80, who includes Mitchell's notes of Hoover's views expressed during a Business Cycle Committee meeting.
54. Herbert Hoover, foreword to Business Cycles and Unemployment, v. Hoover's initial experience in trying to mitigate unemployment came when Warren Harding called for a conference on the subject when four to five million people were unemployed. The President's Conference on Unemployment met in September 1921. It was a combination of businessmen, labor leaders, economists, and statisticians. It proposed an "exhaustive investigation" be made of the causes of unemployment and "methods of stabilizing business and industry so as to prevent the vast waves of suffering which result from the valleys in the so-called business cycle."

55. Dennison, "Management and the Business Cycle," 20–31.
56. Report quoted in Alchon, *The Invisible Hand of Planning*, 107.
57. Schumpeter, *Business Cycles* (New York: McGraw-Hill, 1939). On Schumpeter, see Thomas K. McCraw, "Schumpeter's 'Business Cycles' as Business History," *Business History Review* 80, no. 2 (Summer 2006): 231–61.
58. See J. Adam Tooze, *Statistics and the German State, 1900–1945: The Making of Modern Economic Knowledge* (Cambridge, UK, 2001) for similar developments in Germany.

Acknowledgments I would like to thank David Moss, of Harvard Business School, for his comments on this paper and Felice Whittum for editing the text. Some of this material was previously published in my book *Fortune Tellers: The Story of America's First Economic Forecasters*, copyright © 2014 by Princeton University Press, reprinted by permission.

Author Biography

Walter Friedman is a Lecturer and Director of the Business History Initiative at Harvard Business School. Walter is an editor of the *Business History Review*, and author of *Fortune Tellers: The Story of America's First Economic Forecasters* (Princeton, 2013) and *Birth of a Salesman: The Transformation of Selling in America* (Harvard, 2004). He is currently writing a history of American business from 1945 to 1980.

On a Certain Blindness in Economic Theory: Keynes's Giraffes and the Ordinary Textuality of Economic Ideas

C.N. Biltoft

"*In the days when everybody started fair, Best Beloved, the Leopard lived in a place called the High Veldt. … This was very bad for the Giraffe and the Zebra and the rest of them….*" -Rudyard Kipling, *Just So Stories.*

Ways of Seeing Knowledge and Blindness

Well over a hundred years ago, the American psychologist and philosopher William James explored the contours of an increasingly bewildering industrial, capitalist, and post-Darwinian modernity. In that fin de siècle bazaar of goods, people, and ideas, James remarked upon what he called "a certain blindness in human beings." Blindness implied the difficulty of achieving tolerant intersubjectivity in the face of novelty and difference. However, this nearsightedness grew not just from encountering difference, but also in the striving to prevent those encounters from rattling previously held beliefs. Tied to his general

C.N. Biltoft (✉)
Graduate Institute, Geneva, Switzerland
e-mail: carolyn.biltoft@graduateinstitute.ch

R. Fredona and S.A. Reinert (eds.), *New Perspectives on the History of Political Economy*, https://doi.org/10.1007/978-3-319-58247-4_11

theory of truth, James perceived a continual to and fro, the casting aside of certain concepts, and the re-entrenchment of others. In life as in science, people struggled to step away from and perhaps even needed the warmth of their own inherited perspectives or hard fought certitudes.[1]

Of course, James was neither the first nor the last to point out how all manners of epicycles are built to preserve comfortable tropes and ways of apprehending. In the world of economic ideas, both contemporary and historically anchored critiques have tended to fall on the side of assessment and evaluation. The objective has been to discern the speck in the economic field of vision, in order to remove it. This is a laudable goal. Still, even rigorous critiques of epicycles might unintentionally gloss over some matters of potential interest to historians. Namely, they might miss the unique circumstantiality of those specks and blind spots, including (following James) the needs they emerged to meet or serve. To simply point out the shortcomings of any economic paradigm risks subtly reinforcing the premise that economic life or theory can ever stand outside of human desires, fallibilities, or power relations.[2]

Public debates on the Keynesian Revolution have tended to center on the idea that governments (guided by experts) should or should not intervene into markets either on behalf of economic stability or in order to moderate economic inequalities.[3] Professional economic debates, on the other hand, have centered on the technical rightness or wrongness of the many permutations of macroeconomic models from Keynes forward, including how we measure growth and prosperity.[4] In each case, contemporary arguments in favor of or against Keynesian paradigms have often proposed a "solution" while eliding the original contexts and assumptions.

Against that trend, I look elsewhere at how the worldviews and biases of J.M Keynes helped give content both to the blind spots and also to the insights of modern macroeconomics.[5] Borrowing and extending some of those claims, this essay considers Keynes's 1926 essay *The End of Laissez-Faire*. More specifically, it ponders Keynes's use of the giraffe as a metaphor for a vision of social economic welfare dynamics that challenged neoclassical orthodoxies. Before he had uttered the phrase animal spirits, Keynes used the giraffe to paint a picture of the suffering that could befall the victims of even the most "creative" free-market destructions.[6] Focusing on the giraffe provides a pointed lens for revaluating Keynes's own political cosmology, which in turn shaped his theoretical interventions. As we shall see, giraffes carried all kinds of implicit allusions and connotations, from evolutionary theory, to the longer histories of British imperialism. As such, considering the connotations of the metaphor helps to elucidate how even as Keynes attacked certain orthodoxies, he reinforced others, especially imperial ones.[7]

Methodologically, declaring the "ordinary textuality" of economic ideas treats economic theory as a point from which to observe the lumps, knots, and fissures of a given economic system.[8] It is a way of asserting that economic texts are like any other texts, in that they have a social and cultural life, and thus can be interpreted rather than merely tested.[9] In a sense then, it treats economic theories as commodities produced and consumed in a range of complex contexts that gain layers of meaning as they travel from one geographical or temporal point to the next.[10] Borrowing this point for economic theory makes space for a history of economic ideas that seeks to understand and yet remains disconnected from the goals of economic science.

To those ends, this essay places one of Keynes's key texts within a canon of other ambiguous imperial authors, such as Rudyard Kipling. Unlike Kipling, whose more explicit apologues circled and struggled openly with the ideologies of the "White Man's Burden," Keynes contended with imperialism mostly in the subtexts. It is in order to locate Keynes's ideas within matrices of British imperialism that we begin with the many resonances and repetitions of an old point of wonder and curiosity: the giraffe and its long neck.

Regression and the Herd

The End of Laissez-Faire, began as two lectures, which Keynes gave in Oxford in 1924 and in Berlin in 1926, respectively. The essay marked Keynes's first outright attack on the neoclassical assumptions that individual actions would lead naturally to the best possible collective outcomes. In that text, Keynes borrowed from socialism and claimed that holistic attention to society was necessary to ensure the well-being of individuals rather than the reverse. The Russian experiment had given new urgency to the question, amid the rising specter of the dissatisfied, including anticolonial protests and labor discontentment. Like many of his liberal colleagues, Keynes hoped that promises of immediate reform would hold back revolutionary tidal waves.[11]

Earlier in *The Economic Consequences of the Peace*, Keynes had warned that the whole tempo of waiting and saving for some future promise of satisfaction might no longer hold. There, Keynes stated that economists and captains of industry and states had made lofty promises: "In that day overwork, overcrowding, and underfeeding would come to an end, and men, secure of the comforts and necessities of the body, could proceed to the nobler exercises of their faculties."[12] However, Keynes warned that the First World War's gains and losses followed by revolutionary waves had strained the patience of all classes.[13]

By 1926, some of the initial postwar upset had settled, though certainly not completely. That year, legions of British workers went on strike, protesting the conditions under which they worked and the pay they received.[14] In that context, Keynes set out more directly to undermine the widespread devotion to the concepts of self-interest-driven and self-correcting markets.[15] The question was how could the economy satisfy more of the wants of more of the people, in the right here and right now. As several of his biographers have emphasized, while Keynes saw intervention as vital to soothe the disaffected and dissatisfied, he had no desire to destroy capitalism. Rather, he hoped to improve it, resuscitate it, and imbue it with more grace.[16] Here, Keynes looked to the war's lessons in productivity and wealth creation.[17] In order to gain support for the idea of applying the lessons of war socialism in peacetime, Keynes set out to show the holes and logical fallacies within the doctrines of laissez-faire capitalism.

For Keynes, it had been economists who tainted Enlightenment efforts to release individuals from the stranglehold of the monarch and the church. Where Rousseau, for example, had offered the appealing promise of social contract, economists assured political theorists that the pursuit of economic self-interest provided the surest route to social welfare. According to Keynes, however, the worst modification came after

1858, when the Darwinian logic of fitness had become tangled with free-market orthodoxies. Keynes restated that synthesis co-copyrighted by economists and politicians: "The economists were teaching that wealth, commerce, and machinery were the children of free competition—that free competition built London. But the Darwinians could go one better than that—free competition had built man."[18]

The later part of the nineteenth century had seen a great deal of mutual inspiration between evolutionary biology, the social sciences (including economics), and political theory.[19] Thomas Malthus' *Essay on Population* had reportedly influenced Darwin who in turn had influenced the thinking of the likes of Herbert Spencer and the British economist, Walter Bagehot.[20] These tides of mutual inspiration had taken on a number of different forms, including their well-known uses in justifying racial hierarchies and imperial conquest.[21] However, in 1926, Keynes's primary concern was with the way politicians, captains of industry, and economists had together used Darwin to claim that social intervention undermined the natural mechanisms of progress.[22]

It was in the context of challenging Darwinian justifications for laissez-faire that Keynes first raised the figure of the giraffe. He criticized the premise that "the object of life" was to "...leave the giraffes with the longest necks to starve out those whose necks are shorter."[23] Keynes then continued to revisit the full range of assumptions underpinning the pre-WWI laissez-faire paradigm. He stated:

> Thus, if only we leave the giraffes to themselves, (1) the maximum quantity of leaves will be cropped because the giraffes with the longest necks will, by dint of starving out the others, get nearest to the trees; (2) each giraffe will make for the leaves which he finds most succulent amongst those in reach (3) the giraffes whose relish for a given leaf is greatest will crane most to reach it. In this way more and juicier leaves will be swallowed, and each individual leaf will reach the throat which deserves it most effort.[24]

He then continued to argue point-by-point against the idea that unhindered natural selection could ever lead to progress.[25] Keynes claimed that the very idea of the Darwinian laissez-faire model ignored the existing conditions of "risk and uncertainty" as well as daily aberrations from ideal economic forms, such as monopoly conditions.[26] In addition to these blind spots, Keynes pointed out another fallacy, namely the parallel between "natural selection" and the "love of money." For where true natural selection was a matter of chance, the idea that individual effort motivated by the love of money could forge the greatest good for the greatest number overlooked, according to Keynes, some basic principles of human psychology. Namely, Keynes described what he would later call more neutrally "the liquidity preference" and more metaphorically the "Freudian love of money"; a primordial obsession that would lead to hoarding as much or more than to positive striving.[27]

It was in that frame, that Keynes outlined the basic tenants of what he would later call animal spirits.[28] He had no doubt that individual effort affected the fate of the whole. However, Keynes claimed that the fear of scarcity multiplied (bank runs, stock dumping, hiding money under the mattress) had more power to undermine growth, than the desire for wealth (investment and consumption) had to ensure social welfare. Keynes thus refuted the related claim that providing any outside help would reduce competition, which in turn would reduce desire, which would eventually eliminate the vibrant propensity to hunger (self-interest) necessary for maximizing social welfare.[29]

Indeed, Keynes's objection to laissez-faire mirrored in striking ways Sigmund Freud's concept of regression.[30] Freud too drew from evolutionary and specifically Darwinian metaphors in outlining this specific human neurosis. He stated: "In other words, with the universal tendency of biological processes toward variation, it must necessarily happen that not all preparatory phases of a given function are equally well passed through or accomplished with comparable thoroughness."[31] Freud emphasized natural variation in the human condition, rather than a steady linear progress. In other words, a good many minds might not only get stuck on the journey of growth (inhibition), but also could go backward in emotional or psychological development (regression). Freud continued: "Having attained to this later and more highly developed form, the impulse is forced to a regression when it encounters great external difficulties in the exercise of its function, and accordingly cannot reach the goal which will satisfy its strivings."[32] That is to say, that external difficulties might prevent people from even trying and send them backward developmentally.

Keynes borrowed and developed this idea, implying that too much material discomfort could keep people from striving. Furthermore, Keynes argued like Freud that, left to their own devices, people could sink into their own fears and inhibitions even in more prosperous conditions. These more basic regressive urges meant that some people (giraffes) could not move forward without the help of the trained scientist, in this case the psychoanalyst. We know that Keynes's companions in the Bloomsbury circle were reading and discussing psychoanalysis.[33] Thus, we might perceive a borrowing, where Keynes came to see the role of the economist as akin to that of the therapist. Just as the "talking cure" was needed to move some minds past regressive tendency, the economist needed to help politicians get people past their tendencies to "hoard" and to "herd." It was not safe to assume that "each giraffe will make for leaves he finds most succulent." Nor was it certain that "those whose relish is greatest will crane the most, and so the best leaves will reach the most eager throats." To the contrary, on their own, panicked giraffes might drive the whole economy off a cliff, trampling each other in the process.

In a limited sense, the Freudian factor brings another dimension to the idea that Keynes stood on the side of an interventionist "social welfare" and against individualistic "free markets." It also highlights the depth of Keynes's anticipation of and influence on the nonrational choice heterodoxies of approaches such as behavioral economics.[34] However, of all the possible animals Keynes could have chosen to pilot his point about the nature of herds, he chose the giraffe. While it may seem a minor point to linger upon, the giraffe had a long history of significance both in evolutionary theory and within the framework of colonial civilizing missions. Exploring these resonances highlights some less apparent dimensions of the ideological currents in which Keynes was swimming and thinking.

All Animals Are Equal, Some More Than Others

In the early nineteenth century, Jean-Baptiste Lamarck, French evolutionary biologist/natural philosopher, described his theory of evolutionary change by explaining the worldly reasons for the otherworldly appearance of a giraffe's neck. In his theory, if a herd of giraffes encountered a paucity of grass and yet an abundance of lush leaves, their hunger would encourage them to stretch and strain their necks. First, they would stretch toward the leaves within their reach and then if still hungry further still toward the leaves beyond their reach.[35] In stretching, their necks would lengthen little by little, and that length once acquired would become inheritable. Thus, Lamarck's evolution occurred as a process of passing on to the next generation, those traits that species acquired in the course of their daily struggle for existence.

According to Stephen Jay Gould, shortly after 1859, the curiosity of the giraffe's neck became an often-cited case to demarcate the fundamental differences between Lamarckian and Darwinian theories of evolution. Gould examined a multitude of biology textbooks both past and present, and in so doing noticed that each and every one lingered on the same illustration. He stated: "All texts then use the same example to illustrate Darwinian superiority—the neck of the Giraffe."[36] According to those texts, Charles Darwin had challenged Lamarck's charming view of evolution as tied to the active strivings of necessity. It was not a matter of effort but of chance; the giraffes with the shorter necks simply died out in conditions where grass was scarce and leaves were plentiful, while the longer necked giraffes survived and reproduced. The problem with that illustration, according to Gould, was that it was based on a misreading of Darwin to begin with.

Gould went back to the canon to prove his point: "When we turn to the horse's mouth, the first edition of Darwin's *Origin of Species*, we find no mention whatever of the giraffe's neck as an illustration of natural selection."[37] Subsequent editions of the Origins made a few passing reference to giraffes, but focused on the use of the giraffe's tail.[38] Only in the sixth edition did Darwin include a more extended discussion of the giraffe's neck, and it was there Gould encountered a revelation. He stated: "Darwin does speculate about the adaptive advantage of giraffe's necks, but he cites both natural selection and Lamarckism as probable causes of elongation."[39] Gould suggested that while Darwin was not in favor of the "just so stories" mode of illustration, it was precisely in that vein that subsequent defenders of natural selection drew a sharper distinction than had actually existed between

Lamarck and Darwin. Darwin was also, at least partially, a Lamarckian in the end.

The aim of Gould's essay was to assert two points. Firstly, that "...repetition need not correlate with truth value." Secondly, Gould reminded his readers "...that the current importance and utility of a phenomenon gives us no particular insight into the circumstances of its historical origin."[40] Interestingly, since the publication of Gould's article, biologists have recently revisited Lamarckian theory; it seems there is evidence to support the claim that species indeed sometimes pass on acquired characteristics to their offspring.[41] All the more reason in the words of Gould "...that even the most pious certainties should be periodically scrutinized right down to their foundations."[42] As it is with biology, so it is with economic theory.

More to the content, rather than the methodology of this piece, however, Keynes too apparently accepted that the giraffe marked a point of contention between Lamarckian and Darwinian models. While Keynes did not refute Darwin's mechanism in biology, he objected to its application to questions of the economy. Thus, in using the giraffe, Keynes stood metaphorically on the side of Lamarck.[43] In that key, he explained an "anti-Darwinian" thesis about how to best preserve the welfare of the herd.

> If we have the welfare of the giraffes at heart, we must not overlook the sufferings of the shorter necks who are starved out, or the sweet leaves which fall to the ground and are trampled underfoot in the struggle, or the overfeeding of the long-necked ones, or the evil look of anxiety or struggling greediness which overcasts the mild faces of the heard.[44]

Keynes insisted that "costs of the struggle" mattered, and intervention could help prevent those costs, including the violent highs and lows of the business cycle.

Before looking more closely at the solutions Keynes offered for the welfare of the giraffe, however, we first need to explore the extra-evolutionary resonances that this particular animal carried in the history of imperialism.

Two years after Keynes's essay appeared, the Field Museum in Chicago commissioned a study called *the Giraffe in History and Art.* According to that text, it turns out that giraffes had played a significant role, especially in international relations since the fifteenth century.[45] For example, giraffes had served as valued diplomatic gifts in the early modern world. The gentle, awkward elegance of the creature made them highly prized items for potentates' menageries, which displayed power amid expanding geopolitical horizons and encounters with the "exotic other."[46]

More pointedly, as Erik Ringmar has argued, giraffes began appearing in European courts as signifiers of occupational mentalities. Ringmar cites two cases where the acquisition of giraffes for the menageries of European leaders served as prequels to acts of imperial conquest. Lorenzo Medici acquired a giraffe for his menagerie in 1486, just years before the wave of European expansion to and occupation of the "new world." Secondly, Muhammad Ali gifted a giraffe to Charles X of France in 1827, only three years before France's conquest of Algeria.[47] The point is not that the giraffe served as a kind of "writing on the wall" for the imperial subjugation of others. Rather, it was a signal of mentalities, as growing interest in the exotic reinforced orientalist narrative arcs, whereby fetish and desire at once served to justify, and also grew out of conquest.[48]

Along those lines, nineteenth-century France witnessed a veritable giraffe craze. The giraffe that Mohammed Ali gave to Charles X, "Zara," came to live in the *Jardin des Plantes* after a dramatic march across the French countryside: "She was embarked at Alexandria, wearing round her neck a strip of parchment inscribed with several passages from the Koran and purposed as an amulet to safeguard her health and welfare."[49] She landed at Marseille in November 1826, then arrived in Paris in June of 1827. During Zara's march, hundreds of thousands of spectators flocked to gaze upon this otherworldly creature from afar.[50] In the same moment, as part of his own diplomatic effort to retain control of his territories, Mohammed Ali also gave a gift of a giraffe to George IV of England. Unlike Zara who enjoyed a long life, George's giraffe only survived a few months in the gardens of Windsor palace. In the face of that disgrace compared to France, the British Zoological

Society set out to and eventually acquired four young giraffes, which they housed in the London Zoo.[51] These animals became symbols of British worldliness, scientific acumen, and power and presence on the world stage.

Zoos were just one of many spaces, including colonial exhibitions, world fairs, and various ethnographic displays, by which scientific societies moved in step with corporations and imperial institutions to commoditize the exotic.[52] These displays were the public face of century-long efforts of "liberalism and empire" whereby the will to know and the will to rule came together, generating and acting upon taxonomies that organized every plant, animal, and race in hierarchies.[53] These spectacles also gave credence to the rhetoric of civilizing missions and also allowed the viewing public to feel a part of the sprawling global "community" through what Peter Hoffenberg calls "cultural bonds and shared fantasies."[54]

Of the utmost importance here, however, are that these acts of displaying the "primitive and exotic" alongside the material progress of Western empires, had a way of making imperialism seem both exciting and also perfectly natural.[55] Before returning to Keynes's own use of imperial "taxonomies," we can first look at other more literary iterations of the British Empire and its primitive animal kingdoms. Rudyard Kipling, deemed "poet of the British empire," also dwelled on exotic animals and primitive human characters, whose various storylines invariably illuminated the well-intentionedness and importance of British imperialism. In his "Just So Stories," the narrative told a series of children's fables, which outlined the nonscientific evolutionary development of the appearance of exotic beasts of all kinds, including the fates of giraffes.

In one fable "How the Leopard Got its Spots," Kipling told the story of the brown and gray African "High Veldt." The giraffe, the zebra, the eland, the koodoo, and the hartebeest lived there, along with the leopard, and they were all the same "'sclusively sandy-yellow-brownish all over" color.[56] This monochrome was, in the words of the narrative, "very bad for the Giraffe and the Zebra and the rest of them" because the leopard would lie down and blend in and then sneak up on those grazing unsuspecting vegetarians. And too, the Leopard's friend the Ethiopian (also beige from head to toe) would always hunt the High Veldt game with his spears and arrows.

After being wholly terrorized, one day "the yellowish-greyish-brownish game ran off to the forest." It was there, as they hid in the trees, half in light and half in shadows, that the giraffe got its spots and the zebra its stripes. And there in the peace of the forest, the animals were finally enjoying their lives, while the Leopard and the Ethiopian were bereft "wondering where all their breakfasts and their dinners and their teas had gone." But soon hungry, following their noses, the Ethiopian and the Leopard came to the forest, but all the animals were cleverly camouflaged now compared to the monochromatic hunters. The Ethiopian said: "I can smell Giraffe, and I can hear Giraffe, but I can't see Giraffe."

It was not long, however, before the Leopard and the Ethiopian wised up to what they had to do. The Ethiopian, once beige, turned himself black. He then proclaimed: "It will be the very thing for hiding in hollows and behind trees." Then with the "left over blackness" still on his fingers, he applied spots to the skin of his friend, the Leopard.

> Now you are a beauty!' said the Ethiopian. 'You can lie out on the bare ground and look like a heap of pebbles. You can lie out on the naked rocks and look like a piece of pudding-stone…!' 'But if I'm all this,' said the Leopard, 'why didn't you go spotty too?'

And then, the harsh reentry of the racial hierarchy: "Oh, plain black's best for a nigger," said the Ethiopian.

Through childish turned racially charged language, Kipling suddenly revealed the distance that the narrator perceived between himself and the "primitives." Throughout all of the fables in the collection, Kipling made the hinterland both intimate and foreign, a matter of curious simplicity, easy to grasp, easy to conquer. There is a vast body of work dealing with Kipling's imperialism.[57] For example, Edward Said's introduction to Kipling's *Kim* delineated the existential quality of Kipling's imperialism: "The variously qualified pleasure we can derive from reading Kim today, therefore, is that in it we can watch a great artist blinded in a sense by his own insights about India, confusing the realities before him, which he saw with such colour and ingenuity, with the notion that these realities were permanent and essential."[58] And indeed, in one of his many speeches that he gave during his career, Kipling recited his own imperial position on the empire's naturalness and permanence: "If the charge be true, then 'Blessed are the meek for they shall inherit the earth.' We hold to-day one square mile in every four of the land of the globe, and through our representatives we are responsible for the protection of one person in five out of the entire population of this little planet."[59] In Kipling's world, the British Empire was a gentle and worthy master.

This point offers a way back to the question of economic theory. As Olivier Accominotti et al. have argued, even when economists have paid attention to questions of imperialism, they have often failed to account fully for the "mismatch" between the interests of colonial populations and those of imperial administration.[60] This inability to perceive a mismatch happened in part because the normative claims of one single universal, linear path to "development" was imported into a great deal (not all) of economic theory.[61] Even in theories geared toward uplift, many economic models saw the "rule of experts" on behalf of underdeveloped societies as equally natural.[62]

This tendency to elide, or even fail to acknowledge a deviation of interests between the colonizer and the colonized, was certainly present in Keynes's worldview. So much so in fact that it takes effort to fully identify Keynes's position on empire, as it was simply in the air he breathed.[63] In this way, the giraffe opens one door for further contemplation. Even if Keynes used the giraffe in a Lamarckian frame, the giraffe remained a pregnant imperial metaphor. For example, in the 1920s, the British Uganda Railway chose a giraffe to advertise the promise and excitement of train travel through Africa.[64] However, the history of that railway did not appear in those advertisements, where the placid grazing giraffe beckoned the would-be tourist. The Uganda Railway had been built as part of the scramble for Africa in the late nineteenth century, and the attending labor, loss of lives, and violent altercations between colonizer and colonized disappeared behind advertisements proclaiming industrial progress.[65] As with the giraffe in the Uganda Railway advertisement, we might need to inquire into the history behind the surface of what was advertised, or said explicitly.

While we cannot say for certain what pushed Keynes to pick his long-necked metaphor, we do know that Keynes's Bloomsbury friend (and anti-imperialist) George Orwell had "praised," Kipling for the courage to "speak the truth" about Empire. Orwell argued of Kipling: "He sees clearly…that men can only be highly civilized while other men, inevitably less civilized, are there to guard and feed them."[66] Given that *The End of Laissez-Faire* spoke explicitly of efforts to "guard and feed" the giraffe, we can think of how Keynes absorbed imperial categories into the very heart of his concept of "intervention."[67] A careful examination of the texts reveals that Keynes belongs in a longer tradition (with Kipling) of Fabian socialism, which had long framed imperialism in terms of uplift. That tradition was part of a larger effort—that included zoos and colonial exhibitions—to present empire as a moral and cultural project rather than a coercive state.[68]

Looking back at Keynes's own work before *The End of Laissez-Faire*, there is evidence that Keynes too saw Western imperialism as "natural and essential." In the *Economic Consequences of the Peace,* for example, Keynes expressed concern at the prospect of stripping Germany of its colonies at the end of WWI.[69] In the first case, he worried about what the breaking up of Germany into smaller states would mean for European economic exchange and recovery. However, more than this, Keynes was horrified at the liquidation of Germany's overseas territories: "The Allied and Associated Powers reserve the right to retain and liquidate all property, rights and interests belonging at the date of the coming into force of the Present Treaty to German nations, or companies controlled by them" within the former German colonies.[70]

As Susan Buck Morss has argued, since the nineteenth century, respect for property rights had been a sacrosanct principle of international relations. Any transfer of territory between great powers, even if by conquest, usually made provisions to respect the rights of property of businesses and inhabitants. That was never the case, however, for colonial peoples, whose territories could always be expropriated at will.[71] Keynes expressed concern about the precedent of a Western power being treated as colony. This seems to imply that Keynes—like Kipling and unlike Orwell—felt that some distinctions needed to remain sharp, like those between "civilized" and "backward" people. Undermining that distinction might eventually threaten imperial projects at large. There was, after all, already enough dangerous anticolonial ferment surrounding the "Wilsonian moment."[72]

Moving back even earlier in time, Keynes began his career as an economic policy advisor as a member of the Royal Commission on Indian Currency and Finance of 1913–1914.[73] That commission was tasked with devising a monetary policy for India. As Manu Goswami reminds us: "The large surpluses in the colonial Indian balance of payments, for instance, were a crucial source for sustaining London as the center of world finance."[74] The report that Keynes produced in that capacity, his 1913 *Indian Currency and Finance*, offers a fertile starting point for thinking through these issues.[75] There, Keynes even cited the "propensity to hoard" as an early justification of state intervention into monetary matters. He stated:

> India, as we all know, already wastes far too high a proportion of her resources in the needless accumulation of the precious metals... By the elimination of both precious metals, to the utmost extent that public opinion will permit, from amongst the hoards and the circulation of the country, they ought to counteract an uncivilized and wasteful habit."[76]

Here, Keynes relied on familiar mise-en-valeur imperial rhetoric, which spoke of "training" and "educating" Indians toward a sounder and wiser set of monetary practices. Yet in the very next moment, Keynes warned his imperial colleagues of the dangers of what might happen if Indians learned those lessons too quickly. He stated, "On the other hand, if a time comes when Indians learn to leave off their unfertile habits and to divert their hoards into the channels of productive industry and to the enrichment of their fields, they will have the money markets of the world at their mercy."[77]

Again, we can gain insight by recalling the metaphor of the economic advisor in the role of the psychoanalyst. In the context of colonial policy, the metaphor takes on yet another dimension. For, where the empire (therapist) claims to desire to help the patient (colony) through their regressions and inhibitions, they encounter a dilemma; the moment the patient heals, so ends the therapist's revenue stream.[78] We can see the working of this logic in Keynes's ambivalent description of Indian monetary policy; he argued that Britain needed to help India out of its wasteful habits, but that they should not teach those lessons too quickly or the colony might evade the empire's grasp. Keynes relied on the logic of gradual development, asserting that direct (undemocratic) intervention was indeed serving the interests of the Indian population. This is particularly clear when examining Keynes' 1913 suggesting for the opening of an Indian Central Bank. Keynes' proposal would create a Western-style institution that Britain would control, and that subsequently—far in the future—might pass into Indian hands. While some scholars have tried to see a "pro-Indian" stance in this measure, this overlooks the longer history of the role that central banks played in first consolidating national economies and then supporting the financial coordinating of imperial outposts.[79]

In reading *Indian Currency and Finance,* it is clear that Keynes forged some of his ideas about the aggregate dangers of "hoarding" and the benefits of intervention by studying the Indian case. What is more, he also consolidated his preference for a gold exchange rather than metal standard. In this way, the spirit of reforms that Keynes pursued in the 1920s and 1930s drew to a certain extent from imperial practices.[80] Going forward, Keynes focused less explicitly on imperial policy and more on the interventionist policies he perceived as appropriate for the West.[81] However, he also assumed that the West would continue to have recourse to its colonies.

With these statements in mind, we can look again with new eyes at the specific solutions that Keynes offered for intervening on behalf of the herd in 1926.[82] For example, we see that Keynes emphasized the importance of certain liberal institutions that were in fact crucial to the relationship between Britain and its colonies. He listed the "naturally socialized" models of joint-stock corporations (think the East India Company), the Bank of England, the press, and the universities such as Oxford and Cambridge. With those partnerships in place, he then mapped out the main tenets that he saw as a vital aspect of any interventionist "agenda" on behalf of the "herd."

First, he spoke out for, "… the deliberate control of the currency and of credit by a central institution," namely, the Bank of England.

It is not a coincidence that Keynes chose the Bank of England as his ideal model, which was not only a joint-stock corporation but also the monetary lever of the British Empire.[83] The second point on Keynes's agenda was that of savings and investment. Here, the giraffe helped Keynes to make this point. The animal spirits of the desire for expansion and wealth (investment) and the herding propensity to hoard (savings) stood at cross-purposes. So this is precisely why savings and investment offered one domain in which states could get their hands dirty in ways that would have a tremendous positive impact not only on welfare, but in mitigating the deep depths of recession. Keynes stated: “I believe that some coordinated act of intelligent judgment is required as to the scale on which it is desirable that the community as a whole should save, the scale on which these savings should go abroad in the form of foreign investments, and whether the present organization of the investment market distributes savings along the most nationally productive channels.”[84] Upon close inspection, the description of the “coordinated” effort at collective savings echoed closely the way London interacted with certain imperial and commonwealth financial networks.[85]

The final point on Keynes's agenda for targeted state intervention included population dynamics.[86] Keynes asserted: “The time may arrive a little later when a community as a whole must pay attention to the innate quality as well as to the mere numbers of its future members.”[87] Since eugenics had lingered in discussions of population questions since the nineteenth century, refering to the “quality” of population, raises questions in retrospect.[88] For example, how did Keynes imagine that states might control population numbers with an eye toward “quality?”

In this final point, Keynes was once again very much part of the global status quo. In a world where an unprecedented mixing of people had come about through trade, migration, travel, and imperialism, even ostensibly democratic societies, especially in Europe, tended to seek to define more clearly their identities in terms of the exclusion of others.[89] In turn, excluded groups rallied on behalf of class, ethnicity, and gender to make collective claims for rights.[90] Faced with these dynamics, legal systems in much of the Western world were wrestling with the question of whether political rights belonged to individuals or groups and *ethnos*.[91] It seems that while Keynes remained skeptical of social-Darwinian paradigms, he still retained the typically imperial and typically nationalist beliefs in the importance of the "fitness" of populations.[92] In this way, we might consider Keynes's attention to fitness as subtly tied to the ways that racial criteria served imperial governments in justifying different modes of government in the metropolis and the colony. [93]

As a final point, the same year that Keynes published *The End of Laissez-Faire*, in 1926 the British Imperial Conference was convening. It was during that conference that the British Empire defined its vision of the "commonwealth." In so doing, it drew a distinction between those powers sufficiently developed to be "autonomous but affiliated," while others still needed to be governed from the outside.[94] As we have seen, these taxonomies of more and less civilized, more and less capable of autonomy, also informed Keynes's perspective on the nature and kinds of intervention that states should undertake.

When the depression hit and spread to varying degrees in 1929, the need for economic answers became ever more pressing and the idea of managed economies less shocking. Suddenly, the question of herd dynamics, echoed in market loss and bank failures, gave more credit and credence to Keynes's articulations. In a world hungry for and more open to economic advice, Keynes edited and reprinted the *The End of Laissez-Faire*. Thus, we will end by asking why, in 1931, the giraffe suddenly disappeared from sight.

By Way of Concluding: Or the Case of the Disappearing Giraffe

In his self-collected and straightforwardly titled *Essays in Persuasion*, Keynes asserted: "I have thought it convenient to choose this date of publication, because we are standing at a point of transition. It is called a National Crisis. But that is not correct—for Great Britain the main crisis is over." That date was 1931, and it was just a few short years after the market crash in the USA had created varied levels of depression and unemployment across the world. Keynes used the opportunity to recount how far Western society had progressed since 1919. He continued triumphantly: "Scarcely any one in England now believes in the Treaty of Versailles or in the prewar Gold Standard or in the Policy of Deflation. These battles have been won—mainly by the irresistible pressure of events and only secondarily by the slow undermining of old prejudices." Keynes no doubt saw his own work as vital to that "slow undermining" of old orthodoxies.

Keynes asserted that while the idea of capitalist yet managed economies had gained ground, the question of how to manage them remained to be fully settled in the details. He admitted: "But most of us have, as yet, only a vague idea of what we are going to do next, of how we are going to use our regained freedom of choice." To further the goal (in addition to sitting on the Macmillan Committee on Finance that same year), Keynes collected and collated a series of his own works for publication.[95] Keynes explained how he chose and edited each text within his *Persuasions*: "The method has been to omit freely (without special indications in the text) anything which appeared to be redundant or unnecessary to the main line of the argument or to have lost interest with the passage of events; but to alter nothing in the text which has been retained."[96]

Keynes included *The End of Laissez-Faire* in that volume, but in a highly abbreviated form. For the most part, the 1931 version re-itemized his "agenda." Namely, he spoke of the need for the central control of currency, credit, savings, investment, and finally, population. Remarkably, however, neither the Darwin-laissez-faire synthesis, nor the call to provide leaves for the herd remained. Thus, in reading through the reprint, a reader aware of the previous editions finds themselves in a similar position to Kipling's Ethiopian: *"I can smell Giraffe, and I can hear Giraffe, but I can't see Giraffe."* The question of course is why? Here, we have an opportunity to apply a literary insight into economic texts: namely, we have to ponder both the presences and the pregnant absences.

Perhaps Keynes simply perceived that evolutionary metaphors were not as important as they had been a few short years earlier. Or, perhaps he simply selected the elements of the text that he believed to be of the most immediate practical interest. Both are perfectly reasonable assumptions. Beyond authorial intent, however, we might conclude that the absence of the giraffe makes it even harder to perceive Keynes's imperial values and commitments. In that reprint, he restated the importance of "wise" expert interventions on behalf of the community, yet he further whitewashed the question of how precisely that community was constituted and organized both locally and globally. As he erased the giraffe, he erased the only (albeit admittedly implicit and metaphorical) reference to the fact that Britain depended on the resources of its empire.

Keynes concluded the 1931 reprint with the following statement: "Material Poverty provides the incentive to change precisely in situations where there is very little margin for experiments. Material Prosperity removes the incentive just when it might be safe to take a chance."[97] For Keynes, this was a renewed call to bravely act in conditions of poverty. It also formed the basis of one of the primary insights of macroeconomic intervention so often repeated since the Keynesian revolution, namely "Spend in moments of crisis and save moments of prosperity."[98] Yet, in thinking of Gould's quest to overturn the often-repeated myth that Darwin opposed Lamarck on the question of the giraffe's neck, we can end on the following reflection: What have we missed about the original contexts of Keynes's theories, in repeating them? The point here is neither to reject nor to support Keynes, but rather to suggest that there is a need to ask historically grounded questions of economic assumptions, such as: Whose welfare does the theory protect and to whose welfare ("domestic" or "foreign") does it remain blind?

So if there is a moral to this story, it is simply this. William James—who spoke out against the US occupation of the Philippines—spoke out in favor of intellectual pluralism.[99] "Everything you can think of, however vast or inclusive, has on the pluralistic view a genuinely 'external' environment of some sort or amount."[100] That is to say, all theories have contexts, all sight is limited, and no totalities hold. It is thus against absolutes that we ponder the ordinary textuality of economic ideas. For according to James: "The pluralistic world is thus more like a federal republic than like an empire or a kingdom."[101]

Notes

1. William James, *Essays in Radical Empiricism* (Memphis: Bottom of the Hill Publishing, 2012); William James, *Pragmatism: A New Name for Some Old Ways of Thinking: Popular Lectures on Philosophy* (Cambridge: Cambridge University Press, 2014).
2. The literature on the necessity of embeddedness as an approach to economic thought is vast. For a small sampling of such perspectives historically see Francesco Boldizzoni, *The Poverty of Clio Resurrecting Economic History* (Princeton, NJ: Princeton University Press, 2011); William H. Sewell, "A Strange Career: The Historical Study of Economic Life," *History and Theory* 49, no. 4 (December 1, 2010): 146–66; Wolfgang Streeck, "How to Study Contemporary Capitalism?" *European Journal of Sociology/Archives Européennes de Sociologie* 53, no. 1 (April 2012): 1–28.
3. For a summary of those debates, see Barry J. Eichengreen, *Hall of Mirrors: The Great Depression, the Great Recession, and the Uses-and Misuses-of History* (Oxford: Oxford University Press, 2015).
4. "The Trouble With Macroeconomics—Paul Romer," accessed November 12, 2016, https://paulromer.net/the-trouble-with-macro/; Diane Coyle, *GDP: A Brief but Affectionate History* (Princeton: Princeton University Press, 2014); and Joseph E. Stiglitz et al., *Mismeasuring Our Lives: Why GDP Doesn't Add Up; the Report by the Commission on the Measurement of Economic Performance and Social Progress* (New York, NY [u.a.]: New Press, 2010).
5. C. N. Biltoft, "Eliding the Empire: J.M. Keynes's World View before the Micro-Macro Divide, 1913–1936," article under review.
6. Joseph A. Schumpeter, *Can Capitalism Survive?: Creative Destruction and the Future of the Global Economy* (New York: Harper Perennial, 2009); see also Robert Skidelsky, "Creative Destruction: Keynes, Hobson, Marx - and the Crisis of Capitalism," *New Statesman*, April 12, 2013.
7. Others have identified Keynes's enduring (if sometimes *liberally* compassionate) sympathy for the British imperial project. For the view that Keynes was ultimately mostly indifferent to the idea of Indian independence, please see Robert Skidelsky, *John Maynard Keynes* (New York: Viking, 1986). For an alternative view, please see Anand G. Chandavarkar, *Keynes and India: A Study in Economics*

and Biography (Basingstoke: Macmillan, 1989). For the colonial implications of Keynes' thoughts, see Timothy Mitchell, *Rule of Experts: Egypt, Techno-Politics, Modernity* (Berkeley, CA and London: University of California Press, 2012).

8. For an example of this mode of interpretation, please see Andrew Sartori, "Global Intellectual History and the History of Political Economy," in *Global Intellectual History*, ed. Samuel Moyn and Andrew Sartori (New York, NY: Columbia University Press, 2013). See also, for example, Sophus A. Reinert, *Translating Empire: Emulation and the Origins of Political Economy* (Cambridge, MA: Harvard University Press, 2011). Also Sewell, "A Strange Career."
9. In this view, theories hold a similar place in the history of global capitalism as commodities, so economic ideas emerge at the intersection of the "social" and "cultural" meaning-making and the international division of labor. Arjun Appadurai et al., eds., *The Social Life of Things: Commodities in Cultural Perspective* (Cambridge: Cambridge University Press, 1986). See also Gary Gereffi, Miguel Korzeniewicz, and Political Economy of the World-System Conference, eds., *Commodity Chains and Global Capitalism* (Westport, CT: Greenwood Press, 1994). Steven Topik, Carlos Marichal, and Zephyr L. Frank, *From Silver to Cocaine: Latin American Commodity Chains and the Building of the World Economy, 1500–2000* (Durham, NC: Duke University Press, 2006). For a particularly effective look at how global commodities studies might equally give us ideas for thinking about economic theories and the history of capitalism, please see the classic by Sidney W. Mintz, *Sweetness and Power: The Place of Sugar in Modern History* (New York, NY: Viking, 1985). Sven Beckert, *Empire of Cotton: A Global History* (New York: Knopf, 2014). For a heterodox but still economic exploration of how the world of commodities offers insights into economic theory, please see Piero Sraffa, *Production of Commodities by Means of Commodities; Prelude to a Critique of Economic Theory* (Cambridge: Cambridge University Press, 1960).
10. For other examples of scholarship based on similar methodologies, please see Emma Rothschild, *Economic Sentiments: Adam Smith, Condorcet, and the Enlightenment* (Cambridge, MA: Harvard University Press, 2001); Reinert, *Translating Empire*.
11. Carlo Cristiano, *The Political and Economic Thought of the Young Keynes: Liberalism, Markets and Empire* (London: Routledge, 2014).

12. John Maynard Keynes, *The End of Laissez-Faire; The Economic Consequences of the Peace* (Amherst: Prometheus Books, 2004), 68–69.
13. Keynes, *The End of Laissez-Faire; The Economic Consequences of the Peace*, 69–70.
14. Charles Ferrall and Dougal McNeill, *Writing the 1926 General Strike. Literature, Culture, Politics* (Cambridge: Cambridge University Press, 2015).
15. See Robert L. Heilbroner, *The Worldly Philosophers: The Lives, Times, and Ideas of the Great Economic Thinkers* (New York: Simon & Schuster, 1999); Nicholas Wapshott, *Keynes Hayek: The Clash That Defined Modern Economics* (New York: W.W. Norton & Co., 2011); and Skidelsky, *Keynes the Return of the Master.*
16. Skidelsky, *John Maynard Keynes*; Robert Cord, *Keynes* (London: Haus, 2007).
17. Ibid., 33.
18. John Maynard Keynes, *The End of Laissez-Faire* (Signalman Publishing, 2009).
19. For a brilliant explication of the intermingling of social science, material interests, and empire, please see Marc Flandreau, *Anthropologists in the Stock Exchange: A Financial History of Victorian Science* (Chicago: University of Chicago Press, 2016); See also Bernard V. Lightman, *Victorian Science in Context* (Chicago: University of Chicago Press, 1997).
20. Thomas Cowles, "Malthus, Darwin, and Bagehot: A Study in the Transference of a Concept," *Isis* 26, no. 2 (1937): 341–48; Olivier Accominotti et al., "Black Man's Burden, White Man's Welfare: Control, Devolution and Development in the British Empire, 1880–1914," *European Review of Economic History* 14, no. 01 (2010): 47–70. Marc Flandreau, "The Descent of Central Banking: Bagehot, Darwin and the Foreign Debt Market" (Third CEPR Economic History Symposium, Oslo, 2015).
21. John Darwin, "Imperialism and the Victorians: The Dynamics of Territorial Expansion," *The English Historical Review* 112, no. 447 (1997): 614–42; Paul B. Rich, *Race and Empire in British Politics* (Cambridge and New York: Cambridge University Press, 1986); Kalpana Wilson, *Race, Racism and Development: Interrogating History, Discourse and Practice* (London and New York: Zed Books, 2012).
22. Keynes, *The End of Laissez-Faire; The Economic Consequences of the Peace*, 29.

23. Ibid., 29.
24. Ibid., 30.
25. Ibid., 31.
26. Ibid.
27. E. G. Winslow, "Keynes and Freud: Psychoanalysis and Keynes's Account of the 'Animal Spirits' of Capitalism," *Social Research* 53, no. 4 (1986): 549–78.
28. Wapshott, *Keynes Hayek*.
29. George A. Akerlof, *Animal Spirits: How Human Psychology Drives the Economy, and Why It Matters for Global Capitalism* (Princeton, NJ: Princeton University Press, 2010). See chapter on Keynes in Heilbroner, *The Worldly Philosophers*.
30. Akerlof, *Animal Spirits*.
31. Sigmund Freud, *The Complete Introductory Lectures on Psychoanalysis* (New York: W.W. Norton, 1966), 298.
32. Ibid., 299.
33. Winslow, "Keynes and Freud"; Skidelsky, *John Maynard Keynes*.
34. Gary S. Becker and Kevin Murphy, *Social Economics: Market Behavior in a Social Environment* (Cambridge, MA: Harvard University Press, 2003); Edward Cartwright, *Behavioral Economics* (London and New York, NY: Routledge, 2011).
35. For a summary of Lamarck's life and concepts, see L. J. Jordanova, *Lamarck* (Oxford and New York: Oxford University Press, 1984).
36. Stephen Jay Gould, *Leonardo's Mountain of Clams and the Diet of Worms* (Harvard University Press, 2011), 302.
37. Ibid., 306–8. Geoffrey M. Hodgson, "The Mystery of the Routine. The Darwinian Destiny of An Evolutionary Theory of Economic Change," *Revue Économique* 54, no. 2 (2003): 355–84.
38. Gould, *Leonardo's Mountain of Clams and the Diet of Worms*, 309–10.
39. Ibid., 312.
40. Ibid., 304.
41. Various web articles on epigenetics' reconsideration of some aspects of Lamarck's theory. "Lamarck's Bizarre Theory of Evolution May Turn out to Be Right after All," *io9*, accessed October 26, 2013, http://io9.com/5866001/lamarcks-bizarre-theory-of-evolution-may-turn-out-to-be-right-after-all.
42. Gould, *Leonardo's Mountain of Clams and the Diet of Worms*, 312.
43. Hodgson, "The Mystery of the Routine." For a description of the economists who have identified with Lamarckian metaphors, see also

Geoffrey Martin Hodgson, *Economics and Evolution: Bringing Life Back into Economics* (Ann Arbor, MI: University of Michigan, 1999).
44. Keynes, *The End of Laissez-Faire; The Economic Consequences of the Peace*, 31.
45. Berthold Laufer, *The Giraffe in History and Art* (Chicago: Field Museum of Natural History, 1928), 14.
46. Ibid., 69.
47. Erik Ringmar, "Audience for a Giraffe: European Expansionism and the Quest for the Exotic," *Journal of World History* 17, no. 4 (October 30, 2006): 375–97, 377–88.
48. Edward W. Said, *Orientalism*, 1979; John M. MacKenzie, *Orientalism: History, Theory and the Arts* (Manchester and New York: Manchester University Press, 2007); Raymond Corbey, "Ethnographic Showcases, 1870–1930," *Cultural Anthropology* 8, no. 3 (1993): 338–69; and Timothy Mitchell, *Colonising Egypt* (Cambridge [u.a.]: Cambridge University Press, 2007).
49. Laufer, *The Giraffe in History and Art*, 88; Michael Allin, *Zarafa: A Giraffe's True Story, from Deep in Africa to the Heart of Paris* (New York: Walker Publishing Company, 1998).
50. Ringmar, "Audience for a Giraffe," 385.
51. Laufer, *The Giraffe in Art and History*, 90–91; Takashi Ito, *London Zoo and the Victorians, 1828–1859* (Woodbridge: Royal Historical Society, 2014), 63; and Ringmar, "Audience for a Giraffe," 387.
52. Peter H. Hoffenberg, *An Empire on Display: English, Indian, and Australian Exhibitions from the Crystal Palace to the Great War* (Berkeley: University of California Press, 2001), 54.
53. Uday Singh Mehta, *Liberalism and Empire: A Study in Nineteenth-Century British Liberal Thought* (Chicago: University of Chicago Press, 1999); Andrew Sartori, "The British Empire and Its Liberal Mission," *The Journal of Modern History* 78, no. 3 (2006): 623–42; Harriet Ritvo, "Zoological Nomenclature and the Empire of Victorian Science," in *Victorian Science in Context*, ed. Bernard V. Lightman (Chicago: Chicago University Press, 1997), 334–54, 334.
54. Hoffenberg, *An Empire on Display*, 2–3.
55. Corbey, "Ethnographic Showcases, 1870–1930," 339.
56. "Just So Stories, by Rudyard Kipling," accessed November 16, 2016, https://www.gutenberg.org/files/2781/2781-h/2781-h.htm#link2H_4_0004.

57. Caroline Rooney, *Kipling and Beyond: Patriotism, Globalisation, and Postcolonialism* (Houndmills, Basingstoke and Hampshire: Palgrave Macmillan, 2010).
58. Rudyard Kipling and Edward W. Said, *Kim* (London: Penguin Books, 1989), 45.
59. "The Ritual of Government—A Book of Words–Rudyard Kipling, Book, Etext," accessed November 16, 2016, http://www.telelib.com/authors/K/KiplingRudyard/prose/BookOfWords/ritualgovernment.html.
60. Olivier Accominotti et al., "Black Man's Burden, White Man's Welfare: Control, Devolution and Development in the British Empire, 1880–1914," *European Review of Economic History* 14, no. 1 (2010): 47–70, 48.
61. Wilson, *Race, Racism and Development*; Gilbert Rist, *The History of Development: From Western Origins to Global Faith* (London: Zed Books, 2014).
62. Mitchell, *Rule of Experts*; Flandreau, *Anthropologists in the Stock Exchange*; and Bernard S. Cohn, *Colonialism and Its Forms of Knowledge: The British in India* (Princeton: Princeton University Press, 1996).
63. Cristiano, *The Political and Economic Thought of the Young Keynes*.
64. Laufer, *The Giraffe in History and Art*, 93.
65. Clarence B. Davis, Kenneth E. Wilburn, and Ronald Robinson, *Railway Imperialism* (New York: Greenwood Press, 1991); F. L. O'Callaghan, *Uganda Railway* (Chatham: Royal Engineers Institute, 1900).
66. Quoted in Jonah Raskin, *The Mythology of Imperialism: A Revolutionary Critique of British Literature and Society in the Modern Age* (New York: Monthly Review Press, 2009), 70.
67. Duncan Bell, *The Idea of Greater Britain: Empire and the Future of World Order, 1860–1900* (Princeton, NJ: Princeton University Press, 2007).
68. Hoffenberg, *An Empire on Display*, 20.
69. Keynes, *The End of Laissez-Faire; The Economic Consequences of the Peace*, 107.
70. Ibid., 109.
71. Susan Buck-Morss, *Dreamworld and Catastrophe: The Passing of Mass Utopia in East and West* (Cambridge, MA: MIT Press, 2002), 15–16.

72. Erez Manela, *The Wilsonian Moment: Self-Determination and the International Origins of Anticolonial Nationalism* (Oxford; New York: Oxford University Press, 2014); Cemil Aydin, *The Politics of Anti-Westernism in Asia: Visions of World Order in Pan-Islamic and Pan-Asian Thought* (New York: Columbia University Press, 2007).
73. Cristiano, *The Political and Economic Thought of the Young Keynes.*
74. Manu Goswami, *Producing India: From Colonial Economy to National Space* (Chicago: University of Chicago Press, 2013), 69.
75. Cristiano, *The Political and Economic Thought of the Young Keynes*; Chandavarkar, *Keynes and India.*
76. John Maynard Keynes, *Indian Currency and Finance* (London and New York: Macmillan & Co. Ltd, 1913), 63.
77. Ibid., 64.
78. For germane case studies where this dilemma is particularly clear, please see Marc Flandreau, *Money Doctors: The Experience of International Financial Advising, 1850–2000* (London and New York: Routledge, 2003).
79. For a summary of the first position, please see Chandavarkar, *Keynes and India.* For a view of the relation between central banks and imperialism, please see Steven Bryan, *The Gold Standard at the Turn of the Twentieth Century: Rising Powers, Global Money, and the Age of Empire* (New York: Columbia University Press, 2010); Marcello De Cecco, *The International Gold Standard: Money and Empire* (New York: St. Martin's Press, 1984).
80. Charles S. Maier, *Recasting Bourgeois Europe: Stabilization in France, Germany, and Italy in the Decade after World War I* (Princeton, NJ: Princeton University Press, 1975).
81. Schumpeter made a similar claim in 1919; please see Joseph A. Schumpeter, *Imperialism and Social Classes* (New York: A.M. Kelly, 1951).
82. Ibid., 173–74.
83. Keynes, *The End of Laissez-Faire: The Economic Consequences of the Peace*, 41.
84. John Maynard Keynes, *Essays in Persuasion* (Cambridge: Cambridge University Press for the Royal Economic Society, 1913), 173–74.
85. P. J. Cain and A. G. Hopkins, *British Imperialism: 1688–2015* (London: Routledge, 2016).
86. For a history of Keynes's views on population, please see John Toye, *Keynes on Population* (Oxford: Oxford University Press, 2000).

87. Keynes, *Essays in Persuasion*, 173.
88. Roger Luckhurst and Josephine McDonagh, *Transactions and Encounters: Science and Culture in the Nineteenth Century* (Manchester, UK and New York: Manchester University Press, 2002); Donald J. Childs, *Modernism and Eugenics: Woolf, Eliot, Yeats, and the Culture of Degeneration* (Cambridge: Cambridge University Press, 2006).
89. Keynes, *The End of Laissez-Faire*; *The Economic Consequences of the Peace.*
90. Jeffry A. Frieden, *Global Capitalism: Its Fall and Rise in the Twentieth Century* (New York: W.W. Norton, 2007); James Foreman-Peck, *A History of the World Economy : International Economic Relations since 1850* (Totowa, NJ: Barnes & Noble, 1983).
91. See Mark Mazower, "Minorities and the League of Nations in Interwar Europe," *Daedalus* 126, no. 2 (Spring 1997): 47–63.
92. Ann Stoler, *Carnal Knowledge and Imperial Power: Race and the Intimate in Colonial Rule* (Berkeley, CA: University of California Press, 2010); Heather Streets-Salter and Trevor R. Getz, *Empires and Colonies in the Modern World: A Global Perspective* (Oxford: Oxford University Press, 2015).
93. Alison Bashford, "Population, Geopolitics, and International Organizations in the Mid Twentieth Century," *Journal of World History* 19, no. 3 (2008): 327–47; Alison Bashford, "Nation, Empire, Globe: The Spaces of Population Debate in the Interwar Years," *Comparative Studies in Society and History* 49, no. 1 (2007); Matthew Connelly, "Seeing Beyond the State: The Population Control Movement and the Problem of Sovereignty," *Past and Present* 193, no. 1 (2006): 197; and M. Connelly, "To Inherit the Earth. Imagining World Population, from the Yellow Peril to the Population Bomb," *Journal of Global History* 1, no. 3 (November 2006): 299–319.
94. *Imperial Conference 1926* (Dublin: Publications Sale Office, 1926).
95. H. P. Macmillan, Great Britain, and Committee on Finance and Industry, *Committee on Finance and Industry: Report* (London: His Maj. Stationery Office, 1931); Cunliffe Committee and Macmillan Committee, *British Parliamentary Reports on International Finance. The Cunliffe Committee and The Macmillan Committee Reports. Repr. of the Ed. London 1918, 1931* (New York: Arno Pr, 1978).

96. John Maynard Keynes, *Essays in Persuasion* (Cambridge: Cambridge University Press, 2013), 2.
97. Ibid., 175.
98. Paul R. Krugman, *End This Depression Now!* (New York: W.W. Norton & Co., 2012).
99. Howard M. Feinstein, *Becoming William James* (Ithaca, NY: Cornell University Press, 1984).
100. William James, *A Pluralistic Universe* (London: Longmans, Green, and Co., 1909), http://public.eblib.com/choice/publicfullrecord.aspx?p=1672691. I want to assert however that the "pluralism" to which I refer is not what Timothy Mitchell calls "easy pluralism," but rather a pluralism attuned to the impossibility of universalism. See the introduction of Timothy Mitchell, *Questions of Modernity* (Minneapolis: University of Minnesota Press, 2000).
101. James, *A Pluralistic Universe.*

Acknowledgments My sincere thanks to the participants of the Global Studies seminar at Lehigh University (especially Bill Bullman, Nitzan Lebovic, and John Savage) for an extremely valuable discussion of an earlier version of this text. I also want to thank Betsy Carter, Francesco Bolidzonni, Robert Fredona, Marc Flandreau, Susanna Hecht, Sophus A. Reinert, Wolfgang Streeck, and Corey Tazzara for feedback at various stages. Finally, as promised, Justin from Kavarna Coffeehouse, whose espresso macchiato made this piece possible.

Author Biography

Carolyn N. Biltoft is trained in modern world history (Princeton, 2010), and her work approaches the dynamics of global capitalism since 1850 through the lenses of intellectual and cultural history. In particular, Carolyn is interested in the ways that individuals and institutions have responded to, made sense of, and then influenced the bundle of interconnected phenomena collated under the term globalization. Her forthcoming book, *Global Flesh and Spirit: The Information Age as seen from the League of Nations, 1918–1939*, situates the rise and fall of the world's first intergovernmental organization within the riptides of a global modernity where markets and societies became entangled with information systems.

Between Economic Planning and Market Competition: Institutional Law and Economics in the US

Laura Phillips Sawyer

In 1926 John Maurice Clark published a seminal text in institutionalist economics, *Social Control of Business*, surveying the ways in which business was subject to control by a variety of formal and informal constraints.[1] The text rejected mainstream ideas in neoclassical political economy by explaining how individual self-interest and competition could be manipulated not only through legal rules but also by custom, habit, codes of ethics, and morals. Representative of the institutionalist movement, Clark discarded presumptions of an individualistic economy based on market competition. Instead, he posited that long-term public goals of prosperity and equity could be achieved through the public and private study of "industry itself," which existed "on the frontier where new policies are being worked out."[2] The book fused the development of the regulatory state, giving particular attention to administrative law, with self-regulation by businesses and trade associations. Both public

L. Phillips Sawyer (✉)
Harvard Business School, Boston, USA
e-mail: LSawyer@hbs.edu

R. Fredona and S.A. Reinert (eds.), *New Perspectives on the History of Political Economy*, https://doi.org/10.1007/978-3-319-58247-4_12

and private regulations, he argued, advanced codes of conduct to standardize business activities and control competitive practices. Building on the work of Richard Ely, John Commons, and Dean Roscoe Pound, Clark's *Social Control of Business* extended progressive liberals' initiatives for regulatory state expansion through administrative agencies and it advanced private rulemaking by trade associations as a complement to the development of mandatory public regulation.

Social Control of Business epitomized the first great law and economics movement's challenge to the neoclassical paradigm of academic research and public policy.[3] Rather than pursuing a policy agenda based on a singular model of human behavior or industrial order, the institutionalists believed that social science research should guide policy makers in shaping rules and regulations according to the particular structure of a given industry. The purpose of industry-specific studies was twofold: to understand the economic dynamics of an industry, giving especial attention to social costs or negative externalities, and to construct a detailed account of the macroeconomy as a whole. That approach resulted in a slew of studies and policies that many critics have said amounted to little more than questioning of orthodox economics, rather than a coherent research agenda. Institutional economics, in turn, has been largely dismissed and overlooked by mainstream economic and policy history because of its limited duration in the academy and its very diverse policy prescriptions.[4] Dismissing the influence of institutionalism obscures the intellectual origins and social purposes of the 1920s "new economics" in academic research, regulatory policy, and private self-regulation.

This essay argues that one of the central tenets of institutionalist law and economics—the social control of business—helped structure the research and planning agendas of administrative agencies, such as the Department of Commerce and the Federal Trade Commission (FTC), as well as private research organizations, including Harvard Business School (HBS), the National Bureau of Economic Research (NBER), and the Social Science Research Council (SSRC).[5] The motivation toward social control united progressive liberal economists who sought to reform not only academic research methods but also policy-making outcomes. Their experiences during WWI with domestic economic planning motivated the institutionalists toward postwar collaboration with government officials, regulators, and private research institutes. By the mid-1920s, the first great law and economics movement had embedded a long-term research agenda within both public administrative agencies and private research institutes, both of which pursued social science research in economic planning.

***

Interwar Institutional Economics

At the close of the First World War, the American Economic Association (AEA) convened a small, one-day conference to discuss various aspects of postwar recovery. Sessions covered monetary stability, maintenance of international peace, price fixing during peacetime, and the future of agricultural policies.[6] At that conference, Walton Hamilton coined the term "institutionalist economics" to signal a break with existing US economic thought and policy. In turn, Hamilton emerged as the initial spokesperson for a group of progressive liberal economists who believed neoclassical economics, theory, and regulation could not address the new economic realities of the postwar world. Cosponsored by the American Sociological Society, his panel, entitled "Economic Theory," stood apart from the rest. At that panel, Walton Hamilton laid out a new agenda not only for economic theory and research methods but also for economic regulation.[7]

Hamilton's paper, which appeared in the following year's *American Economic Review*, surveyed the state of the discipline and argued that neoclassical economics' reliance on subjective value theory had led the discipline away from critical analysis and toward becoming nothing more than *status quo* apologists.[8] "Only in recent years has value theory escaped a formal association with *laissez faire* [but] now even its most positive statements bear in such terms as 'utility' and 'productivity' and in the wording of principles [belie] implications about the worthwhileness of prevailing arrangements."[9] Neoclassical economics was not wholly *laissez faire*, Hamilton conceded; however, the subjective theory of value relied upon the premise of free competition and individual choice that Hamilton questioned. The world had changed with industrialization and world war, Hamilton and many other progressive economists argued, bringing new social problems and greater demand for control of powerful economic interests. Institutional economics, he offered as an alternative, was "concerned with industry in relation to human well-being."[10]

Economics had taken for granted the institutions—derived from custom, habit, and formal legal structures—that ordered economic relationships. Hamilton argued that because "institutions are social arrangements capable of change rather than obstinate natural phenomena," economics "should be relevant to the modern problem of control."[11] Whereas neoclassical economists' focus on value theory had been "derived from the classical doctrine of organization of industry [based] upon the principles of free competition," the institutionalist research agenda began not with the presumption of perfect competition but rather focused on the inherent malleability of economic relationships.[12] Rather than seeking out "economics statics" and equilibria to explain the "immutable" laws of industrial economies, Hamilton envisioned administrative agencies and private initiatives capable of identifying the "economic dynamics" that created and distributed value. Partnership between business, government, and the social sciences could temper competition and improve the distribution of wealth. Those new administrative bodies could collaborate with firms and trade associations so as to gather information and help shape business interactions through "conscious control." The purpose of the "social control" of business would be to improve not only efficiencies but also, perhaps more importantly, the distribution of wealth and resources.

For Hamilton, as with the institutionalist movement more generally, not all market competition improved social welfare or maximized efficiencies. In response, his life's work was dedicated to the pursuit of economic models and legal reforms that employed new management techniques for a public purpose. Others in this movement—including Wesley Claire Mitchell, Sumner Slichter, Leo Wiloman, Dexter Keezer, Stacy May, and Morris Copeland—were also concerned with the responsibilities of business to society.[13] Their great insight was that neoclassical economics had failed to incorporate ethical or societal considerations into its economic models, instead presuming that free competition necessarily maximized aggregate welfare.

Several leading institutional economists pioneered studies in business cycles, investigating the causes of economic booms and busts as well as the social costs of economic adjustments. Wesley Mitchell, who developed the most influential theory of business cycles in 1913, provided a trenchant critique of neoclassical value theory and its presumption of rational decision making.[14] Borrowing from Thorstein Veblen's criticism of mainstream economics' portrayal of man as a "lightning calculator of pleasure and pain," Mitchell argued that such a hedonistic conception of man failed to consider the psychological or evolutionary influences on decision making.[15] Rather than fixing prices according to market supply and demand, for example, businesspeople could be driven to "ruinous competition," wherein prices fall below costs, by their desire to destroy rivals. Not only could such behavior reduce competition and facilitate market consolidation, it also increased unemployment, drove down wages, and facilitated underconsumption.[16] Mitchell also examined banks' pro-cyclical lending, businesses' over-leveraging during a boom, and the concomitant bankruptcies characteristic of an economic bust or recession. Mitchell's work on business cycles and prescriptions for macroeconomic "social experiments" to mitigate downturns proved influential during the brief but sharp postwar recession.

Clark's *Social Control of Business* built upon Mitchell's study of business cycles by emphasizing that private rights alone could not satisfy the needs of a complex industrial society. Rather than individuals guiding business decisions, Clark presented six case studies that examined formal industrial regulations, extralegal codes of ethics used by business and professional associations, and informal union rules. In his final chapter, "If I were Dictator," he reflected on how those overlapping rules and mechanisms might be employed to negate the negative externalities of industrial production, including waste of natural resources, unemployment, and underconsumption. Critically, however, Clark believed that the administrative state must partner with business, professional, and labor organizations rather than dictate state-led or top-down regulations. He intended that partnership to preserve the positive benefits of the price mechanism, while also guiding closer coordination between business and government.[17]

The institutionalists appealed to the wider world of progressive reform and political discourse. Despite their critics, they developed several programs for the collection, tabulation, and dissemination of business statistics by appealing to reformers, business groups, and regulators. First, they built on the progressive liberal tradition emerging at the turn of the century that emphasized the interdependencies created by modern industrialization and urbanization. The institutionalists came from a cohort of pragmatic social reformers, such as John Dewey, Herbert Croly, and Walter Lippmann, who supported the expansion of state power to better citizens' lives. Institutionalists built on those impulses and contributed a technocratic vision of expert-led governance through administrative state agencies and trade associations. Secondly, the institutionalists also appealed to a diverse set of businesspeople seeking to rationalize business management practices—sometimes through top-down regulation but more often through deliberative organizations outside of government. Finally, their empirical approach attracted the attention of both business associations and state agencies, creating new collaborations between academic economists, private commercial associations, and government regulators.[18]

In their rejection of universal principles and generalizable economic rules, the institutionalists preferred deductive logic, which required industry-specific studies to evaluate the changing processes of price and wage setting, patterns of employment, and procedures to manage competitive markets. In order to paint "a picture of the pragmatic reality called industry," they pursued present business statistics as well as historical data in search of social and economic trends.[19] Then as now, the great strength and purpose of the institutionalists' research agenda also became its Achilles' heel. The main critique against the institutionalists was their lack of a coherent research method or any generalizable theory of value or competition.[20] But, of course, this was precisely their point—neither economic conditions nor their governing institutions remained static, and the purpose of the social sciences should be to understand how those institutional constraints could be used to govern dynamic economies.

Social Control and the Administrative State

The institutionalists' critique of neoclassical economics and law reflected a pervasive reconsideration of market competition that had resulted from the economic realities of a changing industrial order. Prior to the wartime experience of a coordinated market economy, formal legal rules and administrative agencies had been created to manage a rapidly changing economy. Corporate consolidations around the turn of the century had been met with the consternation of farmers, small proprietors, and laborers who felt disenfranchised from the economic gains made by corporate capitalists. Those social dislocations that accompanied industrialization and urbanization informed the regulatory politics of the anti-monopoly movement, which feared not only the consolidation of market power suppressing competitive markets but also the corresponding malady of undue political influence corrupting democratic political processes. In turn, the passage of the Sherman Antitrust Act of 1890 forbade restraints of trade and monopolization in interstate commerce. Yet, it failed to stem the growth of large-scale corporations or abuses of dominant firm position, such as predatory pricing. Additionally, the US Supreme Court's strict interpretation of the law occluded any associational activities that could be construed as collusive and, thereby, the Court further incentivized vertical consolidation. The institutionalists provided economic reasoning for a political and regulatory movement to further revise the rules of competition through administrative experts, rather than legislative processes. They endorsed new administrative controls intended to manage competitive processes so as to reduce social costs and market externalities associated with these corporate consolidations and market fluctuations.

Although the passage of the Federal Trade Commission (FTC) and Clayton Acts of 1914 failed to settle the uncertainty of competition policy, these did empower an administrative agency to review and prosecute anticompetitive business activities. That legislation created the FTC, which prohibited price discrimination, tying contracts, interlocking directorates, and unfair methods of competition, and also exempted labor unions from antitrust prosecution. President Wilson, who signed the act, asked the US Chamber of Commerce (USCC) to participate in an experiment with the FTC to "match all the facts of business throughout the country and to see the vast and consistent pattern of it," just as the Department of Agriculture did for farmers.[21] Joseph Davies, Commissioner of Corporations at the Department of Commerce, explained that the purpose of the FTC was "to convert the anarchy of unlicensed competition into a condition under law of competitive liberty, which will preserve those seeds of individual initiative and enterprise."[22] The liberal democratic goals espoused by the FTC mirrored the nascent formation of institutionalist research and policy agendas.

During its first years, FTC commissioners promoted uniform cost accounting and information sharing on industrial trade statistics in efforts to promote standardized business practices largely through trade associations and minimal public oversight. FTC Commissioner Edward Hurley, former president of the Illinois Manufacturers' Association, explained that reliable cost information must be the first step in rationalizing intra- and inter-business practices.[23] In an FTC pamphlet circulated to 230,000 businesses and commercial associations, for example, Hurley explained that rather than focusing only on sales volume, managers should determine the costs and revenues of each specific product line and distribute the overhead expenses accordingly. The manual demonstrated bookkeeping methods to actuate product line expense reports.[24]

Uniform cost accounting standardized methods to calculate prices and, thereby, influenced what constituted a fair price according to both the informal rules promulgated by trade associations and the standards enforced through FTC prosecutions. The notion of an enforceable standard of fair competition required basic bookkeeping before the FTC could sufficiently regulate trade practices or act as a clearinghouse for industry information. Training "industrial secretaries" became a focal point of USCC meetings. Paul Cherington, an economist and marketing professor at the Harvard Graduate School of Business Administration, as it was then known, led a special committee on retail prices and cost accounting for the Chamber. For Cherington and other progressive economists and businesspeople, unfair competition carried a destructive edge that cut against independent proprietors. "Destructive" or "cutthroat" practices included secret rebates given to large-scale retailers, sales below cost, and loss leader advertising. These activities, they argued, threatened the long-term viability of competitive markets for quality consumer durables by reducing the number of competitors.[25] Cherington, along with Paul Nystrom (a Wisconsin-educated economist), embraced Brandeisian logic that valued a decentralized economic order and endorsed antitrust exemptions for associations of small proprietors.

Although the institutionalists did not promote restrictions on firm size or scope, they shared progressive liberals' fears that concentrated economic power might lead to predatory practices and monopoly. Searching for a middle ground between conceding to oligopolies of large firms and preserving inefficient firms, the institutionalists' public-private regulatory approach to protecting competitive markets reflected the policy preferences of Louis Brandeis, an architect of the FTC. Those efforts to manage market competition through trade association rulemaking that often bordered on collusive behavior also provoked the ire of some dominant firms. For example, Percy Straus of Macy's, a chain department store based in New York, led efforts against Resale Price Maintenance, a coordinating device used by small and independent proprietors to standardize brand name prices across all retail outlets.[26]

The administrative reordering of public and private interests informed not only President Wilson's stance on domestic competition policy but also mobilization efforts during the First World War. Both progressive economists and leading businesspeople participated in wartime planning efforts, many of whom became advocates for codes of fair competition and greater collaboration between government and business to rationalize markets through standardized business practices and information sharing. Yet, the wartime experience did not create a fully institutionalized order. Initially, smaller businesses had begun efforts at voluntary war preparedness, and later, Bernard Baruch, chairman of the War Industries Board (WIB), led efforts for "cooperative committees of industry."[27] The WIB did not authorize outright price fixing, although military purchasing bureaus enforced price restrictions. It left an ambiguous legacy—it relied on the voluntary collaboration of trade associations and government regulators, creating neither a fully coordinated nor a cartelized economy.

The war's legacy strengthened the appeal of public-private management of competitive industries as a viable model for American regulation and antitrust reform, especially for small and medium-sized firms for whom corporate consolidations appeared most threatening. The war's celebrated legacy of the social control of business galvanized both institutional economists and administrative regulators interested in rationalizing business interactions to institute social and economic reforms.[28] But the FTC's renewed attention to trade association activities and policing competitive business practices almost immediately provoked a jurisdictional dispute with the Court, regarding which branch of government could determine what constituted unfair trade practices.[29] Despite the Court's ruling that narrowed the FTC's authority, businesspeople within the USCC and regulators at the FTC and Department of Commerce continued to pursue rulemaking authority through administrative interventions.

The wartime experience strengthened the institutionalists' research agenda and broadened the appeal of private businesses partnering with public administrative agencies as beneficial to both private concerns and public interest. This confluence of factors helped to rework the conceptual category of market competition. By the 1920s, a distinctly American view of "new economics" captured prominent economic departments, business schools, government bureaus, and USCC debates. Advocates envisioned a system of cooperative capitalism that managed production and consumption so as to maintain price stability, facilitate innovation, and ensure fair play among competitors.

Through the 1920s, this program for managing American competition became part of the administrative role of the Department of Commerce and FTC. With Herbert Hoover at the helm of the Department of Commerce, he took over many of the standardization, conservation, and information-sharing efforts first initiated by the WIB and carried these into peacetime. In his role as US Food Administrator during the war, Hoover had led a team of businesspeople and economic experts to coordinate production and distribution of foodstuffs abroad. "Food will win the war," he promised the USCC.[30] Indeed the widespread success of wartime industry coordination helped popularize the associational movement, not for price controls per se but certainly for the continuation of information sharing and standardization programs. In July of 1921, the Commerce Department began publishing a monthly *Survey of Current Business*, a collection of industry statistics on bids, prices, quantities sold, and orders. The *Survey* lent authority to the "open price association" model, which had received support from Louis Brandeis and Arthur Jerome Eddy a decade earlier as a method by which trade associations might mitigate the so-called ruinous competition through mandatory information sharing.[31] Similarly, Hoover helped reform the Census Bureau to gather and disseminate economic statistics for both private businesses and public regulators. The Government Printing Office published endless pamphlets and manuals on cost accounting, industry standards and statistics, and business cycle reports.[32]

Hoover's influence reached beyond the Department of Commerce as well, extending to the FTC and Department of Justice by mid-decade. Under his leadership, a series of government-sponsored conferences brought together businesspeople, public officials, and reformers to address a range of business problems, including overfishing Alaskan salmon, oil by-products in the Chesapeake Bay, and highway safety. By the mid-1920s, the FTC began hosting industry-wide trade practice conferences, building on the engineer's conviction that standardized practices could eliminate waste in production methods and employment fluctuations. These conferences were intended to rationalize business practices and set standards for what constituted fair competition.

Hoover's close economic aide, Wesley Mitchell, urged the Commerce Secretary to consider how these social costs of doing business were transferred onto the public at large.[33] Hoover's interest in reducing waste and rationalizing industry coincided with Mitchell's institutional agenda to reduce the costs of industry. Although Hoover did not endorse direct economic interventions in most cases, he expanded the federal government's sphere of influence over business through data collection, tabulation, and distribution. Moreover, as chairman of President Harding's Committee on Recent Economic Changes, he adopted Mitchell's language of "social experimentation" to alleviate unemployment endemic to business cycle swings. Although Hoover agreed that capriciousness of the market led to labor unrest and unemployment, transferring social costs from business to society, he was not prepared to accept institutionalists' proposed labor legislation. Nevertheless, the fact-finding missions of the Committee on Recent Economic Changes as well as the capacity building of administrative agencies influenced the range of policy proposals available to President Franklin Roosevelt's first administration.

Despite his initial efforts, Hoover could not stifle Department of Justice prosecutions of such loose combinations under Attorney General Harry Daugherty's leadership; however, Hoover did outlast him. When Daugherty stepped down in April 1924, President Calvin Coolidge nominated Harlan Fiske Stone to replace him. A friend of Hoover and progressive economists alike, Stone, who would join the Supreme Court only a year later, initiated test cases against trade associations in order to clarify what industry cooperation would pass constitutional muster. For example, Stone brought an antitrust suit against the Maple Flooring Manufacturers Association for information sharing on production processes, bids, and output. Then, one year later, as a newly appointed Court Justice, he penned the Court's opinion upholding the association agreements. The trade associations, according to Stone's majority opinion, had collaborated to reduce waste and had also reduced prices, relative to nonmembers. Also, the Court held, the association's collaboration with the Department of Commerce provided important information to the Federal Reserve and other departments of government.[34] Although the institutionalists had not formalized a theory of public-private management of competitive markets, a shift in the American regulatory system had taken place by the mid-1920s.[35]

Academic Experts and Intermediary Organizations

The attention given to Hoover's Department of Commerce obscures the role of a wide range of advocates in public service and private research institutes who also fostered a public-private system of managed competition.[36] The popularity of institutionalist research methods and goals to rationalize internal management and stabilize inter-firm competition spread to leading research universities and institutes. Animated by a belief in the responsibility of business to society and the possibility for new forms of social control, a loosely coordinated movement arose across a variety of newly established research organizations, including Harvard Business School (HBS), the National Bureau of Economic Research (NBER), and the Social Science Research Council (SSRC). These private organizations pursued industry-specific studies to better understand competitive practices and the price-cost relationship according to industry-specific production and distribution methods. Studies focused on the methods used to coordinate industrial development through uniform cost accounting, standardized production and grading systems, and codes of ethics affecting prices and wages. Indeed, there was great hope that rationalizing intra-firm management through research-based rules might stem business cycles, reduce waste, and provide a more equitable system of competition, minimizing social costs. These intra-firm management techniques were often codified by trade associations and sanctioned by FTC regulators, particularly when sponsored through FTC trade practice conferences. Ultimately, these research centers helped establish organizational and professional authority by disassociating such coordinating tactics with private self-interest or cartelization. Instead, research and publicity supported association-based cooperation as an alternative to both free market competition and state socialism.

The Harvard Graduate School of Business Administration promised a new era of business organization and managerial efficiency achieved through expert accountants and managers, which it publicized to the US Chamber of Commerce. For example, Paul Cherington explained, the business school's course "Commercial Organization" had developed its "own system of uniform cost accounting," which "trained recruits" mastered in banking, railroad rate making, commercial law, and general accounting.[37] Students attended discursive lectures by professors and industry leaders and then performed fieldwork as an apprentice of sorts. The scientific accounting methods of these "commercial secretaries" explained pricing policies and provided important legal defense for price protection policies by a single firm or a group of firms. Instituting a uniform system of cost accounting became one of the most important prerequisites to coordinating business group best practices.[38]

The Harvard Bureau of Business Research had been established "for the purpose of assembling and classifying business data and establishing … standards and principles of business action." The school employed the institutionalist research methods, and many of its early leaders subscribed the movement's progressive policy agenda.[39] From its outset, Dean Edwin Gay, a trained institutional economist, complained that "no accounting and statistical standard existed" especially in retail management, where competition between chain stores and independent proprietors frequently drove prices below the latter's costs. The political backlash provoked by highly competitive industries had encouraged campaigns for protective legislation and a sincere questioning of whether or not concentration and consolidation benefited consumers in the long run.

Gay steered Harvard's directors to conduct its first study in the retail distribution of shoes. Given that industry's relatively standardized and stable production methods, retail management techniques could be isolated and analyzed.[40] The "Harvard System" developed a cooperative framework of information sharing—600 participating shoe retailers from across the country submitted sales data to the Bureau's statisticians, who created standard accounting methods and principles. They measured each store's gross profits, total operating expenses (excluding freight, cartage, and interest), buying expenses, sales force, advertising, deliveries, rent, interest, stockturns per year, and annual sales of the average salesperson. The Bureau, then, calculated percentages for each category and circulated comparative charts to show how the least and most profitable businesses operated.[41] The data showed how firm management dictated prices and profitability. Additionally, the data provided the requisite information to sufficiently identify predatory practices, which associations might prohibit. Similarly, Edwin Gay later partnered with the progressive liberal business leader, Henry Dennison, to advance voluntary reforms to corporate governance in support of profit-sharing plans and pension plans.[42] Social science investigations could be used to improve business management techniques as well as to expose the social costs and benefits of competing systems.

During the war, Mitchell had envisioned creating a nonpartisan institute to provide serviceable social science data for both public and private management purposes; antitrust law, however, presented an obstacle. It was not clear what information-sharing constituted an attempt to restrain trade.[43] Under Mitchell's guidance, the NBER partnered with the Department of Commerce and the FTC for information gathering purposes. The accumulation and analysis of such knowledge, Mitchell argued, required permanent public and private institutions to support social science research and guide public policies.[44]

That relationship with government continued after the war; at the behest of Secretary of Commerce Herbert Hoover, Mitchell received an invitation to participate in President Warren Harding's Conference on Unemployment in 1921. Mitchell joined the business cycle committee, along with Owen Young (chairman, General Electric), Joseph Defrees (president, Chamber of Commerce), Matthew Woll (American Federation of Labor), Mary Van Kleeck (Russell Sage Foundation). To avoid future economic recessions, the committee's final report called for greater information sharing between business and government for the purpose of private and public planning.

> The best service Government can render is to collect the necessary information to show us what the present situation in business is, what current trends are, to collect comparatively simple statistics from a very wide circle of industries, to put it in effective form and then make use of it by the business public.[45]

Mitchell, who had been a founding member of the institutional economics school, was perhaps one of the best experts to reach out to the business community and explain the micro- and macroeconomic benefits of cooperative research, rulemaking, and economic planning. His book, *Business Cycles* (1913), had famously explained economic downturns as the result of endogenous shocks that reverberated throughout the economy.[46] He had categorized the variables that determine profits, revenue, and costs, and he explained how each variable responded to stages of a cycle. Mitchell's study concluded that "during the revivals prices of labor rise less than prices of commodities."[47] This wage lag created a problem of underconsumption that could retard recovery.

As a result of his academic work and participation on the conference committee, Mitchell supported "social experimentation" in private and public unemployment insurance programs to protect workers during economic downturns.[48] While not all conference participants embraced unemployment relief and insurance plans, Mitchell urged Hoover to embrace relief in order to achieve recovery. Hoover took credit for creating unemployment branch offices in states with severe unemployment; those offices then partnered with federal agencies.[49] The conference recommendations reflected institutionalists' concerns with uncoordinated economic activities leading to problematic social consequences, like unemployment and waste of natural resources, which required government oversight and coordination of private sector business decisions. The final report also brought together multiple disciplines to achieve macroeconomic stability, appealing to economists, businessmen, statisticians, and social workers. Mitchell remained a part of Hoover's Commerce Department, acting as a lead economist to the Advisory Committee on Statistics aiding in the Department's *Current Survey*.[50]

In addition to the NBER, several other private and university-based research institutes emerged in this period. In 1923, Charles Merriam, a professor of political science, established the Social Science Research Council (SSRC) at the University of Chicago. The SSRC employed similar empirical methods and, by the early 1930s, became influential in national political economy. Like Mitchell, Merriam rejected the rational man theory of value in neoclassical economics. Instead, he pioneered quantitative studies on individual decision making that could be aggregated in order to better understand how democracies think, so to speak. He envisioned these data being particularly useful to political leaders and their social scientist advisors.[51] Ultimately, he is credited with founding the behavioralist approach to the practice of politics, which, similar to institutionalist economics, employed modern psychology and statistical research to understand individual choice and pluralist decision making. His goal with the SSRC and later organizations, such as the Public Administration Clearing House, was to improve government administration through social science research so as to achieve democratic ends, charting a path between free market capitalism and state socialism.[52] Also like Mitchell, those goals brought him back to federal government service, both within President Hoover's Research Committee on Social Trends, in 1929, and President Franklin Roosevelt's National Planning Board, in 1933.[53]

Each of these organizations brought the social sciences closer to business management and public policy making, though in distinct ways. HBS sought to professionalize business management not only in the pursuit of profits but also toward the public interest. NBER's goal to gather and disseminate micro- and macroeconomic data to mitigate business cycles brought its economists in direct contact with both business leaders and policy makers. Likewise, the SSRC's research agenda focused on minimizing the social costs of American capitalism through economic reforms aimed at raising social minima. Although each attempted to retain its impartiality, the thin line between scientific management and social economic planning blurred as social scientists moved between groups, cross-pollinating ideas and institutions.

***

For institutionalists like Mitchell, Hamilton, and JM Clark, institutionalism affirmed that business was broadly "affected with a public interest."[54] Institutionalists also espoused a firm commitment to deliberative processes, following their commitment to social scientific inquiry, economic measurement, and fact-gathering.[55] From that developed the managerial economics of pricing behavior of firms, macro studies of business cycles, organizational theories of ownership and corporate governance, and public-private designs for competition policy. The theme of social control runs throughout each of these categories of inquiry. The idea of social control of business steered institutionalists to develop government regulation toward socially desirable outcomes. This diverse group chose different routes to that end. Hamilton, for example, joined the Yale Law School and focused his efforts on constitutional arguments to abandon the legal formalism of yesteryear.[56] He remained firmly an antitruster who believed in the public-private tradition of managed competition. He reentered government service as an assistant attorney general to Thurman Arnold in 1938. Mitchell continued to gather data and direct research initiatives at the NBER and proposed modest indicative planning.

The crisis of the Great Depression created a catalyst for social-political change in the USA, and under these circumstances policy makers, regulators, and business leaders drew from existing paradigms of economic management. The influence of a more radical strand of institutionalists peaked during the First New Deal with the National Industrial Recovery Act, but outright price fixing failed to pass constitutional muster. Nevertheless, institutional economics and the vision of managed competition as a public-private exchange persisted through piecemeal legislation in the Second New Deal. But it was the continued authority of the FTC as the manager of competition, evolving through administrative law rather than statutory mandate, which provided its truly lasting legacy.[57]

Public-private cooperation between regulators and business groups—for better or worse—has become embedded in American state-building. In addition to various trade associations' success at coordinating industry standards, information sharing on costs and prices, and intra-group monitoring, businesspeople learned that greater political power and legitimacy resulted from collaborating with academics and government officials. But this was not a straightforward "capture" story.[58] These coalitions promulgated a vision for managed competition that must be understood as resulting from that interwar cooperation. In other words, we cannot understand the interest group story of managed competition without appreciating how an alternative vision of American capitalism resulted from an ongoing exchange between institutional economists, public regulators, and private research institutes. We cannot understand the complexity or contingency of US political economy without recognizing the plurality of visions for American capitalism that rejected free market competition but yet did not embrace state socialism either. Within these interstices, the institutionalists helped build the modern American system of public and private economic governance.

Notes

1. John M. Clark, *Social Control Business* (Chicago: University of Chicago Press, 1926). On institutional economics, see Malcolm Rutherford, *The Institutionalist Movement in American Economics, 1918–1947: Science and Social Control* (Cambridge: Cambridge University Press, 2011); Geoffrey Martin Hodgson, *The Evolution of Institutional Economics: Agency, Structure, and Darwinism in American Institutionalism* (New York: Routledge, 2004).
2. Clark, *Social Control*, 65.
3. Herbert Hovenkamp, *Enterprise and American Law, 1836–1937* (Cambridge, MA: Harvard University Press, 1991); Barbara H. Fried, *The Progressive Assault on Laissez Faire: Robert Hale and the First Law and Economics Movement* (Cambridge, MA: Harvard University Press, 1998).
4. See Mark Blaug, *Economic Theory in Retrospect*, 4th ed. (Cambridge, 1985); Malcolm Rutherford, "Understanding Institutionalist Economics: 1918–1929," *Journal of the History of Economic Thought* 22 (2000): 277–308. The conventional history of the institutionalist movement portrays it as disjointed and incoherent; however, Rutherford and other revisionists argue that "institutionalism was associated with a particular research agenda that must, at the time, have seemed full of promise and excitement." Ibid., 278.
5. William J. Novak, *The People's Welfare: Law and Regulation in Nineteenth-Century America* (Chapel Hill: University of North Carolina Press, 1996); Brian Balogh, *A Government Out of Sight: The Mystery of National Authority in Nineteenth-Century America* (Cambridge: Cambridge University Press, 2009). Both Balogh and Novak have demonstrated the long-standing public-private tradition of American governance. This paper emphasizes new methods of public-private economic regulation through administrative agencies and trade associations.
6. "Program for the Thirty-First Annual Meeting," *American Economic Review* 9 (March 1919): 1–4.
7. Rutherford referred to Hamilton's "work on law and economics, industrial organization, and the social control of industry [as] one of the most important lines of institutionalist work." Rutherford, *Institutionalist Movement*, 12.

8. Walton H. Hamilton, "The Institutional Approach to Economic Theory," *AER* 9 (1919): 309–18. The discussants were well-positioned to focus on the postwar adjustments: W.W. Stewart (War Industries Board), L.H. Haney (FTC), and B.M. Anderson, Jr. (National Bank of Commerce).
9. Ibid., 310.
10. Ibid., 311.
11. Ibid., 312–13. "Since the neo-classical doctrine has passed into the inheritance, the formal defense of laissez faire is gone, though it still lingers implicitly in terms and the statement of propositions. Formally it is concerned with the mechanical way in which the values of goods and of shares in distribution emerge in the market. But it has no concern with the organization of that market, the nature of the transactions which occur there, or the less immediate facts of the distribution of opportunity, property, and leisure upon which the size of these shares rest. Its explanatory terms are not matters subject to control." Ibid., 313.
12. Ibid.
13. For example Clark, *Social Control Business*; Sumner Slichter, "The Organization and Control of Economic Activity," in *The Trend of Economics*, ed. Rexford Tugwell (New York: Knopf, 1924); Dexter Keezer and Stacy May, *Public Control of Business: A Study of Antitrust law Enforcement, Public Interest Regulation, and Government Participation in Business* (New York: Harper & Bros., 1930); and Morris Copeland (Ph.D. dissertation, 1921, unpublished manuscript).
14. Wesley Mitchell, *Business Cycles* (Berkeley: University of California Press, 1913). See also Mitchell, "Unemployment and Business Fluctuations," *American Labor Legislation Review* 13 (1923): 15–22, recommending "social experimentation" in unemployment relief to ease the postwar adjustments.
15. Thorstein Veblen (1898), "Why Is Economics Not an Evolutionary Science?," reprinted in *The Place of Science in Modern Civilization* (New York, 1919), 73; Wesley Mitchell, "The Role of Money in Economic Theory," *AER* 6 (March 1916): 140–61.
16. John Maurice Clark contributed to Mitchell's theory of business cycles with his explanation of the "acceleration principle," wherein changes in the economy's rate of growth place disproportionate pressure on capital goods producers as compared to consumer goods producers. See John

M. Clark, "Business Acceleration and the Law of Demand," *Journal of Political Economy* 15, no. 3 (March 1917): 217–35.

17. See also Malcolm Rutherford, "Institutionalism and the Social Control of Business," *History of Political Economy* 47 (ann. supp.) (2015): 77–98.
18. Fried, *Assault on Laissez Faire*, 5–10; Kyle Bruce, "Activist Management: Henry S. Dennison's Institutional Economics," *Journal of Economic Issues* 40 (December 2006): 1113–36.
19. *Price and Price Policies*, ed. Walton Hamilton and Associates (New York: McGraw-Hill Book Co., 1938), 23.
20. See Arthur Robert Burns, "Review of *Price and Price Policies*, ed. Walton Hamilton and Associates," *Political Science Quarterly* 53 (September 1938): 425–28; Blaug, *Economic Theory*, 703.
21. President Wilson, "The Opportunity of the National Chamber of Commerce," *Chamber Records* (February 3, 1915): 78–81, 80.
22. Joseph Davies, "The Federal Trade Commission," *Chamber Records*, Hagley Archive, Accession No. 1960, Series I (February 4, 1915): 155–63, 163. [Hereafter *Chamber Records*.]
23. Edward Nash Hurley, *Helpful Activities to Strengthen American Business* (Washington, DC: Government Printing Office, 1916).
24. Berk, *Brandeis and Regulated Competition*, 121–30. Hurley sent out the FTC publication, *Fundamentals of the Cost System* (Washington, DC: Government Printing Office, 1916); *Annual Report of the Federal Trade Commission* (Washington, DC: Government Printing Office, 1916), 15.
25. Paul Cherington, "Preliminary Report," *Chamber Records* (February 4, 1915), 347–63; Cherington, "Maintenance of Resale Prices," ibid. (February 10, 1916), 210–40.
26. "Minority Report," *Chamber Records* (February 10, 1916), 215–71; House Committee on Interstate and Foreign Commerce, *To Prevent Discrimination in Prices and to Provide for Publicity of Prices to Dealers and the Public: Hearings*, 63rd Cong., 2nd sess., on H.R. 13305, February 27, 1914–January 9, 1915 (Washington: Government Printing Office, 1915).
27. Robert D. Cuff, *The War Industries Board: Business-Government Relations During World War I* (Baltimore: The Johns Hopkins Press, 1973).

28. J. Maurice Clark, Walton Hamilton, and Harold Moulton, eds., *Readings in the Economics of War* (Chicago: University of Chicago Press, 1918); Charles Van Hise, *Conservation and Regulation in the United States During the War* (Washington: Government Printing Office, 1918).
29. *FTC v. Gratz*, 253 U.S. 421 (1920), limiting FTC authority to prosecute antitrust abuses already deemed illegal by law or Court precedent.
30. Herbert Hoover, *Chamber Records* (September 19, 1917), 127–31.
31. See Brandeis, "The Democracy of Business," *Chamber Records* (February 12, 1914), 168–72, 168; Arthur Jerome Eddy, *The New Competition: An Examination of the Conditions Underlying the Radical Change That Is Taking Place in the Commercial and Industrial World—The Change Taking Place from a Competitive to a Cooperative Basis* (Chicago: A.C. McClurg & Co., 1917).
32. "Progress in the Elimination of Waste," in *The Fourteenth Annual Report of the Secretary of Commerce* (Washington, DC: Government Printing Office, 1927).
33. Wesley C. Mitchell, "What Is Stabilization?," *Chamber Records* (April 29, 1931): 117–22, 118.
34. *Maple Flooring Manufacturers' Assn. v. U.S.*, 268 U.S. 563 (1925), 574, 576.
35. William J. Barber, *From New Era to New Deal: Herbert Hoover, the Economists, and American Economic Policy, 1921–1933* (Cambridge: Cambridge University Press, 1985), 2–4.
36. Ellis W. Hawley, "Herbert Hoover, the Commerce Secretariat, and the Vision of an 'Associative State,' 1921–1928," *Journal of American History* 61 (June 1974): 116–40; Robert F. Himmelberg, *The Origins of the National Recovery Administration: Business, Government, and the Trade Association Issue, 1921–1933*, 2nd ed. (New York: Fordham University Press, 1993).
37. Paul T. Cherington, "Training Industrial Secretaries," *Chamber Records* (February 11, 1914): 83–85, 83.
38. On the history of Harvard Business School and its changing curriculum and mission, see Rakesh Kurana, *From Higher Aims to Hired Hands: The Social Transformation of American Business Schools and the Unfulfilled Promise of Management as a Profession* (Princeton: Princeton University Press, 2007).

39. Arthur E. Swanson, "The Harvard Bureau of Business Research," *Journal of Political Economy* 22 (November 1914): 896–900, 896. Swanson, an economics professor at Northwestern University, provided a prescient critique of the Bureau's importance. "The development by the Harvard Bureau of a distinct co-operative plan of organization for conducting business research should be recognized as a valuable contribution in itself. This plan, modified in particulars as a result of further experience, will doubtless serve as the basis for the inauguration of research activities by other institutions." Ibid., 899.
40. Ibid., 897. See also: "Systematizing Drug Store Expense," *Pharmaceutical Era* 47 (April 1914): 143–44.
41. Ibid., 900.
42. Kyle Bruce, "Activist Management: Henry S. Dennison's Institutional Economics," *Journal of Economic Issues* 40 (December 2006): 1113–36, 1129.
43. See Edwin R. A. Seligman and Robert A. Love, *Price Cutting and Price Maintenance: A Study in Economics* (New York: Harper & Brothers Publishers, 1932). This study cataloged all federal cases dealing with information sharing on prices.
44. Jeff Biddle, "Social Science and the Making of Social Policy: Wesley Mitchell's Vision," in *The Economic Mind in America: Essays in the History of American Economics*, ed. Malcolm Rutherford (New York, 1998), 43–79, 46. See also Mitchell, *Business Cycles*, 588–96.
45. Mitchell, *Chamber Records* (May 15, 1922), 632–39, 636.
46. Howard Sherman, "The Business Cycle Theory of Wesley Mitchell," *Journal of Economic Issues* 35 (March 2001): 85–97, 88.
47. Ibid., 90. Mitchell, *Business Cycles* (1913, 1989), 16.
48. See Wesley Mitchell, "Unemployment and Business Fluctuations," *American Labor Legislation Review* 13 (March 1923): 15–22, 18.
49. Herbert Hoover, *Memoirs of Herbert Hoover*, vol. 2 (New York: Macmillan, 1937), 41–42.
50. "Country's Business Continues to Increase," *Wall Street Journal* (December 8, 1921), 2. See also Barber, *New Era to New Deal*, 8. Hoover's Advisory Committee on Statistics included Mitchell, "Edwin R.A. Seligman ([Professor of Economics] Columbia University), Allyn A. Young ([Professor of Economics] Harvard), Walter F. Willcox ([Professor of Economics and Statistics] Cornell), Carroll W. Doten ([Professor of Economics] Massachusetts Institute of Technology), Edwin F. Gay

(then president of the *New York Evening Post*, who had formerly served as the first dean of the Harvard Business School), and William S. Rossiter (formerly the head of the U.S. Census Bureau)."

51. Patrick Reagan, *Designing a New America: The Origins of New Deal Planning, 1890–1943* (Amherst: University of Massachusetts Press, 1999), 72–73.
52. See Charles Merriam, *The Making of Citizens: A Comparative Study of Methods of Civic Training* (Chicago: University of Chicago Press, 1931), for an assessment of European state socialism that is both laudatory of its public goals and critical of the means used to achieve them. See also James Kloppenberg and Richard W. Fox, *A Companion to American Thought* (New York: Wiley-Blackwell, 1995), 449.
53. Reagan, *Designing a New America*, 75.
54. Walton Hamilton, "Affectation with Public Interest," *Yale Law Journal* 39 (June 1930): 1089–112. See Harry Scheiber, "The Road to *Munn*: Eminent Domain and the Concept of Public Purpose in the State Courts," *Perspectives in American History* 5 (1971): 327–402.
55. Dorothy Ross, *The Origins of American Social Science* (Cambridge: Cambridge University Press, 1991), 213. This is also where mainstream institutionalists departed from Veblen's use of evolutionary theory, which did not leave room for social guidance and legislative reform. See Rutherford, *Institutionalist Movement*, 38–39, 44; Rutherford, "Morris Copeland: A Case Study in the History of Institutional Economics," *Journal of the History of Economic Thought* 24 (September 2002): 261–90.
56. Hamilton, "The Regulation of Employment Agencies," *Yale Law Journal* 38 (December 1928): 225–35; Hamilton, "Affectation with Public Interest"; Hamilton, "The Control of Big Business," *The Nation* 134 (May 25, 1932): 591–93. See also Clark, *Social Control of Business*.
57. Sumner Kittelle and Elmer Mostow, "A Review of the Trade Practice Conferences of the Federal Trade Commission," *George Washington Law Review* 8 (1939–1940): 427–51.
58. William Novak, "A Revisionist History of Regulatory Capture," in *Preventing Regulatory Capture: Special Interest Influence and How to Limit It*, ed. Daniel Carpenter and David Moss (The Tobin Project, 2013).

Author Biography

Laura Phillips Sawyer is an Assistant Professor in the Business, Government, and International Economy Unit at Harvard Business School. Laura's work has appeared in *Business History Review, Journal for the Gilded Age and Progressive Era*, and *Capital Gains: Business and Politics in the 20th Century* (2016). Her book *American Fair Trade: Proprietary Capitalism, Corporatism, and the "New Competition," 1890–1940*, has been recently published by Cambridge University Press.

Punishment, Political Economy, and the Genealogy of Morals

Bernard E. Harcourt

Introduction

In previous research on *The Illusion of Free Markets*, I tried to demonstrate how the emergence of liberal economic ideas in the eighteenth century was inextricably linked to the idea of a strong police state, and how this relation has influenced our current political condition of massive, racialized over-incarceration.[1] In that work, I tried to document simultaneously, first, the *diachronic* evolution of two historical ideas—namely that of the free market on the one hand (represented by the left column in the diagram below) and of the police state on the other (the right column)—and, second, the *synchronic* linkage at each historical stage of these two necessarily imbricated notions:

The analysis explored, on the one hand, how the concept of the free market emerged from eighteenth-century notions of "natural order." It traced the transformations and variations from an early divine notion

B.E. Harcourt (✉)
Columbia University, New York, USA
e-mail: bernard.harcourt@columbia.edu

R. Fredona and S.A. Reinert (eds.), *New Perspectives on the History of Political Economy*, https://doi.org/10.1007/978-3-319-58247-4_13

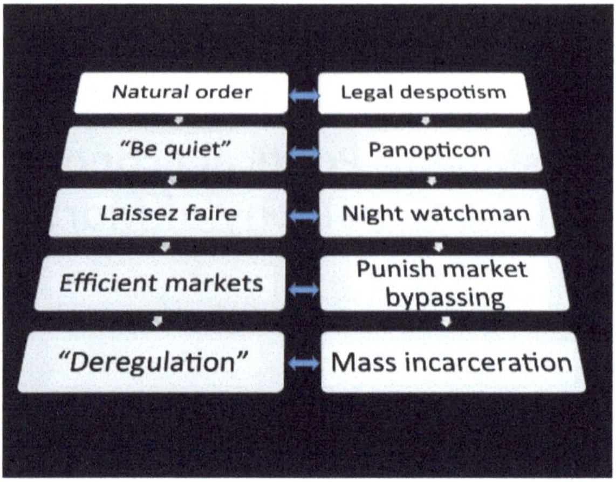

of orderliness tied to natural law in the work of François Quesnay and the physiocrats, through Jeremy Bentham's (admittedly complicated and messy) maxim that the government should "Be Quiet" in economic affairs, through the more secular ideas of self-interest, expertise, and informational advantage reflected in conventional nineteenth-century *laissez-faire* ideas, to the cybernetic notions of "spontaneous order" elaborated by Friedrich Hayek, and finally to the more scientific and highly technical economic theories of the Chicago School of Economics regarding the efficiency of competitive markets. This is the left column.

On the other hand, the analysis demonstrated how these varying notions of economic orderliness have been linked, since their inception and at each stage, with a paradoxical trust in governmental competence when it comes to policing and punishing. This latter concept of the police state, just like the idea of the free market, evolved over time, from early notions of "legal despotism" in Quesnay's writings[2] and in the policing practices of Le Mercier de la Rivière when he was *Intendant* of Martinique (paradoxically, his parting gift to the island was a police force); through the omnipresent, pervasive intervention of the state in Bentham's *panopticon* prison and criminal-law writings (recall that Bentham viewed the penal code as a "grand menu of prices" and invented the *panopticon* for all sorts of institutions of social control, including penitentiaries, asylums, workhouses, etc.); to the conventional nineteenth-century notion of the state as "nightwatchman" in the classical *laissez-faire* approach (the metaphor had never struck me, in fact, until I hit upon this genealogy); to the symbiotic function of the criminal law to efficient competitive markets in Chicago School theory. As my colleague Richard Posner would write, in 1985, precisely capturing this symbiotic relationship:

> The major function of criminal law in a capitalist society is to prevent people from bypassing the system of voluntary, compensated exchange—the "market," explicit or implicit—in situations where, because transaction costs are low, the market is a more efficient method of allocating resources than forced exchange... When transaction costs are low, the market is, virtually by definition, the most efficient method of allocating resources. Attempts to bypass the market will therefore be discouraged by a legal system bent on promoting efficiency.[3]

In fact, Posner would *define* crime as inefficient behavior or market bypassing in 1985. Just like legal despotism in physiocratic thought, the criminal law represents the outer boundary of the free market and natural order. Penal law is its diametrical other, where the state must intervene through punitive practices in order to sustain and guarantee the natural orderliness of the economic domain or free market. This is the right column.

Throughout, the analysis sought to demonstrate the paradoxical linkage of the notion of orderliness in economics with the need for a Big Brother state when it comes to policing and punishing. This is the series of synchronic arrows relating the two diachronic series. In contrast to other critical thinkers who also study what has been called "neoliberal penality" today—namely, the paradox of a supposedly hands-off government and a massive prison apparatus—I argue that the symbiotic relationship preceded the neoliberal turn in the 1970s and was itself inscribed in early liberal thought in the eighteenth century. I resist Loïc Wacquant's suggestion that "the expansive penal state is the distinct creation of *neo*-liberalism, and not an inheritance from or resurgence of classic liberalism."[4] I trace our present political condition further back and argue that this paradoxical set of beliefs—on the one hand, in the incompetence of government in the economic domain and, on the other hand, in the competence and legitimacy of government in the penal sphere—has facilitated the exponential growth of the prison and jail populations in the USA, not only with mass incarceration in the twenty-first century, but also at the birth of the penitentiary during the "Market Revolution" of the Jacksonian era.

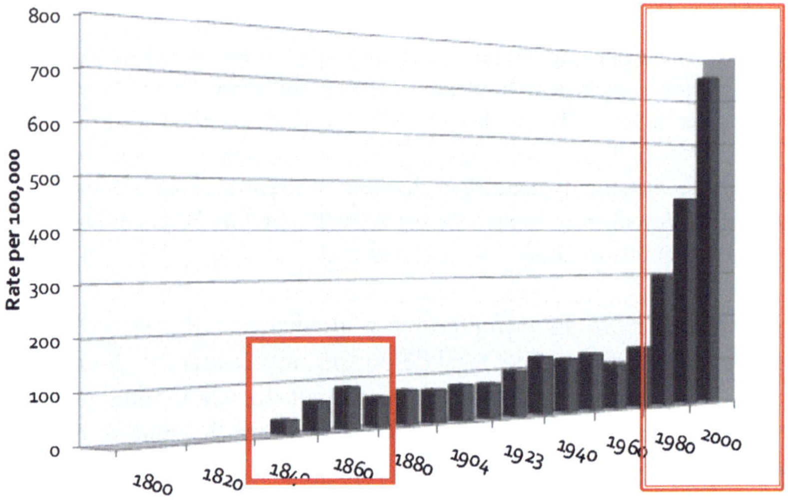

An undercurrent in that work—perhaps one that was too far under the surface, but one that I would like to explore here—concerns the mechanisms and devices by which these concepts of natural order and policing would become accepted, tolerated, and so pervasive. My central concern, throughout, is to explore the production of these truths—more specifically, how they become held as truths. This is especially important in our contemporary times marked by the toxic combination of neoliberalism and mass incarceration. And one vital dimension to this question—one to which we often do not pay sufficient attention—is precisely the issue of moral economies, of the moralization of social relations and behaviors.[5]

One place to start, though this may be surprising, is with E.P. Thompson, whose work on "The Moral Economy of the English

Crowd in the Eighteenth Century," or more generally, on the notion of moral economies, would make us rethink seemingly spontaneous and spasmodic food riots as fully coherent resistance to new forms of economic relations and ideas. Thompson highlighted the extent to which the resistance was itself a *moralized* resistance, grounded in notions of moral fault, responsibility, and blame, of right and wrong, of good and evil. The riots were not merely irregular, spasmodic responses to shortage and hunger; rather, they represented a righteous indignation, a moralistic and thus political response to the shift away from a paternalistic rationality of custom, intended to protect the people, to a purportedly amoral and abstract force of the market. For Thompson, the most compelling proof of the moral underpinnings, you will recall, was that the seditious crowd did not simply steal food, but rather, against their own interests, destroyed the mills, the very instruments that would have provided them with food. The riots, Thompson showed, were aimed at dismantling the instruments of the new political economy.

It should be surprising to start with Thompson because he was moralizing—and justifying—resistance, whereas the task here is rather to show how these new political economies became acceptable and tolerated, in other words to enlist a genealogy of morals as a key element in the eventual acceptance of new economic regimes. These are connected because, sadly, the same crowd that resisted would eventually come to embrace the new spirit of capitalism. But that also would not come naturally, spontaneously, or spasmodically. The men and women of the crowd had to be prepared, tilled, shaped into the kind of subjectivities that would come to embrace the demoralized, free flowing, more fluid market-based and self-interested economies. And this would not happen without a large dose of moralization. In order for it all to become palatable, it had to be made right.

This is where Max Weber—the Nietzschian Weber, the Weber of the *Protestant Ethic* in its original, not Parsonian version—would be so important. The spirit of capitalism would feel so natural to many, like a well-worn glove, because it had been, for many, a calling, as Weber suggested. The ascetic, rationalistic lifestyle, which had been a calling for the Puritans, would become secondhand. "Remember, that *time is money*... Money can beget money, and its offspring can beget more, and so on." Weber's genealogy of capitalism passed through morals—producing new political economies and processes, such as "machine production," that would govern our lives. "[T]he spirit of religious asceticism," Weber wrote, "has escaped from the cage,"[6] but not us, with our materialism and "care for external goods." The modern materialist—the acquisitive capitalist—would remain cloaked in a shell of steel. For how long, or whether forever, Weber could not tell. "No one knows who will live in this cage in the future..."[7] What was for sure, though is that this Nietzschian Weber had utter contempt for these *last men*, these rationalist capitalists, who in their "nullity [imagine] that it has attained a level of civilization never before achieved."[8]

Our Anglo-American reading of Weber's final passage was distorted by Talcott Parsons' translation, with these "last men" becoming, in Parsons' hand, "the last stage"—the Nietzschian reference expunged and cleansed, the genealogy erased, for a while. But only for a while. In the end, though, it is the Nietzschian Weber that returns to show us the extent to which the many are prepared, morally and ethically, for capitalism. The soil has to be tilled; it does not bear the fruit of capitalism spontaneously.

So we have, then, Thompson on the moral economies of resistance, and a Nietzschian Weber on the moral economies of acceptance. Foucault would marry the two in his Collège de France lectures on *The Punitive Society* in the winter of 1973. Foucault would graft a genealogy of morals on a political economy by means of what he called "*illégalismes*."

The core concept of *illégalismes* is a term that has somewhat erroneously been translated as "illegalities" in the English edition of *Discipline and Punish*. It would be more appropriate to use a neologism, such as "*illegalisms*," because "illegalities" is actually the end state, that which, in some sense, resolves the struggle. Illegalities is what represents the culmination of a power struggle that operates through illegalisms.

The idea of illegalisms is that the law itself is a struggle, a negotiation, an agonistic combat, a competition over the very question of defining the line of illegality—the line that divides deviations, disorderliness, rule-breaking, rule-interpretation, from illegality and the sanction.

Foucault elaborated, in 1973, a political economy based on this notion of illegalisms—a theory in three steps. As you realize, I am giving you the theory and not the historical details.

Foucault starts with the idea that illegalisms were widespread throughout the eighteenth century and well distributed across the different strata of society: the different classes practiced strategic games at the borders and interstices of the law. "[I]n every system, different social groups, different classes, different castes each have their illegalisms," Foucault would declare.[9] In the eighteenth century, he would identify not only the popular illegalisms—the illegalisms of the popular classes—but also the illegalisms of merchants and men of commerce, as well as "illegalisms of the privileged who escape by status, tolerance, as an exception to the law," and even illegalisms of power—of *the lieutenant de police*, of the *commissaires*, etc. These illegalisms were nested, sometimes in conflict, often in symbiosis, both working together and in tension. But for the most part, the privileged in the eighteenth century tolerated popular illegalisms because they also practiced their own forms of deviance against the monarchy, and the relationship "worked" in a certain way. "It seems to me that in the late eighteenth century," Foucault said, in February 1973, "a popular illegalism was not only compatible with, but useful to the development of the bourgeois economy. [But] there came a time when these popular illegalisms that had meshed with the development of the economy became incompatible with it."

Second, then, Foucault identifies a break, toward the end of the *ancien régime*. As the nineteenth century approached, the popular illegalisms not only began to be perceived as a threat, a danger by the more privileged in society, the merchants, aristocrats, and bourgeois in France, but also in England and Russia (where Bentham's brother, Samuel, was inventing the *panopticon*). The new forms of wealth accumulation, of moveable goods, of stocks and supplies—as opposed to landed wealth—exposed massive amounts of chattel property to the workers who came in direct contact with this new commercial wealth. The accumulation of wealth began to make popular illegalisms less useful—even dangerous—to the interests of the privileged. "These illegalisms ceased, at a certain time, to be tolerable to the class coming to power, because wealth, in its materiality, was spatialized in new forms …"

Foucault then identifies, in a third moment, a turn to the penal sanction. In the late eighteenth century, the commercial class seized the mechanisms of criminal justice to put an end to these popular illegalisms—not only the depredation of material property and private wealth, but also the "dissipation" of their own time and bodies, of the strength of the workers themselves, of their human capital (dissipation that took "the form of absenteeism, delay, laziness, parties, debauchery, nomadism.") In this way, the privileged would seize the administrative and police apparatus of the late eighteenth century to crack down on popular illegalisms. The result would be a turn to the penitentiary and the prison form—which was not so much a model of confinement for violations of a statute, so much as imprisonment for irregular behavior.

So far, though, we are still at the level of an explanation in political economy. But a genealogy of morals would come next. For it was only through the *moralization* of those acts of debauchery and absenteeism that the managerial classes would be able to transform formerly tolerated behaviors, even encouraged behaviors, into illegal acts.

Foucault would excavate and discover this move first in the writings of the Quakers and other dissenters. He located there a moralized discourse that would introduce the idea of the penitentiary, of penitence, into the sphere of punishment. He found echoes of this discourse among the more privileged classes of the early nineteenth century, echoes revealing how certain writers in France and England—Colquhoun in London, for instance—would use moral notions of fault, guilt, and penance to facilitate the construction of the capitalist enterprise.[10]

The transformation of popular illegalisms into illegalities operates first by means of their conversion into morally reprehensible acts that deserve penance, into moral failings and failures. Foucault unearths these brutal passages, written by early nineteenth-century reformers, about the moral inadequacies and failings of the working class—here, for instance, he minutely dissects this text by a jurist and reformer from the Napoleonic era regarding revisions to the penal code, a brutal text referring to the popular classes as that "bastardized race":

> There, hard souls, dry, fierce, devoid of moral ideas, will only obey their gross sensations; laziness, immorality, greed, envy will prove the irreconcilable enemies of wisdom and labor, of the economy and of property. There will thrive misdemeanors and crimes of all kinds, less in the masses of the nation than in the dregs of the foreign tribe in general, which is formed next to the real people by the force of circumstances and habits accumulated for centuries. Almost always, for such a nation, the punishments must be measured against the nature of this bastardized race, which is the source of crimes, and the regeneration of which can barely be glimpsed, after many years of the wisest government.
>
> Là, des âmes dures, sèches, farouches, dénuées d'idées morales, n'obéiront qu'à leurs grossières sensations; la paresse, la débauche, l'avidité, l'envie, se montreront ennemies irréconciliables de la sagesse et du travail, de l'économie et de la propriété. Là, pulluleront des délits et des crimes de toute espèce, moins dans la masse de la nation que dans la lie de cette peuplade étrangère au caractère général, qui s'est formée à côté du vrai peuple par la force des circonstances et des habitudes accumulées pendant des siècles. Presque toujours, pour une telle nation, les peines doivent être mesurées sur la nature de *cette race abâtardie*, qui est le foyer des crimes, et dont la régénération se laisse à peine entrevoir, après une longue suite d'années du gouvernement le plus sage.

Foucault would unearth and dissect this other, equally violent passage from the rural context:

> The peasant is an evil, cunning, ferocious beast, half-civilized; he has neither heart nor integrity, nor honor; he lets himself be led to ferocity, were it not that the other two estates crushed him mercilessly and reduced him to not being able to commit the crime he would want to commit.
>
> Le paysan est un animal méchant, rusé, une bête féroce, à demi-civilisée; il n'a ni coeur, ni probité, ni honneur; il se laisserait souvent entraîner à la férocité, si les deux autres états ne fondaient impitoyablement sur lui et le réduisaient à ne pouvoir exécuter le crime qu'il voudrait faire.

And in a fictitious dialogue between the popular class and the privileged, Foucault asks on behalf of the workers: "What has changed? Did not we together violate the law, and circumvent the rules?" To which the privileged respond, "under the *ancien régime*, we were all together fighting power, unjustifiable abuses of the monarchy, we were taking on sovereign power. But now, you are just attacking private property. Formerly, we fought together against abuse of power. Now, you are violating the law. And it manifests a complete lack of morals." And in his manuscript, Foucault ends this dialogue with a marvelous exclamation: "Allez et faites pénitence."

"Go, and do your penance": this is the moment where Foucault would turn from an archeological method, which had been inadequate to explain the generalization of the prison form, to the genealogical method. For Foucault, the prison form could not be derived from an archaeological examination of the penal theories of the great reformers of the eighteenth century. It traced instead to the moralized notion of penitence.

***

The thesis in *The Illusion of Free Markets* may not have paid sufficient attention to this dimension, namely to the moralization that is necessary for so many of us to swallow neoliberal penality. But it was certainly present. The traces of a moral struggle, of a battle, of what Foucault described in *The Punitive Society* as a civil war, the idea of the criminal as social enemy, these are all over the texts, from the eighteenth to the twentieth centuries.

Beginning with François Quesnay, who referred to "*les hommes pervers,*" "*les voleurs et les méchants.*" Quesnay would write:

> The natural and fundamental laws of societies … imprint themselves on men's hearts, they are the light that illuminates and masters their conscience: this light can only be weakened or obscured by their disordered passions [*leurs passions déréglées*]. The principle object of positive laws is this very disorderliness [*dérèglement*], to which they oppose a severe punishment to those perverse men [*une sanction redoubtable aux hommes pervers*]. For, on the whole, what is it that is truly necessary for the prosperity of a nation? To cultivate the land as successfully as possible and to keep society safe from thieves and evil people [*des voleurs et des méchans*].

The first part is governed by self-interest, the second is entrusted to the civil government.[11]

Dupont de Neumours as well would moralize his discourse. As you may recall, Beccaria had included a chapter on contraband in his little tract from 1764, *On Crimes and Punishments*, where he had advocated severe penalties, including the galleys, for smuggling. "Such a crime deserves a fairly heavy punishment," Beccaria wrote, "even up to imprisonment or penal servitude." In the case of a tobacco smuggler, for instance, Beccaria prescribed a prison regime including "toil and exertion in the excise service which [the smuggler] wished to defraud."

Du Pont's reaction in the *Éphémérides* was visceral and it centered on the moral righteousness associated with private property. To Du Pont, the real criminals are not those who smuggle contraband, but those who regulate commerce: "If there is, then, a true offense that deserves prison and penal servitude, it's not that of the smugglers, but that of the Regulators who have proposed and still propose, who have compelled and still compel the adoption of royal edicts that hamper trade, of fiscal inquisitions, and of monopolistic threats to the natural rights of citizens, to their property, to their civil liberty, deterring useful work, and as fearsome for public as for private wealth." The notion of the "real" criminal, of the "real enemy of society"—this moralization of crime infuses Dupont's response to Beccaria.

Fast forward to the present. Once again, my colleague Richard Posner is another one who does not mince his words. I have often been struck by his statements about criminals—especially about the moral rightness of hating criminals. Posner's personal views surrounding the hatred of criminals are displayed best in his 2012 article on James Fitzjames Stephen titled, "The Romance of Force: James Fitzjames Stephen on Criminal Law."[12] In the course of rehearsing Stephen's views that popular hatred of criminals is morally justified, Posner goes further and develops an entire utilitarian justification for it.

According to Stephen, popular hatred is an important aspect of law, because it motivates the (vengeful) enforcement of justice. If criminal injury did not cause outrage, Stephen reasons, there would be no impetus for revenge through the legal system. Law, he writes, is "an emphatic assertion of the principle that the feeling of hatred and the desire of vengeance … are important elements of human nature which ought … to be satisfied in a regular public and legal manner."[13] Posner notes that it "was natural" to think of criminal justice in terms of personal vengeance in Stephen's day due to the smaller, less-bureaucratized character of criminal justice back then; but Posner then argues that the view is still valid *today* as well. Posner writes, "the criminal law *is* rooted in vengeance. Vengeance is the stage in the control of antisocial behavior that precedes law and leaves its shape upon law." Emotion is what makes law function, in Stephen's time and ours:

> This is still the case, because while our criminal law system (and England's as well) is now dominated by professionals, who chase and prosecute and punish criminals not out of hatred but because they are paid to do those things, these professionals depend heavily on private citizens for aid in enforcement, including crime victims, the victims' families, bystanders, jurors, and others who usually have no pecuniary stake in assisting in the apprehension and prosecution of criminals. The widespread popular support for capital punishment and other severe punishments, and the widespread popular opposition to legislators and judges perceived as "soft on crime," are based to a great extent on hatred of murderers; and so if you fear crime and believe in deterrence, *you think it morally right to hate criminals.*[14]

Posner not only offers an updated justification, he actually apprises us of our own hatred of the criminal: anyone who believes in deterrence, anyone who is in that sense rational, already does hate the criminal and should think it is morally right to do so. In effect, Posner's view regarding the hatred of the criminal is that it serves a moral role insofar as it contributes to a utilitarian calculus that ensures the efficient functioning of legal pursuits. It is a valuable aspect of our social psychology because it provides the impetus for the enforcement of law.

Posner has other interesting things to say about the accused—innocent as well as guilty—particularly in the context of the legal representation of indigent persons:

> I can confirm from my own experience as a judge that indigent defendants are generally rather poorly represented. But if we are to be hardheaded we must recognize that this may not be entirely a bad thing. The lawyers who represent indigent criminal defendants seem to be good enough to reduce the probability of convicting an innocent person to a very low level. If they were much better, either many guilty people would be acquitted or society would have to devote much greater resources to the prosecution of criminal cases. A bare-bones system for the defense of indigent criminal defendants may be optimal.[15]

Gary Becker presented a somewhat more nuanced view, but one that paradoxically also moralized delinquency. Becker, of course, claimed to have extracted all moralization and morality from his theory of crime and punishment, and to have rested it instead purely on economic reasoning. Yet, there remains a clear notion of individual responsibility in his thought—of the placement of responsibility on the individual delinquent. Here, we could turn to his theory of human capital, which retains a notion of individualized responsibility for investments in the self. Each and everyone of us is ultimately responsible for our own returns on investment. In the end, we are each responsible for what happens to us, individually.

Becker revealed this notion of individual responsibility in the first of two conversations we had at the University of Chicago on Foucault's 1978–1979 lectures, *The Birth of Biopolitics*, where Foucault discussed Becker's work. At one juncture in the discussion, Becker was defending the implications of human capital theory, and stated:

> How it links to power relations… well … if I look at the United States, how can I understand what young African-American men are doing? To me, this theory—and I'm not saying I fully understand what they're doing—but the theory says, well, they have a lot of different options available.
>
> What we're pointing out *to them* is, if you drop out of high school in the United States, you're pretty much destined to be unemployed, to have low earnings, to be in poor health, to have low marriage rates, and the like. That's what the theory points out *to them*. And what it then points

> out to them is that you can overcome that in various ways. Not you alone, but with the state and so on. So to me it's a very much uplifting theory, where again, we're putting the individual—what they do—at the center, rather than as the instruments of what others are doing. They're the center. And it's their interaction with each other and with the power relationships that give us the outcomes. So I find it very difficult to agree with the notion that it's a demeaning view of the individual.[16]

Here again, economic rationality has slid into a notion of individual responsibility that has significant moral overtones.

The moralization of criminality and of delinquents has a long, storied, and troubled history in the twentieth century in this country. Katherine Beckett, David Garland, and others have demonstrated how the very category of crime was produced as a political category in the 1960s—in both a racialized and moralized way—as a political response to the Civil Rights gains, and we see reflections of that even today with renewed claims about a supposed "Ferguson Effect."[17] Dorothy Roberts has explored the production of a moralized discourse over "Black criminality" and its role in justifying the massive incarceration of young black men.[18] Others have analyzed the moralized tropes of the "welfare queen" in relation to the evisceration of the welfare state and the shift from welfare to workfare; of the "disorderly" in relation to the Broken-Windows Theory; of the "ne'er-do-well" in relation to parole prediction instruments; or of the "present oriented" in the writings of Edward Banfield—a category that overlapped squarely with race and poverty.[19] The 1960s, especially, were scarred by a moralized discourse that linked race, poverty, and liberalism to violence, crime and immorality. Richard Nixon's acceptance speech in 1968 captures that well:

> For the past five years we have been deluged by Government programs for the unemployed, programs for the cities, programs for the poor, and we have reaped from these programs *an ugly harvest of frustrations, violence and failure across the land.* And now our opponents will be offering more of the same—more billions for Government jobs, Government housing, Government welfare. I say it's time to quit pouring billions of dollars into programs that have failed in the United States of America.

One need only think back to John DiIulio's earlier interventions in the 1990s—a time when he developed (and would later regret) the theory of "superpredator youths," what he referred to as that "new generation of street criminals" who are "upon us": "the youngest, biggest and baddest generation any society has ever known."[20] "Based on all that we have witnessed, researched and heard from people who are close to the action," Dilulio wrote with two coauthors, "here is what we believe: America is now home to thickening ranks of juvenile 'superpredators'—radically impulsive, brutally remorseless youngsters, including ever more pre-teenage boys, who murder, assault, rape, rob, burglarize, deal deadly drugs, join gun-toting gangs and create serious communal disorders."[21]

These are some of the moralizations that make us tolerate the paradoxes of neoliberal penality and blind us to the reality and devastating consequences of mass incarceretion today.

Let me close with this. The importance of moralization should not be underestimated. The idea of "the criminal as social enemy," the notion of perverted men, of brutally remorseless youngsters, of the righteous hatred of the criminal—these must alert us to the seriousness of the struggle. So I will end with a particularly striking passage from Foucault's lesson of February 28, 1973. After having engaged the ruthlessly brutal texts about the "bastardized races" of rural peasants and unearthed their violent premises, Foucault tells his audience at the Collège de France:

> We're always used to talking about the "stupidity" of the bourgeoisie. I wonder if the theme of bourgeois stupidity is not a theme for [artists, for intellectuals, for philosophers]: those who think that merchants are dim-witted, that financiers are obtuse, that those in power are simply blind. Sheltered by these caricatures, in fact the bourgeoisie is remarkable in intelligence. The lucidity and intelligence of this class, which has captured and retained power under the conditions that we know, produces many effects of stupidity and blindness, but where? - if not exactly among intellectuals. We might be able to define intellectuals as those upon whom the intelligence of the bourgeoisie produces an effect of blindness and stupidity.[22]

And then, he adds in the margin of his manuscript: (« *Ceux qui le nient sont des amuseurs publics. Ils méconnaissent le sérieux de la lutte.* »)[23] "Those who deny this are public entertainers. They don't recognize the seriousness of the fight."

One gets a sense of this when one rereads Dilulio or Banfield, or when one goes all the way back to Quesnay and Dupont. Our understanding of the political economy of punishment today must be twined to a genealogy of morals—that is the only way to understand the new political economy of mass incarceration, or in effect how the intolerable becomes tolerable.

Notes

1. Bernard E. Harcourt, *The Illusion of Free Markets* (Cambridge, MA: Harvard University Press, 2011).
2. See generally Scott Horton, "Quesnay: The Despotism of Natural Law," *Harpers*, November 22, 2011, http://harpers.org/blog/2011/11/quesnay-the-despotism-of-natural-law/.
3. Richard Posner, "An Economic Theory of Criminal Law," *Columbia Law Review* (1985), http://chicagounbound.uchicago.edu/journal_articles/1828/.
4. Loic Wacquant, "Three Steps to a Historical Anthropology of Actually Existing Neoliberalism," *Social Anthropology/Anthropologie Sociale* 20, no. 1 (2012): 66–79, at 76n. 9.
5. This is a topic that Didier Fassin has explored in depth. See http://www.cairn-int.info/article-E_ANNA_646_1237--moral-economies-revisited.htm.
6. Max Weber, *The Protestant Ethic and the Spirit of Capitalism*, trans. Talcott Parsons (New York: Scribner, 1958), 181.
7. Ibid., 182.
8. Ibid.
9. Michel Foucault, *La Société punitive. Cours au Collège de France. 1972–1973*, ed. Bernard E. Harcourt (Paris: Gallimard/Le Seuil, 2013), 293–94, 167, 160, and 160 n.a for the subsequent block quotations.
10. This is so important; it is precisely why I placed Foucault's remarkable passage about Colquhoun on the jacket of the 1973 lectures, an utterly riveting passage: "Unfortunately, when we teach morality, when we study the history of morals, we always analyze the Groundwork of the

Metaphysics of Morals and do not read [Colquhoun], this character who is fundamental for our morality. The inventor of the English police, this Glasgow merchant … settles in London where, in 1792, shipping companies ask him to solve the problem of the superintendence of the docks and the protection of bourgeois wealth. [This is a] basic problem …; to understand a society's system of morality we have to ask the question: Where is the wealth? The history of morality should be organized entirely by this question of the location and movement of wealth."

11. François Quesnay, *Oeuvres économiques complètes et autres textes*, eds., Christine Théré et al. (Paris: Institut national d'études démographiques, 2005), 1016–17, "Les loix naturelles et fondamentales des sociétées … s'impriment dans le cœur des hommes, elles sont la lumière qui les éclaire et maîtrise leur conscience : cette lumière n'est affaiblie ou obscurcie que par leurs passions déréglées. Le principal objet des loix positives est ce dérèglement même auquel elle[s] oppose[nt] une sanction redoutable aux hommes pervers. Car en gros de quoi s'agit-il pour la prospérité d'une nation? *De cultiver la terre avec le plus grand succès possible et de préserver la société des voleurs et des méchans.* La première partie est ordonnée par l'intérêt, la seconde est confiée au gouvernement civil."
12. Richard Posner, "The Romance of Force: James Fitzjames Stephen on Criminal Law," *Ohio State Journal of Criminal Law* 10 (2012): 263–75.
13. Posner 2012, 268.
14. Ibid. (emphasis added).
15. Richard Posner, *The Problematics of Moral and Legal Theory* (Cambridge, MA: Harvard University Press, 2002), 163–64.
16. Gary Becker in Gary Becker, François Ewald, and Bernard E. Harcourt, "Becker on Ewald on Foucault on Becker: American Neoliberalism & Michel Foucault's 1979 *Birth of Biopolitics Lectures*," *The Carceral Notebooks* (2011): 7 at http://www.thecarceral.org/cn7_Becker_Ewald_Conversation.pdf.
17. Katherine Beckett, *Making Crime Pay: Law and Order in Contemporary American Politics* (Oxford: Oxford University Press, 1999); David Garland, *The Culture of Control: Crime and Social Order in Contemporary Society* (Chicago: University of Chicago Press, 2001); "Don't believe the fictitious crime trends used to undermine police reform. The 'Ferguson Effect' is part of an ugly history of using crime to delegitimize civil rights movements. That's why we must be especially vigilant against it," at http://www.theguardian.com/commentisfree/2015/jun/06/dont-believe-ferguson-effect-fictitious-undermine-police-reform.

18. Dorothy Roberts, "Race, Vagueness, and the Social Meaning of Order-Maintenance Policing," *Journal of Criminal Law and Criminology* 89 (1999): 775–836.
19. See http://colabradio.mit.edu/broken-windows-again-3/; Bernard Harcourt, *Illusion of Order: The False Promise of Broken Windows Policing* (Cambridge, MA: Harvard University Press, 2005).
20. See generally http://www.nytimes.com/2014/04/07/us/politics/killing-on-bus-recalls-superpredator-threat-of-90s.html?_r=0.
21. William J. Bennett, John J. Dilulio, and John P. Walters, *Body Count: Moral Poverty … and How to Win America's War against Crime and Drugs* (New York: Simon & Schuster, 1996).
22. *La Societé punitive*, Leçon du 28 février 1973, 168.
23. Ibid., note d (App. cours no. 9, premier feuillet).

Author Biography

Bernard E. Harcourt is Isidor and Seville Suzbacher Professor of Law, Professor of Political Science, and Director of the Columbia Center for Contemporary Critical Thought at Columbia University. Bernard is the author of numerous books, including, most recently, *Exposed: Desire and Disobedience in the Digital Age* (Harvard 2015) and *The Illusion of Free Markets: Punishment and the Myth of Natural Order* (Harvard 2011).

Epilogue

Published after 1570 by the Antwerp printmaker and engraver Jan Galle, Pieter Bruegel the Elder's *Battle of Moneybags and Strongboxes* (or *The Fight over Money*) depicts a chaotic battlefield: bags, banks, chests, and barrels of money attack one another with pikes, lances, swords, and knives; above the armies fly standards emblazoned with the "savage hook (*efferus uncus*)" capable of cracking these containers open and revealing what is barely contained within; coins spill like blood and gore on the ground, heads are split open, limbs are severed.

Galle's print was based on an earlier engraving of Bruegel's drawing by Pieter van der Heyden,[1] to which Galle added, in Latin, French, and Flemish, a paraphrase of Ecclesiasticus 8:3, "gold has destroyed many," a shattering truth bound not by language nor place nor time. Both Galle's version and the original also included, along the lower margin, two sets of distinct verses in Latin and Flemish. "Forward, you piggybanks, barrels, and chests," the first Flemish verse declares, "It's all for money and goods, this fighting and quarreling. Even if they tell you something different, don't believe it!" The print, intended for a popular audience, was part of what Simon Schama has called "an uninterrupted flow of polemics against wealth from Flanders to Holland, from

R. Fredona and S.A. Reinert (eds.), *New Perspectives on the History of Political Economy*, https://doi.org/10.1007/978-3-319-58247-4

Antwerp to Amsterdam."[2] Even if greed and violence are universal flaws, some places and times—like Antwerp in the sixteenth century, made unimaginably prosperous by the new global commerce—became fertile breeding grounds for debates about the formidable tension between the public interest and private interests, and for polemics against the violence, both systemic and explosive, so long at the heart of political economy.

We are once again living in such a time and place. Sergey Tyukanov's 2006 painting *Battle of Money Sacks and Safes* depicts a fantastical and vibrant landscape of violence, of which Bruegel's print now seems a mere snippet or detail. The battle rages across a winding river, with barrels of coins warehoused in buildings on either side. And the viewer cannot but imagine that Tyukanov's painting is itself a snippet from an even larger image, one not yet created: in this work of art, perhaps approaching in size that of the map described in Borges's parable "On Exactitude in Science," and likely surpassing Bosch in invoking the infernal night lit by fire and brimstone, somehow the whole world is seen at once, the battle is being fought everywhere, the ground strewn with dollars, and euros, and all the currencies of the world.

We reproduce *The Fight of the Money-Bags and the Coffers* from the Bleichroeder Print Collection, Kress Collection of Business and Economics, Baker Library, Harvard Business School (CF b4 xx/ olvwork308229).

The editors also wish to thank Sergey Tyukanov. The *Battle of Money Sacks and Safes* (2006) is reproduced courtesy of the artist.

Notes

1. On the print, see Manfred Sellink, *Bruegel: The Complete Paintings, Drawings, and Prints* (Ghent: Ludion, 2007), 265, which is also the source of the Flemish translation.
2. *The Embarrassment of Riches: An Interpretation of Dutch Culture in the Golden Age* (New York: Knopf, 1987), 329.

Index

R. Fredona and S.A. Reinert (eds.), *New Perspectives on the History of Political Economy*, https://doi.org/10.1007/978-3-319-58247-4

The manufacturer's authorised representative in the EU is Springer
Nature Customer Service Centre GmbH, Europaplatz 3, 69115 Heidelberg,
Germany. If you have any concerns regarding our products, please
contact ProductSafety@springernature.com

Printed and bound by CPI Group (UK) Ltd, Croydon, CR0 4YY
05/10/2026
02228138-0005